LET'S PLAY TWO

THE LEGEND OF MR. CUB,
THE LIFE OF ERNIE BANKS

—— RON RAPOPORT ——

hachette
BOOKS

NEW YORK BOSTON

Hachette Books

Hachette Book Group

1290 Avenue of the Americas

New York, NY 10104

hachettebooks.com

twitter.com/hachettebooks

First Edition: March 2019

Hachette Books is a division of Hachette Book Group, Inc.
The Hachette Books name and logo are trademarks of Hachette Book Group, Inc.

The publisher is not responsible for websites (or their content) that are not owned by the publisher.

The Hachette Speakers Bureau provides a wide range of authors for speaking events. To find out more, go to www.hachettespeakersbureau.com or call (866) 376-6591.

Library of Congress Cataloging-in-Publication Data

Names: Rapoport, Ron, author.
Title: Let's play two : the legend of Mr. Cub, the life of Ernie Banks / Ron Rapoport.
Other titles: Let us play two
Description: First edition. | New York : Hachette Books, [2019] |
Includes bibliographical references and index.
Identifiers: LCCN 2018044409| ISBN 9780316318631 (hardcover) |
ISBN 9781549175527 (audio download) | ISBN 9780316318648 (ebook)
Subjects: LCSH: Banks, Ernie, 1931-2015. | Chicago Cubs (Baseball team)—History. |
Baseball players—Illinois—Chicago—Biography. | African American baseball players—Illinois—Chicago—Biography.
Classification: LCC GV865.B24 R36 2019 | DDC 796.357092 [B]—dc23
LC record available at https://lccn.loc.gov/2018044409

ISBNs: 978-0-316-31863-1 (hardcover), 978-0-316-31864-8 (ebook)

Printed in the United States of America

LSC-C

10 9 8 7 6 5 4 3 2 1

For Edna Banks Warren
Big sister, keeper of the family flame

"*Everybody plays two forever. Love, hate. Give, take. There's always the yin and the yang. Everything in life.*"

—Ernie Banks

Contents

Contents

Prologue

Omaha

On the morning of September 11, 2001, former Illinois State Senator William Marovitz was awakened in a hotel room in Omaha, Nebraska, by the sound of a ringing telephone.

"Turn on the TV," the voice in his ear said.

"It's early," Marovitz said. "You woke me up."

"Turn it on."

Together, they watched smoke billowing from the North Tower of the World Trade Center in New York and the chaos in the streets below. Then they gasped in unison as a second plane struck the South Tower.

Marovitz hurriedly dressed and took a cab to a golf course not far away. There he joined more than one hundred others who had been invited to attend an outing arranged by Warren Buffett, the businessman, investor, and philanthropist and one of the world's richest men. Buffett held these events regularly, inviting politicians, heads of corporations, celebrities, athletes, and friends to Omaha for a weekend of golf, conversation, and his own informal comments on the state of the economy and the nation. In the clubhouse, Marovitz stood with dozens of people watching television, all of them still in shock at what had taken place earlier in New York. Soon they were joined by their host.

"For the first time in my life, I'm speechless," Buffett said. "I'm sure a lot of you don't feel like playing golf, but would rather stay here watching things unfold on television and calling your families." But those who had flown to Omaha should entertain no thoughts of returning home any time soon, Buffett warned. "I know many of you have your own planes," he said, "but it doesn't matter. The sky is closed." As for himself, he was going to play golf. Many of those in attendance decided that, however odd it might seem, they would join him.

Marovitz looked around for the two men he had previously arranged to play with: Stedman Graham, a Chicago businessman who was best known as the fiancé of Oprah Winfrey, and Ernie Banks, the Hall of Fame baseball player who had spent his entire career with the Chicago Cubs. As they made their way around the course, they could see Buffett visiting with each group of golfers and giving them updates on the attacks. As he approached them, Buffett's walkie-talkie crackled. "Mr. Buffett, Air Force One has just landed in Omaha."

"At that point, we don't know if we're in the safest place in the world or the most dangerous," Marovitz says of the fact that the plane carrying President George W. Bush had arrived nearby at Offutt Air Force Base, the headquarters of the United States Strategic Command, which contained an underground bunker built to withstand a nuclear blast.

Buffett's guests spent the evening watching television, discussing the implications of the attacks, and, more immediately, how to get home. At breakfast the next morning, Graham told Marovitz and Banks that Winfrey would be sending a plane, but as the day wore on it became clear that not even Oprah Winfrey would be able to breach the closure of the nation's air traffic, and for two more days Buffett's out-of-town visitors remained stranded.

On the third day, Marovitz began making calls and found a rental agency that had a car available. He invited his golfing companions to join him, but Graham held firm. He would wait for Winfrey's plane, he said. But Banks said, "I'm coming with you," and, after getting directions from the hotel, the two men set off on a trip to Chicago they were told would take about seven hours.

———

Marovitz and Banks had been friends in Chicago for thirty years. Banks and his fourth wife, Liz, had attended Marovitz's wedding in 1995 to Christie Hefner, the chair and CEO of the Playboy publishing empire, which had been founded by her father. He and Banks had played golf many times, often at Cog Hill, a course thirty miles southwest of Chicago where Banks had been a regular during his playing days when it was one of the few clubs where black golfers were welcome. And occasionally they did favors for each other.

Banks enjoyed the company of prominent people, and Marovitz, who, along with his political career, was active in Chicago's business real estate market, would often invite him to elite social gatherings. He also brought Banks to Chicago Bulls games—this was during Michael Jordan's heyday when the Bulls were the hottest ticket in town—and Banks would usually bring a box of baseballs for autograph-seekers. "He never said no," Marovitz says. "The ushers would have to stop them from coming down because it was interrupting other people's view of the game."

Banks in turn would make personal appearances at Marovitz's request. "Somebody would call me and say, 'My friend is turning fifty and he's the biggest Cub fan in Chicago. Could Ernie Banks come by his birthday party for just a few minutes and sign a ball and say hello?'" Marovitz says. Banks was invariably accommodating and often stayed longer than the promised time. Banks had a photographic memory and often surprised people he had run into years earlier when he greeted them by name and inquired about their wives and children, whose names he remembered, too.

In 1996, Marovitz bought a building on Chicago's Near North Side that housed a museum dedicated to Al Capone, which he planned to turn into a sports bar. The city's mayor, Richard M. Daley, detested the presence of the museum, as did its Italian community, which considered it a civic insult. "I still have a union card so if they need someone to operate the wrecking ball, I hereby volunteer," Dominic DiFrisco of the Joint Civic Committee of Italian Americans told Gene Siskel, the movie critic for the *Chicago Tribune*. Marovitz had a better idea. He invited Banks to join him on the sidewalk in front of the museum and handed him a baseball bat. As the television cameras rolled, Banks began the destruction of the museum with a home run swing through one of its windows.

But despite Banks's constant public display of good cheer, Marovitz and others who knew him well were aware of another, more complicated, side of his personality. Upon meeting people, Banks would always ask a question and then follow up with more. Only later would those talking to him realize that he had not said a single word about himself. "He'd ask me, 'How's Judge Abe?'" Marovitz says, referring to his uncle, Abraham Lincoln Marovitz, who was a legend in Chicago's legal circles. "Or, 'How that new restaurant doing?,' 'Are you going to run for office?,' 'Have you seen the mayor lately?'" Over the years, the people closest to Banks had learned that these questions—and especially his two best-known greetings: "Are you married?" and "How's your wife?"—were a defense mechanism. As long as he was asking questions, he didn't have to answer them.

People who spent time among professional athletes marveled at this because the favorite subject of so many of them is themselves. They revel in talking about the obstacles they overcame, the achievements no one fully appreciated, the slights they endured, the managers, executives, and media who did them wrong. But Banks was at the other end of the spectrum. He was widely hailed as baseball's greatest ambassador. He exuded happiness and insisted there was nothing he would rather do than play baseball. He never refused to give an interview or sign an autograph, and he saw his signature line—"It's a beautiful day for a ball game; let's play two"—become a much-quoted, and much-parodied, part of the American vocabulary. But he would not talk about himself.

Marovitz was not sure why it was different this time. Perhaps it was because Banks was stuck in a car and had nothing to divert him. He couldn't play golf. He couldn't speak on the phone. He couldn't move around the room and talk to somebody else. He couldn't just disappear. Or perhaps 9/11's body blow to America's central nervous system had shaken him deeply, broken through his defenses, and made him want to reach out to an old friend. But whatever the reason, as the two men rode through the flat Midwestern landscape, Banks began to talk. And for the first time since Marovitz had known him, and the last, he talked about himself.

He talked about growing up as the oldest boy in a family of twelve in Dallas and the responsibilities that entailed. Once, he had missed a year of school to help his father pick cotton. He talked about playing football in high school, but not baseball until he was well into his teens because his school had no diamond. He talked about playing for the Kansas City Monarchs as the Negro Leagues were in their final years because the best young black players were following Jackie Robinson and the other pioneers into the major leagues. He talked about Buck O'Neil, Cool Papa Bell, and all the others who had missed their chance because they had been born too soon and how they compensated by teaching those who came after them everything they knew.

He talked about the women in his life and the mistakes he had made with them, one after another. He talked about his distant relationship with his three children and how he wished he had been a better father. He talked about his finances and how too often he had trusted people who had taken advantage of him. He talked about his teammates—Billy Williams, Ron Santo, Ferguson Jenkins, Don Kessinger, Glenn Beckert, Randy Hundley, Ken Holtzman, Bill Hands, and the rest—who had become as close as family during their playing days. He talked about Leo Durocher, who had humiliated and mocked him while Durocher was managing the Cubs, and how he had responded with silence and runs batted in.

He talked about the piercing disappointment of the Cubs' fabled, fated season of 1969, when the city and its fans had been on fire until the all too bitter end. He talked about the pain of never having played in a

World Series and the fear that he would be remembered more for that piece of bad luck than for the great player he had been. He talked about his belief that nobody really knew him and about the myths, tall stories, and falsehoods—some of which he had perpetuated himself—that had become accepted as fact. He talked about the pleasures and burdens of being the very symbol of his team, a one and only, Mr. Cub.

———

The hours rolled by, and Marovitz, fascinated by Banks's stories about himself—fascinated that Banks was *telling* stories about himself—glanced up and saw a sign that said Claire City. This doesn't seem right, he thought. He had been distracted by Banks's monologue, he realized, and not paying attention to where they were going. He had better stop and check the directions he'd been given back at the hotel.

"Chicago?" the man at the gas station said, and burst out laughing. "You came the wrong way, fella."

Marovitz had not driven east from Omaha toward Illinois, he was told, but north into South Dakota. He had driven *through* South Dakota, in fact, almost to the North Dakota border. The seven-hour trip he had planned would now take at least fourteen. Laughing at the absurdity of it all, he gave his passenger the bad news, turned the car around, and headed for home, Ernie Banks talking about himself all the while.

I

A BLESSED CHILD

Chapter 1

1717 Fairmount

The Dallas Arts District is a proud statement of progress and achievement in a great American city. It covers twenty square blocks in the city's downtown, and its architecturally significant buildings are home to the Dallas Museum of Art, the symphony orchestra, opera, theater center, ballet, black dance theatre, chamber symphony, youth orchestra, and other organizations devoted to the fine arts. It also contains museums of nature and science, sculpture, and Asian art.

The district claims to be the largest contiguous urban arts center in the United States—perhaps only New York has as much culture crammed into an area of similar size—and it boasts elegant restaurants and shops, green space, churches, and a high school for the performing and visual arts. The surrounding residential and commercial real estate has risen in stature over the years, and in price, and the district is high on every list of places visitors to Dallas should not miss.

Longtime residents of Dallas and civic historians marvel at the area's transformation into one of the city's finest areas from one of its most abject. Though the construction of the Central Expressway in the 1950s destroyed the original neighborhood and makes precise calculations difficult, John Slate, the city's archivist, believes the arts district sits on ground that after the Civil War was part of an area known as Freedman's Town. Slate can be sure, however, that the Dee and Charles Wyly Theatre, a building designed by the world-famous architect Rem Koolhaas, now occupies the site of a wooden house of uncertain vintage where, on January 31, 1931, Ernie Banks was born.

Life was precarious for recently freed slaves in and around Dallas after the Civil War. Some gathered in Freedman's Town near a slave cemetery outside the city limits, where they sought mutual protection from their former owners, who had not taken kindly to the war's outcome. Though residents of Freedman's Town who crossed into Dallas risked being arrested for vagrancy, the area served as a source of labor, particularly women working as domestics in white homes, for more than a hundred years. Nor would many other things change for the city's black residents during the coming century.

Dallas's schools remained segregated, of course, and black children often used textbooks discarded by their white counterparts and were taught by teachers paid far less than their white colleagues. Streetcars and buses, restaurants and water fountains, movie theaters and cemeteries were also kept separate. There were no black policemen, judges, or city officials, and black voters were barred from the Democratic primaries, the only elections that mattered. During the 1920s, the Dallas chapter of the Ku Klux Klan, whose membership included judges and city officials, boasted that it was the largest in the country. Many areas downtown were forbidden to blacks, and the state fairgrounds were off-limits except on Juneteenth, the black holiday celebrating the end of slavery, and the second Monday in October, which some called "nigger day at the fair." The practice continued until 1960.

Still, there were opportunities. The coming of the railroads in the 1870s provided good jobs for black workers laying tracks and as conductors while others prospered as farmers. Though blacks were for the most part not allowed to own property, white entrepreneurs bought cheap land on both sides of the Houston & Texas Central Railway tracks and built rickety houses to rent to them. Some of these areas remained unchanged for many years.

A survey conducted by the Dallas Housing Authority of the city's black districts in 1938, for instance, cited the lack of sanitation, absence of sunlight, leaky roofs, broken and boarded-up doors, and sagging floors and walls in most of the houses, and called them "unfit for human habitation." "Fire hazards in these areas endanger the entire city," the report concluded. "The insanitary conditions threaten the lives of the people as a whole, especially in the event of an epidemic. The depressing effect of the slums on the morale of the inhabitants of the areas endangers the social stability of the entire community."

To Eddie and Essie Banks and their growing family, it was home.

"There were three rooms from the front clean through to the back—a front room, a middle room, and a kitchen," says Edna Warren, the first of the Bankses' twelve children, of the family home at 1717 Fairmount, which they rented for twenty dollars a month. "There were double beds in each room and there were always two or three kids in each bed."

There was no indoor plumbing, just a faucet behind the house where the outhouse was also located. To wash dishes, Edna took a dishpan outside, filled it with water, brought it back in, and heated it on the stove. To rinse them, she repeated the process. Baths were taken in a big iron tub, which was also filled with water and heated on the stove. The laborious process restricted baths to one or two a month.

Essie Banks supervised laundry day in the backyard, using what she called a boiling pot, lye soap she made out of fat, and a "rub board." She pushed the clothes through the water with a stick, then transferred them to another pot, where Edna rinsed and hung them on a clothesline. Ironing was done with a smoothing iron, a flat piece of metal that was placed on the stove until red hot. What light there was inside the house came from kerosene lamps with glass chimneys containing small wicks. "I was the chimney girl," says Edna, whose job was to keep them clean.

As a treat for his ever-growing number of children, Eddie would sometimes string three or four extension cords together and give a quarter to the woman in the house next door, which had electricity, and they would listen to the adventures of Superman, Batman, and *The Shadow* on an old radio the woman had given them. When Eddie ran out of quarters, the radio fell silent. Not until Essie, during a brief respite from having children, took a cleaning job at the Dallas Medical Center could the family finally afford their own power. "It was an event to be remembered when we switched from lamps to electricity," Ernie Banks would recall.

The house was heated by two wood-burning stoves fueled by large logs provided by the WPA, the New Deal agency whose trucks also delivered flour, meal, cheese, corn, and other staples, and occasionally used articles of clothing. The logs would be sawed into chunks, and by the time Edna was ten years old her father had taught her how to split them with his double-bladed axe into four pieces small enough to fit in the stove. Why, she wondered, was it her job and not that of her brother, who, though he was two years younger, was taller and stronger than she was? "Daddy, I'm a girl," she complained. Eddie Banks pointed out that Ernie had other chores, including carrying the chopped wood inside, and that everybody had to contribute.

Feeding the family was a challenge. Essie grew greens in her backyard garden and made biscuits and small round tea cakes that Ernie particularly enjoyed, using lard instead of butter, and powdered eggs, and filling them with syrup and jelly. By far the biggest staple of the Banks family diet was red beans, which came in fifty-pound sacks. "My mother was a genius with money," Ernie would remember. "She could make a little bit of money talk. She would take a big can of lard, a big can of beans, a big can of flour, and fix the same meal for months." Still, a boy could get tired of beans, and once he had money of his own he never ate them again.

One source of bounty was a nearby Safeway where the men stocking its shelves would let out a whistle signaling that deliveries were being made. Neighborhood families would wheel wagons around to the back and go through crates of rotten and bruised fruits and vegetables. "If they would get a truck in with grapes, maybe a few of them on the top would be rotten, but they'd get rid of the whole crate," says Edna, who, along with Ernie and their younger brother Ben, was part of the pickup crew. "Mama got rid of the bad part and we ate the good part. Then she would take the rotten grapes and make jelly out of them." Wednesday was chicken-delivery day and Essie would ask for the feet, and perhaps some neck bones and pig's feet that were about to be thrown out.

This foraging once had unintended consequences for Edna. When she and Ernie were attending Booker T. Washington High School, which was diagonally across the street from their home, one of her teachers paid a surprise visit. "I saw you at the garbage can the other day," the woman said. "I'm going to give you and your brother tokens for your lunch so you won't have to be out there doing that." Mortified, Edna tried to explain the food wasn't exactly garbage, but the teacher was unmoved. She would be getting a free lunch now. She should stay away from garbage cans. The story quickly spread through the school, and she began hearing catcalls from her classmates—"I heard about y'all digging through garbage cans"—and her humiliation increased. Nor did she understand how Ernie, who was as much an object of the taunts as she was, could simply ignore them. Why didn't he ever get angry? she wondered. Why didn't the way they lived bother him as much it did her? Why did she sometimes have the feeling that black people didn't have anything to live for, while her brother just shrugged it off?

Ernie would always remember these days with fondness. The rusted wheels he found that he attached to a scooter he fashioned out of boards and raced through the neighborhood with his friends. The BB gun he used to shoot rats, which were never in short supply. The prom jacket his mother bought for fifty cents at Goodwill and his date, a girl named Judy, leaving the dance with somebody else. Miss Della, who lived across the street and sat in a rocking chair on her porch all day, watching him when he went to school and again as he came home. As an adult, he would enjoy rocking chairs himself, and he would think of Miss Della whenever he sat in them.

There was also the Thanksgiving Day chicken his mother left in the backyard while she fetched a pail of boiling water after wringing its neck. When he was sent to retrieve it, there was nothing but a trail of blood. Ernie told this story in different ways over the years; its most colorful version has him following the blood to the thief's lair and, after a wrestling match, returning triumphantly with the chicken intact and his clothes torn and bloody.

"I never said, 'Why do they have that and I don't?'" he said many years later. "We didn't look at other folks. We just lived for the moment and had fun."

"We didn't know we were poor," says Ernie's childhood friend Jack Price. "We didn't know we were living in shotgun houses. We thought outdoor facilities were the norm. We just accepted it."

Banks never entirely overcame this part of his childhood. "I don't look forward to too much," he told an interviewer in 1963. "Even now, I haven't geared myself to extreme heights because of the way I was brought up. I was taught that whatever I had, to be happy with it—even if it was a small thing."

Edna felt different. "I was tired of hard times," she says. "I was tired of being neglected, of people looking at us as poor WPA kids." She and her brothers and sisters had been taught to do without, to accept being poor, not to nag their parents for things they couldn't have. She had heard her father's stories about when times were *really* hard—about soup kitchens and bread lines when the Depression was at its worst. And besides, they were a family, with a mother and a father who loved them, did their best for them, and, poor or not, were respected in the community. "His father, all of them, were very nice people," says Dr. Robert Prince, one of Ernie's classmates. "Ernie may have been poor, but he was one of the nicest, most respectable young men around."

———

Eddie Banks and Essie Durden made their way to Dallas from smaller towns in the South—he from Marshall, Texas, she from Greenwood, Louisiana. Eddie's father was a minister, but it would be Essie who took the family to church on Sundays. He'd done enough churchgoing as a boy, Eddie said. According to family lore, Eddie's grandmother was a slave who worked in her owners' kitchen and had been promised some small property upon their deaths. "But because she couldn't read or write, they took it all away from her," Edna says.

Eddie had three brothers who came around from time to time, but little was said about his life in Marshall or any other family there. Essie's relatives in Greenwood were another story. Her family tree was a thick entanglement of branches carefully tended by relatives who sought out and documented Durdens wherever they had scattered. There were picnics and other get-togethers over the years, but it wasn't until 2002, when Essie was ninety years old, that she finally returned to Greenwood. "Mama wanted us to go to Louisiana to learn her folks," says Walter Banks, the eighth of Eddie and Essie's children, who was born sixteen years after Ernie.

They were all surprised at the turnout—hundreds and hundreds of Durdens and their descendants, it seemed—when suddenly Walter got the shock of his life as he found himself staring at O. J. Simpson and Johnnie Cochran. "I didn't know that O. J. and I were cousins," Walter says about learning that Essie Banks and Simpson's mother were first cousins. "All I knew was O. J. running the football and running through the airport." His astonishment increased when he picked up a booklet made for the reunion that included an in-memoriam page with a number of photos. One of them was of a smiling blond woman with a caption that read: "In loving memory, Nicole Brown Simpson, wife of O. J. Simpson. Daughter-in-law of Eunice Durden Simpson."

Essie left Greenwood when her eighteen-year-old brother, who was living in Dallas, was shot. Her mother, who traveled there to care for her son, wanted to leave Essie at home, but her father insisted that a young girl needed her mother. The marriage ended shortly thereafter, and mother and daughter took up residence in the servants' quarters of a white family's home. At the age of seventeen, Essie met Eddie, who was thirty-five, at a baseball game, and they began keeping company. Finding herself pregnant, she promptly married him and just as promptly began having more children. "The only reason she married Daddy was to get away," Edna says. "She said she never had a young lady's life because she was too busy having babies. She told me, 'I'm not going to have a life of my own.'"

Essie was seventeen when Edna was born and forty-four when she gave birth to her twelfth child, Donald. Edna had the distinction of being born in a hospital—and a white one at that. Essie had little money, and the family her mother worked for generously arranged to have her admitted to Baylor Hospital. This would cause problems later when Edna submitted her birth certificate while applying for a job and was suspected of forgery since everybody knew Baylor Hospital didn't admit black patients, pregnant or not.

Essie's other children were born at home with the assistance of a midwife who had her own ideas about childbirth. "She told me about delivering her babies on an ironing board," says Dolores Law, the daughter of Ernie's younger sister, Estella. "She would sit on it and the midwife would help her." In later years, Essie couldn't remember which of her children were delivered in this fashion, but it is quite possible that Ernie Banks came into the world on an ironing board.

Essie had ambitions of being a nurse but couldn't spare the time away from her family it would have required, so she worked when she could as a domestic in white families' homes. "She was having babies so fast she never did get to work on a solid job," Edna says. Still, she could earn as much as twenty-five dollars every few weeks, which was often more than her husband earned washing cars, shining shoes, and, for more than twenty years, loading and unloading trucks, and cleaning out offices and storerooms at Wyatt's Grocery, which would later become part of the Kroger chain.

"I remember him leaving at five in the morning and coming back at seven at night," Ernie said. "Sunup to sundown, dark to dark. He'd come home, give the money to my mother, play some dominoes or checkers with his brothers, then go right back to work the next day. I used to visualize having a job where I worked only in the daytime."

Eddie never joined the crowd at the local honky-tonks that were part of North Dallas's nightlife. Dipping snuff and pulling from a two-dollar half pint were the extent of his vices, and he was content to practice them at home. Occasionally, Essie would show frustration at her husband's lack of ambition. Why didn't he think about buying a house or a car? she would ask him. Eddie would respond with a shrug and a smile. He was satisfied with what he had, uncomplaining about what was missing. This acceptance of his fate was, Ernie thought as he listened to their arguments, something to think about.

Besides, it wasn't as if Eddie just sat around the house. He was always fixing something—the porch, the roof, the outhouse door, the latch that kept it shut. He built cabinets inside the house, a mailbox outside, and a fence to keep his growing number of children from wandering away. He was a decent mechanic, too, and once nursed an old Nash somebody had brought him into running condition. He probably shouldn't have left the jar of kerosene he used to clean sparkplugs within reach of his six-year-old son, though. "Daddy turned his back and before you knew it Ernie had picked that jar up and drunk it," Edna says. "They had to rush him to the hospital."

Eddie kept busy in others ways, too. He had a wagon—"Call it a junk wagon," says Jack Price—which he would push through the neighborhood and pick up items people had thrown out that he could repair and sell or use himself. Ernie, who was in elementary school at the time, would help his father on his rounds, though the messiness of the job, combined with Essie's busy schedule at home, could have unfortunate results.

"Ernest, where are you going?" Price's mother called out one day when she saw him walking home during school hours.

"I'm going home to wash my clothes, Mrs. Price," he said. "My teacher said I was dirty. But I'm going back to school tomorrow." If he was embarrassed, he showed no signs of it. Eddie enlisted Ernie in another task, too, one that required his absence from school for more than a day.

Long after the Civil War ended, cotton remained king in the South. "We'd drive from Memphis to Dallas several times a year," Robert Prince says, "and all you saw on the side of the road all through Arkansas was cotton." "Hot blazes, son," Prince's father once told him at a certain point in the drive. "You see that tree out there? I used to hurry up and pick to where I could sit under it and rest a while."

The land surrounding Dallas, notes historian Darwin Payne, contained some of the most fertile cotton fields in the world, which had been planted and harvested without slave labor. Soon, the city became a huge inland cotton market that required many hands to do the picking. Prince's father, who had become a math teacher at Washington High, resisted his son's pleas to give it a try—"You're not cut out for it, you're a city boy"—but Eddie Banks and his son joined the labor force.

"They'd bring a truck through the neighborhood at four in the morning to pick the people up," Ernie says. "They gave us a sack and I'd just get down and go at it. The older men could pick with both hands and toss the cotton in the sack in one huge motion. I crawled on my knees. Five or six dollars was pretty good for a day's work. I never made that much."

Years later, Ernie would apply a nostalgic glow to his days in the cotton fields. There was the breakfast of milk and coffee cake or sweet rolls—a rare meal away from home—and the pleasure of doing something with his father that did not include his sometimes overbearing older sister. During his playing career, Banks once heard Dizzy Dean, the former major league pitching star whose radio broadcasts often wandered from the action on the diamond, say he had picked five hundred pounds of cotton a day. "He could really pick it then," Banks told reporters. "The best I could do was three hundred pounds." One thing Banks did not mention in these reminiscences was the full year of school he missed while helping his father in the cotton fields. This worried some of his friends, and they were relieved when he returned to the classroom.

Eddie Banks had another skill that gave him pleasure all his life. He could take an old baseball glove that was all but falling apart and breathe new life into it. "We had three-fingered gloves back then," says Walter Banks. "He'd say, 'Let me fix that webbing,' and he'd sit up all night sewing it up, fixing the thumb, fixing the pocket, until the ball would stick right in there."

Baseball was Eddie's passion, the one thing that could break through his usually placid nature. He had once been the catcher for the Dallas Green Monarchs, a semipro Negro League team sponsored by a neighborhood market, that played at local ballparks on weekends. Back home in Marshall, there were those who thought Eddie could have played for the Kansas City Monarchs or one of the other storied Negro League teams, but if he had any regrets he never shared them with his sons. His finest moment, certainly the one he talked about the most, came when he caught Satchel Paige in a game whose details are obscure—the legendary pitcher may have been making one of his many solo barnstorming appearances—in which Paige made it clear that Eddie's job was not to call pitches but to catch them.

"Satchel would do his fingers some kind of way," Edna says of the stories her father told her. "He would let him know what kind of pitch was coming and where."

One day as Eddie headed to the ballpark, Essie said, "Why don't you take Ernie with you?"

"I was eight or nine," Ernie said of his first appearance on a baseball diamond. "They made me the bat boy."

"He was the most batless bat boy you ever saw," Eddie said. "He'd be playing catch with the players when he should have been doing his chores."

Until then, Ernie had not been particularly moved by his father's love for the game. Years later, he would often tell how Eddie had paid him a nickel to play catch with him. But he did not say how hard he tried to avoid it. Edna remembers that after Essie bought him a glove and Eddie carefully oiled it, Ernie promptly hid it. But Edna quickly retrieved it and issued an ultimatum.

"You listen to me because I'm the oldest and I'm cutting all this wood," she said. "You're going to go out there and you're going to practice and you're going to get that nickel and you're going to give me two cents and we're going to go to the store and get peanut packs."

"What are you, my business partner?" responded Ernie, helpless against his sister's onslaught.

"We would go to the store and he'd get the five pennies," Edna says, "and I made sure he counted me out my two."

But once Ernie got a glimpse of baseball as it was played by the Green Monarchs, his attitude toward the game, and his father, began to change.

"Throw that ball harder!" Eddie would yell at him when he and his friends were playing. "*Throw* it! That's not the way to hold a bat! Hold it square it on your shoulders! Open your legs wider! Naw, naw, naw, squat, *squat*! You can't catch that ball standing up! You got to put your glove down on the dirt to catch it!"

Observing from the sidelines, Ernie's friends would smile and say, "Ooo-*wee*, Mr. Banks is working him out today."

———

Ernie's father had one more lesson for his son, one that would make him uneasy and haunt him the rest of his life.

"I don't want my son working for no white people," Eddie told Essie. "Whatever he does in his life, I want him to do it on his own."

"He wasn't prejudiced," Ernie said. "It was just all the things he had seen in his younger days. They lived through the age of the Ku Klux Klan and lynchings. He never said exactly what it was, but he'd seen enough. He just thought white people weren't trustworthy, that they were sly and slick and weren't fair." Many years later, Eddie's feelings proved to be too deeply held to be mollified by the fact that his son had triumphed in the white world through the game he had taught him.

May 11, 1955, should have been one of the great days of Eddie's life. He had just taken his first plane ride, and now he was at Wrigley Field, having his picture taken in the Cubs' dugout with his son and shaking hands with a swarm of strangers who wanted to meet Ernie Banks's father. The game had barely begun when Banks hit a grand-slam home run off Brooklyn Dodgers pitcher Russ Meyer. The crowd roared with delight and Banks smiled with the knowledge that he had given his father a thrill. But as he rounded the bases, he noticed something strange—Eddie wasn't in his seat. "I had to keep looking for him," Banks says. "He was up and walking. There weren't many blacks at Wrigley Field and white folks chasing him for an autograph was a new experience for him. He just could not sit down."

When the game ended, Banks dressed quickly, left the locker room, found his father, hustled him out of the ballpark, and drove him in silence to a nightclub on the South Side where black players often met after games.

"My God, Ernie," Eddie said when at last he could relax. "That was so *hard*."

Ernie's first exposure to school was less than promising. Preternaturally shy, he had few friends at J. W. Ray Elementary School, which was several blocks from home, and said so little that some of his classmates thought he was deaf and dumb. He sat in the back of the room, seldom raised his hand, and hoped his teachers wouldn't call on him. For the most part, they accommodated him. "I didn't say much," Ernie remembered. "I just didn't get into it. I was kind of an introvert, really."

He was not without curiosity, though, and sometimes hung around after school simply watching what the other boys were doing and occasionally joining them on the playground. "We had a game called tackling ground," Jack Price says. "We threw a ball up in the air and whoever caught it, everybody would try to tackle him. That's how we found out who was the toughest."

Ernie also became involved in more dangerous pursuits. "The school was right next to the railroad tracks," Robert Prince says. "When the train went by, the teacher would have to wait until it passed." The trains would slow down as they approached an embankment, which provided an irresistible temptation for eight- and nine-year-old boys. "The boxcars were open and empty and the train would just crawl," Prince says. "We'd jump in a boxcar and ride a block or two and then jump off. You were a sissy if you didn't do it." Prince's boxcar-riding days ended painfully when his father learned about them. "He wore me out," he says. Fortunately for Ernie, Eddie remained in the dark.

Safer forms of recreation were found in the Moorland branch of the YMCA, a three-story redbrick building eight blocks from home that was the closest thing North Dallas had to a neighborhood meeting place. In 1937, Joe Louis stopped by before boxing in an exhibition at Steer Stadium in Dallas, and over the years many black dignitaries and sports personalities who were unwelcome in the city's segregated hotels—Muhammad Ali, Thurgood Marshall, Duke Ellington, the Harlem Globetrotters, and others—occupied some of the building's thirty-seven sleeping rooms. In later years, the Y became home to the Young Adults, a group of young black professionals, who brought in speakers and discussed civil rights and the fight for desegregation.

For Ernie and his friends, Moorland was a place to swim—strictly in the nude, no bathing suits allowed—play basketball, checkers, and dominoes, shoot pool, and, occasionally, study. Even when they moved on to high school, they returned to the Y to play basketball, a sport Washington didn't offer because it had no court. Ernie was never the fastest man on the floor, but he was a prolific shooter. "It's too bad we didn't have three-point shots then," Price says. "Ernie could shoot from half court and make it."

Years later in his autobiography, *Mr. Cub,* Banks would say sympathetic instructors would turn a blind eye when the boys who couldn't pay for a Y membership sneaked into the building. But Price says no subterfuge was required, because a local banker collected money from his employees and sponsored them. Whatever the case, Ernie would remember the Moorland Y as "the place that developed me as a young man."

He would soon enter an institution that would do even more toward accomplishing that goal.

Chapter 2

Booker T.

In 2013, not long after Scott Rudes moved from Tampa, Florida, to Dallas to become the principal of the Booker T. Washington High School for the Performing and Visual Arts, he received a call from the city's mayor, Mike Rawlings.

"Scott," Rawlings asked, "who's the most famous alum of Booker T.?"

Rudes knew the school had produced many well-known musicians and artists since becoming an arts magnet high school in 1976. Among them were Norah Jones, the pop and jazz icon who had won multiple Grammy Awards and sold tens of millions of albums; Erykah Badu, the singer-songwriter whose work spans multiple genres; Roy Hargrove, the celebrated jazz trumpet player; Edie Brickell, the popular musician and singer who would write a Broadway musical; and other writers, actors, artists, and film and television directors and producers.

Rudes also knew a trick question when he heard one.

"Ernie Banks," he said.

"Good," Rawlings said. "You passed the test."

Visiting art, drama, and music teachers from around the country entering the gleaming new wing of Dallas's performing arts high school might find themselves weeping with envy. The dozens of girls lined at the ballet bar, the art gallery of students' work, the photos of students painting, sculpting, tuning violins, applying theater makeup, and peering through microscopes: Together, they present a statement of aspiration and accomplishment, of the best that a public high school education can offer.

Intensely competitive in its admission process—all students must submit a portfolio, play an instrument, perform a monologue, or provide other evidence of their talent—Washington admits only about one in four applicants and their highly credentialed teachers are supplemented by a noteworthy support group. "There's not a place in the Dallas Arts District that our students don't use," says Sharon Cornell, the school's publicist, of its interaction with the surrounding museums, theaters, galleries, and performance halls. "Every arts organization here has an influence on our students. We're like their little brothers and sisters." Surveying the school during a visit, the singer and musician Harry Connick, Jr., called it a Willie Wonka factory for artists.

But Washington also has another less exalted wing, which was built in 1922 and is connected to the bright and airy new addition. It is where Ernie Banks went to high school.

Long before Dallas's only black high school received its new name and was moved to its present location, it had a much simpler designation: Colored School Number 2. Many of its students walked five or six miles to reach it, often passing white schools closer to their homes. Counties outside of Dallas that didn't have high schools for black children bused them to Washington and later to Lincoln High School, which opened in North Dallas in 1939. When Dallas's schools were desegregated in 1969, Washington was closed and the building was used for storage until, in an extraordinary act of civic imagination, it became an arts magnet high school.

Homes like those the Banks family lived in were long gone by then, and the area consisted of parking lots, liquor stores, and the occasional barbeque shack. White parents had their doubts about sending their children to this part of town, and powerful forces in the city wanted the new school located in the city's more upscale Fair Park area. But in the end it was placed in the refurbished Washington building, and over the years it was joined by other arts institutions and became a part of the Arts District.

The original wing of the building is an architectural misfit among the

modern structures that surround it. Its redbrick façade is indistinguish-
able from elementary and high schools of a certain era all over the country, as are the narrow hallways lined with lockers on both sides and lit by
rows of large single fixtures descending from the ceiling on long poles.
A trophy case commemorating past glories lines one wall—the school
no longer competes in interscholastic sports—and in one corner there is
a glass cabinet that contains a tribute to Ernie Banks. The sense of new
connected to old continues in front of the original wing where girls in
leotards take yoga classes in the late-morning sun. The plot of grass they
sit on, which is divided by a cement walk leading to the front entrance, is
where Banks and his grade-school friends first played football.

"It was the only grassy area in the neighborhood," says Jack Price,
who would go on to play football at Washington with Banks. "The sidewalk was out of bounds so we called time and moved over to the grass,
but somebody would always try to get in a good lick. When we played
football in high school we practiced on gravel and dirt—I still have scars
on my hands—but when we were kids playing by ourselves we had this
nice green grass." Since none of the boys could afford a football, an empty
tin can of the approximate size had to do. "You had to know how to catch
the can just right or you could cut yourself," Price says.

The boys found another unlikely practice field on a lot at a pecan
shelling factory behind Banks's home on Fairmount Street. After the
nuts had been removed, the shells would come flying out of a chute and
form their playing surface. The only thing that could stop the action was
the discovery of a nut that hadn't been opened, which was quickly eaten.
"We'd be all raggedy and dirty and Mrs. Banks would come out of the
house and say, 'Get out of those shells,'" Price says. "'Come on in. Look
at your clothes. Jack, you go on home and wash your clothes. Ernie, you
come over here and wash yours up.'"

———

North Dallas might have been poor, but it had its own set of rules about
raising children that were not to be trifled with. Rule number one said

any adult could discipline any child at any time and that the miscreant's parents would back them up. "You knew that if you got in trouble somebody would go tell your mama," says Joe Kirven, another of Banks's future football teammates at Washington. "The last thing you wanted to hear was 'Boy! Stop doing that!' because you knew they were going to tell your parents." This community watch system could also work to a child's advantage. Gloria Foster, Kirven's wife, remembers when a classmate jumped her on a sidewalk and Gloria rolled on top of her and held her down. Luckily, a woman across the street had seen the incident and spread the word. "Before I could get home, she had called my mother and explained what happened," Gloria says. "Otherwise, I would have been in big trouble for fighting." Since many Washington teachers lived in the neighborhood, they were on unofficial duty away from their classrooms. "They would be up and down the street watching," says Price. "Even on weekends when school was out. You never got away from them."

A few years later, when Banks and his friends exchanged their tin cans for real footballs and joined Washington's team, they found themselves under surveillance by men with a more nefarious interest in their welfare. As far back as the 1870s, gambling had been a major factor in the Dallas economy, and city historian John William Rogers notes that efforts to outlaw the practice were considered bad for business. When a zealous district attorney moved to drive gamblers out of town, "a delegation of businessmen called upon him to point out how ill-advised such a move was for the [city's] prosperity and that Fort Worth with a shrewder policy was offering the gamblers free rent and thirty-five hundred dollars to remove to that city."

Such Wild West leniency was long gone by then, but gambling was still pervasive in North Dallas and everyone knew who the gamblers were. "They'd come up to you and say, 'Hey, didn't I see you wearing that uniform.'" Price says. "'It's nine o'clock. What you doing out this late? Get off these streets. I'm going to tell the coach. I'm going to tell the principal.' Then he'd turn to his friend and say, 'He's out here losing my money.' There was no such thing as hanging out at night. They would run you home."

The players took these and other warnings seriously because they knew their neighborhood's dangers. White people hardly ever ventured into their part of town and the few brave souls who did were wary. Edna recalls the man who regularly brought his laundry to her mother and waited outside until it was ready. "He wouldn't come in and sit down," she says. "Mama would go to the fence and hand him his clothes and he would get in his car and leave."

Guns, drugs, alcohol, and theft were a constant presence in North Dallas, and Ernie was well aware of them. One of the first business trans-actions he ever witnessed was in a pawn shop where his friend Rastine Goodson sold watches and rings that Ernie suspected belonged to his mother. When Ernie returned home from the army some years later, he was not surprised to learn Goodson was in prison for selling drugs. Ernie ran with Rastine and his larcenous friends for a while, but more as an observer than a participant. "They'd come around the house and say, 'Come on, let's go,'" he recalled years later. "I'd go with them, but I always backed away from trouble. I can't explain why. They'd look around and I was gone." Banks would retain this quality of disengage-ment throughout his life—"I don't like arguments, confusion, drama," he said. "It's just the way I am"—and he never forgot how much it amused Goodson. "You're Casper the ghost," his friend told him. "When things happen, you're like smoke, you're gone."

Goodson told him something else during their wanderings, too, and when many of his friends and family members were ravaged by drugs or met early deaths, Ernie never forgot it. "He said I was a blessed child."

———

He was also a conflicted one, in ways he didn't always understand. Some of the jobs he took in high school upset him for no reason. When he was sixteen, he was hired to mop floors in a hotel, but when the boss began telling him what to do, he quit and went home without collecting his pay. "They can keep the money," he told his mother. A later job as a bell-man in a nearby hotel went more smoothly, perhaps because his superiors left him alone.

There was also an inexplicable and totally out-of-character incident with his older sister. Later in their lives, he and Edna would develop a loving bond and laugh over their youthful arguments, but once, when they were teenagers, her sassiness overpowered his reserve and he pointed a gun at her head and cut her with a knife.

In 2006, while talking to an interviewer at his home in Marina del Rey, California, Banks suddenly recalled this moment and called Edna in Dallas.

"Mama had a gun and somehow I got it," he told her, turning on the phone's speaker so his visitor could hear both sides of the conversation. "You were standing on the porch and I pointed it at you and I pulled the trigger. I knew there were no bullets in the gun."

"Mama was at work," Edna said. "Do you remember cutting me?"

"Yeah."

"On my cheek?"

"Yeah."

"You know that scar?"

"Yeah."

"That put it there."

"So my thing was that you had such a great relationship with Daddy. I was envious of that."

"You were just playing with me, though."

"I was trying to cut your throat."

"Oh, you."

"All right, I'll call you back."

"Bye."

For a moment after hanging up, Banks was silent. How could he explain what he had done? Certainly the way Edna always told him what to do, always acted like she knew everything, could get under his skin.

But that wasn't it. As he had just told her, it was because he was jealous of her relationship with his father. Why did their father always come to *her* with his problems? Why was *she* always the one giving their father advice? All these years later and it still bothered him. It bothered him almost as much as the fact that he had threatened and hurt his sister.

———

Though the front yard of Washington High had been his childhood playground, Ernie remained his usual quiet self when he became a student there. He still sat in the back of the class, never volunteering to speak, but he must have been fascinated when, in addition to the usual high school subjects, he found himself studying black history. The curriculum was instituted by John Leslie Patton, Jr., who became the principal of Washington in 1939 and remained for thirty years. When Patton attended the Dallas Colored High School, he was taught by Portia Washington Pittman, Booker T. Washington's daughter, and became a proponent of Washington's doctrine of black progress through education and entrepreneurship rather than by directly challenging segregation. Patton wrote books about teaching black history and, along with I. B. Loud, a pastor at St. Paul's Methodist Church across the street from the school, no one in North Dallas was held in greater respect.

"My mother talked about how he had so much influence over the whole neighborhood, not just the school," says Karen Ridge, the daughter of Ernie's sister Evelyn. "She would always talk about how they were very hands-on in the community." Patton was hands-on in the school, too. "He was not the type that was going to call your parents first," Ridge says. "He's going to discipline you and then call your parents, which meant you were going to get disciplined again when your parents found out."

———

One afternoon as Ernie stood alone watching the Washington football team practice, a man smoking a cigar approached and, with a few words, changed his life. "Ernie," the man said, "you should be out there playing. Come on. Let's go get you a uniform." Banks still had no interest in organized sports, but he did not dare defy Bill Blair.

Though still in his twenties, Blair was the closest thing the boys in North Dallas had to a hero. He had been a football and track star at Washington and, after briefly attending Prairie View A & M, the historically black college two hundred miles south of Dallas, had joined the army, where he became the youngest black first sergeant to serve in World War II. After pitching for the Indianapolis Clowns and other Negro League teams for five years, Blair returned home and became a conspicuous presence in the community.

To Banks and his friends, Blair was a figure of endless fascination. He regaled them with his stories of life in the Negro Leagues. Of how, when a catcher's glove fell apart, it was repaired with a leftover piece of leather and a sock stuffed in the pocket. Of how his favorite pitch was the 12-6—"hit at twelve, drop at six." And of how it was almost a badge of honor that his career ended when he threw his arm out in a tournament in Denver. "Shit, I'll pitch today, I'll pitch tomorrow, and if we play a third day, I can pitch then, too," he would say.

"He was the pied piper of the neighborhood," says Jack Price. "Wherever he walked, we would all gather around him and listen. I can see him now as a very young man coming up the street. Mama and Daddy would say, 'Okay, you boys, here comes Blair. You listen to what he has to say.' He was a character carrier."

"He walked us straight and kept us out of trouble," says Robert Prince. "He and his family lived on Fairmount so he was always around. If we were out doing mischievous things, somebody would yell, 'Here comes Blair! Break it up!' and we would all scatter. He told us how to live—don't smoke, stay away from that boy, don't go to that place, go to church." Blair also kept up his ties with the Negro Leagues and its semipro offshoots that played in various Texas cities. But his first love remained the Washington football team and no able-bodied neighborhood boy was going to stand on the sideline just watching while he was there.

Ernie and his friends were never exactly sure what Blair saw in Ernie. He was of average height, almost painfully thin, and didn't seem to have the necessary aggressiveness to play football. "He wasn't built like an athlete when he was young," Prince says. "I was surprised Ernie even went out for the team." But the fact that Blair saw something in the shy, skinny youth was good enough for Raymond Hollie, the Washington coach.

Hollie was another Washington High legend—his football and track teams won a dozen state championships over the years—and the very essence of the old-fashioned authoritarian coach. He carried a board on the school's gravel-and-mud field and smacked players on the behind when they made mistakes during practice sessions that lasted until dark. He had another requirement, too. "Before you play football, you've got to run track," he told his players, and soon Ernie was long jumping and running the quarter mile while his teammates competed in other events.

When football season finally arrived, Ernie made several important discoveries. One was that he had a talent for catching balls thrown his way. "He was an outstanding pass-catcher," says Price, who played next to Ernie at tackle. "Any time the ball came near him, he could handle it. He had the greatest hands." Hollie was even more enthusiastic. "He was one of the best-looking athletes I ever saw," he would tell interviewers years later when they came around trying to reconstruct Ernie's youth. "Every move came naturally."

Hollie and his teammates were also impressed by another of Ernie's traits. "He was the cleanest athlete I ever saw," Joe Kirven says. "I never heard him say a bad word about anybody. That's unusual in a football player." Also unusual was the fact he never participated in the usual teenage horseplay. If he was going to play football, he was going to take it seriously. "All of us got into fights," says Prince, who was a substitute on the team. "'You're not going to say that about my mama.' 'Did you hit my sister the other day?' Things like that. But not Ernie. He was always a gentleman, and always quiet."

Becoming a member of the Washington football team had another important thing to teach a boy who liked to stand apart from the crowd and observe. It was the concept of working with others in a common pursuit. "I didn't understand how you could put people together to do something worthwhile because I thought most of them didn't like each other and had different frictions," Banks said years later, recalling the moment when he discovered what it meant to be part of a team. He also learned the worth of having a leader he could look up to. Hollie's demanding ways gave his players a sense of purpose and self-discipline. "They became father figures to these kids," Prince says of Hollie and other coaches in the black community. "They were the only fathers that some of these boys had, and they would provide the advice and discipline they needed. These men were idolized by the black community."

Hollie produced good teams year after year, and the one Ernie played on was no exception. In 1948, Washington won the city championship and played a team from Corpus Christi for the state title. North Dallas's version of *Friday Night Lights* was every bit as intense as it was in the rest of Texas, and Washington's fans would sometimes crowd its small practice field to the point where they ran the risk of being run over by players going through their drills. The school's games against Lincoln were particularly anticipated by the alumni of the city's two black high schools, but the excitement over the state championship game reached a new level. The game was played in Dal-Hi Stadium, a 22,000-seat arena that was a fair distance from North Dallas, and fans from the neighborhood took cars, cabs, buses, streetcars, or simply walked. It was a tense scoreless battle until, with only a few minutes remaining, a Washington player fumbled on his own five-yard line, allowing Corpus Christi to score the winning touchdown.

"Everybody was telling us we played a good ball game," says Price, "but we were very down because it was our last year." Ernie had two years of school remaining, but the game marked the end of his football career. Though he had played well, he had also come to the sideline wincing in pain after catching a pass. He had broken his collarbone, and Essie put her foot down.

"That game is too rough for you," she said. "I don't want you playing anymore."

Ernie enjoyed football, but he didn't protest. It was easier to obey his mother than to argue with her. It would not be the last time he would walk away from a confrontation. In the end, the experience affected Essie more than it did her son. "In all my years in baseball my mom never saw me play," he said. "I guess she was a little superstitious about seeing me in any kind of game after that."

Banks's friends were shocked when, in his senior year at Washington, he began keeping company with Mollye Ector. Though his status as an athlete had brought him out of his shell to a small degree, his friends still viewed him as naïve in many ways and felt protective of him. And the fact he was going with Mollye bothered some of them. A pretty girl with high cheekbones and a fashion model's poise, she had run through a string of boyfriends at Washington, and Ernie's friends were afraid he would be hurt.

"I used to tell him, 'Man, leave Mollye alone,'" says Jack Price. "But he was in love with her."

The girls at Washington were particularly surprised that nice quiet Ernie should be going around with a girl they considered fast.

"We'd been friends earlier, but then she sort of ran past me," says Gloria Foster, a churchgoing girl whose parents kept a close watch over her. "Let's just say her speed was faster than mine."

So was the speed of the girls Mollye ran with, who were rumored to be seen at local beer joints that the neighborhood parents and local watchdogs had declared off-limits. Occasionally, they would even roam the neighborhood and create something close to mayhem.

"Those girls were *bold*," Price says. "They would come by my house, five or six of them, and stand outside and yell, 'We want Price! We want Price!' I would be inside trying to hide and my mother would go to the front door and say, 'You better get away from here, you nasty stinking things! Get away from here right now!' They'd be laughing and going down the street and you'd hear them shouting, 'We want Banks! We want Banks!' Man, they were tough."

Mollye's good looks and mischievous behavior gave her a kind of glamour that appealed to Banks as well as to his younger sister Evelyn, who did not share the disdain of some of the other girls. "She told me she had a lot of respect and admiration for her," says Karen Ridge. "She was always talking about the way Mollye carried herself and that she was a wonderful dresser. She felt that she was a good choice for Ernie."

But Essie Banks had a different view. Mollye was wrong for her son, she thought, and she cast a baleful eye over their relationship as it developed over the next few years, a period during which events were conspiring that would allow Ernie to take his athletic talents to another level.

Chapter 3

On the Road

Long before Bill Blair died in 2014 at the age of ninety-two, he had become one of Dallas's most prominent citizens. He founded the *Elite News,* a publication that serves the black community to this day, became a leader in the city's civil rights movement, and remained so active in politics and community affairs that his grandchildren, noting that he always seemed to be on the move, called him "Stop and Go." But for all his accomplishments, Blair was happy to be best known as the man who delivered Ernie Banks to baseball. In fact, he never let anybody forget it.

"Blair, didn't you discover Ernie?" one of his cronies would tease him as they sat in the barbershop.

"You're damn right I discovered him," Blair would reply. "He was over in that goddamn park playing softball in some saggy shorts. I saw him and I knew he had talent then."

And if he never told the story quite the same way—and never mentioned that he lived near Banks at the time and had steered him toward football—who could fault a man for embellishing and enjoying his memories? In one version, Blair was looking out the door of his home on Fairmount Street and saw Banks hitting softballs with his friends. In another, he was living across the street from Griggs Park, which was some distance away from Fairmount, saw him shagging balls, and was intrigued by the strength of his arm. A third version, one confirmed by Banks, is probably closer to the truth.

While playing softball with his friends, Banks was approached by a man named J. W. Worlds, who managed a church league team. He needed a shortstop, Worlds told him, and soon Banks, who was sixteen, was playing softball against grown men. There is some confusion about the kind of softball the team played. In his autobiography, Banks said Worlds ran "the best fast-pitch softball team in our community." But many years later, Banks insisted that the game was strictly slow pitch—no fast windmill deliveries allowed—the kind of softball he and his friends played in the park after school and on weekends.

Whatever the case, the goal on Worlds's team was to have fun and get everybody into the game. Winning was fine, but nobody on the losing team hung his head, and there were no big stars lording it over the other players. And for a curious young boy, there were lessons to be learned from watching his older teammates. Be patient at the plate. Don't swing at the first pitch. Wait for something you can hit solidly. Banks also learned discipline from Worlds, who expected his players to be on time, line up in rows, take pregame drills seriously, and keep their heads in the game. The Griggs Park playing field was large, with buildings beyond both the right and left field boundaries, and it took a strong batter to hit them. Banks never did.

What Blair saw in Banks was raw talent. He stood in against one of the league's best pitchers and hit him with ease, and Blair was particularly impressed by the way he could catch any ball hit near him. "He could field the ball down low and he could pick it up high," says Blair's son, Darryl. "My daddy said the worst ball to judge is a hop hit right at you and Ernie had a natural instinct to field it." Banks needed work on his fielding mechanics, though, and Blair was just the man to teach him. How to get in position before catching a ground ball. How to line up and point his feet at the target before throwing. They worked on these and other basics and Blair was pleased to see Banks applying himself and taking his instruction seriously.

One day, Blair stopped by Griggs Park to show off his protégé to a couple of friends. One was Hank Thompson, a Negro League player who, now that the major leagues were being integrated, would soon become a fine third baseman for the New York Giants. The other was

Johnny Carter, the owner of the Detroit Colts, a Negro League semipro team in Amarillo some 350 miles from Dallas. Banks knew Thompson, who had played against the Green Monarchs a year or two earlier and impressed him with his swing, particularly the way he used his wrists to power the ball great distances. For the rest of that summer he had copied Thompson's stance and swing and found himself spraying line drives as never before.

So Banks lit up when he heard Thompson say, "That kid over there can really play." But Carter responded with words that meant even more: "I'd like to take him to Amarillo." They all drove to Banks's home, where, since Eddie was at work, they unveiled their plans to his mother. "Make sure he's back for school," she said. Banks hastily packed some clothes, jumped into Carter's car, and rode off to spend the summer of 1948 playing baseball. Remembering the moment many years later, Banks would say that the fact Blair had brought Thompson and Carter to watch him play softball at Griggs Park that day, and that they had seen something in him, was a miracle.

Banks was fascinated by his new surroundings, by the higher quality of ball he was now playing, and by the intense and lengthy drills the team went through. He was also fascinated by Carter, who owned not only the Colts, but also the combination hotel, restaurant, bar, and liquor store where the players lived, ate, and drank for free. The roof of the hotel might leak now and then, but still . . . a black man who owned a thriving business and a baseball team, who booked black entertainers and dance bands in some of the towns they visited? Imagine that.

The cities the team played in intrigued him, too. From Amarillo in northeast Texas, they traveled south to Lubbock and Abilene, north to Topeka, Kansas, and Hastings, Nebraska, and west to Roswell and Hobbs, New Mexico. But the greatest fascination came from some of the teams the Colts played against. Their players were *white* and so were their fans. And nobody seemed to give it a second thought. Within limits, that is. "They were happy to see us come in and play," Banks said, "and they were happy to see us get on the bus and leave."

Black men traveling in a group through the South were bound to encounter problems, particularly when they traveled to small towns that had no restaurants where they could eat or hotels where they could sleep. They coped by driving down the road to more hospitable surroundings or by making a meal of peanut butter and jelly sandwiches, sardines, and fruit, and by sleeping on the team bus or in the homes of Johnny Carter's accommodating friends.

Banks loved every minute of it. He loved listening to his teammates tease each other and tell stories. They were like a large family, something he knew quite a bit about. His teammates were older than he was, more than a decade older in some cases, and they made sure he knew what time practice started, which of the town's establishments he should avoid, and when he should be in bed. "They set the rules and guidelines and they made sure I followed them," Banks said. "It was a real blessing to be in that type of environment."

His teammates taught him some of the perks of semipro baseball, too. "I hit a home run in my first game, and they told me to go into the stands and pass my cap around," Banks said. "I made six dollars in nickels, dimes, and quarters." And when the clock struck midnight and the summer ended, he returned home two hundred dollars richer. He was a celebrity now, teased by his envious friends about being a world traveler and called upon by his teachers to tell the class about his adventures playing baseball. Rastine Goodson was right, he thought. He was a blessed child.

After his second summer with the Colts, as Banks was finishing his final year of high school, two men he had never met were contesting his future. One was James A. Stephens, the football coach at Prairie View A & M, who called in his imposing freshman tackle, Jack Price, and gave him an assignment. Stephens had seen Washington play Corpus Christi for the state championship two years earlier and had recruited Price to Prairie View. Stephens also made note of Washington's skinny but sure-handed pass receiver, who was a year behind Price in school.

"The first thing I want you do when you get back to Dallas is go talk to Ernie," Stephens told Price before he returned home for the summer. "I want him down here next year."

In Dallas, meanwhile, Bill Blair, who was monitoring Banks's progress in Amarillo, placed a call to Kansas City.

"Buck, I got one," he said.

"Blair, can he pick 'em up and throw 'em out?"

"Buck, he can play. If I tell you he's got talent, put your foot on it."

That was good enough for Buck O'Neil, who had also received a glowing report on Banks from James "Cool Papa" Bell, one of the Negro Leagues' greatest stars and manager of a team the Colts had played against that summer. So Blair bought Banks a bus ticket and the first suit he ever owned and sent him off to join the Kansas City Monarchs and their legendary manager. It was, Banks would say, the beginning of his life, but his mother had mixed emotions.

"Oh, Jack, he's gone," said Essie Banks, who would surely have wanted her son to become the first member of the family to go to college, when Price relayed Stephens's message. "When he walked off the stage graduation night, the pros were waiting for him with five hundred dollars. He took the money and gave it to me and he left the next day."

Chapter 4

Leaving Home

Though Ernie Banks visited his family many times over the years, he never lived in Dallas again. In itself, this was not unusual. He had a new occupation in a faraway city that brought with it new colleagues, new friends, and new responsibilities. Soon, he would begin a family, become involved in business ventures, and develop a public profile, all of which required his attention. But there was another reason Banks didn't return home as often as he might have: The more celebrated he became around the country, the less comfortable he felt in the city where he was born.

As his mother continued to have children after he left Dallas, Banks was less a brother to his younger siblings than an uncle who blew into town once in a while and then just as quickly was gone. "He would come in from the airport, pick us up, and take us out to eat, do the family thing," says Walter Banks. "Sometimes, I'd go over to the house and sit around and listen to him tell jokes. Other than that, I rarely saw him." Banks's niece Karen Ridge also remembers how much the family enjoyed his visits, but she never truly understood what they meant until they became less frequent. The lack of a real bond between Banks and his younger brothers in particular led to another reason his trips to Dallas were sporadic and often strained.

"They were a working-class family at best, and he talked about how they were a little demanding on him financially," says Sander Esserman, a Dallas attorney who handled some business matters for Banks after he retired from baseball. "Some of them were borderline impoverished and

Ernie was famous and living in the limelight. They all wanted money. It may have been only fifty bucks here or a hundred bucks there, but he sent them checks."

As the years went by, this situation never seemed to change. Banks's third wife, Marjorie Lott, who was married to him from 1984 to 1997, recalls visits that began with the acquisition of hundred-dollar bills. "We'd have to walk in with money because that's what they wanted," Lott says. "Most of the family was begging for money," says Edna. "One time there was an old-timers' game over at the baseball stadium and they had a suite for Ernie. He came in with a handful of envelopes and he said, 'Edna, I have twenty-dollar bills in those envelopes and I'm going to start passing them out to my brothers.'" Nor was this largesse always appreciated. "It would upset me to hear them do him so bad," Edna says, "to hear them say things like, 'Man, he came in here and I needed gas for my car and he didn't even want to give me that.' He was dishing out money all the time."

Though Banks was uncomfortable in his position as Uncle Bountiful, he was happy to help his mother and his father throughout their lives. "I'd call my mom sometimes and she'd say, 'My money is funny,'" Banks said with a laugh. "I would tell her it was on the way." But his family responsibilities extended beyond putting money into envelopes. He may have escaped the temptations and perils of his upbringing, but many of his younger brothers had not, and he became bound up in their problems. "Due to my lifestyle, I wasn't that close to them alive," he said. "But when they got in trouble or they died, I was always there."

At about the time Banks left for Kansas City, his parents moved into a second row house next door on Fairmount Street. "Daddy had so many children, the rent man just let him have it for not much more money," Edna says, and the family was split up, with the boys sleeping in one house and the girls in the other. "I called our house the dormitory," Walter Banks says.

This arrangement held for five years until, in 1953, the family narrowly escaped disaster. While starting a fire in the kitchen stove, Essie reached for a can that had been mistakenly filled with gasoline. It exploded, igniting her dress and some rubberized curtains above the stove. "Mama said she snatched her dress off right quick and smothered it out," Edna says. "Then she snatched the curtains off the wall."

Essie was unhurt, but a piece of the burning curtain landed on the head of Frances, who was eight, and on the arm of six-year-old Walter, where it began to melt. "I brushed it off and my skin just went to bubbling up," he says. Essie tore the burning curtains off Frances and grabbed three-year-old Glover, who had escaped the flames, and they all ran out of the house.

Frances was the most seriously injured, with second-degree burns, but even though she eventually made a full recovery and the house was not seriously damaged, the message was clear. It was time to leave Fairmount Street. Not long afterward, the family moved to a new home in the housing projects of West Dallas, where Eddie could take pleasure in the fact that his new crop of sons all became involved in church-league baseball. "There were seven boys and we all played," Walter says. "Frances played, too. She could catch and hit and run. I used to eat, sleep, and dream baseball. I'd sleep with my glove up under my head to keep people from messing with it."

But as the boys grew older, their idylls ended, and some of them succumbed to drink, drugs, and, in several cases, unspeakable misfortune. And one after another, five of Banks's brothers died at a young age.

There was Sammy, who was twenty-two years old and at loose ends when, in 1962, Banks tried to convince him to join him at his off-season home in California.

"Come on, you'll get a new job, meet some new people, start over," Banks said. "I'll come to Dallas and we'll drive out."

"Aw, man, I don't want to go out there," Sammy said.

A few days later, Banks's phone rang. Sammy had been at a party where someone was playing with a gun, stupidly pointing it at people.

Sammy was dead, shot in the head. Some people just get stuck in time and places, Banks thought as he flew home for the funeral.

A similar fate was met by his brother Ben, who was two years younger. Ben was a second baseman who had followed Banks to the Kansas City Monarchs, where he played well enough for Banks to convince the Cubs to give him a minor league contract. When he arrived at spring training in Arizona in 1956, the press took notice of a second Banks in camp, and pictures of the two baseball-playing brothers appeared in the Chicago newspapers. "He was more talented than me," Banks said.

But hopes that the Cubs might field an all-Banks double-play combination someday didn't last the summer. The team sent Ben to its farm team in Lafayette, Louisiana, where he met a woman who went with him to California. "He just left the team," Banks says. "All he said was he just didn't like baseball." Thirteen years later, at the age of thirty-seven, Ben died. "They say he was into drugs," Banks said. "I don't know."

Even after Banks left baseball, he returned to Dallas for funerals. One was for his brother Glover—the family called him Buddy—who was nineteen years younger and had bonded with his father through baseball more than his other sons. "Buddy is your daddy's favorite child," his mother once told Banks, wounding his feelings a bit. "When Daddy died, Buddy started drinking…" Banks said, his voice trailing off.

In 1999, tragedy struck again when his brother Eddie, Jr., ran a red light, smashed into a car, and killed a man. Two days later, Edna found him dead in the motel room where he was living, the television still blaring.

"That was real hurtful because he tried so hard to make it in life," Banks said. "He got out of the air force and married a girl and she left him. It just changed his life." Banks hired a lawyer to deal with the aftermath of the crash, did so again when the husband of one of his sisters was sent to jail, and yet again when another of his brothers was accused of a crime. His name alone, Banks discovered, was enough to get him in to see Dallas's sheriff and district attorney. "I didn't like doing it, using my influence from baseball," he said. But in some of these cases he was able to help get the charges reduced or dropped.

Banks's sister Frances also died at a young age after lapsing into a diabetic coma, and the family's troubles extended into the next generation in the person of Banks's nephew Bobby Johnson, whose short career with the Texas Rangers was all too representative of the perils of major league baseball in the 1980s.

Johnson was the catcher Eddie Banks had always wanted. Eddie tutored him from a young age and never missed one of his games from peewee leagues through high school. So when Johnson was drafted by the Texas Rangers in 1977, Eddie was overjoyed. At six foot three and 195 pounds, Johnson was impressive physically and played his position well, but in his first few years in the minors he had trouble hitting. A visit with his uncle in Chicago helped straighten him out. Drop your hands, Banks told him, after seeing how high Johnson held his bat. The results were immediate, and in 1979 he was named the Rangers' minor league player of the year.

Two seasons later, Johnson was called up in September and hit two home runs in six games, one of them with two out in the bottom of the ninth for a 1–0 victory over the California Angels. He was touted as a star of the future, one who would be closely observed in spring training the following year. But the reality of his game-winning homer was much darker.

"Mama, I was so high when I hit that home run I didn't know where I was," Johnson confessed to his mother a few years later.

"*What?!*" she said, having no idea her son was caught up in the drug epidemic then ravaging baseball.

Johnson had been introduced to cocaine by a teammate as they drove to a spring training game, and he hit two home runs that day. But he soon learned he was living in a fool's paradise and his career disintegrated in a series of injuries, missed practices, embarrassing public displays of anger, and trips to drug rehab. After three seasons, in which he appeared in ninety-eight games and had a batting average of .197, the Rangers cut him loose. Banks did what he could, arranging tryouts with the Cubs and the San Diego Padres, but Johnson had nothing left to give.

"I was always a leader in high school," he says, "the quarterback of the football team, the catcher on the baseball team. But when it came to following this devil—that's what I call it—he had me by the tail. I thought getting to the big leagues was the end-all be-all. But when I got there, I was like a deer looking into the headlights."

But if Johnson symbolizes the terrible problems of some of Banks's siblings and their children, he also represents their path to something better. After leaving baseball, he got free of drugs, began selling cars—he even owned a dealership for a time—and wound up in Denver, where he has been living for nearly thirty years. "I don't live in the past," he says. "I'm happily married. I put my daughter through college. I've got everything I need. I see a lot of the guys I played with on TV every day and I wouldn't trade my life with any of them."

Many of the dozens of Banks's nephews and nieces and their descendants followed Johnson's example, but without the trauma that preceded it. They went to college, got good jobs, and led productive lives. The family took particular pride in Acie Law, the son of Banks's niece Dolores Law, who starred in basketball at Texas A & M and became the first player to have his jersey hung from the rafters of the school's arena. He later went on to a fine career in the NBA and in Europe.

And in one especially delicious irony, Ashley Ridge, the daughter of Banks's niece Karen, became the last member of the family to attend Booker T. Washington High, graduating in 2009. The school had assumed its glittering new identity by then, and Ashley studied painting and sculpture and then enrolled at Southern Methodist University, where she earned a degree in creative writing. "When I look at my generation and my children's generation and the lifestyle we have, sometimes it brings tears to my eyes," says Karen Ridge, who grew up listening to her mother's stories of wringing chickens' necks and boiling water for baths in an iron washtub. "That the family's been able to come so far and accomplish so much and we've been able to educate our children, to live in much better homes, and to travel. It's a blessing."

———

Banks's prolonged absences from the city of his birth resulted in one consuming frustration for his family and many of those who remembered him as a boy. He was the greatest baseball player Dallas ever produced, and yet it seemed as if the city had forgotten him. After Banks's death, Robert Prince and some of his other teammates lamented the absence of any statue, marker, or street that bears his name. "I am chagrined that Dallas has never acknowledged Ernie," Prince says. "Dallas gave baseball its greatest gift."

Scott Rudes was disappointed too, but for reasons that went beyond honoring an athlete. Banks, the Washington High principal believes, is the perfect vehicle through which the school's roots can be celebrated. For all of Washington's present glories, all the young artists it nurtures, all the magnificent cultural monuments it sits among, the school's more humble origins should not, Rudes thinks, be forgotten.

It is the school where Raymond Hollie arranged for Jack Price, the burly offensive tackle who had never considered going to college, to receive a scholarship to Prairie View A & M. Price returned home to teach in the Dallas school system for forty years, and in 2005 he was inducted into his alma mater's football hall of fame.

It was the school where Robert Prince, whose father taught him and his friends math, won a scholarship to Wiley College, a historically black school in Marshall, Texas, where he studied chemistry. He went on to attend the University of California at Berkeley and Texas Southern, and, after serving in the Korean War, he became an obstetrician who practiced in Dallas for thirty-five years.

It was the school that also sent Joe Kirven to Wiley College. He returned to Dallas and, after much hard work, bought a small maintenance company that grew until it employed nearly two hundred people and had contracts on projects throughout Dallas and Fort Worth. He and Gloria Foster have remained married for more than fifty years.

It was the school that, along with its younger counterpart, Lincoln

High School, trained a generation of doctors, lawyers, teachers, business-men, civil rights leaders, and others who became an integral part of Dallas's burgeoning black professional and middle class. This led Rudes and others to believe that a memorial to the school's most famous alumnus could serve as both a tribute and a reminder. "There is a real respect for what this school has been to so many," Rudes says. "For a lot of them, it was their first generation of schooling. We don't want to lose that sense of history, and Ernie Banks is a part of it."

For several years after Banks's death, there was talk of erecting a statue on the school's grounds, and in 2017, Jeremy Halbreich, a Dallas businessman who has media holdings around the country, began a campaign to raise funds for its construction. "We decided it would be great if we could get one of the school's former students who might be an accomplished sculptor to do this," says Halbreich, who had known Banks in the latter years of his life.

He quickly found his man in Emmanuel Gillespie, a 1985 Washington graduate, whose public art installations are exhibited throughout Dallas and who was delighted to receive the assignment. "That school made an artist out of me," Gillespie says. "It set the framework for my life." Gillespie enlisted a half dozen current Washington students to contribute ideas and soon came up with a model of Ernie Banks, his bat resting on his shoulder, a smile crossing his face.

The statue was dedicated in September 2018, and there was no argument over where to place it—in a corner of the grass field in front of Washington High's original building where Banks and his friends played football with a tin can, trying to avoid the cement path that bisected their makeshift playground and led to the schoolhouse door.

II

APPRENTICESHIP

Chapter 5

Monarchs of All They Surveyed

When Ernie Banks joined the Kansas City Monarchs in 1950, the Negro Leagues were dying. Though it took the better part of a decade before they finally succumbed, the death knell had sounded on April 15, 1947, when Jackie Robinson made his debut with the Brooklyn Dodgers. Almost overnight the allegiance of black baseball fans to the Monarchs, New York Cubans, Chicago American Giants, Birmingham Black Barons, Memphis Red Sox, Indianapolis Clowns, and the other historic teams that made up the Negro Leagues was replaced by a hunger for news of Robinson and the players who followed him into the major leagues.

Rather than attend Negro League games, these fans organized expeditions to major league ballparks. Their fascination with Robinson, Larry Doby, Roy Campanella, Satchel Paige, and other pioneers was so great that the black press wrote story after story about them, radically reduced their coverage of the teams they had so avidly covered in the past, and even debated whether the Negro Leagues should continue to exist. Sam Lacy, a writer who had campaigned for integration, said they were now a "mongrel puppy licking at the heels of a prospective master." And when the Homestead Grays won the Leagues' 1948 World Series, the team's hometown newspaper, the *Pittsburgh Courier*, ran only a few paragraphs. The Negro National League folded shortly thereafter and the Grays, after trying to survive as an independent team, went out of business three years later.

Although only six major league teams had integrated by the time Banks joined the Cubs in 1953—it would take six more years before the final hold-out, the Boston Red Sox, signed their first black player—more than 150 former Negro Leaguers were playing for white minor league teams by then. Their loss and that of the players who followed in the next few years cut the heart out of a once proud institution.

"The big league doors suddenly opened one day and when the Negro players walked in, Negro baseball walked out," said Wendell Smith, one of the leading black sportswriters of the day, who had helped smooth Robinson's path with the Dodgers. "When Major League Baseball says I'm going to take your best black ballplayers, who's going to go to a Negro League game?" asks Larry Lester, a historian and one of the founders of the Negro Leagues Baseball Museum in Kansas City. "As in anything else, when the Walmarts come to town, the mom-and-pops die out." "After Jackie," said Buck Leonard, a Hall of Fame first baseman who played on some of the Homestead Grays' best teams, "we couldn't draw flies."

Some observers mourned these losses, but thought they were inevitable. "We gained something but we lost something, too," said Mal Goode, who became the first black network news correspondent when he joined ABC in 1962. "But what we gained was greater. We got our self-respect, and you have to be black to understand what that means." Also conflicted about these changes was the man who would become Banks's mentor in Kansas City. "When I look at what happened after Jackie, I get a chill up my spine," said Buck O'Neil. "But I also get a bittersweet feeling because I remember that a lot of people lost their whole way of life."

O'Neil and others mourned the black businesses that were destroyed, particularly the hotels that had catered to Negro League teams and the surrounding restaurants and clubs. "The Streets Hotel [in Kansas City] had to close because it couldn't compete with the Muehlebach downtown," he said. "The Vincennes in Chicago went out because the ballplayers and entertainers were staying in the Loop now. Instead of the Woodside in Harlem they were staying in Times Square. A whole way of life came to an end along with black baseball."

O'Neil's Monarchs were afflicted along with the rest. Among the Negro Leagues' most historic teams—between 1923 and 1955 they won thirteen American League pennants and two World Series—the Monarchs limped along until the Philadelphia Athletics moved to Kansas City in 1955, bringing two black players with them. The Monarchs played only two home games the rest of the season and barnstormed their way through the summer. They were sold at the end of the year to Ted Rasberry, a former Negro League player, who quickly realized he had been snookered by their owner, T. Y. Baird.

"When I bought the Monarchs," Rasberry said, "I *thought* I was buying the team, but when I started checking for players, Mr. Baird had sold them all to the majors. All I got was the bus and one player who stayed with me. He was a home run hitter but he was too old. They wouldn't take him." Rasberry patched a club together with players major league organizations didn't want and moved the Monarchs to Grand Rapids, Michigan, where they played other small-market teams and managed to live off their famous name until 1965.

When Banks arrived in Kansas City, he encountered little resentment from his older teammates who had missed their chance at the majors because of the dates on their birth certificates. He often spoke warmly of the players who greeted him and two other young players who would one day cross the color line: Curt Roberts, a second baseman who would become the Pittsburgh Pirates' first black player in 1954, and a promising outfielder and catcher named Elston Howard. "They were happy for us," says George Altman, who played for the Monarchs in 1955 and later spent four years with Banks as a Cub, of the Monarchs' veterans. "I think they enjoyed their careers because the alternative was working in the steel mills."

Howard became Banks's first baseball roommate, and soon the two men were inseparable—eating together, going to the movies together, sitting together on bus rides. "He had more experience than I did,"

Banks said. "I would follow his lead." It would not be the last time Banks attached himself to an older teammate. Eventually, he and Howard made a deal: The first one to get to the big leagues would call the other and tell him what it was like.

The lack of bitterness on the part of the older Monarchs was not unusual. Player after player interviewed by Brent Kelley in his oral history, *The Negro Leagues Revisited,* spoke proudly of their careers. Despite low wages, long bus rides, accommodations that were essentially brothels, meals of baloney sandwiches eaten on the bus, and the constant presence of racist taunts, a large majority said they would do it all over again. They were, some of them insisted, part of something larger in black society, something noble.

Rube Foster, a great pitcher who was also one of the Negro Leagues' founders, said, "I made baseball a profession, later a business. I have wiped away much of that prejudice, so much so that I know of no men who have not felt it as much an honor to meet me as I have felt it an honor to meet them, from the most prominent men in the churches to our greatest educators and college professors."

John Henry "Pop" Lloyd, a hard-hitting shortstop who may have been the best player in all of baseball, black or white, in the second decade of the twentieth century, said in 1949, "I do not consider that I was born at the wrong time. I felt it was the right time, for I had a chance to prove the ability of our race. And because many of us did our very best to uphold the tradition of the game, we have given the Negro a greater opportunity now to be accepted in the major leagues with other Americans."

"Honestly true, if I had to live over, I'd live the same," said Hilton Smith, who won twenty games in each of his twelve seasons with the Monarchs but was overshadowed in the public mind by Satchel Paige. "No regrets."

When Darryl Blair asked his father if he was angry that he hadn't been allowed to play in the majors, he responded with defiance. "The Negro Leagues *were* the majors," Bill Blair said. "When we'd come to a town on Sunday, preachers would cut their sermons short and people would come to the ballpark." And besides, some of the players felt, discrimination could be a two-way street. "Sometimes I think the good white players got cheated, too, because they never got a chance to play against the black players," said Bob Scott, a pitcher and first baseman for the New York Black Yankees and the Memphis Red Sox. "If you never play against the best, you never know how good you are."

In the end, it was the sense of camaraderie, of playing a game available to only a few, that truly mattered. "The outside world didn't exist," said Ted "Double Duty" Radcliffe, who was given his nickname by Damon Runyon after pitching the first game of a doubleheader and catching the second. "We were just one team, together."

Not everybody was thrilled by life in the Negro Leagues, however— Jackie Robinson was called an ingrate when he criticized "low salaries, sloppy umpiring, and questionable business associations" of some of the owners—and the teams certainly had their share of rascals. In a ceremony at the White House during the Clinton administration, Radcliffe discovered that his reputation had preceded him. How many children did he have "on the road," the president asked him. "Now that's a sixty-four-thousand-dollar question." Radcliffe replied. "I was a hit-and-run man. I didn't like no double plays."

But Bill Blair noted that a number of the league's players became respected members of their communities after they retired. "We didn't have knuckleheads," he said. "A lot of Negro League players were college educated and even those who weren't did something. They were leaders." O'Neil actually thought there might have been more players with some college education in the Negro Leagues than in the majors.

While many of the black pioneers in Major League Baseball were under enormous pressure in often hostile environments, there were others who found that the improvement in living conditions alone made them more than ready to play with and against white players. "Anybody who can play Negro baseball is *over*qualified to play major league baseball," said Monte Irvin, who spent six years with the Newark Eagles before moving on to the New York Giants. "You ain't got the uniform to bother with. You got a good place to sleep. You ain't got to worry about no traveling and all that." Still, Irvin lamented what had been lost. "I made more money when I was in the majors, and the caliber of baseball and the playing conditions were better," he said, "but I had more fun in the Negro Leagues."

Making it to the majors was far from Banks's mind. Still in his teens when he joined the Monarchs, he was happy to learn from such elders as Bonnie Serrell, an infielder who had led the league in hitting in 1942, and Sherwood Brewer, a second baseman who had schooled Jackie Robinson in fielding fundamentals and did the same for him. Altman spoke of another infielder, Hank Baylis, "who was like a mentor to me. He'd say, 'You stick with it. You've got a chance. You can do it.' Of course, Buck was the real teacher."

When Buck O'Neil was in his eighties, he became the face of the Negro Leagues in his role as the eloquent conscience of Ken Burns's television documentary on the history of baseball. But to countless Negro League players, who credited him with boosting their careers and told loving Bunyanesque stories about him, he was already a legend.

Altman remembers his first game with the Monarchs in Indianapolis where they were being shut out until O'Neil, who was forty-three years old, put himself in as a pinch hitter. "He hit a ball out to right center field that almost took the hands off the clock, probably about four hundred feet," Altman says. "I thought, 'Wait a minute. I think I'm in the wrong league here.'" Banks had a similar experience the year he joined the Monarchs when O'Neil sent himself up to pinch-hit in a game in Cleveland. "There's nothing to it," O'Neil said before he left the dugout. "First you lock your shoulders. Then you let your arms do the work." "Here's this guy with gray hair—he looked real fatherly—and he went up there and hit a home run," Banks said. "I couldn't believe it."

But O'Neil's real strength was as a leader, one who favored praise and encouragement, which Altman couldn't help but compare with another manager he and Banks would play for. "He inspired his players," Altman says. "That was in contrast to Leo Durocher, who if you don't do well, he's going to back up the truck. Buck was very inspirational. I just enjoyed playing for him."

So did Banks, who would recall fielding the ground balls O'Neil hit to his left, to his right, and straight at him, over and over again, in the withering Kansas City heat. O'Neil's instructions on how to complete a double play were instructive, too. When the runner on first base is coming at you, he said, "Just look dead at him and start that ball right at his face. He's going to get out of the way and it's a perfect strike to first base."

O'Neil also had plenty to teach Banks about hitting as he passed down lessons he had learned from such old Negro Leaguers as third baseman Newt Joseph and Wilbur "Bullet Joe" Rogan, a pitcher who once led the league in wins while also hitting .411. Stand back in the batter's box and away from the plate so you can step into an outside pitch, O'Neil told Banks. Speed up your swing when the ball comes inside. Hit off the balls of your feet, not your heels. Banks came to love these practice sessions even more than the Monarchs' games. "I always liked *digging* for the gold rather than the gold," he said. "Without Buck, I don't think I would have made the big leagues so quickly."

O'Neil was also a mentor off the field, and his wisdom and equanimity helped his players cope with their sometimes fraught circumstances. When the Monarchs were approaching a city, he would stand in the front of the bus and give pointed travelogues that would include tips on which neighborhoods to avoid, which stores not to enter, and which towns had an active chapter of the Ku Klux Klan. "Before we got to one city in Kansas, he said, 'Hey, they just had a lynching over here,'" Banks said. "That got our attention. I was looking around and wondering what's going on. I mean, is this America?" The Monarchs played the game without incident before an appreciative audience, then drove to the next city. O'Neil had another warning for the younger players, particularly those who had grown up in all-black neighborhoods. Speaking to white women was strictly to be avoided and so were lingering glances. "Reckless eyeballing was a big thing with him," Banks said. "You couldn't look at a white woman too long or she could report you and you could be arrested."

O'Neil had one more example to set for a shy nineteen-year-old away from home for the first time. It was his love for the game. To O'Neil, baseball was more than an occupation. It was a way of life, and they were among the lucky few who had been chosen. It was something to be celebrated openly, repeatedly, and without shame. "Be alive, man!" O'Neil would sometimes shout at him. "You gotta love this game to play it!"

"Buck was the ultimate politician," says Jack Hiatt, a catcher for several major league teams who knew O'Neil as a major league scout long after the Negro Leagues disbanded. "He did a marvelous job of presenting himself as a model baseball man. 'Hey, how you doing? Beautiful day for baseball, isn't it?' Ernie was the same way. You would never hear him say anything negative." "I already loved baseball," Banks would say years later. "But Buck showed me how to express that love."

Beneath this ebullience, however, it was possible to see how O'Neil projected a carefully calculated sense of distance when he was around white players, coaches, and executives. "He was a performer, putting on a show," Hiatt says. "You never really knew what was on his mind. I think the group of black players who entered baseball at that time had to do that. They had to fight to get there and they had to fight to stay there. They had to win your hearts every day." Banks learned that lesson from O'Neil, too.

———

There was so much about Banks's first season with the Monarchs that was new and exciting. The team conducted its spring training at Morehouse College in Atlanta, where he was introduced to a thriving, prosperous community that contained institutions run by and for blacks. He marveled as he saw restaurants, stores, parks, schools, insurance companies, banks, construction firms, and the college itself. "Gosh, all black," he thought. "This is different."

His enjoyment increased as the Monarchs began their season. The bus rides were full of stories, camaraderie, and even the occasional song with some of the players accompanying themselves on mouth harps and guitars. The cities they visited—Birmingham, Cincinnati, Indianapolis, Memphis, Detroit—were new to him but familiar to his veteran team-mates, who were paying return visits to the hotels, restaurants, and clubs where their public awaited. And if problems did crop up, O'Neil and the older players handled them without the rookies even noticing. There were times, in fact, when Banks felt as if the outside world didn't exist. He was part of a team now that was making all his decisions for him. And he was creating friendships that would last for many years.

Occasionally, the Monarchs would travel to Chicago for games against the Chicago American Giants in Comiskey Park. They would approach from the south, traveling through northern Indiana, and Banks was fas-cinated by the steel mills of Gary, which were then the world's largest, and the imposing stone columns that marked Chicago Vocational High School, where many aircraft mechanics had been trained and which later offered diplomas to veterans returning from the war. The Chicago skyline was a source of wonder, as was the friendliness of the people who served the Monarchs at the Evans Hotel restaurant, which quickly became one of his favorite haunts.

But though he found himself fitting in, Banks was still his shy, quiet self in social situations. When his teammates dressed up for a night on the town, wearing suits and ties and hats cocked just so, he was content simply to observe. "Some of the older players would meet up with the ladies who had come to the game," he said. "I was kind of on the side-line, just watching. They didn't come after me. I always thought it was my looks. I was very skinny and I think a lot of people looked at my face and thought, 'Oh, you look homely and lonely. Uh-uh, no chance I'll fool with this guy.' And of course I didn't approach them."

Along with their league schedule, the Monarchs played a number of exhibition games, and one day in Des Moines, Iowa, Banks found him-self taking batting practice against none other than Satchel Paige, who had pitched to his father in Dallas so many years earlier. Paige, whose spectacular debut with the World Series champion Cleveland Indians in 1948 at the age of forty-two had settled the debate over whether he was one of the greatest pitchers who ever lived, had been out of the majors for a year and was playing for the Philadelphia Stars. And just as he had with Eddie Banks, Paige told Ernie where his pitches would be coming. Recounting this experience in a conversation with Banks in 1968, Paige said that given the chance he would approach him differently. "Know how I'd pitch to you?" he said. "I'd throw you that necktie ball. You can't hit on your back."

Banks also faced a young pitcher for the Memphis Red Sox named Charley Pride who made the mistake of throwing him a changeup. "Whoosh, it's still going," Pride says. "He hit me everywhere but on the bottom of my feet." Pride claims to have gotten his revenge during a barnstorming appearance in Mississippi, and for years he would claim to have struck Banks out. "Ernie said, 'Hell, no,' when I asked him about it," says Robert Prince. "It was the first time I ever heard him curse."

Pride made it as far as spring training with the California Angels in 1961 when, realizing he was about to be cut, he summoned up his courage and approached the team's owner, the famous movie cowboy Gene Autry.

"Mr. Autry, don't let them send me home," he pleaded.

"I don't run the team," Autry said between bites of a hamburger. "I own the team."

His baseball dream over, Pride picked up a guitar he had been fooling with and began a career that would make him one of the most popular country music singers in the world. Years later, as Autry was receiving an award in Nashville, he told the crowd, "I was sitting over there at a table with Johnny Cash and June, and Eddie Arnold and his wife, and a young fellow that was almost an Angel."

One indication of the dire condition of the Negro Leagues came at the end of Banks's first year with the Monarchs. Though the team had won the first-half title of the West Division, it forfeited its right to play the Chicago American Giants, who had won the second half, for the championship. T. Y. Baird said he couldn't afford to rent a stadium, but O'Neil knew better. Baird had sold too many of the Monarchs' best players to the major leagues and their minor league affiliates, and they had lost even more players to Latin America. He would not, O'Neil said, field a non-representative team. The American Giants were easily beaten by the Indianapolis Clowns in the championship series.

Another casualty of the reduced coverage of the Negro Leagues in the black press was accurate statistics. With the *Kansas City Call* not covering the Monarchs, Larry Lester was reduced to checking out-of-town papers to see how the players were doing. "It was very poorly done," Lester says. "Some of it was nonexistent." For this reason, it is difficult to determine just how well Banks played during his first season with the Monarchs. One report says he hit .255, and Banks confirmed that he hardly set the world on fire. "I didn't do a lot, didn't hit a lot of home runs, didn't have a great batting average," he said. "I was just an average type player." His physical appearance didn't exactly inspire confidence, either. "You should have seen him," said Radcliffe, who was managing the American Giants in 1950. "So skinny and little."

But Buck O'Neil knew better. The first mention of Ernie Banks in *The Sporting News*—a publication that called itself the Bible of Baseball—reported in 1953 that the return of the now twenty-two-year-old shortstop to the Monarchs after two years in the army had brought a smile to his manager's face.

Chapter 6

Army Life

Barnstorming in the off-season was a baseball tradition that stretched back to 1888 when Albert G. Spalding, one of the game's first stars, who also founded the sporting goods company that bears his name, took twenty players on a tour that stretched from Egypt to New Zealand. In a later era, Babe Ruth led all-star teams around the country after the major league season was over, and was once briefly suspended by Commissioner Kenesaw Mountain Landis for doing so. Barnstorming in the Negro Leagues was a way of life, too.

After their first game of the 1942 Negro Leagues World Series against the Homestead Grays, for instance, the Kansas City Monarchs played several exhibitions in small towns on their way to Pittsburgh. "It might seem odd, but that's the way it was done," said Buck O'Neil. "I guess you could say to the folks in those towns the World Series was seeing their team play the Kansas City Monarchs."

Barnstorming also provided the only chance for Negro Leaguers to be on the same field with white players. During the 1930s and 1940s, Satchel Paige's all-stars played against major league teams led by Dizzy Dean and Bob Feller and drew large crowds. "People wanted to come out and see these black boys play these white boys," says Larry Lester. "There was no TV then so people said, 'I can't wait to see this. I'm going to take off work.'"

The teams split the gate, and because they didn't have to share the receipts with the owners of their teams, the profits could be considerable.

Monarchs pitcher Hilton Smith said the 1946 postseason barnstorming tour featuring teams led by Paige and Feller drew large crowds and the players' share was about $6,000 apiece. This upset Stan Musial, who was invited to play on Feller's team but had to pass when his St. Louis Cardinals played the Boston Red Sox in the World Series. Musial's share for winning the Series was less than $4,000. "He raised all kind of heck about it," Smith said.

Banks's mentor Hank Thompson, who spent four seasons with the Monarchs and then seven more with the New York Giants, said he made $7,500 playing for Paige's team on the tour, far more money than he did during the season. "We all wanted to join up with Satchel," O'Neil said. "Satchel was a money tree for all of us."

Major league barnstorming teams also gave fans in smaller towns throughout the country their only chance to see the stars they had read about, and grueling schedules of thirty games or more were not uncommon. This practice lasted well into the 1950s as Willie Mays, Roy Campanella, and Don Newcombe led teams through the South, while such white major leaguers as Richie Ashburn of the Philadelphia Phillies and Spec Shea of the Washington Senators led all-star teams on lengthy tours. Some major league owners worried that their top players might be injured while barnstorming, but since they only gave one-year contracts, the players were free to spend the off-season doing what they did best.

Jackie Robinson's entrance into the major leagues took barnstorming to a new level. Though he was not wild about playing in the off-season, Robinson's major league salary was small, and black fans throughout the country, particularly in the South, all but demanded that he play in their towns. "It's Robinson they came to see," promoter Ted Worner said. "I don't have any doubts about that."

In 1949, Robinson made $15,000 barnstorming, and in 1950 he put together a first-rate all-star team that included Campanella, Larry Doby, Newcombe—and Ernie Banks. "I was flabbergasted," Banks said when the invitation was passed on to him by Buster Haywood, the manager of the Indianapolis Clowns, who were the opposition for Robinson's team on the tour. Play shortstop alongside the great players who had left the Negro Leagues for the majors and proved they belonged? Banks thought he must be living in a dream, one that became even better when Robinson took a personal interest in him. "Why, I don't know, but he really cared about me," Banks said years later. "The most important thing he told me was to listen. Don't talk, just listen."

Robinson also gave him tips about making double plays—get rid of the ball faster, make your throws high enough so the second baseman can make the pivot to first base easily—and complimented him on his hitting, particularly on the way he got around on inside pitches. When the month-long tour made a stop in Dallas, Eddie Banks was in the crowd and beamed with pride when Robinson, Campanella, Doby, and Newcombe all said nice things about him. "My father smoked two cigars during the time it would normally take him to smoke one," Banks said.

At the end of the tour, Banks was given $400 and expenses—he had never bothered to ask what he would be paid—which he took to the nearest clothing store and bought a red shirt and sweater and pearl-gray slacks. He changed clothes in the store, took the train home—he'd seen enough of buses—walked into the house, threw a wad of bills on the dining room table, and said, "We're rich."

"God almighty, son," Eddie Banks said. "I've never seen that much money. And look at you—dressed for high society."

A few weeks later, Banks was brought down to earth when a letter arrived from his draft board. He was to report to a Dallas army induction center and then be sent to Fort Bliss in El Paso, Texas, where he would join an all-black unit that was part of the 45th AAA Gun Battalion, an anti-aircraft unit that had seen heavy action in World War II. The Korean War had begun that summer—Banks's childhood friend Robert Prince was one of the nearly 1.8 million Americans sent to fight in "The Forgotten War"—but the overseas headquarters of the 45th were in Bremerhaven, Germany. This was the first and the most important of several breaks he would receive during his two years in the army.

Banks was less fortunate when, just before he was to begin basic training, his left knee unaccountably locked into one position and he was unable to put any weight on his leg or even get out of bed. After hearing the inevitable jibes from his fellow soldiers about malingering, he was confined to Beaumont army hospital, where he overheard doctors discussing an operation. Instead, he was confined to bed with heavy weights on his leg to keep it immobilized.

"He probably had torn cartilage in his knee," says C. Lowry Barnes, the chairman of the Department of Orthopaedics at the University of Arkansas for Medical Sciences, who specializes in knee surgery and replacements. "Most likely, a little piece of cartilage slipped in the knee and that's why he couldn't get his leg straight. Over time, it removed itself outside the joint and got stuck in between, like a newspaper in a doorjamb."

It is conceivable, Barnes says, that the damaged cartilage healed on its own to some extent or moved away from the knee, alleviating the pain. But it could return at any time, and in fact Banks's knees would trouble him off and on for decades. As for placing heavy weights on his leg, Barnes says, "That's certainly not what we would do now. Today, he'd have an MRI, have arthroscopic surgery, and quickly get on with his life." After three weeks in bed, Banks joined his unit, where he was trained as a cannoneer, one of the soldiers who passed along ammunition used in anti-aircraft artillery.

The highlight of his time at Fort Bliss came when the Harlem Globetrotters played a game in El Paso. Marques Haynes, the Globetrotter great who astonished audiences with his ability to dribble a basketball six times a second, had heard of Banks's athletic ability from friends on the Dallas Colts and the Monarchs, and invited him to join the team as a part-time player. Banks enjoyed the Globetrotters' famous crowd-pleasing antics, though he said he didn't contribute much. His most lasting memory of the evening was a conversation with the team's owner and coach, Abe Saperstein.

"Sit here next to me and I'll describe our plays to you," Saperstein said. "That way you'll know what to do when I put you in." Saperstein's instructions were easy enough, but Banks had a hard time processing them. It was, he said, the first time he had ever sat next to a white man and he wasn't sure what to do. Only when the Globetrotters' comic routines got him and the rest of the crowd laughing was he able to relax.

When Banks arrived in Germany, he benefited from another break. He was on KP duty one day when he was approached by an officer whose words were music to his ears. He was being assigned to another outfit that wanted him for its baseball team, the 242nd AAA Group Barons. "That's when my life in the army began," Banks said.

Playing baseball was a privileged position in the army, one envied by other soldiers. "We had our own floor in the barracks," Jim Knutson, a catcher from La Crosse, Wisconsin, remembers. "We ate meals before the others."

"Their duties other than baseball were very limited because they traveled to play against the other bases," says Ted Knutson, Jim's son. "My dad said when he wasn't playing baseball, he drove supply trucks from one base to another. It was a little embarrassing what good duty it was. I think they felt bad that others were in Korea and they weren't seeing combat."

The games were not particularly well attended—some of the fields had no spectator seating or outfield fences—nor did there seem to be much pride or support from other soldiers on the base. But the competition wasn't bad, and it didn't take long for a consensus to form among the players and those who did follow the games. "Everybody knew right away that he was sensational," Jim Knutson says of Banks. "He could hit, he could run, and he could throw." A reporter for the military newspaper *Stars and Stripes* thought so, too, noting Banks's relaxed attitude at the plate, his quick moves in the field, and his "shotgun-accurate arm."

Banks spent the rest of his tour playing baseball and later, after being promoted to company athletic director, organizing football teams and other athletic activities. His only setback was a recurrence of the locked knee he'd had in Texas. Once again, he was confined to bed where, with weights attached to his leg, he listened to the 1952 World Series in disappointment as the New York Yankees beat Jackie Robinson's Brooklyn Dodgers in seven games.

The army had been integrated only two years before Banks was drafted and he sometimes wondered if he might have been the first black man to supervise white and black soldiers playing together. Though he discussed his time in the army in some detail in his autobiography and later with interviewers, he did not publicly acknowledge that it was his first daily exposure to white people. Once again, he was content to take things as they came, to stand on the outside alone, observing.

With all his needs taken care of, Banks sent much of his army pay home to Dallas, where, though it was often no more than five dollars at a time, it was more than welcome.

"Boy, they was waiting on that money every month," his sister Edna told him.

"I just saw how hard it was for them," Banks said, "and I wanted to help."

After his discharge in 1953, Banks returned to Dallas, where, to his mother's consternation, he and Mollye Ector were married. Edna says Essie Banks was worried about Mollye's reputation and told her son, "Ernest, you're not marrying Mollye because she's not going to make you a good wife." And when I. B. Loud, the pastor at St. Paul's Methodist, told her Mollye was pregnant, Essie dug in her heels even further.

"Well, I do not believe it," she said.

"Believe it or not, they need to get married," the minister replied, and that settled it. The ceremony took place on April 6, 1953, at Loud's home. Not long after the marriage, it became clear that Mollye was not pregnant after all, which upset Essie all over again.

"She tricked him into marrying her," she told Edna. Essie lived to the age of ninety-seven and would see Banks through all four of his marriages, which would cause him and the women involved no end of grief.

Buck O'Neil greeted Banks warmly when he returned to Kansas City, but he was still troubled by his ailing left knee and got off to a slow start. The season didn't begin until late May, and Banks missed ten straight games in June and three more when he tried to return too early. Frustrated by his injury, tired of the long bus rides, and missing his new wife back in Dallas, he left the team and went home to think things over. O'Neil followed a few days later, told him he was making a big mistake and that his team needed him. Mollye came back with him and they moved into an apartment in Kansas City. "I finally got to see him play," she said. "He didn't get a hit that day."

But despite his problems early in the season, Banks was making his mark. His restraint at the plate impressed one opponent, who said, "He can wait on a pitch until the catcher's almost ready to throw it back to you," while another perceptive, if unlikely, observer noted a maturity and wisdom about him. "He seemed like an old man, even though he was young," said Toni Stone, an infielder for the Indianapolis Clowns.

Stone was an exceptional athlete who was frustrated that the Clowns kept her on their roster only as an attendance-boosting publicity stunt: the first woman to play in the Negro Leagues. She played for a number of black semipro teams before joining the Clowns in 1953, where she replaced a nineteen-year-old second baseman named Hank Aaron. Stone surprised her teammates and opponents with a .243 batting average, and by getting a hit off Satchel Paige, and she took a perverse pride in the fact that many of them viewed her as a threat to their masculinity and that some even tried to injure her. After being spiked by a player trying to take her out at second base, she showed off the scars on her wrist and said, "He was out."

Stone joined the Monarchs in 1954, where O'Neil confined her to the bench. "It was hell," she said. But Banks's curiosity about Stone soon turned to admiration. Her isolation from her teammates struck a chord, perhaps serving as a reminder of his own loneliness. "I didn't see all of her struggle, but I saw some of it," Banks told Stone's biographer, Martha Ackmann. "She stood tall, didn't give up, and was very determined. It was rugged for her, but she dealt with all her stuff."

While teams like the Clowns were resorting to oddities like women players and comedy routines out of the Harlem Globetrotters' playbook, the Monarchs retained some dignity. "Kansas City was the Cadillac of the Negro Leagues," says Hank Mason, who pitched for the Monarchs in 1953 and 1954. "We lived in some of the best hotels in the country; they just happened to be black hotels. We ate in some of the best restaurants in the country, only they were black. I don't know about the other teams, but the Kansas City Monarchs were a first-class operation."

No amount of luxury travel could disguise the hodgepodge nature of the Monarchs' schedule, though. They played few games in their hometown, no more than one or two a month, and spent the rest of their time on the road, playing in towns big and small, often on the same day. Mason recalls many Sundays that began with afternoon games in major league ballparks—Crosley Field in Cincinnati, Briggs Stadium in Detroit, Comiskey Park in Chicago, Yankee Stadium in New York—and ended with night games elsewhere. "We'd play a local team or if we were traveling with the Memphis Red Sox maybe we would play them in a smaller town," Mason says. Nor did the Monarchs go home when their regular season ended. Instead, they spent up to six weeks barnstorming with the Clowns. The idea was to keep moving, keep playing, and, for the players who were young enough, keep hoping the major leagues were watching.

Not long after returning from his brief exile in Dallas, Banks began tearing the league apart. On June 28, he hit a bases-loaded triple in the first game of a doubleheader against the Clowns in Detroit, and by mid-July he was among the league's top hitters with a .400 batting average. Several weeks later, *The Sporting News* noted that "the 22-year-old sensation of the Monarchs is leading the league in batting with an average of .408." In less than two months he had become one of the hottest young prospects in baseball for major league teams that were hiring black players, or were thinking about it.

The legends, tall tales, and self-serving falsehoods about the scouting and signing of Banks began in the mid-1950s after he had become one of baseball's most electrifying players, and they continued for many years. The

scouts who had seen him play and the executives who had let him get
away seemed to have a compulsion to explain themselves. Master story-
tellers like baseball executives Frank Lane and Bill Veeck would publicly
bemoan their failure to act while the Cubs, glorying in their good fortune,
would embroider their own accounts and polish them to a high gloss.

After Robinson's breakthrough, many major league teams began
looking at Negro League players in earnest, and since there were only
four teams left in 1953—the Monarchs, Clowns, Red Sox, and Birmingham Black Barons—it is likely that Banks was seen by any number of
scouts that year. But his unremarkable performance in 1950 and his two-
year absence might have made his short and sudden burst of hitting seem
suspect to major league scouts, particularly the old-timers who were
having trouble adjusting to integration. Racist comments on scouting
reports, especially those filed by southerners, were common for many
years after Robinson's debut.

So when Cool Papa Bell and Quincy Trouppe, a nineteen-year veteran of the Negro Leagues, tried to interest the St. Louis Cardinals in
Banks, they were overruled by a scout whose report said, "He can't hit,
he can't run, he has a pretty good arm, but it's a scatter arm. I don't like
him." Lane, the general manager of the Chicago White Sox, also said he
received a report saying Banks couldn't throw, field, or hit. "Now every
time I see he has hit a homer, I get sick remembering how easily we could
have had that kid," Lane said in 1956. He tried to exonerate himself by
saying the Cincinnati Reds and New York Yankees had also passed on
Banks. But the truth is Lane simply wasn't listening to the people inside
his organization and out who were begging him to sign Banks.

O'Neil said John Donaldson, a former Monarchs pitcher and White
Sox scout, was so enraged when his recommendation was ignored that
he quit his job. Connie Johnson, a former Monarchs pitcher then in the
White Sox farm system, also begged the team to sign Banks. "He seems
to be more concerned about getting a chance for Banks than he does for
himself," said White Sox manager Paul Richards. But it was Johnson,
not Banks, who joined the White Sox in 1953 for the beginning of what

would be a five-year career in the majors. Negro League umpire T. H. Jefferson also said he recommended Banks to the White Sox. "They weren't interested," Jefferson said during a visit to Chicago in 1967. "So right here in Comiskey Park, I called time in a game to tell the crowd that one of the players, Ernie Banks, had been signed by the Cubs."

Veeck's stories about trying to sign Banks are fanciful in the extreme. According to Banks's autobiography, Veeck wrote Banks while he was in the army in Germany inviting him to try out with the Cleveland Indians when he returned. (Banks said he received a similar letter from the Brooklyn Dodgers, but was so excited about returning to the Monarchs he ignored them both.) But Veeck said he heard about Banks from a scout during the 1953 season and called T. Y. Baird to ask how much he wanted for him. The price, Baird said, was $35,000.

"Gee, I don't have thirty-five thousand dollars," Veeck said. "I'll give you thirty-five hundred dollars down and the thirty-one thousand five hundred dollars when you catch me."

"That's the way I'm doing business myself, Bill," Baird said. "I have to get thirty-five thousand dollars for Banks to pay off my own debts."

The story ends with Veeck extracting a promise from Baird not to sell Banks to an American League team and quickly tipping off the Cubs about the great young player with the Monarchs. Thus did Veeck, a great spinner of yarns and self-described hustler, claim to be the man who sent Ernie Banks to the Cubs.

The truth is he had less to do with it than the neglectful executives and incompetent scouts who had let Banks get away, because the Cubs, aided by some blind luck from an unlikely source, had been in the front of the pack all along.

Chapter 7

"Going to Chicago, Sorry I Can't Take You"

When it came to selling the contracts of his players, T. Y. Baird was as cagey as they came. A baseball player himself until he was sidelined by a fractured knee, Baird ran a billiard parlor in Kansas City, booked games for local semipro teams and the famous House of David team that barnstormed the country from its base in Michigan, and picked up whatever promotional work he could. In 1929, Baird bought a share of the Monarchs from their founder, J. L. Wilkinson. The two men were the only white owners of a Negro League team.

Wilkinson had long worked with Rube Foster, who was known as the "father of black baseball," for the betterment of the Negro Leagues, but it may have been for the best that his new partner's membership in the Kansas City branch of the Ku Klux Klan went unnoticed. It was, people who knew Baird said, a business decision, as he feared customers at his pool hall might rebel if he didn't have a Klan membership to offset his association with black baseball players.

Baird and Wilkinson ran the Monarchs together during the boom-and-bust years of the next two decades, but when the Negro Leagues had their existential crisis after Jackie Robinson entered the majors, Baird bought Wilkinson out and quickly established a new and perverse business model. The only way for the Monarchs to stay in business, Baird decided, was not by winning pennants but by selling off the contracts of their best players.

Still smarting from the fact that Branch Rickey hadn't paid him for

Robinson, who had played for the Monarchs in 1945, Baird began signing his players to legally binding contracts and, over the next decade, selling them to major league teams and their minor league affiliates. The revenue from these transactions could be the difference between profit and loss. In 1950, Baird earned $21,750 in player transactions and realized an overall net profit of $20,157. In 1952, sales were $14,000 and his net profit was $9,952.

Overall, Baird sold the contracts of thirty-eight players, twenty-nine of whom played in the majors, and the Monarchs soon became known among young black players as their quickest path to the majors. Any of Baird's players was available if the price was right, and the price was often quite low. Five hundred dollars might be enough for a major league organization to get a look at a prospect, with additional small amounts payable if the player made the team, stayed on the roster past a certain date, and advanced to a higher minor league. One team that happily played by Baird's rules was the Chicago Cubs.

Baird's papers contain extensive correspondence with Cubs executives dating back to 1949, and though it would be four years before they would promote two of his protégés to the majors, their farm system soon became a revolving door for black players. Starting with veteran Monarchs pitcher Booker McDaniels, black players came and went—some from Kansas City, some from other organizations—with no apparent plan in mind, certainly no plan of bringing them to Chicago.

Baird's descriptions of his players reveal his own strictly business attitudes about race and the black men who were working their way into white baseball. Writing to Jack Sheehan, the director of the Cubs' farm system, in 1949, he said that catcher Earl Taborn and pitcher Allen Bryant were "very light in color and could pass for white men." When Sheehan expressed interest in Taborn but only for a team in the low minors, Baird said that "he would not play in that low of a classification. This will show you how chesty he is." Baird also recommended that the Cubs check out Monarchs pitcher Gene Robinson, who was "a swell kid, very light in color, and looks like a white man from up in the stands." Sheehan had better hurry, though, because Brick Laws, the president of the Pacific Coast League's Oakland Oaks, had told Baird "he was going to notify the papers that he had signed him because they had been on him to hire a Negro and seemed peeved because I would not accept his offer." And when the Cubs said they were thinking of hiring Harold "Yellowhorse" Morris, who had pitched for the Monarchs in the 1920s, as a scout, Baird replied, "he was above average intelligence for a Negro." That was good enough for Sheehan, and Morris got the job.

The Cubs' dive into the Negro Leagues player pool led to some initial failures that served as an omen for the troubles they would have building a competitive team in the years ahead. One was caused by a monumental failure in judgment, the other by the machinations of T. Y. Baird.

In 1949, the Cubs acted on a scout's enthusiastic recommendation and bought the contract of a twenty-year-old infielder named Jim Gilliam from the Baltimore Elite Giants. Though there was no profit in the deal for Baird, he told Sheehan that Gilliam was "a hell of a good ballplayer" and one of the two best infielders in the Negro Leagues. But Gilliam, who was born and raised in Nashville, Tennessee, had been happy in Baltimore and was uncomfortable adjusting to his first integrated setting. Rather than try to ease his transition, the Cubs saw only a player who wasn't hitting, and, after demoting him from their AAA team in Springfield, Massachusetts, to Class A in Des Moines, Iowa, Sheehan returned him to Baltimore. Four years later, Gilliam began a fourteen-year career with the Brooklyn and Los Angeles Dodgers during which he played in seven World Series, made two All-Star teams, and became one of his team's most reliable and admired players.

But if Sheehan's talent-evaluation skills sometimes failed him, there were other occasions when he got it just right. In March 1950, he offered Baird $1,000 each for a month-long look at a shortstop named Gene Baker and Ernie Banks's old Monarchs roommate, Elston Howard. "Let me know what your asking price is on each one," Sheehan wrote, "and don't scare me off." Baird was happy to let Sheehan give Baker a trial— and to say it would cost $5,500 if he passed it—but said he wanted to hold on to Howard for a while. He had already sold the contracts of five play-ers from his 1949 team, the Monarchs were short of catchers, and he needed "a good club to keep up our reputation so we will continue to be an attraction." Sheehan understood, but told Baird to let him know when he was ready to make a deal for Howard. In June, Sheehan said he would keep Baker, whom he had assigned to the Cubs' Pacific Coast League team in Los Angeles, and again asked about Howard. A month later, he picked up a newspaper and read the worst possible news: Baird had sold Howard to the New York Yankees.

Sheehan was furious. Baird had promised "that you would notify me whenever you were ready to sell him," he wrote. "My disappointment is not in failing to get the player but because you did not keep your prom-ise to me." Baird's response was that the Yankees had paid $2,500 as a down payment on Howard's contract, which was more than the Cubs had offered. Howard would become the Yankees' first black player, the American League's first black Most Valuable Player, and an eight-time All-Star.

If Gilliam and Howard ever wondered what their careers might have been like with the Cubs, it is unlikely they did so with regret. Between 1953 and 1967, they played in a total of seventeen World Series, three of them against each other, while in all but the last of those seasons the Cubs finished no higher than fifth place.

Sheehan's anger at Baird did not prevent the Cubs from continuing to do business with him, and early in the 1953 season they turned their attention to another young Monarch—a shortstop whose name they first heard during a convoluted process that involved the nervous head of a team in Macon, Georgia, a young outfielder in the Cubs' system, and an infielder playing for the Milwaukee Braves' farm team in Jacksonville, Florida.

Tom Gordon wasn't sure the Macon Peaches were ready for Solly Drake, and Drake might have had a few misgivings of his own. After breaking the color line at the Cubs' Class A farm team in Topeka, Kansas, in 1951, Drake had endured his share of racial taunts before becoming a fan favorite as the team's top hitter and a key player in their march to the league's title. When he scored two runs in the last game before he left for the army in August, the crowd passed a hat and presented him with $191.51. Two years later, Drake returned home, and the Cubs assigned him to their Southern Atlantic League in Macon. Concerned about how his city would react to a black player, Gordon, the team's general manager, called Gene Lawing, the Cubs' new farm director, and presented his problem. Lawing was sympathetic and sent Drake to the team's farm team in Des Moines instead.

But while Gordon hesitated, two other Sally League teams decided to break the color line once and for all. One was the Savannah Indians, who named two black players to their roster. The other was the Jacksonville Braves, who added three, including a particularly promising infielder who had played the previous year with the Indianapolis Clowns, Hank Aaron.

Aaron and his teammates would remember their 1953 season in vivid detail. "Places like Macon, they'd come to the ballpark with coolers of beer and they'd be half drunk by batting practice," first baseman Joe Andrews told Aaron's biographer, Lonnie Wheeler. "It was amazing the way Henry could handle it. I'd be standing next to Henry in the infield and some yahoo would call him a nigger or something, and I'd turn to Henry and say, 'Did you hear that?' He'd look back at me and say, 'What, do you think I'm deaf?' "

This was of no concern of Tom Gordon, however, particularly when Aaron went on a hitting tear that showed he was a major league star in the making and ballparks throughout the Sally League began filling up with black customers. The Braves drew so many when they came to Macon that the rope separating them from white fans had to be moved to accommodate them, and the Peaches played before three consecutive sellouts. "Suddenly, the general manager decided that maybe a black player or two wouldn't be such a bad idea," said Aaron, who went on to bat .362

with twenty-two home runs and prompt a sportswriter to say, "Henry Aaron led the league in everything except hotel accommodations."

Gordon made another call to Lawing and said he wouldn't mind having Solly Drake on his team after all. It was too late, said Lawing, who suggested Gordon look for a black player of his own. "Where do I start?" Gordon asked. Lawing noted that the Monarchs would be playing a couple of hours away in Columbus, Georgia, the following night. Why didn't he take a look at their players and discuss it with T. Y. Baird? "He's a good friend of our organization and I'm sure he'll help you if he can," Lawing said.

Gordon was no impressionable novice when it came to scouting young ballplayers, but the moment he saw Banks he was smitten. "Sometimes you have to see a boy two or three weeks to check him from all angles," he said. "That night this shortstop did it all. He came in on slow rollers, had to go in the hole, covered near the left-field foul line, and made the double play. He made it all look so easy. Then, late in the game, he hit a curveball over a sixty-foot fence that was three hundred and fifty feet from home plate. That was enough for me."

Gordon met with Baird after the game, but the Monarchs' owner said he wasn't interested in selling Banks's contract to the minor leagues. When the time came, he said, he would deal directly with the Cubs, or other major league teams. Gordon didn't bother to argue, probably because he realized that no minor league team could afford the price Baird had in mind for the last great Monarchs player he would send to the majors. Gordon called Lawing in Chicago to relay his disappointment and to rave about the shortstop who had gotten away. Lawing in turn passed Gordon's report on to the Cubs' general manager, Wid Matthews.

Perhaps because Banks had spent the previous two years in the army, the Cubs had no record of him, and it isn't clear why Matthews became so determined to pursue a player he had never heard of based on the report of a man who had only seen him play a few times. One possibility is that he did it to compensate for his own lack of judgment in the past.

Before the Cubs made Matthews their general manager in 1950, he'd had a long association with Branch Rickey that began with the St. Louis Cardinals and continued when Rickey became general manager of the Dodgers in 1942. Though Matthews had a solid reputation as a scout, he was not at his best when it came to assessing black players in the early days of integration. When Rickey sent him to look at Jackie Robinson while he was playing for the Monarchs, Matthews expressed reservations about Robinson's "demeanor on the field" and said "he was too much of a hot dog in his mannerisms." Some years later, when Robinson and Roy Campanella recommended a young outfielder they had seen in Birmingham, Alabama, on one of their barnstorming tours, Matthews reported back that he couldn't hit a curveball. So the Dodgers passed on Willie Mays. But when Matthews heard about Banks he immediately dispatched three scouts to check him out. Their reports were unanimous: Banks was the real thing.

"Good accurate arm," wrote Ray Hayworth. "Fielding ranges from good to outstanding. Has good form with quick wrists and level swing." "Really floats around shortstop and fields ball well from any position," Jimmy Payton wrote. "Will become good hitter," wrote Hugh Wise. "Doesn't swing at bad pitches...Outstanding arm and good hitter... No outstanding weaknesses. This player has got it and I strongly recommend we negotiate for his services. Am strong for this boy because I believe he can do the job and has future."

Wise was so impressed that he took it upon himself to take Baird out for a snack and ask him to set a price on Banks's contract. "Of course, he wouldn't," Wise reported. "He definitely wants us to make an offer so he can use it to bait other clubs."

After reading these reports, one of which also mentioned an eighteen-year-old Monarchs pitcher named Bill Dickey, Matthews asked for one more from Ray Blades, the most conservative man on his scouting staff. Blades's assessment was short and lacked the specifics the other scouts had provided. "You wouldn't believe it if I told you," Blades wrote. "Go see him for yourself."

Matthews took Blades's advice and saw Banks play, first in Des Moines and then in Kansas City, where, though he may have spoken with Baird, there are no reports suggesting any negotiations. But when Matthews saw that Banks had been named to play in the Negro Leagues' annual East-West All-Star Game in Chicago in August, he was determined to make his move.

Like the Negro Leagues themselves, the East-West Game had seen better days by the time Banks played in one. In its glory years from the late 1930s through most of the 1940s, the game not only filled Comiskey Park but brought together the largest gathering of African Americans in the United States for what became an unofficial black holiday. "We kept the game in Chicago because it was in the middle of the country and people could get there from all over," Buck O'Neil said.

Railroads arranged for special trains to bring people from New Orleans, Mississippi, and elsewhere in the South; from Kansas and other points west; and from New York and other eastern cities. Hotel rooms sold out, stores lured customers with signs reading "East-West Tickets Sold Here," and nightclubs were filled to overflowing as Duke Ellington, Ella Fitzgerald, Lena Horne, Billie Holiday, and other black entertainers brought their acts to town. Comiskey Park was decorated with red, white, and blue banners, a jazz band played between innings, and the stands were jammed with famous faces and regular folks alike.

"I was twenty-two years old and I couldn't wait to get to Comiskey Park," Monte Irvin said of being named to his first East-West Game in 1941. "Count Basie had written a song called 'Goin' to Chicago Blues.' They were playing it on the radio during our train ride and everybody in our car was singing along. 'Going to Chicago, sorry I can't take you.' You didn't go to Chicago to sleep."

Adding to the buildup was the fact that the game's players were selected by fans who clipped ballots out of black newspapers by the millions, thereby one-upping the major leagues, which didn't let fans choose its All-Star Game rosters until 1947. "That was a pretty important thing for black people to be able to vote, even if it was just for ballplayers," O'Neil said. And the games themselves were serious business, as baseball's finest black players knew they would never play on a larger stage and gave their very best.

But while the East-West Game was a joyous gathering, some saw a greater significance. "Right away it was clear that our game meant a lot more than the big-league game," O'Neil said. "Theirs was, and is, more or less an exhibition. But for black folks, the East-West Game was a matter of racial pride."

"More than anything else," said Monte Irvin, "our games gave black Americans hope all across the country."

The first sign that the East-West Game was in trouble came in 1948 when some of the more than 42,000 people who came to Comiskey Park carried portable radios so they could listen to games involving Jackie Robinson and Roy Campanella with the Brooklyn Dodgers and Satchel Paige and Larry Doby with the Cleveland Indians. Eleven days earlier, the Indians had drawn more than 51,000 fans to the same ballpark—and turned away another 15,000—to see Paige shut out the White Sox. Attendance at the East-West Game declined rapidly during the next few years, and while the crowd at the 1953 game was announced at 10,000, some thought it might have been only half that number.

Banks would later say he had three hits in the game and O'Neil would invent a tale about a late-inning tie, the teams nearly running out of baseballs, and Banks saving the day by hitting a game-winning home run. But the truth was more mundane. Banks went hitless in four at-bats, although the *Chicago Tribune* said he "lived up to advance notices in the field as he accepted seven chances without error and made one of the game's fielding gems with a spectacular stop of Verdes Drake's smash in the third inning, taking the ball on a short hop and throwing Drake out from deep short."

But if Banks's performance at the plate was less than impressive, Matthews was undeterred and told Baird he wanted to talk business. "I'm not ready," Baird said. "I'll let you know when I am." Three weeks later, as the Monarchs were nearing the end of their season and about to play in

Chicago, Baird suggested a meeting at the Conrad Hilton Hotel, during which he got straight to the point.

"Make me an offer," he said.

"I never had any luck dealing that way," Matthews said. "Let's trade tonight. I'd like to walk out of here with Banks and Bill Dickey or leave the field to somebody else. Tell you what I'll do. Put a price on the two boys. I'll take it or leave it within five seconds and that'll be the end of our negotiations."

Baird named his price: $15,000 for Banks and $5,000 for Dickey. Matthews accepted on the spot, and while he later admitted he might have gone higher, perhaps to $30,000, Baird was satisfied. He had just pulled off the biggest sale in the history of the Negro Leagues, one that ensured the Monarchs a five-figure profit for the season.

Later that evening, O'Neil found Banks watching television in the lobby of the Pershing Hotel on Chicago's South Side and delivered a cryptic message. "Get hold of Bill Dickey and the two of you meet me in the lobby at seven tomorrow morning."

Seven in the morning? The Monarchs' bus wasn't due to leave for the team's next game in Muskegon, Michigan, until noon. Had he done something wrong? Banks wondered. Were they going to cut him? The season was almost over. It was time to go home, see his family, look for a job. It didn't make any sense. No longer interested in what was on television, Banks went for a walk.

The following morning, O'Neil was silent during the cab ride north. Banks and Dickey sat in the backseat, discussing their plans for the winter and saying how good it would be to go home. Then, as they arrived at their destination, Banks saw a big red sign. "Welcome to Wrigley Field," it read, and for a moment he was struck dumb. "What is this, Buck?" he finally said. Until that moment, he had never heard of the fabled ballpark.

The intimidation Banks felt increased as he and Dickey followed O'Neil through a side door and up a flight of stairs to Matthews's office. Dickey was nervous, too, and they both remained silent, waiting to see what would happen next. "He was from Shreveport, Louisiana, and I was from Dallas," Banks said. "We come out of the black community, so being around whites was totally different for us."

Matthews spoke rapidly—Banks was fascinated by the small red bow tie that bounced up and down as he talked—as he explained why they were there. Dickey would join the Cubs' Class B farm team in Cedar Rapids, Iowa, when the Monarchs ended their season in Pittsburgh the following week. Banks, however, would report directly to the Cubs. "We like you as a player and know that you can play here at the major league level," Matthews said. But since the Monarchs weren't part of organized baseball, he needed the players' approval. "Just answer yes or no," he said.

"I was hearing what the man said," Banks said, "but I wasn't believing it. We both answered a very nervous yes." The anxiety continued when a contract was put in front of him. "I had to hold my right hand with my left as I scribbled 'Ernest Banks' on a document that seemed to be a mile long," he said.

Banks was still disoriented during the ride back to the Pershing. Only when O'Neil told him he would be making $800 a month as a Cub did he realize he hadn't asked about money. His confusion continued when he found Jim Enright of the *Chicago American*, who had received a tip from the Cubs' front office, waiting for him at the hotel. The resulting interview contained mostly yes and no answers except for one display of self-confidence he may not have completely felt. "Naturally I'm pleased over becoming a major leaguer and I'll do my best to help the Cubs," he said. "I know I can field, and I'm confident I can hit major league pitching."

"Cubs Sign Banks, Negro Star," read the headline over Enright's story, which was quickly picked up by the wire services and spread around the country. Banks called his father in Dallas and said, "We're rich."

"Yeah, son, I know," Eddie Banks said with a laugh. "I read about it."

In Dallas, Banks's old friend Jack Price exulted—"They got the right one," he told everyone he knew—while in Korea, Robert Prince heard the news on a short-wave radio that could have earned him a court-martial had he been discovered carrying it while on guard duty. ("You could see the CO coming for miles," Prince says. "You just put it under a rock.")

"Hey, that's my homeboy!" he shouted.

It was all happening so fast, and Banks understood so little. "There was no baseball in Dallas when I was growing up," he said. "No major league teams came through there. I had no contact with the major leagues and I didn't know anything about it, except for Jackie Robinson. I was so naïve."

Did he really have to leave the Monarchs, for whom he enjoyed playing so much? "I was in my own comfort area and I liked being with the guys," he said. "We cared about each other. They were like my family. I didn't want to leave them."

Sherwood Brewer set him straight. "You've got to go," the Monarchs second baseman, who had done so much to help him get adjusted, said. "It's the major leagues. That's as high as you can go. You'll be playing with Ralph Kiner and Hank Sauer."

"I don't know them," Banks said.

"You will when you get there. Just go, Ernie. It's where you want to be."

A week later in Pittsburgh, O'Neil gave Banks ten dollars and put him on a bus headed west.

III

ERNIE BANKS AND MR. CUB

Chapter 8

North Side, South Side

After he retired from baseball, Ernie Banks would sometimes claim that he was the only athlete who had played his entire career in one ballpark in one city for one owner under one mayor. That wasn't quite right—Banks arrived in Chicago in 1953 and Richard J. Daley didn't become the city's mayor until 1955—but it was close enough.

A visionary builder responsible for a significant portion of today's Chicago skyline, Daley took over the most segregated large city in the United States and saw to it that it remained that way. Daley preserved and enhanced the city's racial makeup by placing every one of the dozens of public housing units built during his administration in black neighborhoods. And though there were some calls for integration of Chicago's housing, schools, and businesses—employers in the Loop, the city's main business district, didn't hire blacks until well into the 1950s—the separation of races was generally accepted by its black residents.

When Jackie Robinson made his Chicago major league debut in May 1947, for instance, many black fans drove or took the "L" to Wrigley Field early in the morning to buy tickets. With no place in the white neighborhood surrounding the ballpark where they could comfortably wait, they returned home and made a second trip north that afternoon to cheer for black America's newest hero. "It was amazing to the other people in the grandstand that we were rooting for Brooklyn," says Timuel Black, a revered educator, historian, and civil rights activist who came to Chicago during the Great Migration of 1919 and was still going strong well into his nineties. "They said, 'What's wrong with you?' They wondered how we could cheer for a non-Chicago team. We told them, 'Wait until the Cubs get some Negro players and we'll be cheering for them.'"

Even accidents of integration were fiercely resisted by white Chicago. Several months before Banks arrived, an administrative error gave a black family an apartment in the Trumbull Park Homes in South Deering on the far South Side. Shortly after they moved in, an advance party of about fifty teenagers gathered outside their building grew to become a mob of more than a thousand people who threw rocks and bricks and trapped the family inside. The protesters included several ethnic groups—Italians, Irish, Slavs, and Poles—and the *Chicago Defender* noted that "although there was no unity in the language background, they had a common hatred for Negroes." The new tenants moved out the following spring, but a few other black families had moved in by then, and the resulting battle for Trumbull Park became so violent that it required a large police presence for several months and made news around the country.

So there was no question where Banks would live in Chicago. It would be in a black neighborhood on the city's South Side from where he would commute to Wrigley Field over the years with a succession of his black teammates who lived nearby. "We lived south, the other players lived north," Banks said. "There was no interaction at all, other than on the field, in the locker room, and on the train."

In the years ahead, the search for adequate housing by the Cubs' black players was not restricted to the city limits, nor were the gains made during the civil rights movement in the 1960s always helpful. "There were victories in court cases and legislation," Black says, "but from a practical point of view there were certain areas where black people didn't move."

As late as 1974, Banks's teammate Billy Williams saw these realities when he moved his growing family to the western suburb of Glen Ellyn only to learn a petition was circulating among his neighbors protesting his presence. "A woman wrote my wife a letter saying they don't have any black people here and they would like it if we didn't come here,"

Williams says. "I'm hitting home runs, people are cheering me, and all of a sudden you find out they don't want you in their neighborhood." Williams ignored the protest and got some measure of satisfaction when he threw occasional parties for his teammates. Word of the Cubs players' presence quickly spread, thrilling young boys in the neighborhood who rode their bikes down his street, hoping to get a glimpse of their heroes. Williams could only wonder if some of them were the sons of the adults who had signed the petition telling him he was not welcome.

But Banks never challenged the status quo. His first living quarters were at 72nd Street and South Wabash Avenue, where he received a small reminder of the adult supervision his neighborhood had provided back in North Dallas. "They knew I was a baseball player," Banks said, "and their main concern was that I stay out of trouble—'Don't stay out late. Don't do this. Stay away from that.' I listened to them and I stayed out of trouble." In 1955, Banks and Mollye moved into a house at 8123 South Michigan, and in 1958, he bought a spacious, attractive two-story home on a corner lot at 8159 South Rhodes, where he lived for most of the rest of his Cubs career.

The Cubs' black players established a reasonably comfortable lifestyle on the South Side, often gathering with their families in a restaurant in the Southmoor Hotel on the corner of Stony Island Avenue and 67th Street. The hotel had a ballroom where their children's birthday parties were celebrated, and it served as home to a number of the black Cubs, as well as some players for the Chicago Bears. The result of this was a feeling of closeness that a succession of the Cubs' black players would share for many years.

During the early days of integration, some young black baseball players struggled when they were sent to new and sometimes hostile environments. But the Cubs were wise enough to realize they shouldn't send Banks out to fend for himself in the big city, so they brought up another black player who became his primary lifeline to his new surroundings.

Gene Baker should have been the Cubs' first black player, and in a sense he was. The team bought Baker's contract from its Los Angeles Angels farm team on September 1, 1953, which made him the first black man on their major league roster. Banks's contract was purchased from the Monarchs a week later, and though both men reported to Wrigley Field on September 14, Baker had a pulled muscle in his left side, so Banks became the first black man to play for the Cubs.

Baker had been in the team's organization since 1950, and his talent earned him a promotion to the majors well before it finally came. He spent three years in Los Angeles, where he hit well, drove in runs and scored them, and played superbly in the field. "I believe Gene was as good a shortstop as I've ever seen—and that includes Pee Wee Reese," said Bobby Bragan, the manager of the Angels' biggest rivals, the Hollywood Stars. And luckily for Banks, Baker was the perfect guide as he adjusted to his new team and city.

Baker was six years older than Banks and his polar opposite in personality. While Banks remained shy and withdrawn, Baker, who had grown up in an integrated setting in Davenport, Iowa, was comfortable talking to just about anyone, black or white. "I kind of followed him around because he had so much more experience than I did," Banks said. "He had a lot of instinct for the game and for people. He nurtured me along."

Banks needed quite a bit of nurturing because there were things about his new team and his new city he simply didn't understand. The fact that he and his teammates only got together at the ballpark took some getting used to. So did adjusting to urban sprawl. "In Dallas and Kansas City, everything was convenient and the closeness was there," Banks said. "But in the majors, things were spread out—different players, different communities, different cultures." This disparity was driven home one day when he and Baker caught a train to St. Louis at the 63rd Street Station on the South Side after their white teammates had boarded downtown. Looking around at a part of the city he had previously only ridden through at high speed, one Cub rolled his eyes and said, "Where are we, South Africa?" Stunned by this remark, Banks turned to Baker, who quietly told him some people shouldn't drink so much.

Getting used to his new work environment was also a challenge. What was the big deal, he wondered when he got his first look at Wrigley Field, which was smaller than some of the ballparks the Monarchs had played in. Why, it looked like anybody could hit a home run here, and he proved it by driving the first batting practice pitch he saw into the left-field bleachers. Then there were his teammates, who seemed so solemn, so lacking in the pride he was used to in Kansas City. The Cubs were coming to the end of a dreadful season—after they made 111 errors in their first eighty games, someone proposed the slogan "On the floor by '54"—and with just a few weeks left they were playing out the string. "The quality of play wasn't as good as where I came from," Banks remembered. "The Monarchs were more lively and had more energy. The pace was slower with the Cubs and everything seemed so disorganized. Nobody seemed like they wanted to play."

This was most apparent during the final week of the season when Baker told him some of his teammates were upset by the way he ran back and forth from the dugout to his position in the field at the beginning and end of each inning, as the Monarchs had always done. "They think you're showing them up," Baker said. Unsure how to respond, Banks said nothing. He had no complaints about how he was received, though, and he was just wide-eyed enough to revel in it. Ralph Kiner and Hank Sauer, the aging home run kings, smiling and shaking his hand. Phil Cavarretta, the Cubs' beleaguered manager, extending a welcome. The other players sizing him up with interest. How could that not be exciting?

But he quickly learned that he was still a bit of a rube. Yosh Kawano, the legendary clubhouse man who would spend sixty-five seasons with the team, whispered in his ear that he might want to ditch his yellow shoelaces and handed him a pair of black ones. Hal Jeffcoat, the Cubs center fielder, loudly asked, "Ernie, where'd you get that glove, at the five and dime store?" Cubs second baseman Eddie Miksis loaned Banks a glove more suitable for big-league play. Thankful for the gesture, Banks would use it for many games to come.

————

On September 17, 1953, three days after Banks arrived in Chicago, he was standing behind the batting cage when Cavarretta walked up and delivered a short message: "You're in there today."

"He said it very slowly and I was a little shaky," Banks remembered. "It was like someone telling you you're going to war."

He looked it during the game, going without a hit in three at-bats and committing an error when he failed to stop a ground ball as the Cubs lost ignominiously to the Philadelphia Phillies, 16–4. The crowd of 2,793 seemed about right for a seventh-place team nearing the end of a season in which they would finish forty games out of first place.

Banks's first road trip began the following day with one instruction from Bob Lewis, the Cubs' traveling secretary: Stick close to Gene Baker. Banks was puzzled until the team arrived in St. Louis and headed to the Chase Hotel without its two newest members. Banks and Baker took a cab to the Olive Hotel in a black neighborhood, where they found comfortable beds, a well-stocked refrigerator, and an obliging manager asking if they needed anything more. Once again, Baker explained the facts of life to him. But a day later, even the older man proved naïve when they took a cab downtown to see a movie only to have the ticket-seller wave them away.

Banks played better in his second game, driving in two runs with singles in a 5–3 win over the Cardinals in Sportsman's Park. The next day, September 20, Sauer, the most popular Cub of his time, who had won the National League's Most Valuable Player Award in 1952, offered Banks some intelligence about the Cardinals' starting pitcher, Gerry Staley. When he gets ahead of a hitter, Sauer said, Staley likes to throw a knuckleball, and it was important not to overswing. "Just try to meet the ball," he said. "Don't kill it."

The Cubs were trailing 11–4 in the eighth inning when Banks faced

Staley for the fourth time. He had already hit a triple and a single and driven in two runs when he saw Staley's knuckleball coming toward him. Following Sauer's instructions, he took a nice, easy swing and was surprised when the ball jumped off the bat and flew into the left-field bleachers. In itself, the home run was nothing much, a meaningless late-inning hit in a game the Cubs would lose by five runs. But there are some things a baseball player never forgets. His first big-league home run and the name of the pitcher he hit it off are among them.

Banks played all seven of the Cubs' remaining games and finished the season hitting .314 with two home runs. (When he finally left the lineup with an injury three years later, he had set a record by playing in 424 consecutive games following his first major league appearance.) The Cubs and their fans could only cross their fingers and hope they had finally found the shortstop they had been seeking for so long.

The fact that the Cubs hadn't had a competent shortstop in more than a decade was a sore spot with their fans, some of whom would call the roll of those who had been found wanting over the years: Dick Bartell, Lennie Merullo, Jack Cusick, Emil Verban, Bob Ramazotti, and others. When Banks arrived, the incumbent was Roy Smalley, who had been their whipping boy since 1948.

Smalley was erratic in the field at best—he led the league in errors three times—particularly when throwing to first base. Fans sitting behind first were known to take cover when Smalley wound up, and Chicago columnist Mike Royko said he was a legend because he could "snatch up ground balls and fling them at the sun." The frequency of these mistakes put a target on Smalley's back and the fans took constant aim. "What I remember most about him," said Ira Berkow, a sports-writer for the New York Times who grew up in Chicago, "was the abuse he endured." Years later, Smalley even heard boos when he appeared at Wrigley Field for an old-timers' game.

Banks's success at shortstop caused a problem for Gene Baker, who had played the position his entire career. When he was finally well enough to return to the lineup, he was sent to second base, a position he had played only about a half dozen times in his life. "I was sort of in a fog out there," Baker said. "Everything seemed backwards to me. But I managed to survive."

Baker's struggles at second base would continue—he led the league in errors three times—and Banks had his problems in the field, too. In a game against St. Louis in the final series of the 1953 season, he caught a sharp ground ball and threw to second base to start a double play. But he hadn't realized the bases were empty and he should have thrown to first. Baker, who wasn't expecting the ball, did well to catch it and make the throw in time to get the runner for an unusual 6–4–3 putout. Banks would be teased about his lapse for some time.

But despite their problems, the Cubs could see the two men adjusting to each other and gaining in confidence. Banks was covering a lot of ground at shortstop and making strong accurate throws. Barely a month into the 1954 season he and Baker were being hailed as one of the best double-play combinations in the National League and drawing comparisons with Billy Jurges and Billy Herman, the shortstop and second baseman for Cubs teams that had played in three World Series in the 1930s. Some even went so far as to mention Joe Tinker and Johnny Evers, who had been celebrated in Franklin P. Adams's famous Tinker-to-Evers-to-Chance doggerel during the Cubs' glory days in the first decade of the twentieth century. Banks and Baker were even given their own joint nickname, Bingo and Bango.

"It just seems to fit them, the way they've been playing for us," said their teammate, catcher Joe Garagiola. "They've got rhythm."

Chapter 9

The Master Builder

The Cubs were playing their final intrasquad game of the spring in Mesa, Arizona, in 1954 when, in an instant, everything stopped. A fastball had gotten away from rookie pitcher Don Elston and hit Ernie Banks squarely in the back of his head. "My heart almost stopped when I saw Ernie crumple to the ground," said manager Phil Cavarretta. "He went down like he was shot," said Ralph Kiner. "I thought we'd lost him."

After a brief stay in the hospital, Banks returned to the team and became a spring training sensation. In his first twenty-three times at bat after being beaned, Banks had eleven hits, including a home run, double, and triple. Soon, rival managers, coaches, and players were standing and moving forward in the dugout when it was his turn to hit so they could have a good view.

Banks's poise seemed remarkable to them, as did his ability to hit a curveball, often the downfall of promising young hitters. "He's the best batter against breaking stuff of any rookie I've ever seen come to the big leagues, and I'm not barring anybody," said Wid Matthews, who was delighted that his bet on Banks was paying off. Cavarretta was equally enthusiastic about Banks's patience at the plate. "Lots of kids are afraid to take a strike and see what the pitcher has," he said, "but not Ernie."

Clyde McCullough, the Cubs veteran catcher who had seen every National League hitter since 1940, offered a detailed early assessment of Banks at the plate. "That kid throws his bat at the ball like Jack Dempsey used to throw a punch," McCullough said. "It travels only a few inches and when the bat connects the ball just seems to jump to the outfield. He cracks that bat like a whip just before contact." McCullough was also impressed by Banks's ability to wait until the last moment before swinging, allowing him to pull the ball with power when most hitters would be trying to deflect it to the opposite field.

Banks was applying himself at shortstop, too, taking ground balls by the hour from Roy Johnson, the Cubs' head scout, and the results added to the excitement he was creating during the normally placid exhibition season. Banks had played in no more than a few dozen major league and spring training games since joining the Cubs the previous September, yet he was being widely hailed as a star in the making. The only dissent came from Baltimore Orioles manager Jimmy Dykes, who bet Chicago sportswriter Edgar Munzel a box of golf balls that Banks would be out of the league by June. On March 20, the Cubs put all their chips on Banks by trading the luckless Roy Smalley to the Milwaukee Braves.

But Banks's first spring training wasn't an unqualified success. No sooner had he arrived in Arizona than he discovered that when it came to finding a place to live, he was on his own.

In the years following the integration of baseball, many of the hotels that housed major league teams during the season moved reluctantly toward allowing black players to stay with their white teammates. Not until 1954, when the Chase Hotel in St. Louis agreed to let Jackie Robinson register, did the last rampart fall.

Spring training took much longer.

As late as 1961, Wendell Smith wrote an article in the *Chicago American* quoting "an outstanding Negro player" saying, "We are tired of staying in flophouses and eating in second-rate restaurants during spring training. If we are good enough to play with a team, then we should be good enough to share the same facilities and accommodations as the other players, both in spring and summer."

Smith, the most influential black sportswriter of his generation, who had recently integrated the *American*'s sports staff himself, was writing about teams training in the South, where segregation was legally enforced. But black players on teams in Arizona had trouble finding places to live, too. Banks, Gene Baker, and those who followed were barred from the Maricopa Hotel in Mesa, where the white Cubs stayed, and the team left them to fend for themselves. The practice went on for years.

"Hell no, they didn't find me a place," says Billy Williams, who first stayed in the Cubs' minor league barracks at Rendezvous Park but had to scramble once he made the major league roster and brought his new wife, Shirley, to Arizona in 1961. He considered himself lucky to find housing in the office of Mesa's first black physician, Louis Alston, several blocks from the ballpark.

Banks's living arrangements were more conventional, but they were still apart from his teammates in a motel across the street from the Maricopa. Eventually, the hotel allowed all the Cubs in its doors, but only with the understanding that the black players would not enter the dining room. They could order room service, they were told, or they could eat elsewhere. And as late as 1964, Banks and Cubs shortstop Andre Rodgers were told they were not welcome at the Mesa Country Club, where the white Cubs played golf for free. They could come on the day of the annual team outing, they were told, but the club's no-blacks policy was in effect the rest of the spring. Hearing of this, Cubs field boss Bob Kennedy declared the course off-limits to the entire team, and the club quickly changed its policy.

But for all the difficulties it presented, spring training in Arizona held some advantages for black players. The ballparks and training facilities of the various teams were in close proximity in Phoenix and its suburbs, which allowed a camaraderie to develop that was not available in Florida, where spring training cities were many miles apart, and there were a number of gathering places they could get to easily. One was a run-down hotel in Tempe, where established stars and minor-leaguers mingled and traded stories over games of tonk, a card game that was popular in the Negro Leagues. "I'd sit there and watch them throw five or ten dollars on the table," Williams says. "Growing up in Alabama, I thought that was a lot of money."

Mrs. White's, a soul food restaurant in Phoenix, was another favorite meeting place, as was a pool hall where such New York—and later San Francisco—Giants as Willie Mays and Willie McCovey joined the Cubs to shoot pool with one eye on the clock. "Everybody had to be in at midnight," Williams says. "We would leave about eleven-thirty and since there was only one stoplight between Phoenix and Mesa, we could make it back in twenty-five minutes. We timed it just right."

But there was another benefit for a young player at a time when relatively few blacks were in the majors and those that had made it were under close scrutiny. Standards of performance and behavior were passed down by example and occasionally in informal seminars. In the years to come, some of these were held—quite surprisingly, given his reputation for seldom having much to say—by Ernie Banks.

"After the day was over, Ernie would hold court in Mesa where all the black players would get together," says Jesse White, a young infielder who joined the Cubs in 1957. "He would share with us how we should conduct ourselves, what we should expect, and that we should commit ourselves to being the best that we could be. Ernie was like the Godfather. He treated us like we were part of his family."

Banks never spoke publicly of these mentoring sessions, but in his autobiography he gave a clue to what inspired them when he told of a ride Roy Campanella gave him and Gene Baker back to their hotel following a game in Brooklyn early in their careers. "Just remember this, fellows," the great Dodgers catcher said, "and at your age it's easy to forget. The higher you climb in baseball, the greater your responsibility will be all up and down the line, both on and off the field."

———

Early in his first spring training, probably sometime before he was beaned, Banks was surprised to receive a letter. "My coaches say you're not trying," it said, "and where there's smoke there's fire. I want to hear your side of it." Banks was told to be at the ballpark at nine a.m. the following day, where he would meet with the man who wrote the letter,

Philip K. Wrigley. Banks read the letter in disbelief. Not trying? Was somebody trying to get rid of him? Somebody who had taken his case all the way to the Cubs' *owner*? It did not make for a restful night.

Banks arrived at the ballpark fifteen minutes early and waited until, at precisely nine a.m., a limousine drove up and its occupant, somewhat overdressed for the desert in a brown suit and hat, joined him in the stands. It was the first time Banks had ever met the man who would be his employer, advisor, booster, and protector during his baseball career and beyond.

"I'm P. K. Wrigley," he said. "I sent you that letter and I just want to hear your side of things."

"Mr. Wrigley," Banks said, looking him in the eye. "I'm doing the best I can."

"That's all I want to know," Wrigley said, and he returned to the limousine and drove off.

Nothing more was ever said about the contents of the letter or who had made the complaints that prompted it. It is conceivable, in fact, that Wrigley had not heard anything negative about Banks, but was simply curious about the young player he had heard so much about, the player who had made Cubs history the first time he swung a bat wearing their uniform.

———

Wrigley's feelings about the integration of baseball were anything but progressive. Taking his cue from Commissioner Kenesaw Mountain Landis, who denied the game had a color line while rigorously enforcing it, Wrigley said in 1942, "I would like to see Negroes in the big leagues. But I don't think the time is now. The public must be prepared to accept Negro players." And in 1946, after Branch Rickey had signed Jackie Robinson, Wrigley was one of four major league owners who wrote a report that revealed baseball's fears in the starkest terms.

The game, they said, was being hounded by "political and social-minded drum beaters." Black players simply weren't good enough to play in the majors. Integration would threaten the existence of Negro League teams, not to mention the money major league owners made renting out their ballparks to them. And if black fans started coming in large numbers to major league games, white fans might stay away. The report was supposed to be kept secret, but Rickey revealed its existence two years later and said all copies had been destroyed. Wrigley and his fellow owners were furious, but he never denied the report's existence or his participation in writing it.

———

Banks's first encounter with Wrigley was typical of the Cubs owner's personality, or at least one side of it. Once, in accepting an award from Chicago's baseball writers at their annual winter banquet, Wrigley's response was, "Thank you." When the writers honored him again some years later and urged him to expand on his remarks, he complied by saying, "Thank you very much."

Wrigley's shyness in public occasionally reached legendary proportions. In 1969, the *Chicago Tribune* dug up a photo of him and his wife sitting in box seats at Wrigley Field in 1938 and said it may have been the last one of him ever taken at the ballpark. Rumors that Wrigley had shown up on opening day in 1969 created a frenzy among the press, which conducted a search and zeroed in on a man in a box seat. He turned out to be Wrigley's cousin. It was said that Wrigley occasionally sneaked into a seat in the back row of the grandstand, where he was sometimes challenged by ushers who didn't recognize him, but for the most part he was content to watch the Cubs on television, either at his office or at his home in Lake Geneva, Wisconsin. In both venues, he stopped whatever he was doing and stood for the seventh-inning stretch.

Even in the late 1960s, when, after many years of mediocrity, the Cubs began playing winning baseball and were the toast of the town, Wrigley couldn't bring himself to come to games. "I've been so wrapped up in this team, and so anxious about it, for so many years that sitting out in the ballpark was a burden I just couldn't take," he said. "Frankly, I just get too nervous and I've gotten to be a pretty old man, you know." He was also aware how fickle the public could be. "When the team is going good, the Cubs belong to the fans," he said. "When the club isn't going so good, they belong to me."

Wrigley seldom gave speeches and refused all requests for radio and television interviews. "It's the difference between information and show business," he said. He never appeared in the Cubs' locker room or took a road trip with the team. Asked if he would go to the World Series if the Cubs ever played in one, he demurred. "My ambition," he said, "is to go live in a cave somewhere with no telephones and a big rock over the door."

But there was another side to Wrigley that belied his image as a baseball hermit. His office in the Wrigley Building was open to visitors, with or without an appointment. "If the door is open, go on in," the receptionist would say. "If it's closed, just sit and wait." Wrigley answered his own phone, answered letters from fans, and was available to newspaper reporters and members of the public, whom he would listen to patiently as they told him what was wrong with the team. He liked to tell the story of the fan who called while watching television in a bar and insisted that he instruct Cubs manager Leo Durocher to remove the pitcher. "Just as I hung up," Wrigley said, "I saw Durocher coming to take the pitcher out and all I could imagine was that guy in the bar saying, 'Boy, did I get fast action.'"

Wrigley had an avuncular relationship with his players, paying them reasonably well by existing baseball standards and offering to help with investments. Banks took him up on it and put half his salary in a trust fund Wrigley set up. By the time he was fifty-five years old, Banks said, the fund was worth four million dollars. And when Hack Wilson, the Cubs' great slugger in the 1920s and early 1930s, died destitute in 1948, Wrigley made the funeral arrangements. When the baseball commissioner's office offered to share the costs, Wrigley said, "I've never seen half a funeral. The Cubs will pay all expenses."

Wrigley's paternalism also extended to the Cubs' fans. Even when

Wrigley Field was filled to overflowing in the late 1960s, he insisted on holding back a number of tickets for sale on game day so anyone could buy them. He angered the owners of other teams by allowing children into the ballpark at half price, and he continued the Cubs' longstanding tradition of letting women into the ballpark free on certain days. Their largest crowd during their 1969 season, for instance, was 42,364, but the paid attendance was 29,866. The rest were women who were taking advantage of Ladies' Day and occupying seats the team could have sold many times over.

When he decided that Wrigley Field's box seats were too narrow, Wrigley had them ripped out, replaced with wider chairs, and the aisles between them expanded. The changes reduced capacity, and potential revenue, by 20 percent. Later, he performed a similar service for the fans in box seats near the right- and left-field foul poles. The seats were facing toward center field instead of home plate, he said, and he had them torn out and turned slightly inward. "A man who pays for a box seat has a right to see the game without getting a pain in the neck," he said. His reason for refusing to put lights in Wrigley Field was similarly succinct. "You wouldn't want to live where twenty thousand or thirty thousand people are hollering up to midnight," he said.

In 1941, Wrigley Field became the first ballpark to install an organ and when, in the same year, Cubs batters complained that fans wearing white shirts in the center-field bleachers made it hard to see pitches, Wrigley closed those seats off. The ballpark's center-field bleachers remain empty to this day. Wrigley also installed moving ramps to Wrigley Field's upper deck and had the massive center-field scoreboard flash "hit" or "error" on close plays and employ yellow numbers to note runs scored during an inning in progress. And in the early 1950s, when most teams' owners refused to televise home games, Wrigley saw the promotional value of the broadcasts and for a number of years allowed several local stations to air the games for free. Later, he made a deal with WGN, which would become a superstation that broadcast the Cubs' games around the country.

Wrigley took over ownership of the Cubs in 1932 after his father, William Wrigley, Jr., died. He saw the team win three National League pennants in that decade and one more in 1945, but as one losing season followed another in the ensuing years, his commitment to the team came into question. He was disengaged, it was said, uninterested in baseball, holding on to the team only because of a promise to his father.

The elder Wrigley was as flamboyant as his son was reserved. Starting out in Philadelphia as a "soap-crutcher," someone who mixes hot kettles of soap with a paddle, he had gone on to build the chewing gum company that bore his name. It made him one of the richest men in America and one of the most conspicuous citizens of Chicago, where there was talk of his running for mayor. Wrigley adored his Cubs—when they won the pennant in 1929, he told them to celebrate with the warning that he wouldn't pick up any check for *less* than fifty dollars—and when he died the team was bequeathed to his son along with instructions not to sell it. "Phil Wrigley assumed the burden out of his sense of loyalty and duty," Bill Veeck, who had worked at Wrigley Field when his own father was the team's president, wrote in his autobiography. "If he had any particular feeling for baseball, any real liking for it, he has disguised it magnificently."

But this harsh judgment does not tell the whole story. At some point during the forty-five years he owned the Cubs, during much of which he was the object of civic mockery, Wrigley might have fairly concluded that he had discharged his debt to his father, sold the team, and retreated into the privacy he held so dear. The reasons he held on to the Cubs were more complicated. So was Wrigley.

Growing up rich did not deter him from making his own way and pursuing his own interests. As a young man, he rode a motorcycle to work, flew gliders towed by speedboats on Lake Geneva, roped steers, bred Arabian stallions, and became skilled at craps, a game that taught him an important lesson. "When the dice are against you, there's nothing you can do about it," he said. "I suppose in many ways it's like baseball. Sometimes you can't do anything wrong and sometimes you can't do anything right."

Wrigley was also a master mechanic and electrician with a fascination for cars, both new and old. He loved nothing more than equipping his cars with devices the auto industry hadn't considered: four-barreled carburetors, overhead cam shafts, automatic chokes, turn indicators, and double taillights among them. "I can remember when he had maybe a dozen old cars—a Stutz Bearcat, a Cord, a Locomobile, the classic cars—stored away in machine shops all over the country so he could go and work on them whenever he pleased," said one of his mechanics. "I've seen him take a brand-new car and drive it right up to a garage so he can start taking it apart," a friend said. He did this, Wrigley said, because, "It's the nearest thing to creation I know."

Wrigley was also a prolific inventor—a non-slip screwdriver was one of his creations—who would assign his patents to coworkers in the machine shops and garages where he worked. He wore white gloves when he visited his home workshop, and if he found grease on his tools he reprimanded the supervisor. As a child, he learned to fix broken clocks his parents gave him "just to keep me quiet for a while," and he continued the practice into adulthood. "I've seen him take a broken wristwatch and work over it for fifteen or twenty minutes and hand it back to you all fixed," said one of his vice presidents. Wrigley also enjoyed physical labor such as digging potholes and removing roots and rocks at his Lake Geneva estate. "There's a lot more exercise in handling a chain saw and working on logs than in playing a game of golf," he said. And besides, when the Cubs lose, "I take it out on the roots and rocks."

But it was as a businessman that Wrigley truly excelled. In thirty years as the head of his father's gum company, he increased sales to such an extent that in the 1960s it could claim to be selling twenty *billion* sticks of gum a year in ninety-one countries. He furthered the development of Catalina Island off the Southern California coast, which his father had bought in 1919 and where the Cubs conducted spring training for nearly thirty years. He was also in on the ground floor of a mail transport company that would become United Airlines.

There was one thing more that distinguished Wrigley from his corporate peers. During the course of his stewardship of the William Wrigley Jr. Company, he proved to be a remarkably humane and far-sighted capitalist. In 1934, Wrigley instituted a guaranteed annual wage similar to those economic theorists would propose many years later to make up for jobs lost to automation and globalization. Under this plan, any Wrigley worker making under $6,000 a year would get at least thirty weeks' pay if they were laid off. "We didn't see it as anything radical," Wrigley said. "We simply felt we owed an obligation to our employees and set up our income assurance plan to take care of them in the event we had to shut down." He also instituted one of the earliest and best pension programs of its time.

In 1932, Wrigley took an even more radical step: raising the wages of his employees at a time when the Depression was putting tens of millions of workers on the street. "It was so electrifying an act that it made headlines around the world," said Arthur Meyerhoff, a Wrigley Company advertising executive. "He thought it would become contagious, that it would help get the American economy going again." This act of priming the pump came before the United States government began applying such Keynesian economic theory in any meaningful way. "He was the symbol of big business and the way he could contribute to society was by giving people money to spend," Meyerhoff said. "He recognized the symbolism of starting things in the other direction. Then two or three weeks later he declared an extra dividend for the Wrigley Company. He wasn't afraid of *that* symbolism either."

"Maybe I'm a socialist or something," Wrigley said, "but I think that the more people we have who own homes and cars and have a chance to go to college, the better off we'll all be." Wrigley also became one of the first businessmen to sign up for the National Recovery Administration, a hallmark of Franklin Roosevelt's New Deal that was anathema to most corporate executives. He committed further heresy by admitting he had even voted for Roosevelt—once.

During World War II, when sugar rationing cut production, Wrigley made another attention-getting decision with his eye on the future when he took his gum off the market and had it packed in the army's K rations and sent to workers in war-production plants. A "Remember This Wrapper" ad campaign featuring pictures of empty packs of gum kept the absent product in the mind of the public, and when Wrigley's gum was again available after the war, it dominated sales for decades. "It is a brilliant example of how marketing intelligently in a difficult time, and keeping a long term perspective, can pay off," Crux Research, a marketing firm near Rochester, New York, would write years later. There was also the fact that in the early 1970s a pack of Wrigley's gum cost what it had fifty years earlier, five cents, with no loss in quality or size. If Wrigley was that good at defying inflation, a Cincinnati newspaper suggested, maybe he ought to be president.

So Wrigley's insistence on retaining ownership of the Cubs can be seen as having less to do with a sense of obligation to his father than with his fascination with how things work and how new ideas can reinvigorate old institutions. Far from being disengaged, Wrigley viewed the Cubs as one of his workshops where he could tinker with the machinery, examine the parts, and try to see them in a different way. During the nearly half century he owned the Cubs, Wrigley would come up with many ideas of how baseball could be changed. Some of them were intelligent; others were ahead of their time and would be adopted much later; still others were preposterous.

If there was one lesson Wrigley would learn over the years, it was that owning a baseball team was not the same as taking apart a watch and putting it back together again.

Chapter 10

Future Shock

As Ernie Banks continued to impress everyone who saw him in his first spring training, the team around him showed serious deficiencies. The Cubs hadn't finished in the first division of the National League since 1946—they'd finished last three times and in seventh place twice during that period—and showed no signs of improvement as the 1954 season approached. Phil Cavarretta was particularly worried about their pitching. "They're just throwing a lot of junk," the Cubs manager said after his pitchers gave up fifty-three runs and thirteen home runs in the first four exhibition games. "In the old days you didn't throw that stuff until you lost your fast one."

Cavarretta was the closest thing to a homegrown hero the Cubs ever had. After winning a fourth straight city baseball championship at Chicago's Lane Technical High School in 1934, he went straight to the Cubs the following year, joining the team in Boston where Babe Ruth, playing his final season with the Boston Braves, stared at him and said, "You know, kid, you should be in high school." The following year, at the age of eighteen, Cavarretta played first base in the 1935 World Series. He went on to spend twenty seasons with the Cubs, playing in three World Series and three All-Star Games and picking up a Most Valuable Player Award along the way. He also set a record for most games played by a Cub and was revered by the team's fans. So managing the team seemed the logical next step.

The way he got the job should have been a warning, though, as Philip

Wrigley, in his finest tinkering mode, imposed an unusual condition: The job was only temporary. Cavarretta would be a fill-in manager for Frankie Frisch, Wrigley said in his announcement of the change in July 1951, after Frisch was fired following a noisy argument with Wid Matthews. "We will definitely replace Phil after the season is over," Wrigley said. "He fully understands that and has taken the job on that condition."

Wrigley's plan was to have Cavarretta go to the minors the following season to gain experience, thereby turning the usual managerial promotion system on its head. The only thing that could change his mind, Wrigley said, was if the Cubs won the pennant. In the meantime, Cavarretta would also continue playing first base. But less than a month later, Wrigley made another surprise announcement: Cavarretta would manage the team in 1952 after all. It was not that the Cubs were playing much better—they were in seventh place when Cavarretta took over and finished last—but Matthews had convinced Wrigley that the team was showing more spirit and he deserved to stay.

The Cubs did a little better the following season, winning as many games as they lost and finishing fifth, but they sank to seventh place in 1953 and, as spring training of 1954 progressed, it was Cavarretta whose spirits needed a lift. The Cubs lost fifteen of their first twenty games, largely because the pitching staff was giving up more than six runs a game, and they needed help in center field, at first base, and behind the plate. Wrigley needed to know how bad things were, Cavarretta decided, and he requested a meeting. "I didn't call the ball club lousy," he said. "All I did was give him the plain unvarnished facts. And that, I believe, is the duty of a manager."

At first, Wrigley seemed to take his manager's report in stride. "This is the first time in all the time I've owned the club that any manager has spoken to me on these grounds," he said. "I'm really glad that we talked." Cavarretta was pleased about having unburdened himself, too, but Matthews saw things differently. He had built the Cubs' roster and didn't appreciate the manager going over his head to complain. On March 29, after the Cubs blew a 3–1 lead to the Baltimore Orioles in the ninth inning of an exhibition game in Dallas, and lost by a run, Matthews told him he was being replaced by Stan Hack. "Phil seems to have developed a defeatist personality," Wrigley told the press. "We don't believe he should continue in a job where he doesn't think success is possible. I felt he was licked before he started."

The news rocketed throughout baseball. Fire a manager in *spring training*?! For telling the *truth*?! Ridiculous. Cavarretta was mortified, and when he heard Wrigley's accusations he exploded. "I was never a defeatist in my life," he said. "I never have quit."

Banks, who had taken advantage of the stopover in Dallas to visit his family, was as stunned by the news as everyone else. He admired Cavarretta for his aggressive attitude and for having asked him over to his house in Dallas during the winter, an invitation he called "especially significant because in Dallas a Negro didn't often make a social visit to a white man's home."

"What's wrong?" he whispered to Gene Baker as he entered a silent clubhouse where Cavarretta was wandering aimlessly, talking to himself.

"Cavarretta has been fired," Baker whispered back.

Banks thought Baker was pulling his leg and asked, "Who's the new manager?"

"I don't know," Baker replied. "Nothing has been said. Maybe they'll make you the new boss."

Banks, who had just received his first glimpse of the dysfunctional team he had become a part of, rushed to the bathroom to hide his laughter.

Cavarretta rejected Wrigley's offer to manage the Cubs' Los Angeles farm team—in effect, to switch jobs with Hack—and signed to play for the White Sox instead. He took little consolation from the fact that he was right about the 1954 Cubs, who fell into seventh place in May and remained there the rest of the season.

Years later, Cavarretta said, Wrigley apologized, saying, "I'm sorry, Phil. I never should have fired you," but their relationship never recovered. Wrigley liked keeping retired Cubs stars in the family—Charlie

Grimm, their former first baseman and manager, always seemed to be around in one capacity or another—but though Cavarretta managed, coached, scouted, and served as a hitting instructor for many teams after his playing career ended, he never worked for the Cubs again. The only tribute the Mr. Cub of his era received was a silent one as Yosh Kawano refused to assign his uniform number, 44, to another player for many years.

―――――

The Cubs were never competitive in 1954, but nobody could say they weren't entertaining. Hank Sauer, now thirty-seven years old, had the last good season of his career, batting .288 with forty-one home runs and 123 runs batted in, while Ralph Kiner hit .285 with twenty-two homers and seventy-three RBI. But most of the attention was centered on the team's new double play combination.

Gene Baker homered on opening day, went on to hit .275 with thirteen home runs, and remained a steadying influence on Banks at shortstop. Banks finished his first full season in the majors hitting .275 with nineteen home runs and seventy-nine RBI, and by September Hack was calling him the best shortstop in the National League. "Most rookies make bad throws and misplay in the clutch, but not this boy," Hack said. "He covers as much ground as any shortstop I've seen in years. He's sure on a ground ball and he throws great. He plays the hitters like a veteran now."

Hack was also impressed by Banks's ability to control his emotions— "He's so calm and businesslike when he comes back to the bench you couldn't tell whether he hit a homer or struck out," he said—and by something else he had never seen in a power hitter. "After he hits a homer," the Cubs manager said, "he comes back to the bench looking as if he did something wrong."

Hack advocated Banks's candidacy for National League Rookie of the Year, but he finished second, far behind Wally Moon of the St. Louis Cardinals, who hit seven fewer home runs than Banks but had a .304 batting average. When the season was over, Hack said he was prepared to trade just about anybody on the team with the exceptions of Baker and Banks, who was beginning to show signs of the relaxed manner and puckish good humor that would become his hallmark in the years ahead. Asked to name a few highlights of the season, Banks mentioned his first trip to New York. He and Mollye had visited the United Nations and the Empire State Building, he said, and taken a moonlight cruise. "We like to dance," he said.

But it was during a later trip to the New York in September that something more important happened. Standing at the batting cage in the Polo Grounds with Monte Irvin, he saw one of his old friend's bats lying on the ground. Picking it up and hefting it in his hands, Banks noted two things. The first was that it had a thinner handle than his own bat did; the second was that, at thirty-one ounces, it was four ounces lighter.

"This feels good," Banks said as he took a few tentative swings.

"You ought to use one like it," Irvin told him.

Banks took it into the batting cage and was immediately impressed by the way his natural wrist action allowed him to swing harder and how the ball seemed to jump off the bat. He was also able to get around on outside pitches, which had been giving him trouble, with ease. His own thirty-five-inch bat felt like a telephone pole in comparison, Banks thought. When the new season rolled around, he would have to give a lighter bat a try.

Chapter 11

MVP! MVP!

Nineteen fifty-five was Ernie Banks's breakout year.

In his second full season with the Cubs, he broke the National League record for home runs by a shortstop, which had stood for twenty-five years, and then broke the major league record as well. His forty-four home runs were one fewer than those hit by all the other National League shortstops combined and more than the total hit by every shortstop in the American League. He became the first player ever to hit five grand-slam home runs in a single season, led all National League shortstops in fielding, won a Gold Glove, and a poll of major league managers rated him and Gene Baker as the best double-play combination in baseball.

This began a six-season period during which Banks was the most productive power hitter in baseball. He had more home runs, 248, and more runs batted in, 693, than Willie Mays (214, 611), Hank Aaron (206, 674), Mickey Mantle (236, 589), Eddie Mathews (226, 605), and every other hitter in the major leagues. In those six seasons, Banks won two home run championships, two RBI titles, and two Most Valuable Player Awards.

Frank Lane, the general manager of the White Sox whose inattention had allowed Banks to slip through his fingers, may have spoken for the rest of baseball in 1955 when he said, "If you give me the choice of any player in the National League, I wouldn't hesitate for a second. Banks would be my man."

Banks also showed a flair for the dramatic that excited Cubs fans and even, on a few rare occasions, himself. In a game against Pittsburgh on

August 4, two days after his fourth grand slam, the Cubs blew a 9–2 lead and trailed 10–9 in the eighth when Banks hit the first pitch he saw for a two-run home run that gave them an 11–10 victory. It was his third homer of the game. But perhaps Banks's most electrifying moment came on July 8 when, as he was waiting in the on-deck circle in the first inning, it was announced over the Wrigley Field public address system that he had been named the National League's starting shortstop in the upcoming All-Star Game. He shyly acknowledged the cheers, then stepped to the plate and hit his twenty-second home run of the season into the left-field bleachers, tying him for most home runs by a National League shortstop. "That made me feel real good," Banks said. "I wanted to repay all those fans who voted for me." In the eleventh inning, he hit his twenty-third home run to break the record and give the Cubs a 6–4 win over the Cardinals.

Banks could point to another accomplishment early in his career as he secured his place among the game's great sluggers. Along with Aaron, he transformed the nature of power hitting.

Baseball was startled that a player as thin as Banks could hit so many home runs. Cubs trainer Al Scheuneman spoke for many in the game when he said, "When you look at his almost skinny frame and muscular structure, you wonder where he gets his home run power. Most of the power hitters were or are big men. Take them down the line—Ruth, Gehrig, Foxx, Greenberg, Wilson, Kluszewski, Kiner, Mathews, Sauer."

But others pointed out that his slim build—Banks weighed just 160 pounds early in his career—was deceptive. "From here to here," said Bob Scheffing, the Cubs manager from 1957 to 1959, grabbing his wrist and then his elbow to demonstrate, "Banks is bigger than anybody in baseball. His forearm is bigger than the top part of his arm. That's how come he's so strong. You grab hold of him and it's like grabbing a piece of steel."

"If you had a ring on when you shook hands with him, you were in trouble," says George Altman. "His strong hands and wrists enabled him to pull the ball, even when they pitched him outside. I didn't see many players with that ability."

"Ernie swings in a much shorter arc than I do," Sauer said. "With those quick and powerful wrists, he can wait a split second longer than a 'body' hitter like myself and so many of the longball hitters. A fraction of a second is a long time when you're swinging at an object sixty feet away."

"Give me his wrists," Cubs first baseman Dale Long told several of his teammates as they discussed the source of Banks's power, "and I'll spot each of you ten home runs before the season starts." When asked by other hitters how he could wait so long on a pitch, Banks said he didn't watch the pitcher's motion, but instead kept his eye on the ball so he could pick it up the instant it was released.

Banks's excellent eyesight also played a role in his hitting ability—tests on a number of players by the eye-care firm of Bausch & Lomb showed he had 20/14 vision—as did his ability to hit the ball where it was pitched. "A pitcher never knows what to throw Banks," Los Angeles Dodgers catcher John Roseboro said. "It's like pitching to a new batter every time. He hits high, low, fast, slow." Dodgers first baseman Wes Parker marveled at Banks's ability to lay off bad pitches, to anticipate what was coming next, and to get a hit, or even a home run, when he had two strikes against him.

The easy, almost gentle manner in which Banks held his bat also fascinated hitters throughout his career. "He would lightly rap his fingers on the bat," said Kiner. "He looked like he was playing the flute. I liked watching him."

Dusty Baker, who reached the majors in 1968 and became one of the National League's most prominent sluggers, had a similar reaction. "He never had any tension," Baker said. "His fingers were always moving. I always tried to keep my hands loose so I could 'throw' the bat versus 'swing' the bat. I got that from Ernie."

"When he would hit, it appeared his two thumbs were wiggling on the bat," says Joe Amalfitano, who has spent more than fifty years in baseball as a player, coach, manager, and scout. "I've seen a lot of players, but I've never seen that."

There was something else that set Banks apart, Amalfitano says, something that could bring batting practice to a halt. "He was one of the very few players that when the ball hit the bat there was a different sound," he says. "I would call it pure, hitting it on a sweet spot of the bat like they say about a golf club. When we heard that sound in batting practice, we would just stand and watch."

Player after player also spoke of Banks's utter calm while standing at the plate. "He didn't have this smashing, powerful, overwhelming approach," says Jeff Torborg, who spent ten years in the majors as a catcher, most of them with the Dodgers, and eleven more as a manager. "He was not the kind of guy who jumped at the ball or swung so hard his helmet came off or the bat flew out of his hands. He was very loose. That's the way he played the game and that's the kind of person he is."

"He is so relaxed," said Tommy Davis, who won two National League batting titles with the Dodgers. "When I think of myself hitting, that's the image I get."

Banks's composure also impressed umpires. "He never argued a pitch," says Doug Harvey, who, after a thirty-year career, became the ninth umpire to be elected to baseball's Hall of Fame. "Strike three. Walk off. Not a word." Banks was also the only hitter Harvey can remember who never so much as turned his head after a called strike on a close pitch. "Usually, I'd call a guy out and he'd turn around and look at me like I was crazy," Harvey says. "But not Ernie. I can't remember him ever complaining."

Nor did Banks ever, as far as anyone can remember, throw his bat after striking out. And when he did hit a home run, Amalfitano noticed something he else had in common with other great hitters of his generation. "He never ran the bases like it was his first home run or his last one," Amalfitano says.

Banks's teammates were also fascinated by his attitude after games. "You never heard him complaining after the Cubs lost or if he had a bad game," says Rich Nye, who pitched for the Cubs from 1966 through 1969. "There was never any whining: 'You made a bad call out there.' 'How could you make that throw?' 'I left five men on base today.' I never heard that from Ernie."

When questioned about his calm, almost peaceful approach to the game, Banks could only smile as if one of his innermost secrets had been exposed. "There's a lot of time to relax in a baseball game," he said in 1959 as he got off to a blazing start en route to his second consecutive Most Valuable Player Award. "It's not like football, where if you have some free time you say to yourself, 'That guy's been whipping my head. How can I whip his head?' There's no time out in soccer. Basketball keeps you busy. But you really have time to relax in baseball. Maybe that's why I'm so fond of it."

Banks recognized that his attitude was not for everybody. He could never play with the intensity of players like Mays, he said, and he recalled a barnstorming tour he had taken with the Giants star and Monte Irvin. "Willie was playing his usual reckless game and Monte reminded him to take it easy, that his career with the Giants was more important," Banks said. "And Willie said, 'This is the only way I can play.' Well, the only way I can play is relaxed."

At the same time Banks was making this comparison between Mays's approach to the game and his own, Wendell Smith was noting the difference between Banks and Jackie Robinson, whose entrance into the majors he had championed a dozen years earlier. "Although cut from the same ebony texture," Smith wrote in *The Sporting News*, "they are as different as night and day. Banks's most striking characteristic and virtue is his humility and natural modesty. In comparison, Robinson was a roaring extrovert, a stormy petrel throughout his career. Jackie Robinson stormed his way through the major leagues. Ernie Banks is breezing his way through."

But for all the theories about how a man with Banks's slender build and relaxed manner could have become one of baseball's best power hitters, there was little question about the most important reason. It was his bat.

———

In 1920, Babe Ruth hit fifty-four home runs, more than the total hit by every other *team* in the American League that year, and baseball would never be the same. Within a few years, home runs dominated the game, and the players who hit them, big men who swung big bats, became its biggest stars. "When I broke in, somebody handed me a bat that weighed thirty-eight ounces," said Lew Fonseca, who won the American League batting championship with the Cleveland Indians in 1929. "You were a sissy in those days if you didn't use a big bat. Babe Ruth used a forty-eight-ounce bat for years."

When he became a manager, Fonseca was one of the first to use film to analyze players, and he later ran baseball's motion picture bureau, where he produced the earliest World Series highlight films. Over the years, he became something of an oracle, leading baseball into an era in which film would be used to study every facet of a player's performance. As he watched Banks blossom into a home run hitter who belied his skinny frame, Fonseca was fascinated by the fact that he was using a lighter bat than virtually every other power hitter he had ever seen, and he decided to conduct an experiment.

He broke down film of Banks using a thirty-four-ounce bat during the 1954 season and compared it to the 1955 footage of him swinging the thirty-one-ounce bat he had been introduced to by Irvin. The difference, Fonseca discovered, was enormous—Banks had added as much as twenty-five miles per hour to his swing. "This may sound improbable," Fonseca said, "but a bat swung by a hitter of Banks's type actually gains on the ball. The bat at impact is traveling faster than the ball. When the home runs pile up, you invariably hear talk of the lively ball. In my book, it's the live bat."

Banks's long, light bat with the thin handle acted almost as a whip, Fonseca said. Few of Banks's home runs were of the tall, towering variety. Most began as line drives and just kept traveling. "The level swing and the incredible wrist action do the trick," he said.

With Aaron achieving similar results using a bat that weighed only thirty ounces, many of baseball's other power hitters, large, strapping men who had always taken pride in the size of their bats, began to take note. In the years ahead, Mays, Mantle, Ted Williams, Stan Musial, Hank Sauer, Ted Kluszewski, Joe Adcock, and others all moved to lighter bats, which led *New York Times* sports columnist Arthur Daley to wonder what would have happened if Ruth had used one. "If the modern buggy-whip bat had been invented earlier," Daley wrote, "the Bambino might have had 100 home runs a season, his blistering line-drive singles going all the way to the fence—and beyond."

But if baseball's best hitters were delighted with the results of their light bats, the man who supplied them was horrified. The new bats "break like crazy," said John Hillerich, the president of Hillerich & Bradsby, the company that has made the famed Louisville Sluggers prized by hitters since the nineteenth century. They were ruining his company's good name. "We've spent nearly 100 years building up a reputation as makers of fine, sturdy bats and it could be torn down in a few years," Hillerich told *The Sporting News* in 1960. "And it won't be our fault. It could stop in an instant if the hitters would use heavier bats, but they won't. They want the long ball."

Compounding the problem, Hillerich said, was that amateur players began demanding lighter bats, too, with disastrous results. "One team broke two dozen in one weekend," he said. "They were shipped back to the factory and we found nothing wrong with them. They simply were too light, not enough guts in them. The impact broke them. We want to keep the hitters happy—that's our business—but it hurts us when the long ball breaks our bats. What can we do? Nobody will use the Ruth weight anymore."

Banks, for his part, took pride in the revolution he and Aaron had wrought. "By the time Hank and I were through," he said with a smile, "there were a lot of guys ordering light bats and playing handball."

———

While Banks was changing the way baseball thought of power hitters, his position on the field was disconcerting to the game's traditionalists. Perhaps the one great irony of his playing career was that, just as he was thought to be too slight to hit home runs, he was considered too big to play shortstop.

Throughout baseball history, shortstops had generally been little men, dependent on their range, the strength of their arms, and their ability to turn double plays. At the plate, they tended to be singles hitters who sprayed the ball to all fields, while their speed made them effective base stealers. So when someone who defied this stereotype came along, his reputation as a fielder often suffered. "I think it is generally true that all power-hitting shortstops get a bad rap as defensive players," Bill James, the influential baseball historian and statistician, wrote in *The Bill James Historical Baseball Abstract*. "People have trouble reconciling the image of the power hitter—the slow, strong muscleman with the uppercut—with the image of the shortstop, who is lithe, quick and agile."

Banks didn't fit that image. He didn't move particularly quickly. His arm was extremely accurate—"Ernie throws strikes to first base no matter where he fields the ball," said Dale Long—but not strong. He just didn't *look* like a shortstop. And there was one thing more. The best fielding shortstop in baseball was playing only a few miles away.

Luis Aparicio was everything Banks was not. A key member of the "Go-Go White Sox" in the mid-1950s, he was, with a slender five-foot-nine, 160-pound build, the very model of a major league shortstop. Aparicio led American League shortstops in fielding for eight consecutive years, and when he retired he was the leader in games played, double plays, chances, and assists. He also led the league in stolen bases nine times in a row, and in four of those seasons he had as many or more steals as Banks did in his entire career. With Aparicio, one of the few players voted into baseball's Hall of Fame almost entirely because of his fielding and base-running ability, so nearby, the comparisons were inevitable. And while no one could argue with Banks's production as a hitter, there were naysayers who insisted he didn't belong at shortstop. The management of the Cubs was among them.

Manager Stan Hack's praise of Banks after his first full season ("Most rookies make bad throws and misplay in the clutch, but not this boy") did not keep the Cubs from searching for someone else to play shortstop, whether through a trade or in their minor league system. In 1956, Wid

Matthews said the team would bring six shortstops to training camp, as if to indicate the position was wide open. A year later, as the Cubs got off to a terrible start, they moved Banks to third base for fifty-eight games, replacing him first with Ed Winceniak, who was hitting all of .121 for the Havana Sugar Kings and lasted only six games, and then with Jack Littrell, who had played decently in the minors the previous year, but hit just .190 for the Cubs. Banks eventually returned to shortstop, and neither Winceniak nor Littrell ever played in the majors again.

This flailing about made it clear that the Cubs simply didn't know what to do with their best player. Nor do they ever appear to have asked him. If they had, they'd have heard a mouthful. The truth was Banks *liked* playing shortstop—fielding ground balls, making double plays, taking cutoff throws from the outfield and making relays. It kept him in the game, kept his mind occupied, and, more importantly, kept him from worrying about his hitting. "If I were in the outfield," he said in 1959, "I'd have too much time to think up a lot of hitting strategy that would probably foul me up. I'm sincerely convinced this makes me a better hitter." But rather than try to make their best hitter comfortable by showing confidence in him in the field, the Cubs continually kept him off-balance and guessing. It was the first time Banks was made to wonder about his place with the team. It would not be the last.

The Cubs' dismissive attitude did have one positive effect on Banks, though. It made him work harder. Rather than complain about the lack of respect the team was showing him, he quietly and methodically applied himself to becoming one of the best shortstops in baseball.

Whereas Banks seemed to know what to do with a bat in his hands almost instinctively, playing shortstop required thought, creativity, and practice. It also meant seeking out those who could help him. Some of the advice he received was technical. Alvin Dark, a fine shortstop in his day who was playing third base when he joined the Cubs in 1958, told Banks he was playing too close to third, expecting hitters to pull the ball. The Cubs had a number of hard-throwing pitchers, Dark pointed out, which meant hitters were less likely to hit the ball toward third. So Banks began playing deeper in the field and straightaway, but with his own twist. "In the late innings, I shade a little bit more toward third when it looks as if [the pitchers] might be tiring," he said.

Banks's old friend Buck O'Neil also had some advice for him after watching a few games at Wrigley Field in 1958. Banks was squatting when the batters were taking their swings, O'Neil said, which delayed his ability to react. Stand straight up, he commanded. Walk around a bit. Stay loose. "It helped me immediately," Banks said. "I was ranging farther and fielding the ball more cleanly because I was relaxed."

Gradually over the years, Banks's reputation in the field improved, and those who had taken him for granted began to realize not only how well he played the position but also how wrong it was to believe that a shortstop had to be built a certain way. This was particularly true of veteran players who became his teammates. "The one thing that surprised me when I had a chance to see Ernie play every day," Bobby Thomson said after he joined the Cubs in 1958, "was the fact that he does so well in the field. People think of him only as a hitter. I think he's an outstanding shortstop, too. He'd even be valuable if he was just another hitter."

"Just seeing him play in a few games against me, I never realized his ability," said Don Zimmer, a veteran infielder who was traded to the Cubs in 1960 and would return to manage them three decades later. "I thought he was just an average shortstop without much range. He's shown me something."

The managers of other teams also came around. There was Bill Rigney, the manager of the San Francisco Giants, who said, "They keep on saying he is just a mediocre fielder. Well, he always looks great playing against us." There was also the man who saw Luis Aparicio play every day. "He's always looked like a fine shortstop to me," White Sox manager Al Lopez said. "Aparicio undoubtedly covers more ground, but there's one other important factor in the work of a big-league shortstop and that's steadiness. Banks certainly has that. He's absolutely reliable in the clutch. He won't lose the game for you with two out and a man on third."

In 1959, Banks won his second consecutive Most Valuable Player Award when he hit forty-five home runs and led the majors with 143 runs batted in. But what might have put him over the top in a fairly close race with Mathews and Aaron was his play at shortstop. He made only twelve errors and had a fielding percentage of .985. Both were records for major league shortstops, and the Cubs were forced at last to surrender to the obvious. "Banks will finally be acclaimed a top-flight shortstop by the top brass of his own club," wrote Edgar Munzel in *The Sporting News*. "For the first time in five years they won't be trying to shift him elsewhere. It's a left-handed accolade but an accolade nevertheless. Ernie is like the prophet who is without honor in his own land."

But by then Banks's days at shortstop were numbered. His chronically aching knees were troubling him more and more, and in 1962 he moved permanently to first base, where he would play more games during his career than he had at shortstop. Still, the hard work he put in to prove to skeptics, including those on his own team, that he was a first-rate shortstop must rank high on his list of baseball accomplishments.

On September 27, 1959, a crowd of 28,346, one of the largest the Cubs had drawn all year, showed up at Wrigley Field to witness the final game of the season. The main attraction was not the Cubs, who had long since been eliminated from National League pennant race, but the Dodgers, who were tied for first with the Milwaukee Braves. Banks, who had been hit on the calf by a pitch thrown by the Dodgers' Johnny Podres the day before, was not in the lineup, and his consecutive game streak of 498 games, the longest in Cubs history, was in jeopardy. But in the seventh inning, with the Dodgers leading 5–1, Cubs field boss Bob Scheffing sent Banks up to pinch-hit, and the large crowd, realizing it would be his last at-bat of the season, stood and cheered.

Banks hit a pop fly to Maury Wills at shortstop and was limping back to the dugout when he was stopped in his tracks. The crowd, still up and cheering, grew louder and then louder still. The cheers were for Banks, of course—he would win his second straight Most Valuable Player Award after the season—but perhaps for the dreary circumstances in which he found himself as well.

"They cheered me when I hadn't done anything," Banks said. "It made all my baseball career worthwhile."

Chapter 12

The Slough of Despond

While Ernie Banks's sustained early success created excitement through-out baseball, it could not hide the dilemma that would ultimately define his career. The greater his achievements, the more obvious it became that he was playing in a vacuum.

In 1955, as Banks shot to stardom, the Cubs played fairly well early in the season, rising as high as second place before fifteen losses in sixteen games in July ended any hope of joining the pennant race. They finished in sixth place, twenty-six games behind the pennant-winning Brooklyn Dodgers, and that set the tone for the seasons that followed. None of the Cubs teams Banks played for through 1960 won more games than they lost. None finished in the National League's first division. Collectively, they were 123 games under .500. And as the years went by, there were no signs of improvement, or hope.

Banks was thirty-two years old when he first played for a team with a winning record—the 1963 Cubs were 82–80—thirty-six when the Cubs finished in the first division for the first time, and thirty-seven before he played in front of a million fans at Wrigley Field in a season. So at a time when he was one of the best players in baseball, none of the games he played in when pennants were being decided were of any impor-tance. He was baseball's great afterthought.

Banks's fifth grand-slam home run in 1955 was a case in point. Only ten players before him had ever hit as many as four in one season—Babe Ruth and Lou Gehrig among them—so his fifth, off Lindy McDaniel of the St. Louis Cardinals on September 19, was given a hero's welcome. Lost in the celebration, however, was the fact that the Cubs lost the game, 6–5, in twelve innings. "The wonder isn't that he hit four of them," one Cubs fan said when Banks tied the record, "but that the rest of the team succeeded in filling the bases that often."

This theme was repeated during his Most Valuable Player season of 1959, when Banks had 143 runs batted in, the most in the National League in twenty-two years. "Nobody could have believed the Cubs could have had that many men on base," Chicago columnist John P. Carmichael wrote. The fact that the Cubs had fewer hits than all but one other National League team that season proved the point.

Nothing more clearly sums up the long litany of Cubs failures during Banks's great early years than the 1959 season. Aside from Banks, only one Cubs player, reserve outfielder Bobby Thomson, had more than fifty runs batted in, and only one of their starting pitchers, Glen Hobbie, won more games than he lost. Yet late in July, after winning games against the Los Angeles Dodgers, San Francisco Giants, and Milwaukee Braves, who were all fighting for the pennant, the Cubs somehow sneaked into fourth place, just four and a half games out of first. "Frankly, I don't see much difference between them and us," Bob Scheffing said. "We've got as good a chance as any of them to go all the way." The Cubs promptly lost seven games in a row and sank out of sight.

The final insult of Banks's second Most Valuable Player season came from the Cubs' neighbors seven miles to the south, where, for the first time since they entered baseball lore as the 1919 Black Sox, the White Sox were winning the American League pennant.

For generations, relations between the fans of Chicago's two baseball teams had been fraught as politics, religion, and neighborhood loyalties combined in a sometimes bitter civic mix. Prentice Marshall, a U.S. District Court judge who was once a candidate for commissioner of baseball, traced this phenomenon back to White Sox founder Charles Comiskey, a proud symbol of Chicago's powerful Irish political machine that gave the city a succession of mayors. There used to be a saying, Marshall said:

"Show me an Irish Catholic who isn't a Democrat and a Sox fan, and I'll show you a son of a bitch." And when one neighborhood mother was asked to sign a permission slip for a grade-school field trip to Wrigley Field, she did so reluctantly, adding a note that said, "I do not think this is a proper activity for a child from the South Side."

"I can't possibly work for the Cubs," Arlene Gill, who was raised in a White Sox household, joined the team's fan club as a teenager, and even had a crush on the bat boy, told herself when she was offered a secretarial job in the Cubs' front office in 1967. The lure of spending spring training in Arizona overcame her scruples, and though she worked for the Cubs for thirty-five years, her family was never reconciled. "My brother only came to Wrigley Field once, and that was because Yosh Kawano was my friend and he was getting an award," Gill says. "My father would come to games once in a while but he said, 'You can stand during the seventh-inning stretch, but not me.'"

And now that the White Sox were on their way to the World Series, their fans could celebrate in triumph over the prostrate Cubs, whose own fans were left to sulk in silence. "I don't care if you were South Side, North Side, in Indiana, Wisconsin, or wherever," says Mike Downey, an eight-year-old White Sox fan in 1959 who would later become a sportswriter in his hometown. "The Cubs were a bunch of scrubs while the White Sox were even better than the damn Yankees."

This disparity came to a head on two successive days late in the season. On September 17, just 598 Cubs fans came to Wrigley Field to see Banks hit the forty-second home run of his magnificent season. It was one of the smallest gatherings in the ballpark's history. The following day, 37,352 people went to Comiskey Park to cheer for the White Sox. Overall, the White Sox outdrew the Cubs by more than 600,000 customers in 1959. One great player, even one winning his second consecutive Most Valuable Player Award, was no match for twenty-five men winning a pennant.

But if the Cubs' mediocrity led to frustration—or, worse, indifference—on the part of their fans, Banks paid a personal price as well. Pitchers had long since learned there were two ways to deal with a fine hitter who had little support in the batting order. One was to walk him intentionally—Banks led the league in that department in both 1959 and 1960—and some managers considered desperate measures. "I'm getting sick and tired of Banks hurting us with his bat," Giants manager Alvin Dark said in 1961. "The next time Ernie comes up against us with the bases loaded, two out and the Giants ahead by at least two runs in the seventh, eighth, or ninth inning, I'm going to walk him intentionally and take my chances with the next guy."

The other way to deal with Banks was to try to intimidate him. Over the years, the legend grew that in 1957 Banks was knocked down by four different pitchers and then hit a home run on the next pitch each time. Reminiscing years later, veteran umpire Tom Gorman even named the pitchers: Don Drysdale, Bob Purkey, Bob Friend, and Jack Sanford. Starting with the fact that Banks didn't hit a home run off Friend that year, Gorman was confused. He might have been referring to the fact that Banks hit home runs in the same game he was hit by a pitch three times during his career—twice off Purkey and once off Drysdale. Gorman's story does point to an incident that is true enough, however—the one time Banks became angry at another player and didn't care who knew it.

Banks was hit by a pitch seventy times during his career, and on sixty-nine of those occasions he shrugged it off. Pitchers had to make a living, too, he said. Fair was fair. But in the third game of the 1959 season, he became a marked man, and the result could have been the end of his career—or worse.

Banks hit two home runs in San Francisco on April 14—one into the left-field bleachers, the other out of Willie Mays's reach and over a 402-foot sign in center—and both of them were off Jack Sanford. "Maybe we've been too nice to him," Giants manager Bill Rigney said, adding that he was tired of watching Banks doff his cap after circling the bases. Sanford, who had given up three home runs to Banks the previous two seasons, wasn't happy either, and in a game at Wrigley Field twelve days later he hit Banks with a pitch. The incident went unnoticed, but when the teams met again at Wrigley Field on August 15, there was no hiding Sanford's intent.

"It sounded like a bomb," said Orlando Cepeda, who was all the way out in left field, of Sanford's pitch that hit Banks in the back in the first inning. "Ernie didn't say a word. He just walked to first base." But if Banks was silent, he was seething nonetheless. What particularly infuriated the Cubs was the fact that Sanford had thrown three pitches behind Banks before finally hitting him. "Any time a pitcher throws behind a batter you can be sure he only has one thing in mind," said Dizzy Dean, who was broadcasting the game. "That's the surest way of hitting the batter because he just naturally moves backwards into the ball."

Sanford denied trying to hit Banks—he was only pitching him tight and would continue to do so, he said—but Banks and his manager were having none of it. "I just can't understand that fellow," Banks said. "If he were just brushing me back, that would be different. But there's no question in my mind that he's deliberately trying to hit me." Scheffing pointed to Banks's two home runs off Sanford in April and said, "He has thrown at Ernie in every game he's pitched against us since that first one."

Banks remained in the game until the seventh inning before retiring for the day. "It hurts real bad," he said, and Cubs physician Arthur Metz was not surprised. The ball had missed hitting Banks's spine by no more than an inch. He should consider himself a lucky man. Metz also said it was highly unlikely that Banks would be able to swing a bat for a while, but the following day he took his aching back up to the plate to face Johnny Antonelli, who was on his way to winning nineteen games for the Giants. In the first inning, he hit an 0–2 pitch into the left-field bleachers for a two-run homer run that tied the score and helped the Cubs to a 5–4 victory. It was, Banks said, his biggest thrill in baseball to date.

During the next three seasons, Banks hit three more home runs off Sanford, and on May 2, 1961, the Giants pitcher hit him on the arm one last time in a game at Wrigley Field. Banks took his position at first base, and neither man said a word to the other.

The Cubs' futility had one other lasting effect on Banks in the early years of his career. It set him apart from the four other great power hitters who joined the major leagues along with him in the early 1950s.

Mays, who was born the same year as Banks, was twenty years old when he played in his first World Series and twenty-three when he played in his second one. Mickey Mantle, who was also the same age as Banks, played in three World Series by the time he was twenty-one. Hank Aaron, who was three years younger, played in two by the age of twenty-four. And Eddie Mathews, who was the same age as Banks, played in two by the age of twenty-six. Though still young men, they had all reached baseball's pinnacle and could play out their careers, and live out their lives, with a measure of fulfillment. All of them would hit more than 500 home runs, all of them would become first-ballot Hall of Famers (with the exception of Mathews, who had to wait until his third year of eligibility), and all of them were World Series champions. Except Banks. As the years went by, he became what amounted to a rare creature on exhibition—beautiful to behold, yet utterly alone.

The way Banks dealt with these circumstances would have come as no surprise to his family and friends back home in Dallas or his former teammates in Kansas City. He withdrew, turned inward, resumed his favored pose as a loner. "I played the game as if there was nobody there but me," he told one interviewer after he retired. "It was just me and the ball," he told another. "I don't care who's throwing it, I'm going to hit it. I'm going to catch it. I'm going to throw it. I'm going to do these things as if I'm playing by myself."

Banks would eventually distill this philosophy even further, until it became a kind of Zen where the game itself was almost beside the point. "When I hit a home run, in my mind I was saying, 'I'm going to get inside this ball that's coming at me and I'm going to take a ride in it,'" he said. "So when I hit a home run, I felt like I was floating out of the ballpark."

This did not mean that the game had become unimportant to Banks. Quite the opposite: It was *all* important, a reason unto itself, as he showed while the 1955 season was winding down. On September 4, he pulled a muscle while running out a double-play ball and left the game for a pinch runner. It was the first time he had been out of the lineup since joining it two years earlier, and team physician L. L. Braun recommended that he sit out for a few days to let his leg heal. Stan Hack agreed, and announced that reserve infielder Owen Friend would play in the Labor Day double-header against the Milwaukee Braves the following day. But when the lineup card was posted, Banks's name was on it. He played in both games and didn't miss an inning the rest of the season.

"I didn't want to use him, but he pleaded with me," Hack said. "He said if the trainer would tape him up he'd be all right. I believe if I hadn't relented he would have burst into tears." This was, Hack thought, quite remarkable. Most injured players would have reasoned that with their team out of the race in September, why not take a few days off? "You don't find that kind of spirit very often anymore," Hack said.

Banks also enhanced his reputation for deference—or perhaps he was just uncomfortable with the thought of being singled out—when he turned down a suggestion by Cubs fans for an "Ernie Banks Day" at Wrigley Field late in September. "I've been playing for the Cubs only two years," he said. "I don't want a 'day' until I have proved myself. I just don't think I deserve one yet."

But if Banks learned to accept and even thrive in his dreary surroundings, the man responsible for them did not. The relentless march of failure began to wear on Philip K. Wrigley, and in the late 1950s he began making one decision after another that set new standards for ineptitude. Nobody could say the Cubs hadn't driven him to it.

Chapter 13

The Once and Future Cub

John Holland became general manager of the Cubs at the end of the 1956 season and remained through 1975. Overall, just five of the teams Holland built in nineteen years won more games than they lost and only three came within ten games of first place.

But while Philip K. Wrigley's forbearance with Holland approached the infinite, his patience with the Cubs' managers had long since run out. The day after the 1959 season ended, he announced the first of what would be a series of managerial moves that, one after the other, would leave his listeners straining to believe their ears. He was bringing back Charlie Grimm to manage the Cubs in 1960, Wrigley said, a decision that surprised nobody more than Charlie Grimm.

Grimm had first joined the Cubs in 1929 and was the greatest living repository of their lore. As player and manager, he had participated in four World Series—he had been on the field when Babe Ruth hit his fabled "called shot" at Wrigley Field in 1932—and as "Jolly Cholly" he was beloved as a storyteller, radio announcer, left-handed banjo player, and reminder of better days gone by. "For years, Phil was as addicted to hiring Charlie Grimm as some men are addicted to alcohol," the great New York sportswriter Red Smith wrote.

But Grimm was sixty-one now, breaking down physically, and had not been on the field in ten years. At the press conference announcing his new job, he seemed less interested in discussing his plans for the team than in telling stories about Gabby Hartnett, Lou Novikoff, and Rabbit

Maranville. So it was less than a surprise when his final turn as manager lasted barely a month. With the Cubs off to a 5–11 start in 1960, and with Grimm suffering painful bone spurs in his heels and making panicky moves with his pitching staff, Wrigley mercifully excused him. "I did it to save Charlie's health and maybe even his life," Wrigley said.

Wrigley then made his most flabbergasting managerial move yet. He sent Grimm to the radio booth and brought Lou Boudreau down from that perch to manage the team. Wrigley professed to be surprised by the fact that this move was greeted with such gleeful amazement. He was simply swapping contracts with the radio station, he said. And if Boudreau, whose long career as a manager had ended just three years earlier, ran into trouble, he might make the switch again and return Grimm to the dugout. "We try to have nice guys and good baseball men around," Wrigley said. "I don't think changing the president of the United States causes as much fuss as changing managers."

While Wrigley flailed about in his office in the Wrigley Building, Holland was matching him step for step in the front office's cramped quarters at Wrigley Field. A baseball lifer who had started out as a second-string catcher before succeeding his father as president and owner of the Oklahoma City Indians in the Texas League, Holland had worked for a number of teams in the Cubs' organization and risen to general manager of the Los Angeles Angels, their top farm club. The Angels won the Pacific Coast League pennant by sixteen games in 1956, but, as is the case with many players with promising minor league credentials who are promoted to the majors, Holland was in over his head.

No one could accuse him of not hitting the ground running, but it soon became clear he was running in place. In his first ten weeks on the job, Holland traded a number of men who weren't playing well for the Cubs—Hobie Landrith, Warren Hacker, Harry Chiti, Pete Whisenant, and others—for others who wouldn't play well for them—Charlie Silvera, Tom Poholsky, and Elmer Singleton among them. Holland also decided to shake things up by taking eleven of his pennant-winning Angels to the Cubs' 1957 spring training camp. Five of them were gone by opening day and only one, pitcher Dick Drott, who won fifteen games in 1957 but only twelve more the rest of his career, amounted to anything that season. "Up here, they separate the men from the boys," said Cubs manager Bob Scheffing.

But the biggest mistake Holland made in his first months on the job was one that set the pattern for one of his key failings as Cubs general manager. He announced he was prepared to trade Gene Baker.

Strictly from a baseball point of view, the idea wasn't necessarily a bad one. Losing as consistently as they were, the Cubs needed to do something to change course, and as part of the best double-play combination in baseball Baker could bring a handsome return in a trade. But by making public the fact that one of his best players was on the block, Holland at once reduced Baker's value by allowing other teams to take turns making lowball offers and stamped himself as a baseball naïf incapable of improving his team in private conversations with other general managers.

But the Cubs had another reason for wanting to get rid of Baker that had nothing to do with building a ball club—Baker's outspoken attitude that boiled over when he took an off-season job representing Hamm's Beer. Baker was understandably miffed when the Cubs objected—Hamm's had long been one of the team's broadcast sponsors, and Cubs announcer Jack Brickhouse personally read its commercials—so who were they to say he couldn't work for them? "When I'm in the off-season, I'm on my time," he told them. "In the season, I'm on your time. You're not telling me what to do." What the team was really concerned about, Baker told Banks, was that just as he had been a good influence on his younger teammate when they joined the Cubs in 1953, he might now lead him to have ideas of his own, too. "We played together, we were associated together, and they thought I would be doing the same thing he was doing," Banks said.

So on May 2, 1957, Baker, the man who had done so much to ease Banks's path into the major leagues and to stabilize their infield, was gone. The deal the Cubs made with the Pittsburgh Pirates was decent enough—they obtained outfielder Lee Walls and first baseman Dale Long, who would both provide some power over the next few seasons—but it did nothing to change the fate of either team. As the season was nearing its end, Ed Prell wrote in the *Chicago Tribune* that the Cubs "were involved in a battle to the death for eighth place with the Pirates." In the end, the two teams shared the cellar with records of 62 92.

Nor did Holland have any clear idea of who might replace Baker at second base. In fact, the Cubs seemed convinced they didn't *need* a second baseman. "I believe a good center fielder is far more important than a second baseman," Scheffing said when Baker was on the block. "There are more fly balls hit to the center field area than there are ground balls to second base."

But since somebody had to play second, the job went to Casey Wise, one of Holland's imports from the Angels. Wise responded to the challenge by committing nine errors in thirty-one games at the position—four of them in a single game in Philadelphia in May—and one more in five games at shortstop. His batting average for the season was .179, and he was gone the following year.

Since his attempt to start a youth movement had turned into such a disaster, Holland abandoned it and spent the next few years filling the team with aging veterans. In 1958, he traded for third baseman Alvin Dark and outfielder Bobby Thomson. In 1960, he brought in veteran out-fielders Frank Thomas and Richie Ashburn. They were all fine players, but they were well into their thirties now—Dark was thirty-six when he joined the team—and few believed they would still be around if and when the Cubs ever challenged for a pennant.

Holland seemed to concede the point when, two years after he had acquired Dark, who had played well at third base, he traded him for Ash-burn, who played well in center field for two years. He was spinning his wheels now, and once again naïvely stating his desires in public, even going so far as to chastise Frank Lane, now the general manager of the St. Louis Cardinals, for refusing to make a deal he wanted.

Holland's reputation among his peers hit its low point after the 1957 season when he traded Cubs pitcher Bob Rush to the Milwaukee Braves. For nine long years, during one of the worst stretches in the team's history, Rush had been both the mainstay of the Cubs' rotation and the symbol of their futility. As the team finished in last place three times and seventh four times, he never started fewer than twenty-seven games and nearly always pitched more than 200 innings. And all he had to show for it were three winning seasons, a record of 108 wins and 140 defeats, and the admiration, if not pity, of the baseball establishment. The respect in which Rush was held was such that in 1950, a season in which he would lead the league with twenty defeats, he was selected to the National League All-Star team. But it wasn't until he was traded that Rush really discovered how highly he was valued.

"What did they use on those poor Cubs, a shotgun?" asked Roy Hamey, the general manager of the Philadelphia Phillies, at the news that Rush and two other players had gone to the Braves for pitcher Taylor Phillips and catcher Sammy Taylor. "How do you make a deal like that?" moaned the Phillies manager, Mayo Smith. "We offered them five players in a trade for Rush," San Francisco Giants manager Bill Rigney said. "They were looking for a center fielder and a third baseman. Instead, they settled for a pitcher who won three games and a catcher who hit .257 at [Class AA] Atlanta. How do you figure a thing like that?" Rigney later admitted the Giants hadn't made a bid for Rush, but said they would have offered more than the Braves did had they known he was available.

The fact that the Braves had won the pennant in 1957 particularly rankled Holland's peers. In their view, he had let a championship team get better with the lopsided trade, and in fact the Braves repeated as National League champions in 1958 with Rush making twenty-eight starts, winning ten games, and starting the third game of the World Series. "I understand the Cubs said I wasn't worth much in a trade," Rush said at the beginning of the season. "Well, I think I'm worth more than they say I am." He now had a World Series ring as proof.

As for the Cubs' end of the deal, Taylor moved in and out of the catcher's box for the next four years—appearing in more than 100 games only once—while Phillips posted a 7–10 record starting for the Cubs in 1958 and was traded to the Phillies the following year. He retired in 1963 with a lifetime record of 16–22.

Even when the Cubs did manage to find good young players in the late 1950s, their record was mixed. George Altman, a big, engaging outfielder, performed creditably after joining the team in 1959, but too often Holland's impatience led to decisions like the one involving Tony Taylor.

Born in Cuba, Taylor was only twenty-two when he joined the Cubs in 1958 and, with their attempts to replace Gene Baker the year before having failed, they were determined to put him at second base, a position he had never played. "That first season he did everything wrong," Bob Scheffing said. "He messed up plays in the field, committed every kind of error imaginable and he didn't hit much either. But he never gave up and he had an excellent teacher in Ernie Banks."

Banks reached out to Taylor both professionally and personally. He showed him the ropes in the field, tried to help him relax, and, seeing that his inability to communicate left him feeling adrift, even attempted to speak to him in his native language. "When I first joined the Cubs, I was so lonesome that Ernie tried to talk Spanish with me," Taylor would remember. "Good guy, Banks. Bad Spanish, but good guy." In 1959, Taylor's hard work paid off. He played in 150 games, hit .280, and played well in the field. At the age of twenty-three, it seemed clear that he would be a fine major league infielder for many years. A few months later, Holland traded him.

Taylor cried when he heard the news—"I felt uprooted again," he said—but it was the Cubs who would be melancholy when they thought of him in the future. While they continued to flounder at second base, the Phillies were set at the position for many years as Taylor's talent, infectious personality, and enthusiasm made him one of the most popular players in their history. By the time he retired, the Phillies had held three Tony Taylor Days in their ballpark—in 1963, 1970, and his final season, 1976. "I must be doing something right," Taylor said. "Right?"

The key player the Cubs received in exchanged for Taylor, pitcher

Don Cardwell, spent fourteen years in the majors, but only three of them with the Cubs, for whom he won thirty games and lost forty-four. Once again, Holland's attempt to build a team had blown up in his face. Undeterred, he began to consider lighting a bonfire of his own.

————

In his later years in baseball, when Banks was as much a symbol of the team as he was a player, Philip K. Wrigley made it clear that he would remain a Cub as long as he was wearing a uniform. "Ernie was born and raised a Cub and he'll die a Cub," Elvin Tappe, who had just been named the field boss, said at the end of the 1961 season. But while Banks was in his prime—almost from the moment he became the Cubs' biggest star, in fact—the Cubs were regularly confronted with the prospect of trading him.

Early on, this was expressed humorously, as when, in 1956, Cardinals owner August Busch instructed Frank Lane, his general manager, to offer Wrigley $500,000 for Banks. Rebuffed, Lane told Busch, "Mr. Wrigley needs five hundred thousand dollars just as much as you do." Stan Musial got in on the gag when he told a St. Louis writer, "The Cubs turned down the deal because they couldn't play cash at short." Musial also offered an unwitting glimpse of the future when he added, "But what do you think would have happened if there was no reserve clause and if Lane could have offered that half-million to Banks himself?" Busch, for his part, was not amused and wrote an article in the *Saturday Evening Post* in which he said, "I've never known before of a case where a firm or a man couldn't put $500,000 to good use in a business."

When Holland became general manager in 1957, he at first seemed amenable to at least consider trading Banks. "I would say yes," he said when the question was put to him, "but a lot would depend on the value received." Perhaps having learned his lesson about conducting business in public, Holland would never utter these words again.

"We have not discussed the trading of Banks and we never have had the slightest thought of trading Banks," Holland said in 1960 as the Cubs got off to another dreadful start while Banks was driving in nineteen runs in thirteen games. "We'll trade anybody else, as long as we can help the team. Trading Banks would be utterly silly. You don't trade the number one player in baseball." Even when it was pointed out that the Cubs could demand four or five front-line players for Banks, Holland remained adamant. "Banks is the best all-around player in the game today and we'd never trade him."

But the rumors kept coming, some of them wild speculation, others appearing to contain at least some basis in fact.

In 1958 and 1959, the Los Angeles Dodgers were said to have wanted him. "When I was coaching with the Dodgers and they were still playing their games in the Los Angeles Coliseum, I was convinced the Cubs could have had Tommy Davis and Sandy Koufax for Ernie Banks," said Bobby Bragan. "The Dodgers wanted Banks because they felt he could give them a pennant with shots over that short left-field fence." Koufax, Bragan noted, was "so wild he had trouble playing catch with a teammate and Davis was just a promising but untried youngster in Spokane." It was, Bragan conceded when he told this story in 1965, just as well for the Dodgers that they didn't make the deal.

During the 1960 season, the Milwaukee Braves made a bid for Banks that they were convinced had a chance of success. "When his name popped up, I thought, 'Oh, my God, Ernie Banks,'" Hank Aaron says. "I was looking forward to that."

The deal was to include eleven players—Banks and three other Cubs for Warren Spahn, who was thirty-nine but in the fourth year of five consecutive seasons with more than twenty wins; Joe Adcock, a reliable slugger who was thirty-two years old; Lee Maye, who, at twenty-five, was at the start of a thirteen-year career in which he would hit ninety-four home runs; and several others. In the end, the trade fell through.

After the 1961 season, it was the turn of the Detroit Tigers and Boston Red Sox. The Tigers' plan was to put Banks in the same batting order as sluggers Al Kaline, Norm Cash, and Rocky Colavito. "They may have to give up one of [team owner] John Fetzer's radio stations," a reporter in

Detroit wrote, "but the Tigers are going to make a bid for Ernie Banks shortly." The Red Sox for their part fantasized about turning Banks loose on the Green Monster, their left-field wall that was only 310 feet from home plate. "You make the trade and I'll sign the papers," Red Sox manager Mike Higgins said.

But by then it was too late. Banks's 1961 season was the first troubled one of his career. His eyes, always among his greatest attributes as a hitter, were giving him problems, and his chronically aching knees had forced the end of his playing streak, which had reached 717 games, the longest in the majors, and slowed him down in the infield. Though Banks had some fine seasons and some heroic moments left, he was in his thirties now and no longer one of baseball's greatest players, no longer able to command the four or five good players needed to build a team in trade.

The Cubs, still wandering aimlessly with no sign of hope—they won sixty-four games and lost ninety in 1961—had missed their chance. For all the mundane, thrilling, depressing, joyous, heartbreaking seasons that lay ahead, Banks and the Cubs were stuck with each other.

Chapter 14

Let's Play Two

In July 1962, the Cubs played two doubleheaders in Houston against the Colt .45s, an expansion team in its first season in the National League. The games were played in Colt Stadium, an old-fashioned ballpark with an uncovered grandstand that circled the perimeter of the outfield and didn't offer its customers a hint of shade.

The city's searing summertime heat would soon lead to the construction of the Astrodome, the world's first domed sports stadium, but even after the team was renamed the Astros and moved into its new air-conditioned arena in 1965, it continued to use Colt Stadium for workouts before road trips so its players could adjust to playing in hot weather. They were warned, however, to keep an eye out for rattlesnakes that had taken up residence on the untended field.

Mosquitoes in Colt Stadium were so large and numerous that outfielders sometimes wore towels under their caps that flowed down over their shoulders, making them look like desert nomads. "The mosquitoes were so big we used to say that everybody should move in groups because otherwise a mosquito might carry one of us back to the nest," Buck O'Neil, who had become a coach for the Cubs in 1962, told Kansas City writer Joe Posnanski. But it wasn't the mosquitoes that bothered the Cubs when they arrived in Houston for a doubleheader on July 15. It was the heat, which was reported to be ninety-three degrees, although the players were convinced it was much hotter on the field. "Houston is a city of a million souls and most of them were smart enough to stay away on this blistering day," Ed Prell wrote in the *Chicago Tribune*.

Only 6,909 fans came to the two games, and 2,497 of them were children lured by the chance to win a Shetland pony. The heat was so intense that umpire Al Barlick walked off the field after four innings of the first game, and after Lou Brock, the Cubs' rookie outfielder, scored three runs in as many times at bat, he collapsed in the dugout and retired to the locker room. Ernie Banks left the field after three innings of the second game, complaining of the heat and an upset stomach. The next day, O'Neil assured the team that Banks and Brock were fine. "Ernie ate two big pieces of ham for breakfast and Lou had sausage patties," he said.

The Cubs and the Colt .45s played another doubleheader in Houston on August 18, a day that was even hotter. Banks struck out three times in the first game, fainted before the second one, and was removed from the lineup. He was feeling better as the game went on, though, and was sent up as a pinch hitter with the score tied in the ninth inning. He struck out and the Cubs lost, 6–5.

"Everyone got on him in the clubhouse," Billy Williams says. "A lot of guys were chanting, 'Let's play two! Let's play two! You say let's play two and you can't even play one.'"

"Beautiful day, Ernie?" O'Neil teased as he approached an exhausted Banks at his locker.

"They're all beautiful days, Buck," Banks replied. "It's just that some are more beautiful than others."

———

No one can be sure exactly when Banks first said, "Let's play two," or, in its more complete form, "It's a beautiful day for a ball game. Let's play two." One version has him responding to the complaints of his teammates just before the July doubleheader in Houston by proclaiming his Texas roots and saying, "I've played in this weather all my life. It's not hot. In fact, let's play two." But Williams recalls hearing Banks use the phrase at least a year earlier and says that is why his teammates were so hard on him when he couldn't make it through the two games in August.

Al Spangler, a Colt .45s outfielder who would join the Cubs in 1967, also remembers hearing Banks elaborating on the phrase during one of the 1962 doubleheaders. "You'd get on first base and he'd be over there bullshitting you, telling you it's such a nice place and the weather is so good, we ought to play *three*," Spangler says. "You're trying to get the sign from the third-base coach and you'd tell him to please shut up."

Long after he retired, Banks gave other versions of the origin of the phrase, some of which seemed to reflect his mood of the moment. One detailed explanation came during the players' strike of 1994–95 and, perhaps because he was contemplating a world without baseball, it was as lyrical as it was fanciful. He was driving down Chicago's Lake Shore Drive in 1969 and the temperature had reached 110 degrees. "I just looked at the whole picture of my life and thought about all the people around the world and other planets and how I'm just a little dot on this Earth but I got to play baseball," he said. "It was such a wonderful moment!" When he arrived at the ballpark, he saw his teammates moving slowly because of the heat, and said, "God, it's a beautiful day. Let's play two." Later, he amended this slightly when he told an interviewer, "We were in first place, and all the reporters were already in the locker room when I arrived at Wrigley for a game with the Cardinals. I walked in and said: 'Boy, it's a beautiful day. Let's play two.' They all thought I was crazy."

Banks told another version of this story, but in a different way and in a different year, 1967. He even named a date, July 18. Instead of driving to the ballpark along the lake, he said he "went through some of Chicago's deprived communities to remind myself how lucky and privileged I was to be a baseball player at beautiful Wrigley Field." Again, he found his teammates dragging in the heat and decided to cheer them up by saying, "Boy, it's a beautiful day. Let's play two." Another sunny version came in 1990 when Banks said he first used the phrase in a conversation with Cubs broadcaster Jack Quinlan before the 1960 All-Star Game in

Kansas City in which he hit a home run in the first inning that helped the National League win, 5–3.

In 2010, Banks gave a darker account, which might have reflected the fact that he was separated from his fourth wife, Liz, and bitter, prolonged divorce proceedings were under way. "I was married and [the ballpark] was the only place I could make my own decisions," he said. "When to swing, when not to swing, when to run. I couldn't do that at home. That's why I said let's play two."

And in 1993, Banks gave what was by far his most succinct explanation. "Oh, that," he said. "I said it one day and it got written up."

It was inevitable that Banks's teammates and other players would take delight in teasing him about his signature phrase, which could seem out of place or even annoying when the Cubs weren't playing well. "We'd say, 'You can't feel that good. Have you not been paying attention?'" Cubs shortstop Don Kessinger says. "He would just come back at you with 'Oh, let's play two. Great day today.'"

"One day in August, we were standing out in left field," says relief pitcher Phil Regan, who was with the Cubs from 1968 until 1972, "and he said, 'It's a beautiful day to play, isn't it?' I said, 'Ernie, we're sweating just standing here. Don't you think it's just too hot to play baseball today?' And he said, 'Well, Phil, it would be a lot hotter if we were out picking cotton.' You just couldn't get him to say anything negative."

"I know Ernie isn't a drinking man," said California Angels infielder Jim Fregosi as he listened to Banks chattering during morning drills before a spring training game in Arizona. "If he was, he would not be feeling all that good so early in the day." But there were other times when players could only smile in admiration when the phrase came up. "If you could hit like him, you'd want to play two games, too," Williams says.

"Let's play two" would go on to become not just an inextricable part of Banks's public identity but it would also earn a place in the American vocabulary. And whenever it was used, there was sure to be a reference to Banks, who would often be described as a legend or legendary, while "Let's play two" would sometimes be called immortal.

Whenever a game in any sport took a long time to complete, or two events occurred back to back, or an entertainment contained two performers, or someone expressed joy about almost anything, the words "Let's play two" or some variation of them were likely to be called upon. In 2013, for instance, when the Chicago Blackhawks and Boston Bruins played into three overtimes in the first game of the Stanley Cup Finals, the *Chicago Tribune* called it "an Ernie Banks moment right in his hometown."

It was also inevitable that the adaptability of "Let's play two" would take it beyond sports.

When Bob Dylan and Willie Nelson went on a concert tour of twenty-seven minor league ballparks in 2005, it was called the "Let's Play Two Summer Tour."

When the stock market was doing well in 2005, analyst David Johnson told NPR's *Marketplace*, "I wish I was Ernie Banks. I'd just say, 'Let's play two.' Let's reopen this thing and have a night session."

When Anthony Clarvoe wrote a play in the mid-1990s about a couple who meet while sneaking out of a wedding reception to watch a baseball game on television, he titled it "Let's Play Two."

When the Aero Theatre in Santa Monica, California, which screens older movies, wanted to celebrate the opening of the 2007 season, it scheduled a double bill entitled, "Let's Play Two: A Baseball Celebration."

When the journalist Chris Suellentrop, writing in the online magazine *Slate*, wanted to explain Osama bin Laden's strategy against American forces in Iraq, he wrote that the al-Qaeda leader feels "he already knocked off one superpower in the Soviet Union, and now he's trying to complete the doubleheader. He's an Islamist Ernie 'Let's Play Two' Banks."

When the rock band Pearl Jam made a documentary about two concerts it gave at the Cubs' ballpark in 2016, the title was *Let's Play Two! Pearl Jam Live at Wrigley*.

And when *Playboy* magazine, in an article entitled "The Thinking Man's Guide to Talking with Women," advised men how to behave after sex, it suggested, "Let your lover do the talking for a change. Remember, you can always play again tomorrow, or, as Ernie Banks used to say, 'Let's play two.'"

The phrase was also a natural for politics, and perhaps no public official used it more than Hillary Clinton, who grew up a Cubs fan in Park Ridge, Illinois, a Chicago suburb, and whose childhood affection for Banks was returned years later when he became a supporter of her husband's presidential campaigns, and her own.

"Thank you, Ernie," Clinton said after Banks introduced her at the 1996 Democratic convention in Chicago. "I feel like saying, 'Let's play two.'" Twenty years later, after being declared the consensus winner of her first presidential debate against Donald Trump, Clinton said, "You know, growing up, one of my favorite baseball players was Ernie Banks. He used to get so excited about going to play that he'd say 'Let's play two.' So I'm looking forward to the next debate and then the one after that."

Years earlier, as Bill Clinton's 1999 impeachment trial was ending in an acquittal, White House counsel Charles Ruff delayed the proceedings by restating much of the lengthy testimony. He took "special pleasure" in reviewing the case, Ruff said. "Or as Ernie Banks might have said, 'It's such a nice day. Let's play two.'"

Sometimes, the phrase was turned back on Banks, such as when, prior to a trip with several other major league players in 1968 to visit American troops in Vietnam, Chicago White Sox broadcaster Bob Elson told him, "Now don't get up some morning and tell those soldiers it's such a wonderful day you wish we had two wars."

Banks himself used the phrase ironically when, at the age of fifty-seven, he joined other former ballplayers in an old-timers' game before the 1988 All-Star Game in Cincinnati, where the temperature was ninety-five degrees. "Let's play two," Banks said when the game ended in a 2–2 tie. "Naw, it's too hot."

Writers and composers occasionally found a wistful quality in the phrase they could use to express nostalgia or regret. In *Murder in Wrigley*

Field, a novel by the Chicago writer Bill Brashler, the narrator recalls a moment at the Cubs' ballpark.

> On that day I walked from the concourse into the light and was temporarily blinded, like a vision, I guess. My eyes adjusted, and I once again took in the ballyard: the white chalk on red clay, the natural carpet of clipped grass, the ivy-covered outfield walls, the aged Chicago apartment buildings beyond them with rooftop fans just waiting for a souvenir. There is no more beautiful sight, not to any claret-blooded American raised on Charlie Grimm and Ernie Banks. The words slip off your tongue: Let's play two.

Steve Goodman, the Chicago folk singer whose song "Go, Cubs, Go" became the anthem of the team's march to the 2016 World Series, wrote "A Dying Cub Fan's Last Request" in 1981 as a mock tribute to long-suffering Cubs fans. Imagining the fan's funeral at Wrigley Field, Goodman asked for six bullpen pitchers to carry his coffin, six groundskeepers to clear his path, and umpires to call him out at every base. "It's a beautiful day for a funeral," he said. "Hey, Ernie, let's play two!"

Three years after writing the song, Goodman died of leukemia at the age of thirty-six and his ashes were scattered at Wrigley Field.

"Let's play two" also became a byword for Banks's many nieces and nephews and their children, who were given the education and opportunities their parents had lacked. "I think about how far they've come from Fairmount Street, being as poor as they were," says Banks's niece Karen Ridge. "We all love sports, but when it came to accomplishments that were more educationally oriented or artistic, we always felt the nucleus came from him—the idea to get out there and do your best. 'Let's play two. Let's paint two. Let's write two.' He always inspired us."

But perhaps the greatest effect of "Let's play two" was on Banks himself. The words symbolized the fact that through sheer force of will he had brought about a change in his personality. The quiet loner, the man who disappeared at the first hint of confrontation, had become not only a symbol of relentless optimism, but also a chatterbox whose teammate Ferguson Jenkins would nickname "AM/FM," comparing Banks to a radio that couldn't be turned off.

Banks wasn't often asked to explain his metamorphosis, and when he did the answer was simple—perhaps too simple. It was nothing more than sheer curiosity, he said, the one quality he had possessed back when he hung around the playground at J. W. Ray Elementary School in Dallas, watching his classmates but not joining them. His Chicago surroundings fascinated him in the same way and made him want to learn more from the people around him.

Philip K. Wrigley was one of them, and Banks made it a point to go to the Cubs owner's office now and then to talk to him and listen to his advice about putting money away. Banks was also fascinated by two fans, Sarah and Carolyn, who were always at the ballpark before the gates opened. Before long, he began appearing on the field early, finding them in their seats, and getting to know them. He began talking to other fans, too. There were also the people who lived in the neighborhood around Wrigley Field, which was not the gentrified mecca of upscale homes, restaurants, and bars it would become, but scruffy and down at the heels. And there were the people who rode in on Chicago's L trains from other parts of the city.

Banks's curiosity led him to attend Little League awards banquets, church suppers, B'nai B'rith meetings, and other events he was invited to. In the years ahead, he would become notoriously unreliable about attending functions he had committed to, but early in his career he accepted everything that came his way and was always there on time. He went out so often, he said, it might have cost him a marriage.

Banks was particularly fascinated by Pat Pieper, who had been the Cubs' public address announcer since 1915, the year after Wrigley Field opened. Pieper spent his evenings as a waiter at the Ivanhoe restaurant, six blocks south of the ballpark, and he would regale Banks with stories of the 1918 World Series between the Cubs and the Red Sox—Babe Ruth had pitched for Boston—and of the moment in 1932 when the megaphone he used to announce the starting lineups was replaced by an electronic public address system. Pieper always dressed so well, Banks noticed, and he was helpful in telling him which restaurants would welcome him and which he should avoid.

Banks was out of his shell now. For the rest of his life, he would conduct himself in public in a way that would make him the very symbol of joy and optimism. It was a remarkable act of self-invention, and it had all begun with three one-syllable words.

———

Perhaps inevitably, there was a backlash to "Let's play two." "Maybe it's sacrilege, but I believe Banks was a con artist," Los Angeles Dodgers catcher John Roseboro said. "No one smiles all the time naturally unless they're putting it on and putting you on. Every day of our lives isn't a good one."

Some of Banks's teammates agreed, though they tended to phrase it more gently. "It was all bullshit," says Bill Hands, a member of the Cubs' pitching rotation in the late 1960s and early seventies. "We all understood that. That's the way he was. I liked him for it." Others disagreed, Hank Aaron among them. "If Ernie's a phony, he must be a hell of an actor because he's been fooling me for most of his life," Aaron said.

But the people closest to Banks believed this discussion missed the point. They saw that he had created an image he could use to his advantage when he was out in public, while still being able to retreat ever more deeply into the privacy he craved. This was particularly true on the Cubs' road trips, during which Banks was all but invisible. "I never saw him around the hotel or in the restaurant," says Cubs pitcher Rich Nye. "You just saw him at the ballpark. I don't remember him even taking the team bus. I think he took a cab most of the time." The same was true, Nye says, of the occasional team dinners on the road where the Cubs would celebrate if they were playing well and commiserate if they weren't. Banks never attended.

"I never saw him out at night," says Chuck Shriver, the team's publicity director from 1966 to 1975, and the same was true after games in

Chicago. "My dad would tell me Ernie would do his business and then go home," says Ron Santo, Jr. "My dad would go out with Glenn Beckert and Randy Hundley and some other guys, but Ernie kept to himself."

But if Banks's teammates were puzzled by the contrast between his public and private behavior, some of those who played with him the longest also had a feeling of regret. "I always appreciated his outward presence of loving life and loving the Cubs," says Don Kessinger, "but I always thought there was a side to Ernie that most of us never got a chance to be a part of."

Back home in Dallas, Edna Warren had at first scarcely been able to credit the reports of her shy, retiring brother, the boy who sat in the back of the classroom and seldom spoke up, being celebrated as the very essence of garrulous, smiling happy talk. "I thought it was a put-on," she says. But as the years went by and Banks's life became more complicated, she began to see what he had done. She had listened to Banks talk about the many things that troubled him often enough to realize that, in public at least, he had found a way to handle them. "Even if he was hurting inside you never knew," she says. "He covered it up by being happy."

"He had a great skill at building a façade around him," says Marjorie Lott, Banks's third wife. "I think a lot of his 'It's a great day, let's play two' was a cover-up of his sadness."

Lott occasionally suggested that Banks see a therapist, someone he could talk to about turning his projected happiness into the real thing, but Banks rejected the idea. "He always knew things about other people," she says. "But he never got to know himself."

Some of the people close to Banks felt that maintaining this image took a toll on him, particularly as he got older. "It takes a lot of effort to be happy when you're not happy," says Sharon Pannozzo, the Cubs' public relations director, who worked for the team from 1982 to 2006. "So even though he may have been thinking, 'I'm not happy, I have financial difficulties, I'm having problems with my spouse,' you always got the Ernie that was expected. He was creating a character that people expected to see. That takes a lot of effort."

"I admired him for having the energy and the willingness to make people happy by putting on that happy face because not everybody can do it," says former Dodger Wes Parker. "But I always had the feeling that somewhere in there he was running away from pain."

"I think Ernie was very humbled by the label of Mr. Cub, but it was heavy, too," says John McDonough, the president of the Cubs who spent twenty years as a team executive. "It's the ultimate honor, but to have to appear as this pristine person—'I'm Mr. Cub, I'm day baseball, I'm sunshine, I'm everything that's good about life'—that's hard."

Eventually, says Banks's son Jerry, he became a prisoner of that character. "Once you've put on that façade for so long, you need to live with what you've created," he says. "You can't turn it off, even if you would like to. Basically, you sacrifice your life."

One prominent Chicagoan who spent a great deal of time with Banks summed up the feelings of more than a few people who were close to him. "He was a tortured soul," he said. "He just hid it very well."

To which Lott adds, "I think he would have lived a lot longer if he had not been so sad inside."

Chapter 15

The Rock of the Family

Mollye's divorce filing in 1959 was specific and unsparing. Three times between 1955 and 1958, she said, Banks had hit her "on the face, body and head with violence, bruising and injuring her and causing pain." Two of her friends testified they'd seen the bruises. After the third beating, on December 13, 1958, Mollye said, Banks deserted her and left her "without any means to support herself."

Banks denied hitting her, but quickly agreed to the divorce. The Chicago press reported only the barest of details of the proceedings—and made no editorial comment—and the reputation of the city's biggest sports star, who months earlier had been named the National League's Most Valuable Player, remained unsullied. Banks was never again charged with physical violence.

As Banks's wife, Mollye had kept a low and dutiful profile. She prepared his breakfast, she told an interviewer—fruit juice, eggs, and ham, with the addition of a couple of slices of toast if the Cubs were playing a doubleheader—took their clothes to the Laundromat, brought them home, and ironed them. Asked about the fans who mobbed her husband at Wrigley Field, she said it was all part of the game, though some of the women went "beyond the realm of good manners, such as calling him at home." It didn't bother her, though. All she wanted was success for her husband.

And now that the marriage was over, Mollye's monetary demands were modest. After some legal back-and-forth, she was awarded $65,000

to be paid in three installments per year over a fourteen-year period
beginning at $2,500 each and diminishing to $1,500. In 1963, Banks was
charged with contempt of court for failing to meet this schedule, but the
charges were dismissed when a life insurance policy was set up to make
regular payments. "I think she was paid off by the Cubs and Ernie was
free of everything," Billy Williams says.

The divorce established a pattern of angry disputes and lengthy battles involving numerous lawyers that would mark the end of all four of
Banks's marriages. "He said, 'Edna, I paid Mollye off,'" Banks's sister
says. "Then he turned around and let the others do the same thing. Poor
thing. I felt so sorry for him. He lost so much money."

"Ernie had the same kind of luck with women I did with my first
wife," says Hank Aaron, who considers himself fortunate to have made a
lasting second marriage with his wife, Billye. "I used to tell people, 'You
look for me and if I'm not here I'm probably in the bottom of the ocean.'"

Mollye returned to Dallas, where members of Banks's family believed
she remarried and had a child. Later, she worked as a domestic. "She was
a lovely woman, wise beyond her years and always willing to give good
advice to a young mother in times of need," Maria Brisco, whose house
Mollye cleaned from 1992 to 1997, said in a Facebook post after Banks's
death. "She spoke of Ernie Banks fondly. Spoke no ill. She was thankful
for his success, continued to follow his career long after their divorce. He
always held a special place in her heart."

This affection was not returned, however, as Banks seldom spoke of
Mollye again. In his autobiography, which was published in 1971, he did
not mention her name.

Banks's three subsequent wives—Eloyce Johnson, Marjorie Lott, and Liz
Ellzey—had much in common. They were all intelligent, self-possessed,
capable women who had good jobs and definite opinions. "Eloyce was
a lady that didn't take no shit," Billy Williams says with a smile as he
summons up memories of the woman Banks was married to through the

remainder of his baseball career and beyond and who was the mother of his three children. He might have been speaking of Marjorie and Liz as well.

"Mom was a tough lady," Jerry Banks, one of the Bankses' twin sons, says of Eloyce. "She was very demanding and high-spirited and could match wits with anyone. She wore the pants in the family."

"She was a pistol, a very strong woman," agrees Jerry's brother, Joey. "She wouldn't be pushed around. She was the rock of the family."

There are several different accounts of how Banks and Eloyce met, and they are almost comical in their differences. In his autobiography, Banks says he noticed her as a receptionist in a Chicago office building. In an oral history years later, he said they met in a restaurant. Jerry Banks was told they first noticed each other at a Harlem Globetrotters game where Banks was hosting events during halftime. Eloyce's version is different still. "I was an assistant buyer for thirty-six stores," she said in 1978. "To tell you the truth, I didn't know one thing about the Cubs. When we met at a press party, I thought he played for the Milwaukee Braves. It took him ten years to get over that." Whatever the case, Banks and Eloyce quickly began dating, quickly discovered she was pregnant, and quickly eloped to Las Vegas.

Banks and Eloyce were different in almost every way. Born in Tyler, Texas, she was raised by a family of educators, dated professional men, and was briefly married to a doctor. "Her mother didn't think much of baseball players," Banks says. "She didn't say, 'I don't know what she sees in you,' but she treated me that way."

Because Eloyce had extremely light-colored skin, she exuded an air of mystery. "If you saw pictures of her," says Williams, "you couldn't tell if she was white or black." And *Jet* magazine, which closely followed the lives of black celebrities, spoke of "the barbershop arguments over that recently published photo of the new wife of Chicago Cubs shortstop Ernie Banks. Some folks insist she is white. Actually, the new Mrs. Banks is Negro."

"She was gorgeous. She looked like Ava Gardner," says Martha Black, the daughter of Joe Black, a former pitcher in the Negro and major leagues, whose mother was one of Eloyce's closest friends. "As kids we didn't whisper and I would say out loud, 'You don't look like my family. You're not black.' My mom's like 'Shh,' and I'm like 'She's not,' and finally Mrs. Banks said, 'Baby, I am.'"

This sort of attention could wear on Eloyce, and occasionally she would ask someone to look after Jerry and Joey and her younger daughter, Jan, so she could shop for groceries without drawing stares and whispers. No one could accuse Eloyce of being shy, however. She knew what she wanted and was never afraid to say so. "She was real aggressive," says Jerry Banks. "If people came over to the house to do some work, they were not leaving until it was absolutely done correctly. She would give them a hell of a hard time. On the other hand, she was a southern woman. You couldn't leave the house without getting fed."

Eloyce's fierce determination took many forms. Just try to tell her what to do, Williams recalls, and you were in for a fight. There was, for instance, her ongoing crusade to improve the mediocre living accommodations of the Cubs' black players in spring training. "She used to go around and try to get places for us to stay," Williams says. "She would go in and talk to people and when they wouldn't do it she got pissed off at them."

But Eloyce's most enduring battles in her twenty-two years of marriage were with her husband. Like many baseball wives, she disliked the spotlight and didn't care who knew it. When Banks was approached by fans while they were in a restaurant, for instance, she would respond angrily. "You need to get out of here," she would tell autograph seekers. "We're having dinner now. Don't bother us." To which Banks would invariably reply, "Oh, Eloyce, it's okay. Why are you getting so upset over this? It's not that big a deal."

"It happened all the time," Jerry Banks says. "He would always shush her. He would not turn anybody away for any reason. He would never say no and she would always say no. He was the least confrontational individual I've ever met. My mom was just the opposite. Whatever he couldn't say, she would."

It was not that Eloyce didn't understand the reason for Banks's behavior. "Out in public, Ernie has to be an actor," she said. "*Every* ballplayer has to be an actor, don't you see? They have to please the public." But understanding did not mean acceptance, and in 1978, seven years after Banks had retired from baseball and at about the time she was telling her children she was planning a divorce, she spoke for baseball wives everywhere in a revealing interview with Brent Frazee of the *Rockford Journal-Star.*

"We all have children so we can't go on road trips," she said. "I've had a lot of lonely moments that a lot of women, who are glad their husbands are gone, don't have. I'm not a person who likes to be alone. Yet, when he was a player he was gone continuously. I guess that's just unfortunate for me. There's a terrific strain on the wife, on the children, on the family life period. But you learn to adjust—you have to ... There are times when this kind of life gets on your nerves. We all say, 'I don't know how much longer I can take this.' But we care, so we stay."

Banks's determination to avoid confrontation extended to his life at home. "He was real mellow, very quiet around the house," Jerry Banks says. "He'd go out in the yard and smoke his pipe. We knew when he got home to just leave him alone."

Disciplining her rambunctious young sons was an ongoing struggle for Eloyce, and once again Banks offered little support. "We were maybe fighting or arguing or hitting each other in the head," Jerry says of his boyhood battles with his brother, "and he would let us get away with it. He'd say, 'They're just being boys. Leave them alone.'"

The fact that Banks traveled so much added to the problem, Jerry says. "When he was on a road trip, she'd say, 'Wait till your dad gets home,' and we'd say, 'That's like two weeks.'" On the rare occasions Banks was moved to anger, though, his sons would get an indication of a home run hitter's strength. "Spanking was not his thing," Jerry says. "He was a squeezer. He'd grab your shoulder and once he got his hand on you, you were not going anywhere."

He never saw a hint of physical violence between his parents, Jerry says. His mother's greatest frustration, in fact, came from the fact that she couldn't get Banks to react at all. "He would just shake his head and not say much. I never saw him lose his cool. He never shouted and he would never incite an argument in any way. The most he would do is say, 'I'm gone,' and get in the car and drive away."

One of the great regrets of Joey and Jerry's childhood was how seldom they were able to engage Banks in a backyard ritual enjoyed by fathers and sons everywhere. "I'd say, 'Come on, let's play catch, Dad,' Joey remembers. "We did it a few times, but it wasn't often."

"There was no ball playing," Jerry says. "No 'Let's go to the batting cage,' that kind of thing."

Occasionally, Banks would come to the boys' Little League games, where they would get a taste of how their mother felt when she and her husband were out in public. "People would say, 'Is that him?' and he would get mobbed," Joey says. Soon, Banks would be signing autographs, chatting with strangers, and hitting ground balls to the sons of other men.

Even when the twins did spend time with their father, it was almost always in the company of other people. This began when they were very young and Eloyce decided they should accompany Banks on some of his many public appearances. "My mom really needed a break because my dad traveled so much," Jerry says. "From the time when we were able to walk and put a suit on, my mom would say, 'You just go with your dad.' Boy Scout jamborees, pancake breakfasts, you name it, we're going. And you'd never see us without a suit and tie on."

As they grew older, they learned how to behave and to show they didn't need constant supervision when they were out with their father. "When we wore suits, we knew we were 'on,' like Dad," Jerry says. "My mother would say, 'Don't show out.' It's a southern phrase. We knew that this was not the time to be fighting over a piece of candy. Even if you're on your own, you're not on your own. That's a lot for a little kid to handle, but it all worked out."

When the twins were out with their father in public, they knew they had to share him. They were proud when he would introduce them— "These are my boys"—but the casual warmth he showed to strangers provided a stark contrast to his behavior at home. "There were not a whole lot of 'I love you, son,' moments," Jerry says. "I don't know if that's because of the number of kids in his family or what. He just would not say, 'I love you.' I'd say, 'I love you, Dad,' and he'd say, 'Okay, I love you too.' I kissed him more than he kissed me." As both a child and a young man, Jerry would sometimes find himself being introduced to others as Ernie Banks's son. "My name is Jerry," he would reply, frustrated at not having an identity of his own. "I'm not Ernie Banks's son."

Eloyce had two methods for coping with her unhappiness. One was becoming a Jehovah's Witness, which she practiced with her daughter, Jan. The other was drinking. "I wouldn't call her an alcoholic," Billy Williams says. "But she would drink. Ernie didn't like it much."

"She was a heavy drinker," says Edna. "One night we all went out to a big dinner and she overdrank. I said, 'Oh, Ernest,' and he said, 'Edna, don't worry about it. Jan will put her to bed.'"

Banks was particularly bothered when Eloyce drank in public and members of the Cubs' front office were sometimes called upon to intervene. Chuck Shriver recalls driving Banks and Eloyce to a January banquet in Appleton, Wisconsin, after having been warned about her drinking. "I had to sit with her and make sure she didn't have too many cocktails," Shriver says. "I was a kid, twenty-seven years old, and I was telling her, 'I don't think Ernie would want you to have that.' But she was polite to me. She didn't tell me to go jump in the lake."

Arlene Gill saw Banks's embarrassment over Eloyce's drinking when she showed up during a team party in spring training and began arguing with him. Gill realized Banks hadn't told Eloyce about the gathering, hoping he could get through the evening without her causing a scene.

The one public event at which Eloyce's drinking was the most noticeable was the Chicago baseball writers' dinner, an annual winter ritual held at a downtown hotel during which speeches were given, awards were presented, and liquor flowed. Arguments between Banks and

Eloyce were such a regular part of the event that Williams and his wife devised a method to defuse them. "Shirley would get Ernie and I would get Eloyce and we'd go our separate ways," Williams says. "We'd meet up maybe two hours later, after they'd cooled off."

Several times at these dinners, Mary Dease, a lifelong Cubs fan who became John Holland's secretary, found Eloyce sitting in a lounge adjacent to the ladies room in the Sheraton-Chicago Hotel on the verge of tears and wanting to talk. "She would corner you and sit you down and you could see she had had a few drinks," Dease says. "She would say things like, 'I'm so unhappy. My life is so difficult.' What was I going to say? Here she's talking about somebody you've idolized since you were six years old. She was a very troubled woman. I felt sorry for her."

Of all the complaints Eloyce expressed to Dease in these moments, one in particular may have best summed up her feelings about life with her husband:

"He says yes to everyone but me."

Chapter 16

Bright College Days

Lou Boudreau had no better luck finishing the 1960 season managing the Cubs than Charlie Grimm did starting it. The team won sixty games, lost ninety-four, and Boudreau, who had won a World Series as player-manager for the Cleveland Indians in 1948, was wise enough to see what lay ahead. Probably anticipating Philip K. Wrigley's reaction, he asked for a two-year contract, was turned down, and returned to the team's radio booth, where he would spend the next twenty-seven seasons.

Wrigley seemed to be in no hurry to name Boudreau's replacement. He asked his staff for a "blueprint on the future manager" and then went off on one of his regular tours around the world to meet with the representatives of his gum company. The guessing game lasted into the winter, long after major league teams usually choose their managers.

One persistent rumor had Wrigley choosing Elvin Tappe, a backup catcher who had been in the Cubs' system since 1952 and was a player-coach in 1960. Tappe seemed hopeful when he told a reporter, "If they want a young, energetic and ambitious fellow who knows the personnel, the pitchers and the farm prospects, then I'd fit the bill."

He didn't know the half of it.

Tappe had previously suggested to Wrigley that the Cubs rotate their minor league coaches from team to team so their young players would all receive the same instruction. And in December he participated in a conversation with Wrigley and some of the Cubs' department heads in which the owner stunned them with the question, "Do we even need a manager?" On January 12, 1961, in a chaotic press conference at the Wrigley Building restaurant where reporters jostled for space and tripped over television cables, Wrigley gave his answer. They did not.

Sitting next to a sign on the table in front of him that said, "Anyone who remains calm in the midst of all this confusion simply does not understand the situation," Wrigley said the job of managing a baseball team was too much for one man. "It's like the presidency," he said. "No one man can possibly do all the things required of a manager or the president of the United States." So the Cubs, Wrigley told the bewildered crowd, would not have a manager for the upcoming season "as that position is generally understood." Instead, they would rotate some of their coaches between their major and minor league teams with the likelihood that any number of them could be the "head coach" during a single season. The concept was soon dubbed the College of Coaches.

Wrigley, who had often expressed his doubts about managers, was not acting out of impulse. When he gave Grimm the job two years earlier, he said, "I believe managers are expendable. In fact, I believe there should be relief managers just like relief pitchers so you can keep rotating them." And now he had taken Tappe's sensible suggestion to move the Cubs' minor league coaches throughout the organization, expanded it to include the major league team, and come up with something brand-new. The Cubs would be managed by committee.

As if to sum up the enormity of the experiment, Wrigley said, "There is an old expression. 'He who explains is lost.' Therefore we will not try to explain except to say that we are not departing from tradition rashly or in haste, but only after long and thorough analysis." Such explanation as there was came from John Holland, who said that while the Cubs were naming eight men to their coaching staff, only four would take turns being in charge of the team. A man might "run the Cubs one month, manage in the minors the next month, and then return to the Cubs as a coach the next month. And so on. Nothing is definite yet."

Wrigley's audience hardly knew what to think.

"Do you run your gum business this way?" one dumbfounded reporter asked.

"I've always run the gum business this way," he replied. "No man is indispensable. It's like hiring a man to run a bulldozer. If the man gets sick, that doesn't mean the bulldozer has broken down. You simply have another driver step in."

And as Tappe, who was one of the eight coaches Wrigley named, surveyed the adoption of his now unrecognizable proposal, he said, "We certainly cannot do much worse trying a new system than we have done for many years under the old."

One of the other coaches the Cubs' owner chose had his doubts, though. "I feel I've had too many chances," Charlie Grimm said. "But I'm ready to do anything Mr. Wrigley asks."

Wrigley's plan quickly became the subject of ridicule in Chicago and around the country. *Chicago Daily News* columnist John Carmichael said Wrigley was trying to draw attention away from the Chicago White Sox, who had led the American League in attendance in 1960 and drawn more than twice as many fans as the Cubs. A writer for the *Los Angeles Times* compared the idea to "scientists who are trying to put a man on the moon when they could benefit humanity a whole lot more by discovering a preventative for hangovers." And Arthur Daley of the *New York Times* said the Cubs "may wind up as the most coached and least managed team in baseball."

Baseball's top executives were also skeptical. "If Mr. Wrigley wants to have eight coaches and no manager, then that is his business," said Commissioner Ford Frick.

"Certainly Mr. Wrigley knows what he wants to do," National League president Warren Giles said.

"I've never heard of a team without a manager before," said American League president Joe Cronin. "I'd feel a lot better with one chief and more Indians."

Even President John F. Kennedy took notice in a speech about concerns that automation might lead to unemployment. "Chicago, I might add, also provides the exception to this pattern since it now takes ten men to manage the Cubs instead of one," Kennedy said.

And a businessman in Des Moines, Iowa, Joe Rosenfield, jokingly reflected on his decision to purchase a minority stake in the Cubs. "I would have been just as well off to buy stock in a company that manufactures buggy whips and fireless cookers," he wrote. "People have tried to comfort me by telling me I own 2.73 percent of Ernie Banks. With my luck, if I owned the same fraction of Achilles, I would end up with the heel."

But while the College of Coaches was roundly mocked, it came as no real surprise to those who were acquainted with Wrigley's fondness for experimentation that had been expressed in many ways during his long ownership of the Cubs.

In 1943, he founded the All-American Girls Professional Baseball League against the possibility that World War II would force the major leagues to shut down. "Femininity is the keynote of our league," he said. "No pants-wearing, tough-talking female softballer will play on any of our teams." The league played in a number of Midwestern cities for twelve years and in its best season drew a million fans.

But perhaps Wrigley's singular achievement was the creation of an environment where a number of visionary ideas, good and bad, were tested.

As early as 1938, he hired a psychologist, Coleman R. Griffith, to design a program for improving training methods, charting player development, and making practice sessions more efficient. Predictably, Griffith clashed with the Cubs' dugout culture—Grimm, who was then the manager, called him the "headshrinker"—and only lasted two years. It would take decades before the field of sports psychology would become established and athletes would routinely seek help with their mental approach to the game.

Similarly, in 1962 the Cubs hired a doctor, Jacob Suker, to observe the players' eating habits and suggest ways to improve them. Soon, he was making road trips, measuring how much energy the players expended at the ballpark, and even stationing himself in the hotel dining room to monitor what they were eating. Ernie Banks, Suker noticed, had a steak, eggs, juice, and toast with butter for lunch and pronounced it amazing. "He must have had twenty-five hundred or three thousand calories in that one meal," he said. "That's almost as much calories as I would consume in two days." Suker would remain the team's physician until his death in 1989, and though many of the players had great affection for him, they laughed at his dietary suggestions. Proper nutrition, personal trainers, and individually designed workouts were concepts whose time would come much later.

During his announcement of the College of Coaches, Wrigley held up several examples of another experiment he had in mind: punch cards. The use of IBM machines, he explained, could show how players hit against opposing pitchers, and vice versa. The Cubs thus became the first baseball team to use computers. "It was very simple stuff compared to what's going on now," says Blake Cullen, the Cubs' traveling secretary for many years. "Left-handers versus right-handers, day games versus night games, grass versus turf, that kind of thing."

The operation was so simple, in fact, that it was run not by a computer specialist, but by Wrigley's chauffeur of many years, Gus Settergren. But once again, Wrigley's reach exceeded his grasp as the press scoffed and baseball men were suspicious of anything they couldn't see for themselves. The digital era that would revolutionize baseball remained off in the future.

In 1963, Wrigley announced another unorthodox move that was greeted with derision when he named Colonel Robert Whitlow, a former World War II fighter pilot who had just retired from the air force, the Cubs' "athletic director." At first, it appeared that Whitlow would be in charge of player and managerial moves, but he was quickly moved to the sidelines, where he issued such comments as "We're going to strike fear from our vocabulary" and the Cubs were showing "fine spirit." He became known as the vice president in charge of fine spirit and was gone after two years.

But Whitlow left behind several ideas that again demonstrated the value of a culture that encouraged new ideas, even if their worth was not immediately recognized. He had a weight room installed in the Cubs' locker room, which was uncommon at the time but is universal today, and devised diets that included powdered nutritional supplements. He also introduced the concept of counting and charting pitches.

Using an elaborate diagram he had created, Whitlow would record every pitch thrown in a game by type—fastball, curveball, changeup, and others—exact location in or out of the strike zone, and where it was hit if the batter made contact. The Cubs and the media rolled their eyes at what they considered one more of Whitlow's goofy ideas as well as his attention to how many pitches each pitcher threw in a game. Years later, charting and counting pitches would all but dictate how pitchers were handled, but Whitlow was ignored by the Cubs managers and coaches, and he resigned after the 1964 season, saying he wasn't earning his salary. He was too far ahead of his time, Wrigley said, adding that "baseball people are slow to accept anyone with new ideas."

But for every new idea Wrigley devised or encouraged that would later vindicate him, he had as many or more that were simply laughable. He tried putting wires in the pitchers' jackets so they could stay warm between innings on cold days. He invented a gummed belt to keep the players' jerseys from riding up. He even paid $5,000 to a swami or "evil eye" to sit behind home plate and hex the opposition.

"There's nothing funny about this," Wrigley told Bill Veeck in the early 1930s, not long after taking over the Cubs, when he hired a man Veeck described as a "ferret-faced wizened little guy in a checkered suit." "This man may help us. And don't go talking to your newspaper friends about it. Or anybody else, either." The swami traveled with the Cubs during the season and retreated to their offices on cold Chicago days, where he would stand over the Western Union machine and hex the opposition as the play-by-play came in. He, too, didn't last long.

But while Wrigley remained a wildly inventive owner who had new ideas, good and bad, throughout his life, when it came to building a

winning baseball team he remained stuck in the past. Unlike other owners, he refused to use his own great fortune to improve the team. The
Cubs and his gum company were separate organizations, and he would
not even allow ads for Wrigley's gum to appear on broadcasts of the
games. The Cubs, he insisted, must pay for themselves.

Wrigley liked to make the team's finances public, probably because
they proved how close the margin was between profit and loss. In 1960,
when the Cubs were the fourth-poorest draw in baseball, they made
$27,411. In 1968, when they drew more than one million fans for the first
time in seventeen years, they made $2,047,355, but $1.8 million of that
came in expansion fees from the major leagues' four new teams. Wrigley
was so open about the Cubs' finances that in 1959 he even offered to let
player representative Dale Long look at the books. Long declined, saying it was none of his business and he wouldn't understand what he was
looking at anyway.

But Wrigley's frugality exacted a toll. The Cubs were well behind
other teams in building a minor league organization, and when they
finally got around to it Wrigley seemed more concerned with whether
the farm teams were making money than whether they were developing players. He even allowed his minor league teams to sell players to
other teams if the price was right. And when a player did show promise,
he might suddenly find himself playing in Chicago before he was ready.

"They were rushed through the minor leagues out of a state of
urgency," says Joe Amalfitano. "They were learning their craft at the
major league level when they should have been taking it a step at a time."

Rich Nye, a Cubs pitcher from 1967 through 1969, was surprised to
find himself called up the same season he was drafted out of the University of California. Bill Stoneman, who pitched for the Cubs for two
seasons before going to the Montreal Expos in the expansion draft, similarly found himself in Wrigley Field only a year after he was drafted from
the University of Idaho. "They seemed to think that pitching in college
was good enough experience," said Nye, who lamented the fact he didn't
spend more time in the higher levels of the minor leagues. "They didn't

look like they were working on building a strong minor league system to reinforce the big leagues."

The Cubs' front office was also run haphazardly and on the cheap, with just the bare minimum of personnel. Mary Dease recalls throwing a housewarming party in her new small studio apartment in 1973 where nearly the entire Cubs' administrative staff showed up. "It was crowded," she said, "but they all fit."

Their work space was equally bare-bones—a cramped and dusty office that featured a large old-fashioned PBX switchboard, operated by women who lifted a heavy plug each time a light came on and connected it to the proper extension. "It was like something you'd see in a thirties or forties movie," Dease says. "*The Front Page* comes to mind. I remember holding the receiver on my elbow and working the plugs with my right hand. I had to go to the doctor after a few months with a pinched nerve. They finally got me a headset, which were pretty new in those days. It was not a high-tech operation."

The Cubs' public relations department was similarly behind the times. Chuck Shriver got his first inkling of what he was getting into in 1966 when he discovered the man running the department was Rip Collins, a former member of the St. Louis Cardinals' Gashouse Gang and one of the eight men who had been named to the College of Coaches five years earlier. "All he did was shake hands and sit around the press-room bar," Shriver says. "On my first day, he said, 'You might as well start over there,' and he pointed to a huge cardboard box like the kind toilet paper comes in that was filled with two years of unopened fan mail."

Nor did the Cubs publish a yearbook or a newsletter. A simple media guide, not generally available to the public, was the team's only publication, and for Shriver it came to symbolize one of the supreme ironies of how the Cubs were run. For all of Wrigley's willingness to gamble on the field, his front office was gripped with an almost paralytic fear when it came to making decisions.

In the late 1960s, the public relations department of the commissioner's office requested that every team's press guide be the same rectangular shape, so they would all fit in a binder that could be given to sportswriters and team officials. The Cubs' guide was almost square, and Shriver took the league's request to the team's business manager, Bill Heymans. Heymans said he couldn't make such a decision and told him to talk to Holland. Holland's answer was the same; only Wrigley himself could approve the change. Soon, an astonished Shriver found himself sitting ramrod straight in the owner's office in the Wrigley Building.

"We don't do things just to make the rest of the league happy," Wrigley said after hearing the young publicity director out. Wrigley then asked if it would cost more to make a rectangular media guide. Shriver said the price would be the same. Five minutes of uncomfortable silence ensued as Wrigley thought it over. Finally, he said, "Well, I guess that'll be okay."

"I'm thinking to myself as I'm walking out, 'We had to go all the way to the top guy just to get permission to change the size of the *media guide?*'" Shriver says. "I couldn't believe it."

The Cubs' attitude toward their women employees was similarly rigid. They were expected to wear skirts or dresses at all times, and while they were allowed into the Wrigley Field lunchroom, which was known as the Pink Poodle, the rules changed on game days, when it became a men-only lounge for the press, visiting scouts, and executives. If they hadn't packed a lunch—there were no restaurants fit for unaccompanied women near the ballpark at the time—they were allowed to walk out onto the concourse, buy food at a concession stand, and submit an expense account. It was, some of them thought, the least the Cubs could do.

Predictably, the Cubs' 1961 spring training began with the members of the College of Coaches jockeying for position. Since they didn't know which of them would be named to run the team, or even who would be in the rotation, they took turns trying to gain Wrigley's attention by praising the genius of his creation.

"This is the best thing to happen to baseball since the spitball," Tappe said as drills got under way in Arizona. "When you go to a law office, there are different experts for deeds, for insurance, for civil actions. Hospitals are filled with specialists. If it works for law and medicine, why not for baseball?"

"Look at our advantages," said Gordie Holt, a veteran scout who had joined the Cubs as a coach the previous year. "We will have four minds working whereas the other clubs will have just one."

"Other owners don't have Mr. Wrigley's nerve," said Verlon "Rube" Walker, whose career as a minor league catcher and player-manager in the Cubs' farm system had just ended. "Give us time. They'll follow."

"I thought it was fantastic when I first heard of the idea," said Rip Collins. "Now it makes sense."

"I see no flaws," said Harry Craft, who had managed the Kansas City Athletics for two and a half seasons. "The plan has created harmony."

"It'll work, and sooner than the critics think," said Vedie Himsl, a scout and minor league manager for the Cubs for most of the 1950s.

Even Charlie Grimm seemed energized by the thought of another chance in the dugout. "This is something new and proves to the players we are interested in their future," he said.

Wrigley responded to these bids for his attention like a child with a new toy coveted by his playmates. He offered no hints about who would begin the season as head coach, or even when he would make his decision. The spring wore on with the coaches looking over their shoulders and the players leafing through thirty-eight-page manuals they had been given that contained detailed instructions on such fundamentals as how to execute bunts, pickoffs, and cutoff throws from the outfield. The writers covering the team were given explanatory booklets of their own, each of them numbered like so many secret documents passed out to intelligence officers to make sure they were all returned.

Finally, on April 6, Wrigley called Holland during the ninth inning of an exhibition game with the Boston Red Sox in Dallas. He was naming Himsl the manager, Wrigley said, for no better reason than he was the oldest in point of consecutive service in uniform. Holland gave Himsl the news on the flight to Chicago, where the Cubs opened the season five days later.

———

The experiment spun out of control almost immediately. After the Cubs lost six of their first eleven games, Himsl was replaced by Kraft, under whom they lost eight of their next twelve. Himsl then returned to the dugout, which indicated that Wrigley was already having doubts about his announced plan of using a succession of four different men. The Cubs proceeded to lose eighteen of twenty-one games before Memorial Day, and Wrigley had seen enough. On June 13, he called the merry-go-round to a halt.

"The rotation of coaches into the head coaching position has been temporarily suspended," he said. Tappe would be the head coach for an indefinite period. Asked how long that period might last, Wrigley said, "I have no idea."

By the time the season was over, Tappe would manage ninety-six games to thirty-one for Himsl, sixteen for Kraft, and eleven for Lou Klein, who had managed the Cubs' Class D team earlier in the season. "The system's revolutionary aspects have been considerably dulled," Jerome Holtzman wrote in The Sporting News. Tappe, he said, "often appears alone, a veritable captain at the bridge."

None of the Cubs' four managers in 1961 won more games than he lost—the team finished in seventh place with a record of sixty and ninety-four—and the notion that a variety of coaches would improve the team like so many legal or medical specialists failed spectacularly. The Cubs were seventh in the National League in batting and earned run average and last in fielding percentage.

———

The Cubs didn't have many bright moments in 1961, but one came near the end of June when they won three straight games at Wrigley Field against the Cincinnati Reds, and scored thirty-eight runs while doing so. Banks spent the series on the bench nursing his knee, and after the third game, Tappe made an announcement. "We hate to disturb a winning lineup," Tappe said, "and a little more rest won't do Ernie any harm."

"What! Banks Can't Get in Cubs' Lineup?" asked a headline in the *Chicago Tribune.* Two days later, Banks learned he would not be in the starting lineup of the National League All-Star team for the first time in seven years. These were not the first indignities Banks suffered in 1961, or the last.

Dating back to his days in the army, when his knees first began troubling him, Banks had experienced pain off and on. But he played through it and occasionally had the fluid drained from his knees. Now, however, Cubs' doctors said there was floating cartilage in his left knee and began to talk about an operation.

Thinking the wear and tear of playing shortstop might be aggravating the injury, Banks tried to adjust by playing left field, but the position frustrated him. He had never been an outfielder, he told Tappe, and he never would be. What about first base? Tappe asked him in the middle of June. At least that would get him back to the infield. Banks was willing, but in his seventh game at the new position, he ran into a wall behind first base in San Francisco as he was chasing a pop-up. His knee was drained again, a pint of blood was extracted, and the pain was too great to continue. On June 23, Banks told Tappe he should come out of the lineup. His 717-game playing streak, the longest in the majors and an all-time Cubs record, was over.

Banks was back at shortstop a week later—he just felt more comfortable there, he said—but after fifteen games during which he had only one home run and four runs batted in he returned to the dugout. His knee was still bothering him, but he also admitted to a new and more worrying problem: his eyes.

Banks's excellent eyesight had always played a key role in his hitting ability. So when he first noticed a loss of depth perception in 1957 he was relieved when eye drops and a few simple exercises solved the problem. "As soon as we completed the treatments, Ernie's batting average shot up precipitously," said Dr. Richard A. Perritt, the eye specialist treating him. But now, four years later, the problem had returned and was more persistent.

Perritt gave a detailed diagnosis. Banks was suffering from a spasm of the muscle that controls the internal rotation of the eyes, leading to a lack of coordination. It was, he said, like a team of horses pulling toward each other and stepping on each other's feet rather than moving forward. Another defect Perritt noted was a "small fleeting periodic blind spot in the left eye. We had to do a lot of work to uncover it." The result was a lack of depth perception. "A ball could be right on top of him and Ernie would figure it was farther away," he said.

Perritt was equally forthcoming when asked what was causing the problem. It was Banks himself. "Ernie wasn't hitting as well as he wanted to and he began pressing," he said. "His current eye troubles are the result of the tension and the pressure and the resulting fatigue." All he could offer by way of a cure were more eye drops, more exercises, and a stereoscope, an instrument that looked like a pair of binoculars, that he told Banks to stare into for ten or fifteen minutes each day. Banks said his left eye was particularly bothersome, and he tried to compensate by moving back in the batter's box and waiting longer before he swung his bat, hoping to pick up the ball with his right eye. The reason it didn't work was simple, he said. "My nose was in the way."

Banks was stoic, even philosophical, as he watched his teammates play without him. Walking to the Wrigley Field batting cage on a sunny day late in July, he heard a boy yell from the stands, "Hey, Ernie, if you break a bat can I have it?"

"You can have it if I break it," Banks replied.

A group of Little Leaguers came out on the field and Banks walked over to them, put his glove under his arm, and patted two of the boys on the head.

"What a wonderful day for baseball," he said to nobody in particular. Then, almost as an afterthought, he added, "Too wonderful to sit on the bench."

On July 26, Banks was sent up to pinch-hit with two out in the eighth inning of a game against the St. Louis Cardinals at Wrigley Field. He hit a three-run home run that tied the game, and the Cubs won in twelve innings. Two days later, he hit two more home runs, and another the day after that. He hit six home runs in August and six more in September, all while playing creditably at shortstop.

In all, Banks hit sixteen home runs and drove in forty-one runs in the final two months of the season and finished with a batting average of .274, twenty-nine home runs, and eighty runs batted in. And despite his ailments, he missed only sixteen games. Compared to the six seasons that had come before, the year was a disappointment. For any other shortstop, it would have been a career highlight.

The concern over Banks's eyes faded. Talk of an operation on his knees disappeared. For the first time, Banks had learned what it was like to confront the doubts of those who thought he might never be the player he once was, and his own doubts as well. It was knowledge he would put to good use in the years ahead.

Chapter 17

"He Was Why We Fell in Love with the Game"

On May 25, 1962, in the ninth inning of a game in Cincinnati, Ernie Banks turned away from a high inside pitch he could see coming straight at him. He was unable to get out of the way, and the ball struck him low on the back of his head and knocked him to the ground. Without losing consciousness, Banks was carried off the field on a stretcher.

"I was pitching him inside all the way," said Reds pitcher Moe Drabowsky. "It just got away from me."

Banks was taken to a Cincinnati hospital, where he was visited that evening by a penitent Drabowsky, who had been his teammate from 1956 through 1960. He was made to wait as Banks underwent X-rays.

"Moe, you look worse than I feel," Banks said as he was wheeled back into his room. "I'm going to ask the doctor if it's okay for me to give you this bed so I can visit you."

Complaining of headaches, Banks stayed in the hospital for a second night, then returned to Chicago with his teammates for a series against the Milwaukee Braves. He was back in the lineup four days after he had been hit, wearing a batting helmet for the first time instead of the plastic liner he had used under his cap because the helmet felt uncomfortable.

In his first at-bat in the second inning, Banks hit a pitch by Bob Hendley off the left-field wall for a double. In the third inning, he hit a home run off Hendley. In the fifth inning, he hit a home run off Don Nottebart. In the seventh inning, he hit a home run off Lew Burdette. It was the third time in his career that Banks had hit three home runs in one game, and the Cubs, who had led 9–0 after three innings, held on to win, 11–9.

———

Even before the 1962 season began, Banks's career was reborn. He hit .343 with six home runs in spring training and said that while he was still doing exercises for his knees, his eyes felt so strong he wasn't bothering with the stereoscope anymore. Banks hit a 400-foot home run on opening day in Houston, and his three home runs in the game against the Braves gave him fourteen by the end of May. It was the fastest start of his career, and though his batting average was a modest .269, Banks finished the season with thirty-seven home runs and 104 runs batted in. It was a bravura performance that silenced all talk that he might be slowing down.

The season also marked another milestone for Banks: a permanent move to first base. He had no sooner agreed to Elvin Tappe's suggestion that he give the position another try than he realized it was a godsend. Before the end of spring training, Banks saw that as much as he loved playing shortstop, the position had taken a toll on him. "I never realized just how strenuous a job it was at shortstop until I moved to first base," he said. "There is scarcely a play the shortstop isn't in on. It's a rat race over there, while things are fairly peaceful at first base." His new position might add two or three years to his career, Banks said, and help his hitting as well.

There was another reason for Banks's enthusiasm for his new position. He was a natural. He had some things to learn—how to field ground balls that arrived at different angles than they did at shortstop, how close to hold a runner on first base depending on how quickly he could get to second, how much to cheat in toward home plate if he had a chance for a force play. He also had some early problems learning the proper footwork for tagging first base and getting out of the way when the second baseman or pitcher was making the play there. "Sometimes I seem to have too many feet," he said, "and sometimes not enough."

But Banks had excellent teachers in Charlie Grimm and Buck O'Neil, who had been so adept at the position that for a gag one day in Kansas City he had played barefoot and wearing a hula skirt. "Any good infielder can do a good job at first base," Grimm said. "All he has to do is master the footwork." And by the end of the spring, the Cubs' coaches were satisfied. Give Banks a couple of months, they said, and he would be one of the best first basemen in the league. The prediction was borne out when, in his first year at the position, Banks finished second among National League first basemen in fielding percentage.

In the years ahead, Banks would come to be respected as a first baseman just as he had been at shortstop. In 1969, New York Mets coach Al "Rube" Walker called him the best in baseball at scooping up low throws. "He had great hands," Cubs pitcher Bill Hands agreed. "He didn't have the greatest range, but anything he got to he didn't miss. Anytime a ball was in the dirt, he had it. I can't tell you how many errors he saved us over the years."

As comfortable as Banks came to feel at first base, however, he sometimes exhibited a reflexive longing for the position he had left behind. "When a ball was hit to his right, he would run over almost in front of me," says Joe Amalfitano, the Cubs second baseman in 1964. "I finally said, 'Hey, listen, if I know I've got it, I'm going to yell at you. You get over to first.' He still had the mind-set of playing shortstop."

Banks's popularity in Chicago reached its peak during these years as his long service to a team that seemed incapable of improvement left his fans to exult in his triumphs and agonize with his struggles. He was a reliable, comforting figure who had become a symbol of the way the city liked to feel about itself—always hard at work even when things were at their worst. This was particularly true of his effect on children.

"I used to walk home from grade school and I would turn on the games and score the last couple of innings, always hoping Ernie would get to bat," says Dennis Paoli, who lived near Wrigley Field. "And there was the way he held the bat, straight up. When I played, I used to hold my bat the same way, which was a terrible idea."

"Back in the days when the Cubs usually battled the Pirates for last place and most of the time the upper deck wasn't open because of the small crowds, at least we always had number fourteen," Bob Sirott, a Chicago broadcaster, wrote of a Wrigley Field childhood. "When Ernie hit a high fly ball to shallow left, we roared with expectation. If the ball sailed over the ivy-covered wall, we screamed and jumped and hugged our seatmates."

Banks's young fans also responded to the fact that he remained a Cub year after year while other players came and went. "You identified the Cubs entirely with him," Paoli says. "He was exactly what you wanted your team to be. You wanted a whole team of Ernie Bankses."

In many cases, this youthful infatuation never really went away. In Schererville, Indiana, for instance, Clea McLeod was informed by her new husband, Russ, that he had a statue of Banks that would be placed on top of their Christmas tree. "No angels and no stars," McCloud said. "Just Ernie Banks. It was on the tree for forty Christmases."

Banks responded to this adoration in kind, often standing for long periods before and after games to sign autographs, a habit he kept up for the rest of his life. Years later, when he was asked why he was always so accommodating, he smiled and said, "I signed all those autographs to all those young boys because I always thought one of them might give me a job when they got older."

Banks was a particular inspiration to black youngsters, though there weren't many whose fathers and grandfathers rooted for the Cubs. Because of geography—Comiskey Park was located near Chicago's largest black communities—and the fact that the White Sox had integrated before the Cubs, the city's black fans largely supported the Sox. "I was born and raised on the South Side of Chicago, which means by birthright I was supposed to hate the Cubs," wrote Michael Wilbon, a sportswriter for the *Washington Post,* and later a television commentator for ESPN.

"But there was nobody in the world who could talk me into rooting against Ernie Banks."

As for white children—those who were raised in prejudice-free environments, at least—they simply saw Banks as one of them. "I don't think we even realized he was a black man," says Ned Colletti, a young Cubs fan who lived out by O'Hare International Airport. "He was just our hero. He was why we fell in love with the game."

Still other fans had more elemental views of his appeal. "He don't cuss, he don't bitch, and he don't smoke," one Chicago woman said. "I guess you could call him a saint."

There were times when this adulation could get out of hand, most notably on August 27, 1962, when Banks made a public appearance at a clothing store in Gary, Indiana. The organizers of the event were unprepared when an estimated 7,500 people showed up and began pushing their way forward to get a glimpse of Banks. The crowd broke through a plate-glass window and twenty-three people were injured, many of them children. Four ambulances took the victims to several local hospitals and, thankfully, no one was seriously hurt. When order was restored, Banks remained at the store to sign autographs and then went to one of the hospitals, where he signed baseballs for some of the injured children.

Banks was also involved in another incident that year, one that proved fame and admiration were no protection from Chicago's problems. It happened on July 2 when, as the Cubs were about to travel from Milwaukee to Cincinnati, a bullet was fired through the window of the Banks home on Rhodes Avenue. Eloyce had just returned home from a party at the Palmer House, she said, when she heard two shots at the back of the house. The next morning she found a broken window in the breakfast nook and a bullet lying on the floor.

The Bankses were rattled but not surprised. For three weeks, gangs of young black teenagers—Eloyce estimated that some were as young as ten—had been gathering in the neighborhood and shouting abusive remarks. A week earlier, at least twenty-five of them had stood in front of the Banks house, and two shots were fired. She called the police and the gang dispersed, but it returned after the patrol moved on.

When Eloyce called Banks in Cincinnati, he seemed incredulous that a young man on the South Side of Chicago should even have a gun, let alone use it. "A boy I know in the neighborhood told me just the other day about a sixteen-year-old boy who had a gun, but he wouldn't say who it was," he said. "This upsets me tremendously."

Banks and some other neighborhood fathers had talked about trying to organize activities for youngsters, but nothing had come of it. And now he was worried about being on the road while Eloyce, who was seven months pregnant with their third child, was dealing with gunshots through the breakfast nook window. "If something isn't done to stop the noise and carrying on," he said, "I may have to send Eloyce and the boys to California or to Dallas until our new baby comes." But the incidents ended, and the family stayed together in Chicago.

While Banks's performance on the field in 1962 was heartening, the Cubs were a disaster. They lost their first seven games, won only four of twenty games in April, lost twice as many games on the road as they won, were shut out ten times, and were eliminated from the pennant race more than five weeks before the season ended. A ten-game string of defeats in September assured they would lose 100 games for the first time and finish in the second division for the sixteenth consecutive season. Their final record, 59–103, was the worst in their ninety-one years of existence. They were saved from finishing last only because the New York Mets, in their first year in the league, lost 120 games, the most of any major league team in the twentieth century. "Without Ernie Banks," said Jimmy Dykes, who had once bet a box of golf balls that Banks would be a failure, "the Cubs would have finished in Albuquerque." Unsurprisingly, the Cubs' attendance, 609,802, was the worst in baseball, and on three consecutive days late in September, fewer than 1,000 fans came to Wrigley Field.

The Cubs' futility in 1962 was agonizing and endless. On April 17 at home, they scored five runs in the first inning against Pittsburgh and it appeared they would break a six-game losing streak. The Pirates scored six runs off five pitchers in the last two innings and won 10–6. A week later, Sandy Koufax tied the major league record by striking out eighteen Cubs in a game won by the Los Angeles Dodgers, 10–2. On May 16 in New York, Cubs infielder Daryl Robertson tried to bunt with two strikes and a man on second with the score tied in the eleventh inning. He struck out and the Cubs lost, 6–5, for their second extra-inning loss to the lowly Mets by that score in as many days. Robertson's entire major league career consisted of nineteen games he played with the Cubs in 1962, during which he had two hits in nineteen at-bats.

One other casualty of the Cubs' 1962 season was the College of Coaches. Philip K. Wrigley had insisted that a managerial rotation be given another chance, but the results were even worse than in the season before, and the players were in open revolt. After the 1961 season, Cubs second baseman Don Zimmer called the idea a "joke that was doomed to failure the moment it was created." Different coaches liked different players, he said, and they all "treated the players as chessmen, not thinking, breathing players." As a reward for his honesty, Zimmer was exposed to the expansion draft and was claimed by the Mets. A year later, when pitcher Don Cardwell told John Holland the system wasn't working, he was traded within a week.

"I can't remember much that was good about it," said Don Elston, a Cubs relief pitcher, of the college. "There was jealousy among the coaches. When one guy was the head coach, some of the other coaches did nothing to help him. They sat there waiting for their turn."

"We would go from a manager who would like to bunt and hit-and-run one week to a guy who didn't do any of that the next week," said catcher Dick Bartell. "The system was not good for morale, and there was plenty of tendency toward insubordination on the team," said Lou Brock. "The trouble was, how could you know who to be insubordinate to?"

The one Cubs player who did not express any doubts about the College of Coaches may have been the only one who could have done something about it. "Ernie never let me know what his feelings were," says pitcher Ken Holtzman, who joined the team in 1965 as the experiment was coming to an end. "Due to his special relationship with Mr. Wrigley, he wisely hid his feelings and just went along with it. What I learned was that a two-time MVP commands more respect from the other players than any temporary manager."

Before the season began, Wrigley announced some changes to his master plan. Some coaches are good instructors, he said, while others are better at running a team. The goal was to try to discover who was which. "After all," he said, "you can't find out if a fellow can manage unless you give him a shot at it." By the end of the season, he said, the Cubs might be down to two head coaches, or maybe only one. "But if it's just one coach, we'll still call him coach instead of manager."

The season began with Tappe, who had managed the bulk of the 1961 season, in the dugout. But with the Cubs off to their woeful start, he lasted less than a month and was replaced by Lou Klein. Tappe returned to his role as backup catcher and at the end of the season was named manager of the Cubs' farm team in Salt Lake City, which came as a relief. "It gives me a chance to go out there and work on managing," he said. "It's tough to learn in the big leagues."

Klein's fate was sealed after the two extra-inning losses in New York that so alarmed Holland that he flew in to assess the damage for himself. On June 4, after the Cubs had spent sixteen days in last place, Wrigley handed the reins to Charlie Metro, a veteran minor league manager who had the no-nonsense reputation the owner thought his players needed. Metro promised to shake things up—more running, more practice, more toughness, more pride—and when the Cubs won nine games and lost eight in his first weeks on the job, one writer called it a "dizzy spiral upward." Like Tappe a year earlier, Metro was named head coach for the rest of the season. Reporters pointed out he hadn't spent any time in the Cubs' minor league system and declared the College of Coaches dead.

Metro's modest winning streak didn't last, nor did his hopes of returning in 1963. His final months were beset by sniping back and forth with Tappe and Klein and complaints from the players about such indignities as a ban on golf clubs in the clubhouse to keep them off the links on the mornings of day games. Metro finished the season with a record of 43–69, which gave him the distinction of being the longest-serving head coach in the brief history of the College of Coaches, and he was then fired. Wrigley responded to the demise of his creation somewhat plaintively. "Metro gave us lip service," he said. "He told us he thought it was a good system. Privately, though, he indicated he did not approve or agree." Then he added, "Maybe we are a peculiar organization."

Wrigley also revealed that some of the Cubs had brought their complaints directly to him. "It's the same old story," said the owner, whose history with player-manager conflicts extended back to his father's firing of Rogers Hornsby in 1932 while the Cubs were in second place. "It happened with Hornsby, too. Metro was impatient and too tough."

"Oh, so they have started slinging a little mud?" Metro said when he learned of Wrigley's remarks. A few days later, after the White Sox named him their head scout, Metro was more diplomatic. "I don't wish to say anything detrimental to the Cubs' organization," he said. "I hope Mr. Wrigley finds the Shangri-La type of man he is looking for. My biggest problem now is what to do with five hundred picture postcards of myself in a Cubs uniform."

———

In June 1962, the Cubs announced an addition to their coaching staff. Buck O'Neil would become the first black coach in the history of major league baseball. "The Cubs are to be congratulated," *The Sporting News* said in an editorial. "There was a feeling in some quarters that status beyond that of player would be denied to Negro athletes. The addition of O'Neil to the Cub staff refutes that belief." A writer for the Associated Negro Press saw things differently. "The promotion of O'Neil on a limited basis, although laudatory on its face value, seems a rather timid move in fact." And indeed the Cubs made it clear that O'Neil would never be their head coach. "O'Neil will serve in the ranks along with the rest of the coaches," Holland said. "As a matter of fact, he will be a scout-coach since he will continue the scouting duties among the players of his race."

The Cubs had an important reason for promoting O'Neil, and it had nothing to do with breaking racial barriers. They wanted him in the dugout to monitor Banks's play at first base, and the only way to prevent complaints from other teams was to make him a coach. Their determination to limit O'Neil's role was shown in a game in Houston when both Metro and Tappe, who was coaching third base, were ejected. O'Neil was the logical man to take over at third, but Cubs pitching coach Fred Martin was brought in from the bullpen. O'Neil later learned that Grimm had told the other coaches that he was not to be allowed on the field during a game for fear that he would take a white man's job. Not getting a chance to coach on a major league field was one of the few disappointments in his long life in baseball, O'Neil said. Left unsaid were any thoughts he might have had about never being considered for a job managing in the majors.

In January 1963, Wrigley officially pronounced an end to his experiment. "Despite our grand plans, each of the head coaches had his own individual ideas and the aim of standardization of play was not achieved because of the various personalities," he said. "The players did not know where to turn and the goal was not attained." A month later, Wrigley named Bob Kennedy, the manager of the Cubs' farm team in Salt Lake City, to run the Cubs, with the expectation that he would stay for the entire season. In fact, Kennedy would remain in charge for the next two and a half seasons, but his job title never changed. He was the head coach, which was one last bow to the College of Coaches, now extinct in all but name.

Elvin Tappe would always maintain that the College of Coaches was never given its due. "Today, hitting and pitching coaches and infield coaches are moving from club to club, giving instruction to all of the players in their system," he said. Tappe did admit, however, that his plan had grown out of control. "I never intended it to be used on the big-league level," he said. "Mr. Wrigley got all carried away."

Chapter 18

The Lull Before the Storm

The Cubs had returned to Chicago from a long West Coast road trip in the middle of June 1963, and Ernie Banks was talking to a reporter before the team's first home games in nearly two weeks.

"It's great to be back in the friendly confines of Wrigley Field," Banks said.

"It sounds like there's a cliché in there someplace," the writer said.

"Maybe so," Banks said with a grin. "But you feel better when you're at home."

Aside from his second enduring contribution to the American lexicon, Banks had little to be happy about in 1963. His eyes were bothering him again, his badly bruised right knee took a painful blow from a batted ball, and he suffered a bruised heel when a runner stepped on his foot at first base. Most worrisome of all, Banks was losing weight and complaining of a lack of energy. "I just get tired," he said. "The first time at the plate I swing the bat pretty good, but after that I'm pushing the ball. I don't have any snap in the bat."

At the conclusion of a home stand late in May, Banks was in the midst of a one-for-twenty-five hitting slump and his batting average was barely above .200. He had hit rock bottom, and the rest of the league took notice. During a game in Houston, the Cubs had runners on second and third with first base open when Colt .45s' manager Harry Craft ordered that Banks be pitched to rather than walked intentionally. No Chicago writer could remember such a thing happening since Banks had entered the league.

Banks suffered an even greater humiliation on July 27 at Wrigley Field at the hands of his own team. He had been given the day off, but in the eighth inning he was sent up to pinch-hit. He was swinging several bats in the on-deck circle when the Cardinals brought in a right-handed pitcher to face him. Cubs head coach Bob Kennedy followed with a move of his own. A hush fell over the crowd as Merritt Ranew, a journeyman catcher and left-handed hitter, emerged from the dugout carrying a bat. Swishing his own bats toward the ground in embarrassment, Banks walked off the field. It was the first time since his rookie season when, after Warren Spahn struck him out twice, that a teammate had pinch-hit for him.

"What is wrong with Ernie Banks?" Edgar Munzel wrote in *The Sporting News*. "Could it be possible that Mr. Cub is nearing the end of the road in baseball?" It was a fair question, one that Banks was asking himself. "It's hard," he said. "I need to prove to myself that I'm not washed up."

Banks had a hot streak in June, raising his batting average almost fifty points in just two weeks and hitting two home runs in a game against the San Francisco Giants and three more in one against the Los Angeles Dodgers, two of them off Sandy Koufax. But his final numbers—a .227 batting average, eighteen home runs, sixty-four runs batted in, and twenty-four missed games—represented the worst season of his career to date by far.

Not until late in the season did tests reveal what his problem was. Banks was suffering from the mumps, of all things, a subclinical variety in which the disease remains hidden in the blood with no swelling of the glands, which made a diagnosis difficult. Banks would be used only as a pinch hitter and spot defensive player for the rest of the season, the Cubs announced, and would miss the team's final road trip to Pittsburgh and Milwaukee. His main goal in the off-season, Banks said, was to rest. "I plan to be so lazy this winter they're going to have to wake me up to eat," he said. But Banks was more concerned about his physical condition than he let on.

"He was worried about a low-grade blood infection which he suspected could be cancer," said Vince Lloyd, the Cubs' radio broadcaster, who did charity work for Danny Thomas's St. Jude's Hospital in Memphis, Tennessee, which specialized in blood diseases. Banks never specifically told Lloyd he suspected he might have leukemia, but his questions made his fears clear enough. Lloyd followed Banks's lead by dancing around the subject. "I suspected what he suspected," he said, "but I didn't want to come right out and say it. I can't help recalling how good a front he maintained." After Banks's illness was identified, Lloyd mentioned how impressed he was that Banks had kept his worries to himself. "I just wouldn't want to give my friends any cause for concern," said Banks, who had shut out the outside world once again.

On June 6, 1963, the Giants had the bases loaded with one out in the tenth inning of a tie game at Wrigley Field when Cubs shortstop Andre Rodgers noticed the runner at second base had strayed far off the bag. Rodgers flashed a sign to catcher Dick Bertell, who relayed it to pitcher Lindy McDaniel. McDaniel wheeled and fired the ball to Rodgers, who picked a thoroughly embarrassed Willie Mays off the base. Mays would be fined twenty-five dollars for his transgression. McDaniel retired the final batter and, in the bottom of the inning, ended the game with one of the three home runs he would hit in his twenty-one-year career. Suddenly, miracle of miracles, the Cubs were tied with the St. Louis Cardinals for first place in the National League.

"It is beginning to appear the Cubs are no longer an absolute cinch to finish deep in the league's second tier," Jerome Holtzman wrote in *The Sporting News* as the Cubs made their charge. They promptly lost six of their next seven games, dropped to fifth place, and were not a threat for the rest of the season.

John Holland and Bob Kennedy tried to make something of the fact that the Cubs' record of 82–80 marked the first time they had finished above .500 in seventeen years, but it was a mirage. Because of the disastrous records of the expansion New York Mets (51–111) and the Colt .45s (66–96), seven of the league's ten teams won more games than they lost.

The Cubs' seventh-place finish marked their sixteenth straight season in the second division, the most in the history of the National League.

It strains credulity to imagine that a healthy Ernie Banks could have helped the Cubs make up the seventeen games they finished behind the league champion Dodgers, but the Cubs could not help wondering what if. Neither could Banks. "If I had been hitting like I should, we would have been in it all the way," he said. "It's rough when you're on a club you know would be in contention if you were contributing something."

Banks showed up at spring training in 1964 completely recovered from his illness. He had gained back all the weight he had lost, and trainer Al Scheuneman noted with approval that most of the added pounds were in his seat and thighs rather than across his shoulders and chest, which would have hampered his swing. The only thing bothering Banks now was a hoarse voice, and his teammates took to calling him Louis Armstrong. "I think I'll get myself a trumpet," he said. "That man made a million bucks with that voice, didn't he?"

Even before the season began, it was clear that he was back. In the Cubs' final fourteen exhibition games, he hit .400 with four home runs and fourteen runs batted in. He didn't let up when the regular season began, and by the end of June he was hitting .300 with ten home runs and forty-four runs batted in. "Ernie Banks looks better to me than at any time since 1960," said Harry Craft. "He's got that old snap back in his bat." He would no longer be pitching to him with first base open, Craft said.

Though he tailed off toward the end of the season, Banks hit the tenth grand slam of his career on September 27 and finished the year hitting .264 with twenty-three home runs and ninety-five runs batted in. The deteriorating condition of his knees had robbed him of the speed he needed to hit .300, but there was nothing wrong with the way he was swinging the bat. "It proved to me that I can still play good baseball," Banks said of his comeback. "When you have a couple of poor seasons, it creates tension and doubt." And again, he expressed his greatest concern. "I got to wondering whether I could still play," he said. But Banks's good season did nothing to help the Cubs, and the team backslid into eighth place with a 76–86 record.

In appreciation of his fine season, and perhaps out of concern over how many more he might have left, the Cubs arranged for the Ernie Banks Day that Banks had refused nine years earlier because he didn't think he had earned it. It was the first time the team had ever honored a player in such a manner, and the committee that organized the event contained some of Chicago's most prominent citizens, who presented him with a new car. His teammates gave him a silver tray, engraved to salute him as "Mr. Cub." Philip R. Clarke, the chairman of the committee that arranged the day, said he had seen every great Cubs player back to the days of Frank Chance and that none of them were entitled to be called Mr. Cub over Banks. "I want to thank God for making me an American and for giving me the ability to be a major league baseball player," Banks said.

Perhaps no game symbolized the Cubs' struggles more than opening day 1965 at Wrigley Field. In the bottom of the ninth inning, Banks hit a three-run home run to tie the Cardinals, 9–9. Each team scored a run in the eleventh, and the game was called due to darkness and entered the record books as a 10–10 tie. As they had done so often in the past, and would continue to do in the seasons ahead, the Cubs had hit well, pitched poorly—they used five pitchers in the first five innings—fielded atrociously, committing five errors, and spun their wheels in the standings.

Banks got off to another fast start in 1965. He had thirteen hits and twelve runs batted in during the Cubs' first seven games, and ten home runs, a league-leading forty-four runs batted in, and a .303 batting average by the end of May. Again, he tailed off as the season progressed, and he finished hitting .265 with twenty-eight home runs and 106 runs batted in.

Though Banks and the Cubs were delighted by his revival at the plate, they also realized his career had reached a turning point. For so many years, he had been his team's leading power hitter, uncontestably the finest who had ever worn a Cubs uniform. But now he was just another part of a highly productive crowd. Billy Williams hit .312 in 1964 with thirty-three home runs and ninety-eight runs batted in. In 1965, his numbers were .315, thirty-four, and 108. Ron Santo hit .313 in 1964 with thirty home runs and 114 RBI. In 1965, his line was .312, thirty-three, and 101. The torch, it was clear, had been passed.

Other Cubs also had excellent seasons during this period. Starting pitcher Larry Jackson led the majors with twenty-four wins in 1964, and reliever Ted Abernathy led the league with thirty-one saves the following year. But the Cubs finished in eighth place both seasons as their constantly fluctuating lineup and their lack of pitching depth doomed them to mediocrity; Williams and Santo began to get a feeling for what Banks had been going through all these years.

In the middle of June 1965, Philip Wrigley's patience with Bob Kennedy finally ran out. The Cubs were languishing in eighth place, attendance was down, and after more than two seasons of managerial stability it was once again time for a change. Wrigley announced that Lou Klein, an original member of the College of Coaches, would take over the team. Asked about his future expectations, Klein was optimistic. "When the job was offered to me, my first question was about permanence," he said. "When I was told I'd get a full shot at the job, naturally I took it."

"The obvious conclusion," one writer said, "is that he'll manage the Cubs next year."

It was September 9, 1965, and Byron Browne could scarcely believe his good fortune.

A call had come earlier in the day in Indianapolis where Browne, playing for the Cubs' Salt Lake City farm team, had hit two home runs the day before off Dave DeBusschere, who would soon abandon his attempt to play two major league sports and return to the National Basketball Association, where he would play for thirteen seasons, win two championships, and be elected to the Basketball Hall of Fame.

"Pack your bags," Browne was told. "You're meeting the ball club in Los Angeles."

And now here was Yosh Kawano picking him up at the airport.

"You're in the game tonight," the Cubs' clubhouse man said.

"Who's pitching?" Browne asked. Kawano said he didn't know.

"Leave your bags here. We're going to the ballpark," Billy Williams told Browne when he arrived at the Cubs' hotel. "Congratulations about being in the game."

"Who's pitching?" Browne asked.

"Don't worry about it," Williams said.

"Good to have you with us," Banks said as he shook Browne's hand in the Cubs' locker room.

"Who's pitching?" Browne asked.

"It's fine," Banks said. "Get ready."

Out on the field before the game, Browne felt disoriented by the smell of the smoke he saw casting a dark haze in the Dodger Stadium lights. "I'd never seen anything like that," Browne says of the smoldering remains of the Watts riots that had shaken Los Angeles to its core a month earlier. "It felt like the city was on fire."

"The smell hung around for a long time," says Jeff Torborg, the young Dodgers catcher who was getting a rare start in place of John Roseboro. "We were all concerned about whether the riot would roam any farther. I'm not a gun person, but somebody loaned me a shotgun and I had it lying on the floor near the backseat of my car." Roseboro, who lived not far from where the riots took place, went one step further. Acting on a rumor that protesters might be coming to his neighborhood, he sat by his front door all night, several guns at the ready.

The smooth, measured basso profundo of John Ramsey, the Dodgers' public address announcer, sounded like the voice of God as it wafted down from press box. "Maury Wills...Jim Gilliam...Willie Davis...Ron Fairly..." Ramsey said as he ran through the home team's batting order.

"And tonight...pitching for your Los Angeles Dodgers," Ramsey concluded, pausing for effect..."Sandy...*Koufax.*"

"What?" Browne said to himself. "My first game? You've got to be kidding."

Koufax had trouble with his breaking ball early in the game, and Glenn Beckert hit a hanging curve sharply down the left-field line in the first inning. It landed inches foul.

In the second inning, Browne hit a hard line drive to shallow right center field, where Davis caught it off his shoe tops.

Why was he playing Browne in so close, someone asked the Dodgers center fielder later.

"I didn't know he had power," Davis replied.

In the fifth inning, Browne hit a high curveball for a grounder up the middle. Wills moved quickly to his left, grabbed the ball just before it got through the infield, and threw him out.

As the game continued, Koufax gained control of his curve and began throwing so hard his head was coming out from under his cap.

"He threw one ball high," says Torborg, who had to play almost on top of the batter because Koufax's curve was descending so sharply it would have landed just inches behind home plate. "I had to reach for it so fast it almost yanked my shoulder out of whack."

By this point, Torborg's excitement was such that he began firing the ball back to Koufax between pitches.

"Will you calm down?" Koufax told him. "You're throwing the ball harder than I am." Torborg calmed down.

In the bottom of the eighth, Torborg hit a line drive to left field about as hard as he could hit a baseball.

"I was a lousy hitter, but I got all of that one," says Torborg, whose defensive skills gave him a ten-year major league career despite a .214 lifetime batting average. "I was running from first base to second thinking Sandy's pitching a special game and I'm going to hit a home run and have my picture taken with him. Then the son of a gun caught it right at the gate."

Browne had raced over and, at the last instant, caught the ball at the entrance to the Dodgers bullpen.

In the top of the inning, Browne had become the third of the six batters Koufax struck out consecutively to complete his fourth no-hitter and Major League Baseball's sixth perfect game in the twentieth century.

"He tried to throw the ball right past us," said Banks, who struck out three times without making contact. "And he did."

Asked what he was throwing in the final two innings, Koufax replied, "Everything I had."

In the Cubs' locker room after the game, starting pitcher Bob Hendley was stoic. He had just pitched the game of his life, a one-hitter, and lost, 1–0, on a run the Dodgers scored without a hit or even an official at-bat. A walk to Lou Johnson, a bunt, a steal of third, and an error by Cubs catcher Chris Krug, whose throw sailed over Santo's head, had allowed the game's only run to score.

"This game is the most recognizable thing I've ever done in baseball," Hendley said later. "And I came out a loser."

After the game, Cubs coach Lou Klein approached Browne in the locker room as well as another young outfielder, Don Young, who had also just played in his first major league game.

"Are you *sure* you want to play in the National League?" Klein asked.

Browne and Young could only smile.

Five days later, Hendley got a measure of revenge when he gave up just four hits in a 2–1 victory over the Dodgers at Wrigley Field. Koufax allowed five hits in six innings and left the game for a pinch hitter. It was his eighth and final loss of a season in which he won twenty-six games and the National League's Cy Young Award.

———

The Cubs' record under Klein was no better than it had been under Kennedy, and they finished eighth in the National League standings and ninth in attendance. Klein remained hopeful he would be back in 1966, but the season ended with rumors circulating that someone else was being considered for the job. The gossip reached Wrigley, who responded coyly. "We are making no comments," he said. "We are not especially considering anyone and wouldn't write anyone off." His decision, Wrigley said, would be delayed by sales meetings with the international representatives of his gum company.

On October, 25, 1965, as the Cubs were introducing their latest field boss in Wrigley Field's Pink Poodle press room, they passed out a short mimeographed statement that one sharp-eyed reporter noticed was missing a key element.

"What's your title?" the writer asked the new man.

"I'm the *manager*," Leo Durocher shouted. "I'm not the head coach. I'm the *manager*."

IV

HIMSELF

Chapter 19

Taking Over

Leo Durocher oozed charm and menace in equal measure.

Whether it was true that as a young player Durocher stole Babe Ruth's watch from the New York Yankees' clubhouse hardly seemed to matter. It was the sort of story that defined Durocher throughout his life.

In seventeen years as a player, twenty-six as a manager, and four as a coach, Durocher created more headlines, bawled out more players, kicked dirt on more umpires, fought with more sportswriters, romanced and occasionally married more women, drew the baseball commissioner's attention more often, was involved in more lawsuits, and left more bruised feelings and bitter enemies in his wake than any dozen of his peers.

As early as 1944, Jack Troy of the *Atlanta Constitution* reacted to a story that Hollywood was considering making a movie about Durocher by writing, "That ought to be good if the principal scenes are shot in a cellar." Two decades later, Ray Sons of the *Chicago Sun-Times*, who was known to his colleagues as the gentlest of souls, said, "I couldn't stand the fellow. He was the most selfish, arrogant guy I ever knew."

Durocher thrived on attention. Indeed, there were those who believed he could not live without it. "Durocher wants the spotlight for the nourishment it, in itself, gives his body," wrote the New York sportswriter Dick Young. "He sucks up attention. His ego must be fed more than his stomach, or he will perish."

Possessed of a comedian's timing and an actor's ease, Durocher knew exactly what to do when the spotlight swung in his direction. In the early 1960s, when he was a coach for the Los Angeles Dodgers, he appeared on such television sitcoms as *The Donna Reed Show, The Joey Bishop Show, The Beverly Hillbillies, The Munsters,* and *Mr. Ed,* always playing himself and always acquitting himself admirably. He made guest appearances on shows hosted by such stars as Dinah Shore and Judy Garland, and when he joined Garland in a duet of "Take Me Out to the Ball Game" it was hard to tell which of them was more relaxed.

The people who hated and feared Durocher often told stories that painted him as a dictator, egomaniac, and control freak. So did those who loved and admired him.

Joe Amalfitano reveres Durocher's memory. He speaks fondly of how Durocher converted him from an adequate ballplayer into a coach, manager, instructor, scout, and advisor whose baseball career spanned half a century. "We became very good friends," Amalfitano says. "He came to my wedding. He was gracious to my mother. He had two adopted children and once he said, 'If I had my own sons, I'd want them to be like Joe Amalfitano.' That's pretty nice, isn't it?" It's also a far cry from how he felt about Durocher when they first met.

At the age of twenty, Amalfitano sat on the bench of the 1954 New York Giants, who easily won the National League pennant and then the World Series in a four-game sweep of the Cleveland Indians. Amalfitano was on the team only because of baseball's bonus-baby rule that said any player signed for more than $4,000 must remain with the major league team for two seasons, and Durocher was angry that he was taking up a spot on the roster. "I always sat down on the end of the bench, as far away from him as I could. I was scared of him," Amalfitano says. "I had a deep hatred of him because I was a kid who didn't know how to play and he was saddled with me."

Amalfitano appeared in only forty-five games in 1954 and 1955 and often went long periods without playing. One dry spell ended when, after Durocher was thrown out of a game, Giants' coach Herman Franks put him in as a pinch runner and he made a base-running error and was tagged out. After the game, Amalfitano sat facing his locker, waiting for the inevitable. "I didn't see him coming," he says, "...and then I could smell the cologne."

"What the hell were you doing out there?!" Durocher shouted. "If you ever do that again, I'll send you so far away they'll never find you!"

On another occasion, Amalfitano made a base-running mistake in full view of Durocher, who reacted by throwing a towel in the air as he stood on the dugout steps. "He had a habit of that," Amalfitano said. "It was very embarrassing to be the receiver of that towel."

"What were you trying to do out there?" Durocher demanded when the inning was over.

"Well, I thought—" Amalfitano said.

"Don't think," Durocher interrupted. "I do the thinking around here."

Amalfitano walked down to the water cooler and then, against his better judgment, shouted, "Well, I'll be damned! We're not even allowed to think around here! Just wind me up and send me out there!"

When Amalfitano's two years were up and he was sent to the minors where he belonged, Durocher's image never left him. "I spent four years with Leo's face in my mind," he says. "I was going to prove to him that I could play." Which he did when, after his delayed apprenticeship was over, he returned to play seven years with the Giants, Houston Astros, and, finally, Durocher's Cubs.

"Hey, how about the kid?" Durocher would tell people. "He made himself into a pretty good ballplayer."

"You know, Leo," Amalfitano once told him, "you're not a bad guy after all."

After Amalfitano became a coach, he learned more about Durocher's insatiable need for attention. "I'm going to tell you this and I want you to remember it," Durocher told him. "The front office belongs to me. The media belongs to me. Stay away from the batting cage where the press hangs out. Don't get quoted in the paper. You got it?" Amalfitano got it. He was also fascinated by Durocher's devious way of dealing with an errant player. "If he was mad at something you did, he would attack you while you were out in the field," Amalfitano says. "He'd get near the guy's roommate in the dugout and make sure he heard him because he knew he would share the remark. That's one reason why the players got so pissed off at him."

Once, after a base-running error cut a Cubs rally short, Durocher berated Amalfitano, who was coaching third base, when he returned to the dugout.

"Don't you know that's my winning run out there?" he shouted.

"He didn't say '*our* winning run,'" Amalfitano says. "It was '*my* winning run.'"

Cubs pitching coach Joe Becker had a similar experience. "When we're going good, they're Leo's pitchers," Becker said. "When we're going horseshit, he wants to know what's wrong with *my* pitchers."

Nor did Durocher's need to dominate those around him stop at the locker room door. "We'd be playing gin on the plane," says Jack Hiatt, who joined the Cubs as a catcher in 1970, "and Leo, who was a very good gin player, would come up from behind and watch. Once, he watched me playing for a while and he said, 'Jesus Christ, and I'm entrusting *you* with my pitchers?'"

Durocher's ability to charm women was unsurpassed. His third wife, the actress Laraine Day, wrote that she was put off by him when they first met while boarding a plane. But by the end of the trip, she was planning to marry him.

The young women who worked for the Cubs were equally smitten.

"I loved Leo," says Arlene Gill. "When he came up to the front office, you always knew he was there. He had that rough voice and he was always so funny. He was a pussycat. He wouldn't hurt a fly."

During spring training, when most of the Cubs' organization was thrown together for more than a month, Durocher would occasionally enter the hotel bar late in the evening, see a group of players and staff, join them, and take over the room.

"The game is called Cardinal Puff Puff," he said one night as he introduced them to a drinking game. "I'm a very lenient pope, and in order to make cardinal, you have to do what I say."

"You had a full drink in front of you," says Mary Dease, "and you'd take a gulp and then you had to go through an elaborate progression of tapping your hands on top of the table, on the bottom of the table, and tapping your feet, too. The minute you made a mistake, he'd order you another drink and you'd start over. Of course, the more you drank, the more mistakes you made."

Occasionally after these late nights, Dease would find a note in her typewriter. "Mary Doll, good morning, love. Where were you? Can't stay up all night drinking and get here on time?" The note would be signed "Leo the Lion (Or the lamb!!)."

As Dease's first spring in Arizona was coming to an end, John Holland demanded some paperwork that had been packed away for the trip back to Chicago and, when she couldn't produce it, shouted and cursed at her and slammed the door to his office as two of his assistants stood uncomfortably by. Just then, Durocher walked in, wearing his Cubs uniform, complete with cap and cleats, and found her weeping.

"Oh, Mary, doll, sweetie, don't you cry," Durocher said, and he put his arms around her and brushed away her tears. "Come on. Come on. We're going home tomorrow. This is all going to be over."

"It was like he knew that I'd had my fill for age eighteen and I was ready to stop being this little baby," says Dease. "I'll never forget the degree of comfort I got from this famous person making a fuss over me."

Aware of Durocher's reputation, the young women in the Cubs' front office had their antennae out for any romantic entanglements in their midst, and as far as they could tell Durocher, who was unmarried when he joined the Cubs, was always the gentleman when he was among them.

Except once.

"Let me see your room," Durocher said to Dease as they were leaving the bar one night.

"I fell for it," says Dease, who was just a year out of a Catholic girls' high school. "Suddenly he's chasing me around the bed and I'm thinking,

'Uh-oh. How am I going to get this legend out of my room?' Finally, he took pity on me, and the next day when I was thinking I was going to have to quit my job it was like nothing had happened."

Far from feeling harassed or mistreated, Dease considers the incident a treasured memory. "If it happened to me now," she says, throwing her head back in laughter, "I'd say, 'Okay, let's unzip your pants and you show me what you've got.' I think it's a charming little story."

Many years later, when Durocher died, Dease wrote a letter to the *Chicago Tribune* that attempted in some small way to counter the many notorious stories about Durocher that dominated the obituaries and farewells to one of baseball's most incorrigible figures. She told of Durocher comforting her after Holland yelled at her and concluded, "I'm blowing your image, Leo. God bless you."

—

Durocher hadn't managed a major league team in ten years when he joined the Cubs, and it was widely assumed that he had burned too many bridges over the years to get another job. His leave-taking from the New York Giants was a case in point.

After winning pennants in 1951 and 1954, during which he was credited with engineering the most storied comeback in baseball history and with the ascendance of Willie Mays, Durocher should have been set for many more seasons with the Giants. But after just one more year, he was fired. He had picked silly fights with the team's owner, Horace Stoneham, demanding game tickets that were not available and maneuvering to add the role of general manager to his portfolio. And Stoneham, a prodigious drinker, was still irate over a stag dinner in Los Angeles the previous winter during which Danny Kaye, an old friend of Durocher's, had mimicked Stoneham by staggering around with his clothes disheveled, falling across a table, scattering glasses and silverware, and asking, "Where can a guy take a piss?"

So just one year after claiming his only World Series championship as a manager, Durocher was out of baseball. He spent much of the next decade turning down jobs he considered beneath him, such as from the Cleveland Indians, Baltimore Orioles, and Kansas City Athletics, and publicly criticizing executives and owners who he said had betrayed him. Fred Haney, the general manager of the Los Angeles Angels, had "fouled me up," Durocher said in 1963, by suggesting he wasn't interested in managing the American League's new expansion team. And August Busch, the owner of the St. Louis Cardinals, had offered him a job during the 1964 season when the team was floundering and then reneged when the Cardinals came back to win the National League pennant and the World Series.

In 1961, Durocher became the third-base coach for the Dodgers, which, though it was a demotion, allowed him to live in an exclusive section of Beverly Hills, hang out with his Hollywood friends, and remain in baseball's spotlight. But any thought that he might be mellowing now that he was in his mid-fifties did not last long.

"He was charming and I enjoyed his stories, but he could be mean, really mean," says Wes Parker, the Dodgers' Gold Glove–winning first baseman. "He loved everybody when they were hot and didn't have time for anyone when they cooled off. He loved hanging out with the guys who were the star of the moment." Parker says Durocher went out of his way to bad-mouth Dodger manager Walt Alston. Whenever the Dodgers faltered, rumors arose that Durocher would replace Alston, and Durocher did everything he could to remain in the spotlight.

His first season with the team had barely begun when he got into one of his most famous fights with an umpire, Jocko Conlan, who threw him out of a game for throwing a towel. Furious, Durocher came out of the dugout and, in an attempt to kick dirt at Conlan, kicked him in the shins instead. Conlan kicked back, threw his face mask and chest protector to the ground, and clenched his fists before the other umpires surrounded him while Dodgers pitcher Don Drysdale dragged Durocher away by the collar. Durocher would dine out on the story for years, saying he should have realized that Conlan had the advantage because he was wearing shin guards. Conlan, for his part, called Durocher "the king of complainers, troublemakers, arguers, moaners, the ones who can never, never, never accept a tough decision that goes against them."

A year later, with the pennant on the line in a playoff game against the Giants, Durocher was at it again. Maury Wills stole third base, and when the throw trying to catch him was wild he turned and headed for home. Durocher left the third-base coach's box, ran alongside him, and when Wills slid safely into the plate he went into a theatrical slide of his own. "Durocher got up laughing," Giants outfielder Felipe Alou said. "I wanted to beat them after what Durocher did. Sliding. Like it was a show." The Giants did win the game, and the pennant.

But for all his histrionics, Durocher was never seriously considered as a replacement for Alston, who was amused by him and didn't feel threatened. The only report of a confrontation came in 1962, when Durocher was quoted as saying Dodgers players Ron Fairly and Tommy Davis weren't trying hard enough and should be fined. "You do the coaching," Alston told Durocher, "and I'll do the chewing out."

But if Alston was content to let Durocher be Durocher, the Dodgers players soon grew tired of him. After he annoyed Frank Howard, the team's six-foot-seven outfielder, by tapping his shins with a bat, Howard stood up, lifted him off the floor, and gave him a shove. And as he watched Jeff Torborg working with coach Pete Reiser on blocking the plate, Durocher told the catcher he could jar the ball loose sliding into home. Torborg accepted the challenge, and Durocher went out to the infield and rounded third base as Reiser threw the ball home. Torborg showed what he had learned by shoving his forearm into Durocher's head and knocking him briefly unconscious. "I think you're out," Reiser said as the players on the field, who had stopped what they were doing to watch, laughed.

When Durocher's promised job with the Cardinals fell through after the 1964 season, he spent 1965 as a commentator for ABC, both on the radio and on its national telecast of baseball's game of the week. His tenure with the Dodgers probably would have ended soon anyway. "I have no quarrel with Leo," Dodgers' general manager Buzzie Bavasi said, "but you know how he is and how he wears out his welcome. Having Leo work for you is like using dynamite to build a road." Durocher, who had been involved in a scuffle with a fan after a game at Dodger Stadium and an alienation-of-affection lawsuit in Vermont during his time with the team, couldn't really disagree. "I'm a guy who steps on a lot of toes," he said. "When trouble comes, I can expect the worst."

There were some who suspected Durocher's move to the television booth marked the end of his managerial career, but others, including Jim Murray of the *Los Angeles Times*, weren't so sure. "You can always tell when Leo Durocher is getting ready to get back in baseball when he (a) slugs a fan, (b) gets kicked out of a game and (c) gets sued for stealing some guy's wife," Murray wrote.

Philip K. Wrigley had never thought highly of Durocher. "No, sir! We wouldn't have him as a gift!" he said of reports the Cubs were thinking of hiring him in the late 1950s. So as the Cubs considered their options after the 1965 season, John Holland was startled when Wrigley mentioned his name. Durocher was surprised, too, but when Holland offered him the job he jumped at it. "It was a pleasant enough life," he said of living in Los Angeles and talking about baseball on radio and television. "I was making more money than I had ever made in baseball, and so naturally I couldn't wait to put the uniform on again."

One question neither the Cubs nor any of the other teams that flirted with Durocher during his decade in exile appear to have addressed is how good a manager he was. Many of the players on his teams swore by him—the common refrain was that he was always one step ahead of most managers—and more than a few said they owed their careers to him. But others thought his habits of throwing towels, yelling at players, battling umpires, and indulging his hunches and superstitions were relics of a bygone era. "If a lineup won a ball game," says Hiatt, "you would see the same one the next night. And on one road trip we took to the West Coast, he wore the same alpaca sweater every day. That was a treat."

Durocher's long tenure in baseball and his abilities at self-promotion automatically made him a candidate for every opening that arose, but there were some who wondered if they necessarily made him a good choice. There was, for instance, the matter of his overall record. In twenty-six years, Durocher's teams won three pennants and one World Series. His total of 2,088 wins ranked tenth on the overall list in 2018, but dozens of managers—some of them in the Hall of Fame, others all but forgotten—have won more than one World Series, many of them in far fewer years than Durocher spent as a manager.

There were other curious aspects to Durocher's record. One was that his teams seemed unable to protect a lead. In 1942, Durocher's Brooklyn Dodgers led the National League by nine games in the middle of July, but lost the pennant to the Cardinals. Four of his other Dodger teams were in first place in July but couldn't hold on. The same thing occurred when Durocher moved to the Giants. In 1949, they were in first place early in June and finished fifth. And in 1952, the year after their storied playoff victory over the Dodgers, they led the league late in May before falling into second place, where they remained for the rest of the season. The only exception to these failures came in 1954, when the Giants took the lead on June 12, won the pennant by five games, and gave Durocher his only World Series championship. That one season aside, the record suggested that whenever his teams had the whip in their hands, Durocher would find a way to jar it loose.

Another mark against Durocher was his reputation for playing his regulars relentlessly, not giving them days off during the grind of the long season, turning a deaf ear to the advice of trainers and doctors, and relying on his players' competitive spirit to ignore injuries and fatigue and stay in the lineup. The most infamous episode occurred when he was managing the Dodgers in 1942 and Reiser, whose reckless style of play curtailed what many thought would be a Hall of Fame career, returned to the team just one day after his most recent encounter with an outfield wall, which had sent him to the hospital and prompted his doctor to insist he sit out the rest of the season.

In a memorable article by W. C. Heinz in *Time*, Reiser, who was then twenty-three years old, related how he resisted Durocher's insistence that he dress for the game, but succumbed when the manager said his presence would boost the team's morale and he wouldn't actually play. That promise ended in the fourteenth inning of a tie game against the Pittsburgh Pirates when Reiser, the last man on the bench, drove in the winning runs with a line drive that would have been a triple if he hadn't collapsed as he rounded first base.

"By God, we beat 'em! How do you feel?" Durocher asked Reiser when he woke up back in the hospital a day later.

"How do you think I feel?" Reiser replied.

"Aw, you're better with one leg and one eye than anybody else I've got."

"Yeah, and that's the way I'll end up—with one leg and one eye."

Durocher also had another bad habit that dated back to the 1940s. After Durocher missed a spring training game while managing the Dodgers so he could appear on Milton Berle's radio show, Branch Rickey said, "That young man will have to choose a profession." It was not the last time Durocher would fail to show up for work.

―――――

Durocher's first task when he came to Chicago was to ingratiate himself with Wrigley and erase any lingering doubts the Cubs' owner might still have. He did this by apologizing to Wrigley for his press conference statement that he was the manager, not a coach.

"I hope you haven't been watching me shoot off my mouth on television and think that I've come here to take over everything," he said.

"I wanted you to do that, to take charge," Wrigley replied.

Before long, the Cubs owner was praising his new manager, admitting to his previous concerns, but adding, "Leo's improved tremendously because he's mellowed with age, as we all have. He's mellow enough now. I don't want him to get too nice!" There was no chance of that, as Durocher said he would coach third base when the Cubs opened the

1966 season in San Francisco and Los Angeles. He wanted, he said, "to give the fans a chance to boo me."

As for his relationship with the biggest name on the Cubs' roster, Durocher approached it warily.

"He comes with the franchise," he said of Ernie Banks, "and I'm glad to have him on my side for a change."

Banks's response was equally bland.

"Durocher has the credentials of a successful manager," he said.

And with that, the battle was joined.

Chapter 20

"Daddy, Where Were You?"

At about the time the College of Coaches was coming to an end, Ernie Banks had a brainstorm that was as odd as any that Philip K. Wrigley ever came up with. He would run for Chicago alderman. In a racially mixed district. As a Republican.

"How do you think he's going to finish?" a reporter asked Richard J. Daley after Banks made his surprise announcement in December 1962.

"Somewhere out in left field," the mayor replied.

Banks gave two different explanations about the origins of his quixotic quest. One was that an aide to Illinois's Republican U.S. senator Everett Dirksen had asked him to run. Another is that he approached S. B. Fuller, who had risen from a poverty-stricken boyhood in Louisiana to develop a beauty products empire that made him perhaps the richest black man in America. Fuller owned several black newspapers, was the head of the Chicago branch of the NAACP, and was a proud Republican who believed that government programs harmed free enterprise and promoted socialism.

"I went to him and I said I want to run for alderman of the eighth ward," Banks said. "He said that would be a great idea." Fuller gave Banks a number of tips about how to succeed in politics, one of which was that he should always wear a hat.

Wrigley gave Banks his consent as long as it didn't interfere with baseball—"I don't want a part-time ballplayer," he said—and Banks gave it his best shot. He hired a veteran campaign manager, established a storefront headquarters, and gave as many as four speeches a day. He toured the ward, discussing such issues as taxes and crime, and commiserated with a local principal who said the street outside his school was in desperate need of a sewer.

The jokes about Banks's candidacy were not long in coming. One local wit said Banks would be sure to win if he received the votes of all the Cubs coaches. Another said he should easily win the eighth ward since the Cubs have been wards of eighth place for some time. Even one of Banks's own political advisors couldn't resist the temptation, saying, "He'll finish closer to the top than he ever has with the Cubs."

Banks received support from the editorial page of the *Chicago Tribune*, which called him "an intelligent public spirited citizen" and said he would be a useful rejoinder to "the older generation of Negro politician," who were all Democrats. But Banks blundered when he failed to clear his candidacy with Chicago's small but feisty Republican Party, whose representatives in the eighth ward backed another candidate, Gerald E. Gibbons, by a vote of eighty-four to three. "If he had been running with the Daley machine, he would have been a shoo-in," says Jesse Jackson, the renowned Chicago-based civil rights leader.

But Banks's candidacy was harmed by more than the lack of party support. Only three of Chicago's fifty aldermen were Republicans at the time, and the six who were black came from solidly black districts, as opposed to the 60–40 white-black split in the eighth ward. In the end, Gibbons was soundly beaten by the Democratic incumbent, James Condon, by more than two to one, while Banks finished a distant third. "I don't understand this political game too well," he said. "They try to strike you out before you even get a time at bat."

Banks occasionally talked about giving politics another try, but some years later he put his finger on a problem that prevented him from being successful. "I'm used to saying nice things about other people, not myself," he said. "It didn't come natural. It didn't work."

One question that does not seem to have come up during Banks's campaign is why he bothered. Though he had been taking sociology classes at the University of Chicago, he had never shown much interest in politics, the workings of government, or the one great social issue of the day, which would torment him the rest of his life.

———

Jackie Robinson was nearing the end of his baseball career when Banks arrived in Chicago. Robinson was still honoring the promise he made to Brooklyn Dodgers owner Branch Rickey that he would not fight back against the indignities he faced as baseball's first black player, and this created the template for the pioneers who followed him. They kept a low profile on racial matters and coped with slurs and injustices privately. And while nobody doubted their talent, they were often patronized by a press that remained fascinated by the color of their skin.

In 1955, *Time* magazine referred to Banks as a "Dallas-bred Negro shortstop." In August of that year, Edgar Munzel called him "a brilliant Negro shortstop." In 1958, *Time* called him a "rangy Negro shortstop." In 1959, Munzel took Banks's side after he was beaned by Jack Sanford, noting the "amazing tolerance by this Negro star, who is a wonderful credit to his race."

Later, when Billy Williams and Ferguson Jenkins joined the Cubs, it was often noted how the team's three biggest black stars were symbols of proper comportment. "We had such a great class of black athletes that I played with," says Al Spangler. "They were all first class and everybody got along."

"They were three extraordinary guys in terms of demeanor," says Chuck Shriver, the Cubs' publicity director. "They were very calm, very laid back, very non-confrontational. It was a seamless thing from our standpoint."

The other black players who joined the Cubs in the 1960s also got along well with their white teammates. There are no recorded incidents of racial confrontations during this time, with one uncomfortable exception that occurred on April 4, 1968, the day Martin Luther King was assassinated.

Lou Johnson, the outfielder who had scored the only run in Sandy Koufax's perfect game three years earlier, had been acquired from the Dodgers in the off-season, and the Cubs were delighted when they discovered he trailed merriment in his wake. "Lou could come into a clubhouse and have people laughing in a minute, just because he was Lou being Lou," his Dodger teammate Al Ferrara told Michael Leahy in his book *The Last Innocents*. Yet just as Banks's outward cheerfulness masked his inner insecurities, Johnson's masked the rage he felt about the bigotry he had encountered growing up in Lexington, Kentucky, and during his career in the minors.

Asked why he attacked the ball so hard in batting practice one day, Johnson replied, "Because it's fucking white."

"I had anger," Johnson would say years later. "I had hate."

The Cubs were scheduled to play an exhibition game in Evansville, Indiana, the day King was killed, and when it was canceled several white players got into an elevator to go to the hotel dining room.

"The door opened and Johnson was there and he wouldn't get on the elevator with us," Spangler says. "He just waited for another elevator."

———

Banks was comfortable with his image as the sunny, smiling epitome of baseball brotherhood and so were the Cubs, who cited him as an example for the black players who followed him to Wrigley Field. "They wanted everybody to be like Ernie," Williams said. "Be like him as a ballplayer and be like him as an individual."

How far the Cubs were willing to go to make sure their black players followed Banks's example has long been a subject of conjecture. For years, stories were told of the trading of Oscar Gamble, an outfielder who was rushed to the majors in 1969 at the age of nineteen. A titillating article in the *Chicago Daily News* about the new young bachelor in town, which helpfully included his address, greatly improved Gamble's social life. "Every time I walked out the door, there was another cute girl," he said. And since some of them were white, he became a target of the Cubs' front office, which was uncomfortable with players who tested social boundaries. Caught in the middle of this dynamic was Leo Durocher.

The manager's reputation for championing black players dated back to long before baseball was integrated. As early as 1939, when he was player-manager of the Dodgers, Durocher said, "Hell, yes! I'd sign them in a minute if I got permission from the big shots." He had seen any number of black players who could play in the majors, Durocher said, Satchel Paige and Josh Gibson among them. Durocher was also famous for nipping a revolt against Robinson by Dodgers players in the bud in 1947 by calling a team meeting and telling them they could "wipe their ass with the petition," and for championing a young Willie Mays while managing the New York Giants.

But now Durocher was confronted with a new challenge, which led some of the Cubs to see him in a different light. "You got this sense that Leo might have been a little prejudiced," says pitcher Rich Nye. "I know it sounds strange, but you got that sense."

The same was true of John Holland. "John, God rest his soul, was very bigoted, but that was his era," says Shriver. "He didn't even like Italians, let alone black people. One time, he went into a tirade about Ron Santo because he was Italian and he didn't like his temperament. He just didn't have a lot of tolerance."

But for all the gossip surrounding Gamble, his talent was undeniable, and when he went to the Arizona Instructional League after the 1969 season, he was projected as the Cubs' starting center fielder for the next decade. "He reminds me of Willie Mays when he was breaking in," Durocher said. "What a ballplayer this kid is going to be."

Gamble was traded to the Philadelphia Phillies before the instructional league season ended.

"That son of a bitch," Durocher later grumbled to Blake Cullen, "trying to date my daughter."

Gamble's sin, Cullen says, was not dating white women as much as it was dating the *wrong* white woman: one of Durocher's teenage stepdaughters from his marriage to Lynne Goldblatt in Chicago five months earlier.

"I've always wondered what would have happened if I had played all those years in Wrigley Field," Gamble said later. The Cubs might have wondered, too, as he went on to have a seventeen-year career in the majors during which he hit 200 home runs and played in two World Series with the New York Yankees. In 1977, Gamble returned to Chicago with the White Sox, where his thirty-one home runs, eighty-three runs batted in, and outlandishly oversize Afro made him one of the team's most popular players. Some wondered if he could have worn such a racially infused haircut while playing for the Cubs.

For all the speculation over Gamble's departure, he insists no one on the Cubs ever told him he was traded for dating a white woman. This distinguishes him from Byron Browne, who was told he was banished for that reason by Durocher himself.

After breaking in against Sandy Koufax in 1965, Browne was a regular in the Cubs' outfield a year later, and though he led the league in strikeouts, he hit sixteen home runs, drove in fifty-one runs, and was named to the Topps All-Star Rookie Team. Browne needed improvement in the outfield, but at the age of twenty-four he appeared full of promise. Until early in the 1967 season, when Durocher brought a young woman to the Chicago Playboy Club and found Browne there with a date of his own, who was white. "My night life was pretty good," Browne says. "I had a lot of fun. But I'm a man of color. There were places you didn't go."

"I'll see you in my office," Durocher told Browne, leaving him to fret for the rest of the evening.

"You know what, son?" Durocher told him the following day at Wrigley Field. "I don't care how good you are, you can't play for me."

"Damn, Byron, you're the only ballplayer I know who was sent down when he was hitting .300," Dick Selma, the Cubs' fun-loving pitcher, told Browne, who'd had three hits in his first ten at-bats. Browne hit twenty-five home runs and drove in seventy-two runs for the Cubs' Dallas farm team and was traded to Houston at the end of the season.

Banks stood in direct contradiction to this sort of drama. If there were racist attitudes in the Cubs' front office, it was news to him. He never complained and was never seen breaking any social taboos. "The only race we have in baseball is trying to beat the throw to first for a hit, or trying to steal a base," he said.

Even when Banks told the story of the one racial incident he encountered during his playing days, he made it sound like a lark. In one version, it happened before a spring training game in Mobile in 1954. In another, it was in Birmingham in 1955. In a third, it was in Mobile several years later. The Cubs had stopped at a hotel to change into their uniforms, and Banks and Gene Baker were told it would be best if they dressed at the ballpark. Baker waited in the bus but Banks went to a store to buy a candy bar and a newspaper. The owner greeted him by rushing out from behind the counter, shouting profanity, and threatening to call the police. "I left on the fly and hurried back to the bus," Banks said in his autobiography.

"I see you just learned the facts about southern hospitality," said Baker, laughing at Banks's naïveté.

But Banks learned his lesson quickly. "In those days, we knew we couldn't change things so we rolled with the punches," Baker said some years later. "And nobody was better at rolling than Ernie."

As his popularity grew, Banks was called upon to participate in programs of racial uplift, and he did his part. In 1957, he was named general chairman of membership by the Chicago branch of the NAACP. Later that year, he took a blood test to publicize a Chicago Board of Health's battle against venereal disease, which was on the rise in the city's black neighborhoods. And in 1967, he and such prominent black athletes as Gale Sayers, Bill Russell, and Bill White were named to a national sports committee to raise $100,000 for the NAACP defense committee.

But such good works began to pale as race became a volatile political issue in the 1960s and prominent black Americans were called on to express their support. The few athletes who did speak out were often frustrated by the many who did not. Hank Aaron, who believed strongly in the struggle for civil rights but felt isolated and unheard in Milwaukee and later in Atlanta, reached out for help but couldn't find it.

"I talked to Ernie and I talked to Willie Mays, too," Aaron says. "I said, 'Ernie, you're in Chicago. Willie, you're in California. We can control the press a little bit. We've got to make people realize that things aren't as good as they seem.' But it just wasn't in their makeup. They were not going to say anything. I had some very bad feelings about that. What does it mean if just Hank Aaron is speaking out alone?"

Sometimes, it seemed as if Banks went out of his way to avoid giving offense. In 1971, the Baseball Hall of Fame decided to establish a special exhibit for Negro League players and to make Satchel Paige its first honoree. The reaction was immediate and furious. "They segregated the Hall of Fame!" wrote Jim Murray, who called the separate display "a shocking bit of insolent cynicism . . . Either let him in the front of the hall or move the whole darn thing to Mississippi."

Other writers and a number of players also criticized the decision, which was quickly rescinded; Paige's plaque, and those of other Negro League Hall of Famers, would appear alongside those of the hall's white players. But Banks defended it. "With the rules the way they are," he said, "it's impossible for those players to be recognized for what they did. It doesn't give them all the recognition they deserve, but it does give them some." The idea of changing an offensive rule doesn't seem to have occurred to him.

Over the years, some of Banks's friends and acquaintances would question him about his unwillingness to become publicly involved in the struggle for racial equality. His answers seldom varied. "You have to be grateful for what you have," he told Rebecca Polihronis, the Cubs' community relations coordinator and manager of their charitable arm in the 1990s and the early years of the twenty-first century. "Being bitter is only going to hurt you." The message was the same to Arlene Gill. "There are some things you can't change," Banks told her. "And if you can't change something, complaining isn't going to help."

But some of those close to Banks saw that his unwillingness to become active in the civil rights movement did not mean he was unaware of the issues that were roiling the country. Ken Holtzman, one of the Cubs' most thoughtful players in the late 1960s, said that Banks "was aware of all the cultural conflicts going on in the country and, although very reluctant to be vocal about any political matters, he had a very good understanding about current events."

Banks spoke out about the nascent Black Power movement during the 1960s, calling it silly. "I have problems like everybody else," he said, "but it doesn't do any good to go around spreading the bad news." Black pride was fine, he said, but they needed to be practical. "Black people have to get along in the world, not just among themselves," he said. "If you want to get a good job, or get into business, you've got to live with other people, including the white ones." This attitude did not endear him to more militant blacks, who made him the target of criticism, some of which was particularly harsh. "How can Banks be an Uncle Tom?" one of them told *Sports Illustrated* in 1969. "Why, he's never been a Negro."

Even Robinson, who had traded his non-confrontational stance for uncompromising militancy when he retired from baseball, spoke out against Banks's lack of engagement. In 1969, while he was pushing for baseball to hire its first black manager, Robinson said Aaron, Curt Flood, and Bill White would be good candidates, but Banks would not. "He's still childish in his views," Robinson told Ira Berkow. "A lot of people like his bubbly attitude. I think it's unrealistic."

Banks was wounded by these remarks and those made by Aaron. "It hurt him a lot because he loved these people and respected them so greatly," says Marjorie Lott, Banks's wife at the time. "But at the same time, he thought they didn't understand him. He wanted to be in positive situations and environments, not around adversity. That's just who he was. He was not the person they wanted him to be."

Lott was also frustrated by Banks's reluctance to speak out. She was the equal opportunity employment officer at the Chicago Transit Authority, where they met when Banks was named to its board, and was deeply involved in minority hiring. "Things were opening up," Lott says. "He had a great opportunity to get involved, but he wouldn't do it. His reputation had been established, and he didn't want to go against the grain and ruin it. And he had a certain kind of respect for authority, for the white man who had given him the opportunity to succeed in a white world. He felt a certain kind of loyalty. He was more of a peacemaker. He wanted to please everybody and be happy. I don't think he felt he would be very good at the fight."

In the end, Lott accepted Banks's reluctance to speak out. His insistence on remaining optimistic, shunning negativity, and making people smile was who he was. It was also, she realized, the reason she had married him in the first place.

⸻

As the years went by and the early days of the civil rights movement became the stuff of history and of memory, the actions of Banks and other athletes of his era who had not participated came to be seen in a different light. They had not marched or spoken out, but they had left their mark just the same.

"He played his role because he proved something that we as blacks already knew," says Timuel Black, Chicago's nonagenarian civil rights activist and historian. "It was that given the opportunity, we're just as good as anyone else, and better than most." Banks's insistence on leading by example may have frustrated militants, Black says, but it had merit nevertheless. Black relates it to a distant memory of being on a playground when he was twelve years old and listening to the words of Al Pullins, one of the original Harlem Globetrotters. "Let me tell you something, Shorty," Pullins said. "When everybody is running around, you stay cool. If you stay cool, you'll break up the game."

"It stayed with me," Black says. "Ernie Banks and the black athletes of that time personified it in the world they had to live in. Be cool. Ernie Banks was not just a baseball player. He had to adjust to the social and cultural world he had to live in if he was going to be successful. And he was."

Jesse Jackson is also sympathetic to Banks's approach. "Some heroes, their strength is not talking, it's doing," Jackson says. "Ernie Banks came to symbolize something bigger than life." Jackson, who saw Banks often over the years, was convinced that Banks was concerned about the struggle for civil rights even if he didn't speak out. "Sometimes, people express their pain in extroverted ways and sometimes people internalize it," Jackson says. "Ernie internalized his pain." It is important, Jackson says, to remember the timetable of events on the road toward racial equality and how one milestone led to another. "We knew Ernie Banks," he says, "before we knew Martin Luther King."

As Banks grew older, he reassessed his role in the civil rights movement, and for the first time began to express a measure of regret. "We were there, but we weren't there," he told Timothy J. Gilfoyle of the Chicago Historical Society in 1997. "Our life was in baseball. We didn't get involved in the marches and demonstrations because we were in baseball."

Nine years later, when he was seventy-five, Banks gave his most heartfelt expression of what might have been. "That's a real void in my life," he told Steve Jacobson for his book *Carrying Jackie's Torch*. "I see a lot of people today who struggled and went to jail and the dogs were after them, and I'd look 'em in the eyes and say, 'God almighty, I wish I'd 'a been there.' My children, sometimes they think about, 'Daddy, where were you all the times that struggle was going on?' And I could only answer one way: 'I was playing baseball.' That was the struggle."

Chapter 21

Teammates

All told, there were ten of them—four infielders, two outfielders, three pitchers, and a catcher.

Some were found by scouts for the Cubs as they bird-dogged teenagers from Seattle to Mobile, from Forrest City, Arkansas, to Colton, California. Others were acquired from major league teams by John Holland, who was finally getting the hang of making trades. One by one, they joined the Cubs over a six-year period that started in 1960 and played for them for a total of more than seventy seasons.

Among them were a batting champion, a Cy Young Award winner, two Rookies of the Year, four Gold Glove winners, and some of the most consistent run producers of their era. One of them pitched two no-hitters. Three broke records that had lasted for many years. Four joined Ernie Banks in the Hall of Fame.

Along with other players who joined the team for shorter periods, they participated in some of the greatest thrills, triumphs, and delights in the history of Chicago sports. And some of the greatest mistakes, disappointments, and tragedies.

———

Billy Williams spent five years in the minors after leaving his home in Mobile, Alabama, and when he was finally promoted to Chicago in 1961 he spent most of the early part of the season sitting on the bench while a long-forgotten player named Bob Will played left field for the Cubs.

When Williams was given a chance to play, it was usually as a pinch hitter, and his performance was frustratingly inconsistent. After a game in Philadelphia one night, he sat on the bench brooding until the ballpark lights went out and he realized everyone had left. "I got in a cab and went back to the hotel thinking about how I hit good in Double-A and Triple-A, why can't I hit good in the major leagues?" Williams says.

On June 16, the day after Ernie Banks's brief experiment as an outfielder ended and he moved to first base for the first time, Williams was sent to left field for a game in San Francisco. He seized the opportunity by hitting a grand-slam home run. He remained in the lineup, and by July 1 he had a twelve-game hitting streak and his batting average was above .400. Williams finished the season hitting .278 with twenty-five home runs and eighty-six runs batted in and easily won the National League's Rookie of the Year Award.

Williams went on to bat over .300 five times, to drive in ninety or more runs ten times, to lead the league in hitting when he was thirty-four years old, and to play in 1,117 consecutive games for the Cubs, breaking a National League record that had stood for more than a decade. He was elected to the Hall of Fame in 1987. But because he played for a losing team, and in the shadow of Banks, he was more admired and coveted by other teams than he was appreciated in his own town. "Sure, I'm taken for granted," he once said. "But I don't mind that. Only a few players in the big leagues really draw the fans and I'm definitely not one of them."

In the spring of 1959, a Cubs roving hitting instructor assembled thirty players who had participated in a three-week rookie camp and began making brutal assessments. "You're not going to make it," he said to player after player before coming to a nineteen-year-old infielder who had caught his eye. "You can play in the major leagues right now," Rogers Hornsby, the last National League hitter to bat over .400, told him. Ron Santo went home to Seattle to pick up more clothes and say goodbye to his girlfriend, then returned to Arizona to join the Cubs major leaguers for spring training.

A year later, after the Cubs had lost nine straight games and fallen into last place, they brought Santo up from their Triple-A farm club in Houston and put him in the lineup for a doubleheader in Pittsburgh. He had three hits, two of them doubles, in the two games, drove in five runs, and made two fine plays at third base. Up in the broadcast booth, Lou Boudreau pronounced him ready to play every day.

The following season, at the age of twenty-one, Santo drove in eighty-three runs, and he would have that many or more runs batted in for the next eleven seasons. He also won five consecutive Gold Gloves, and his exclusion from the Hall of Fame until a year after he died in 2010 was a constant source of irritation for Cubs fans. But Santo would perhaps become best known for another quality he brought to his team.

"He was the most emotional man I have ever met in my life," a former member of the Cubs' front office says. "He wanted you to understand things. He was always saying, 'Do you see how I feel?' 'Don't you see that this is important?' 'Don't you agree?' Most people don't care about stuff like that."

Santo understood that his emotions often got the best of him, but all his efforts to control them failed. "Tell your dad he's got to relax," Banks told Santo's son, Ron, Jr., when Santo's passionate reactions to the Cubs' failures spilled over when he became the color commentator on the team's radio broadcasts in 1990. "There was nothing he could do," Ron, Jr., says. "My dad was just that way. That's what drove him to be the player he was. Ernie was the total opposite."

Glenn Beckert was another player whose passions were obvious to everyone who saw him play—and everyone who played with or against him. "You had to watch him all the time," Jesse White says of playing with Beckert on the Cubs' Salt Lake City farm team. "A ball would go up and

I'd say, 'I got it' and he'd plow me over. He'd end up with the ball and I'd end up in the hospital. We used to call him 'The Bruiser.'"

Born in Pittsburgh, Beckert spent many afternoons at Forbes Field, where he would marvel at Banks's play when the Cubs were in town. "Then all of a sudden I was beside him," Beckert said. "For a kid who grew up loving sports, it was the American dream."

Beckert arrived in Chicago in 1965 and immediately made his mark. He was a fine second baseman who won a Gold Glove in 1968 and the sort of hitter who won managers' hearts. He was almost impossible to strike out—twenty-five or fewer strikeouts in more than six hundred at-bats was a normal season—and utterly selfless at the plate. In 1969, Cubs coach Pete Reiser said Beckert gave up twenty to thirty points of his batting average by hitting grounders that moved runners around the bases. Leo Durocher disagreed, saying it might be as high as fifty points. "He's a double pro," said Durocher, who counted Beckert as one of his favorite players. "Pretty hard to give anyone more of a compliment than that."

Don Kessinger could do almost anything with a ball. At home in Forrest City, Arkansas, he was the quarterback on an undefeated football team, and at the University of Mississippi his jump shot was so reliable he had offers from two professional basketball teams. But Kessinger wanted to play baseball, and when a scout from Chicago offered him a bonus he took it because "I thought I could get to the top faster with the Cubs."

Though he was a prodigy at shortstop—"Kessinger makes some plays as well or better than any other shortstop who ever lived," Durocher once said—when it came to hitting major league pitching, Kessinger discovered the one thing he couldn't do with a ball. After batting .201 in 1965, his rookie season, Kessinger, desperate for advice, turned to Alvin Dark, who was spending the season as a Cubs coach. Dark suggested he try switch-hitting, and Kessinger spent the winter in the University of Mississippi gym hitting tennis balls right-handed and left-handed. The following season also began poorly, and after being benched for a time he became so distracted he forgot his first wedding anniversary.

"I didn't say anything," Carolyn Kessinger joked. "I just decided to leave home."

Durocher, who had seen Kessinger switch-hitting in practice, turned him over to Reiser, who several years earlier had had some success turning another light-hitting shortstop into an effective switch-hitter. Kessinger could only hope Reiser would have the same results with him that he'd had with Maury Wills. Two weeks later, Kessinger switch-hit for the first time in a game and was reborn. He finished the season hitting .274 and remained the Cubs shortstop for the next decade, earning a place on six All-Star teams along the way.

On September 25, 1966, the Cubs played their last home game of the season against the Los Angeles Dodgers, who were fighting for the National League pennant. The Cubs were finishing a disastrous season in which they finished in last place and were so lacking in pitching that they started rookies in seventy-four games. One of them was Ken Holtzman, who at the age of twenty led all Cubs pitchers with just eleven victories. Pitching for the Dodgers was Sandy Koufax, and the game, which was billed as a matchup of two Jewish left-handers, drew 21,659 fans to Wrigley Field, one of the largest crowds of the season.

Koufax had pitched his perfect game against the Cubs a year earlier, but the Cubs scored two runs in the first inning, and Holtzman, who was thrilled simply to be on the same field with the great Dodger pitcher, didn't allow a hit until the ninth inning, and the Cubs won, 2–1. Koufax retired at the end of the season, and the two men never pitched against each other again. Holtzman, who later pitched two no-hitters for the Cubs, had a longer career than Koufax, and his 174 wins are the most ever by a Jewish pitcher.

Holtzman was born and raised in St. Louis and came from a family of Cardinals fans, who quickly switched allegiances when he was drafted by the Cubs in 1965. He stayed with the team for six full seasons—and returned for two more at the end of his career—but he spent more than half his playing days with other teams, including the Oakland A's, for whom he became the only veteran member of the 1969 Cubs to play in the World Series. But that is not how he is best remembered. "When you look at my uncle's career," says Holtzman's nephew Douglas, "he won all of his World Series games with Oakland, but most people remember him from the '69 Cubs team."

This is fine with Holtzman, who summed up his feelings not long after Banks died. "My biggest thrill in my major league career was not the World Series I was in or All-Star Games, or no-hitters, but the very first day I suited up and walked on that beautiful green carpet alongside Banks, Santo, Williams, and other players that I had read about as a kid."

In a four-month span between December 1965 and April 1966, John Holland made the two best trades of his nineteen-year tenure as the Cubs' general manager. Both of the players he acquired were major leaguers at the age of twenty-two, both languished with teams that hadn't recognized their value, and both quickly became two of the most reliable players the Cubs ever had.

Ferguson Jenkins might have been a professional hockey player. He played the sport in high school in Chatham, Ontario, where his father, a chef who had emigrated from Barbados, met his mother, whose ancestors had come to Canada via the Underground Railroad. But baseball was Jenkins's preferred game, and he spent his first two seasons in the majors with the Philadelphia Phillies, where he was used as a reliever and was dismissed by one national magazine writer as a "five-inning pitcher."

It was one of the most spectacularly wrong characterizations of a baseball player ever made, yet when Durocher first suggested that Jenkins try starting games, he had some convincing to do. "He surprised me," Durocher said. "Here he was twenty-two years old and he had a chance to be a starting pitcher."

Jenkins overcame his doubts in his very first start on August 25, 1966, when he pitched eight and a third innings in a 3–2 victory over the New York Mets. He lasted until there was one out in the ninth in two of his next three starts as well, but not until September 15, when he pitched a four-hitter against the Phillies, did he finish a game. "I was beginning to wonder if I'd ever make it," Jenkins said.

Jenkins would go on to lead the National League in complete games four times and have 284 career victories and 267 complete games. He won twenty or more games for the Cubs six times, won the Cy Young Award in 1971, finished second and third in the balloting twice each, and, in 1991, become the first Canadian ever elected to baseball's Hall of Fame.

The San Francisco Giants were so eager to get rid of Randy Hundley that they threw a pitcher named Bill Hands into the deal that brought him to Chicago. Hundley, who was born in Martinsville, Virginia, was immediately put into the Cubs' starting lineup and played in 149 games in the 1966 season, breaking a forty-one-year-old major league record for games played by a rookie catcher. He remained the team's catcher for the next eight seasons.

Though Hundley's lifetime batting average was just .236, he drove in sixty or more runs four times and was a superb fielder whose career fielding percentage was .990. He won a Gold Glove in 1967 when he committed only four errors, and he became a part of baseball lore by pioneering the concept of catching pitches with one hand. "My dad was a semipro catcher, and he taught me to protect the bare hand and just catch the ball with the glove," Hundley said. Soon, nearly every other major league catcher was following his example.

Hundley's teammates were astonished by his durability—he caught

90 percent of the Cubs' games from 1966 to 1969—and his pitchers adored him. "Having Hundley catch for you was like sitting down to a steak dinner with a steak knife," Jenkins said. "Without Hundley, all you had was a fork."

———

The kid was pumping gas back home in Hackensack, New Jersey, one day when a scout for the San Francisco Giants pulled in for a fill-up. "Aren't you Bill Hands?" the scout asked. "What the hell are you doing here?" Hands had no ready answer. A star pitcher in high school, he had turned down several major league offers because his parents thought he should go to college. But he soon learned he was "not the book type," and now he was at loose ends. The scout sent him off to the San Francisco Giants' organization, where he languished in the minors for six long years. "Bill was born to lose," one observer said. "He has great stuff much of the time, but he'll find a way to blow a game."

When he came to the Cubs along with Hundley late in 1966, Hands was quickly inserted into the starting rotation of a team that was desperate for pitching. His eight victories were good for second most by a pitcher on a dreadful Cubs team and, since he was a "smart kid from New Jersey," he became a favorite of his teammates, who called him "Froggy" because they thought his pitching motion resembled that of Don Larsen, who hunted frogs in the off-season.

Hands was sent to the bullpen for much of the 1967 season, where he did well enough to earn a promotion. He made the most of it and won seventy-seven games during his next five seasons with the Cubs and finished his career with an all but symmetrical record of 111–110.

Hands, who died in 2017 at the age of seventy-six, remained a Cubs fan, but he preferred to stay in the background. When he came to Shea Stadium to watch the Cubs play the Mets in 1985, Yosh Kawano asked him to come into the clubhouse and meet the current players. "No," Hands said. "They don't want to meet a ghost from the past."

———

As the Cubs were preparing to leave Arizona near the end of March 1962, they had a small if welcome problem. For some years, it had been their custom to give a watch to the outstanding rookie in spring training—Banks won it in 1954—but now, for the first time, they realized they were going to have to award two watches. Both recipients had played in the low minors in 1961, but their performances during the spring, and in a short Arizona rookie-league season the previous fall, persuaded the Cubs not only to elevate them to the majors but also to put them in the starting lineup on opening day.

"They will remain there as long as they can hold on to their jobs," Elvin Tappe said of the two young players: a second baseman named Ken Hubbs, and Lou Brock, who would play in the outfield. Together, they would come to represent the twin demons that haunted the Cubs in the two decades Banks played for them—terrible judgment and rotten luck.

Chapter 22

And Yet So Far

Ken Hubbs was playing shortstop one day when the batter hit a looping fly ball to short center field. Hubbs ran to his left, leaped, stretched out until he was parallel to the ground, and deflected the ball with his glove. As it fell, Hubbs reached over with his bare hand, caught it just above the ground, rolled over onto his right shoulder in the center-field grass, and jumped up with the ball in his hand.

"That's one of the greatest plays I've ever seen," shouted Mel Allen, the legendary voice of the New York Yankees, who was broadcasting the 1954 Little League World Series in Williamsport, Pennsylvania.

Hubbs was twelve years old.

Hubbs grew up in Colton, California, a town of some 20,000 residents in San Bernardino County, east of Los Angeles. In high school, he was president of the student body and the Most Valuable Player in Colton High's league in football and basketball, and he made the all-conference team in baseball as a freshman. During baseball practice one day, Hubbs noticed the track team working out, wandered over, and, still in his baseball uniform, high-jumped six feet. It was the first time he had ever attempted the event.

John Wooden wanted Hubbs to play basketball at UCLA. Notre Dame, the University of Southern California, and a dozen other schools wanted him to quarterback their football teams. His older brother, Keith, who played football at Brigham Young, thought he should play basketball, which he thought was Ken's best sport.

Hubbs talked it over with his father, Eulis, an insurance salesman who had contracted polio as an adult and coached Hubbs's Little League team from a wheelchair. If Hubbs wanted to be a professional athlete, they agreed, he should play baseball. "I figured I should get involved as soon as I can," Hubbs said. "An athlete's life is pretty short."

The Cubs gave Hubbs a $15,000 signing bonus, and after two up-and-down seasons as a minor league shortstop, he was sent to Wenatchee, Washington, in the Class B Northwestern League in 1961, where Cubs coach Bobby Adams had a message for him. He was being switched to second base, and for the same reason Gene Baker had made the change seven years earlier. "Their intention was that Kenny would replace Ernie Banks at shortstop," says Keith Hubbs. "But they realized that Ernie was not going to stop playing there before Kenny was ready for the major leagues."

Working with Adams and other coaches, Hubbs fielded so many ground balls at his new position that it seemed as if he was doing it in his sleep. The twenty-four double plays he was involved in during twelve spring training games were proof that the experiment was working, as was his new watch and his ticket to the majors. Hubbs could only smile at the irony of the fact that Banks, who had been his favorite player ever since he had seen his first major league game during a stopover in Chicago on the way to Williamsport eight years earlier, was now playing first base.

On April 17, 1962, with his father in attendance at Wrigley Field, Hubbs had four singles and a double, but while his hitting showed promise, he struggled in the field. He made three errors in a three-game series against the Giants, and on June 13, when he kicked a ball hit by Roberto Clemente of the Pittsburgh Pirates, it was his ninth error of the season.

He didn't commit another one for nearly three months.

Nobody in baseball knew what to make of it. A *rookie* was closing in on long-standing records for errorless games set by two veteran stars, Red Schoendienst of the St. Louis Cardinals and Bobby Doerr of the Boston Red Sox? A twenty-year-old rookie who had been playing the position for barely a year? How could this be? Nor did Hubbs seem intimidated or protective as he approached Schoendienst's National League record of fifty-seven games, which had stood for a dozen years, and Doerr's major league mark of seventy-three games, which was fourteen years old. "At no time did he play it safe," *The Sporting News* said in an editorial. "He challenged everything within reach. There was no Nice Nelly or Safety Sam type of play. This makes the record all the more impressive."

On September 2 in Houston, Hubbs broke Doerr's record while his father, sitting in his wheelchair, shot movies. "Ken has been doing things like this ever since he was a little boy," said Dorothy Hubbs, his mother. Three days later, in the second game of a doubleheader in Cincinnati, Hubbs fielded an easy double-play grounder hit by the Reds' Gordie Coleman. His relay to shortstop was wide, and after seventy-eight errorless games and 418 chances, both major league records, the streak was over.

Hubbs finished the year batting a respectable .260 and leading all National League rookies in games played, hits, doubles, triples, runs scored, and batting average. He became the first rookie to win a Gold Glove and made a shambles of the race for Rookie of the Year, winning nineteen of twenty votes. Hubbs's heroics had begun too late for him to be named to the National League All-Star team—though the Cubs rewarded his achievements by rewriting his contract twice during the season—but seasoned baseball people knew what they were seeing.

"Ken is intelligent and has the determination and ambition that will carry him to the top," Charlie Metro said. "He is going to be playing second base a long time in the majors and before he's through he'll be playing regularly in the All-Star Game." Banks put it more simply. Hubbs may have been a rookie, he said, but he was already the leader of the Cubs' infield.

Hubbs's second season was less successful—his batting average dipped to .235 and he made seven more errors than in 1962—but he endeared himself to his teammates when, on April 29 in San Francisco, he was hit in his left ear by a fastball thrown by the Cubs' old friend Jack Sanford. The pitch went exactly where he wanted it to, Sanford said. It was Hubbs's fault for not getting out of the way.

With blood flowing from his ear and the Cubs fearing a skull fracture, Hubbs was carried off the field and taken to a nearby hospital. When doctors determined there was no break, he was back in the lineup the following day. A player with that sort of courage doesn't come along very often, John Holland said. Hubbs, it was clear, was going to be the Cubs second baseman for many years to come.

Back home in Colton after the season, Hubbs pondered a family friend's offer to sell him a piece of land he'd had his eye on for $5,000. But he decided to buy a small airplane instead.

Only 9,750 fans turned out for the Cubs' home opener on April 13, 1962, and those who stayed home were the smart ones. Both the temperature and the wind velocity at Wrigley Field were in the thirties, and the Cubs and St. Louis battled nearly five hours before the Cardinals scored three runs in the top of the fifteenth inning to win, 8–5. Those who did attend the game, though, came home with something to talk about—a home run over the right-field stands in the first inning, followed by a triple, single, and stolen base by the Cubs' new center fielder.

Lou Brock was born in El Dorado, Arkansas, and moved with this mother to Collinston, Louisiana, a town of 900 people, at the age of two. One of nine children, Brock acted up in class one day and, as punishment, was assigned to read books from the school's modest library about Jackie Robinson and other baseball players. "I saw that they got eight dollars a day in meal money," Brock told Franz Schulze, the collaborator on his autobiography. "*Eight dollars a day.* Now what in the world, I wondered, were they making a *week*?"

Brock played at Southern University in Baton Rouge, Louisiana, and, after receiving a $30,000 bonus to sign with the Cubs, was sent to St. Cloud in the Class C Northern League where he hit .361, drove in eighty-two runs, and stole thirty-seven bases. Though it was his first season in organized baseball, and in the low minors at that, the Cubs decided to take a closer look.

Brock turned heads in the fall Arizona Instructional League—he "looks like the hottest headline material of the circuit," one writer said— and in his first spring training game he drove in seven runs. He followed with ten hits in his first fifteen at-bats, and by the time the spring was well along he was batting over .400 with ten home runs and twenty runs batted in. The Cubs had seen enough. Brock was given his watch and told he would be their center fielder on opening day.

In retrospect, this may have been a mistake, because for all the excitement Brock was creating at the plate and on the base paths, he was a work in progress in the outfield. He had trouble judging fly balls, fielding grounders, and hitting the cutoff man on throws to the infield. What he needed, he later said, was a year in Triple-A. Those who saw Brock in his rookie year could only agree. "If you have watched all the Cubs' home games thus far," wrote Bob Smith in the *Chicago Daily News*, "you have probably come to the conclusion that Lou Brock is the worst outfielder in baseball history. He really isn't, but he hasn't done much to prove it."

Brock thought this judgment was a little harsh, but he couldn't really deny it. "I was bad news," he said. Part of his problem was nervousness and lack of self-confidence. "I was impatient, unable to control myself," he said. "I'm not sure whether I overrated major league play or not. It was like going from the eighth grade into college."

"Ernie, what does it take to play major league baseball?" Brock asked Banks one day.

"Lou, all you need is one thing," Banks replied. "You've got to relax."

"I can't relax," Brock said. "I don't want to go back to Louisiana picking no cotton."

Making matters worse was the fact that Brock was receiving his on-the-job training in the worst possible place, Wrigley Field.

"A rookie trying to hold down center field in Cubs Park was bound to have a hard time of it," Schoendienst said. "The sun is bad in your eyes out there and the wind runs in circles in the outfield."

Brock's inability to cope with the sun was so great that he kept his sunglasses flipped down while pitches were being delivered, which made it harder to pick up the ball off the bat. Soon, the fans began to react to his misadventures. "Rock, as in Brock," fans would yell after a botched play. "Lou, I hear you're a bum," came a cry from the bleachers one day. "And I hear you're fast. That makes you a fast bum."

"He was booed with considerable gusto," one writer noted. "They razzed him because he was such an ox in the outfield," Banks said. "They expected a lot of him, and he never lived up to what they thought he was able to do."

Brock was not at his best offensively early in his career, either. He hit .263 his rookie year, .258 in 1963, and had just eighteen home runs and seventy-two runs batting in during those two seasons. Still, there were flashes of brilliance. He was capable of hitting streaks—he had ten hits in eighteen at-bats and made several excellent catches in four games in New York—and in any given game he might do something remarkable.

On May 20, 1962, Brock hit a grand slam in a rare doubleheader sweep of the Phillies. On June 24, in a doubleheader against the Pirates, he made eleven trips to the plate and reached base nine times with a triple, two doubles, two singles, and four walks. And in a game against the Mets, he scored from second base while the catcher was fielding a ball hit in front of home plate and throwing the runner out at first.

One of Brock's hitting feats became the stuff of legend when, on June 17, he hit a home run over a forty-foot fence into a portion of the center-field bleachers in the Polo Grounds where no one—not Babe Ruth, not Mel Ott, not Willie Mays—had ever hit one before. Later in the game, Banks hit a home run that just cleared the left-field fence 279 feet from home plate. "Lou, if I chopped up your blast," he told Brock, "I'd have five homers."

There was no doubting Brock's impressive speed, either; his twenty-four stolen bases in 1963 were the most by a Cub in more than thirty years. And as the season progressed, his throws began to gain in accuracy, and he led the National League in double plays and assists from the outfield. In a vote for outstanding second-year player in the league, Brock finished second to Cardinals catcher Tim McCarver.

Once the season was over, Holland said he was in the market for a left-handed starting pitcher, but made it clear there were limits to what he was willing to give up to obtain one. He was not going to break up the Cubs' infield, he said. And he was not going to trade Lou Brock.

Ken Hubbs was afraid of flying. He had never been on a plane until he flew to Morristown, Tennessee, for his first season in the minors, and he couldn't understand how planes stayed in the air. Later, when he was traveling with the Cubs, he would go up to the cockpit and talk to the pilots about safety. After his rookie season, he decided there was only one way to overcome his doubts once and for all—take flying lessons.

"I want you to go with Kenny and talk him out of it," Eulis Hubbs told Keith when they discovered he was learning to fly during spring training of his second season with the Cubs. Keith drove to the small airport in Mesa, Arizona, and sat on the hood of his car as he watched his brother practice takeoffs and landings. "My heart was pounding a hundred beats a minute," Keith says. "It was very nerve-racking for me to watch him." Later, Ken talked Keith into taking flying lessons, too. His instructor, a famous stunt pilot named Art Scholl, told him that he considered Ken to be an excellent pilot, particularly when it came to exercising judgment.

After the 1963 season, Hubbs bought a single-engine Cessna 172, the most popular aircraft ever built, which remains in production to this day. In the first two weeks after receiving his pilot's license, he logged more than seventy hours of flight time, and he was particularly proud of the radio receiver he had installed that allowed him to communicate with his family while he was in the air.

"He'd fly over the house and say, 'Mom, if you can hear me, you can start dinner because I'll be home in thirty or forty minutes,'" Dorothy Hubbs said.

On February 12, 1964, not long after packing his gear for spring training, Hubbs planned his first flight of any real length. He and Dennis Doyle, his best friend since childhood, would fly to Las Vegas, where they would stop for fuel, and then fly on to Provo, Utah, to see Doyle's wife, Elaine, who had taken the train earlier in the week to show her parents their six-week-old daughter. It would be Hubbs's last flight until the end of the baseball season. Hubbs and Doyle stopped at Keith's home, where they watched Ken's favorite television show, *The Fugitive*, before driving to the airport.

"Be careful," Keith told Doyle and his brother as they got into the car.

"Hey," Doyle said, "I'm not going to let my little daughter grow up without me."

Hubbs and Doyle had planned to stay in Provo for just a few hours, but Doyle's wife convinced them to remain overnight because, although she and Doyle had been married for two years, some of her family had never met him. Before leaving the following morning, Hubbs checked the weather report and learned there was a storm coming in from the north, which he was sure would remain behind him on the trip home. What he had no way of knowing—and what satellite imagery that would later revolutionize weather forecasting would have told him in an instant—was that the storm had horseshoed around the Wasatch mountain range and was now approaching from the south.

Hubbs took off into clear weather, but soon the Cessna became enveloped in the storm, and he turned around and headed back toward the Provo airport. A railroad crew reported seeing a small red-and-white plane flying low to the ground and following the train tracks, as if the pilot was trying to get his bearings. Hubbs's plane was painted red and white.

Late that afternoon, long after the two men were expected home, the Hubbs family called Elaine Doyle in Provo, who said they had left many hours earlier. Eulis Hubbs reported the plane missing, and a small fleet of planes began to search over Utah, Nevada, and parts of California. Nothing was heard the rest of the day or the one that followed, and Keith took his wife, Roxanna, to a civic light opera performance in San Bernardino, calling his father during intermission to ask if there was any news. The following morning, Hubbs's father answered the phone and, for the first time that anyone in the family could remember, began to cry.

Harlon Bement, Utah's aeronautics director, and Myron Jense, the manager of the Provo airport, were the first to spot the wreckage some 200 yards from a small island in Utah Lake, about five miles south of the Provo airport. Hubbs had lost track of the horizon during the storm, Bement believed, and had probably been unable to tell which direction and at what angle he was flying.

The front of the plane's fuselage had crashed through eighteen inches of ice while the lighter back portion and the wings and tail were scattered on top. A scuba diver found Hubbs and Doyle, still strapped into their seats, their bodies decapitated and shorn of their arms and legs below the knees. The diver brought up the torsos, which were placed along with the body parts that were strewn on the ice amid the wreckage. "I never told my mom and dad that—ever," Keith Hubbs says of the dismemberment of the bodies, which the diver told him about some months after the crash. "We sometimes joked that Kenny and Denny are in each other's graves."

The news of Hubbs's death stunned the Cubs. From his spring training headquarters in Mesa, Arizona, head coach Bob Kennedy, a marine pilot during World War II, was close to tears, and Robert Whitlow, the team's athletic director, said, "It's just too tragic to believe."

But nowhere did the crash have greater impact than in the small town of Colton. Businesses closed, school was canceled, and the memorial service was moved from the family church to the high school auditorium where Hubbs had once presided as student body president. Every police car in Colton joined the funeral convoy while the San Bernardino County sheriff's department took over their regular patrols. Hubbs's teammates on Colton's 1954 championship Little League team were honorary pallbearers, and every member of the Cubs was in attendance.

Some of them, including Banks, served as pallbearers, before taking the short, sad journey to spring training.

A young woman was in the audience, too, a stewardess as they were called at the time, whom Hubbs had met in Chicago. Pretty enough to have won her airline's "Miss Photogenic" contest, she had flown out two weeks earlier and stayed with an aunt in San Bernardino, going out with Hubbs, and sometimes Keith and Roxanna, in the evenings. The Hubbs family thought she was sweet and a better match for Ken than the local girl he had previously been engaged to, who had spoken about how she couldn't wait to get out of Colton.

The city established an award in Hubbs's name that has been given to the top high school athlete in the area for more than half a century. "Ken Hubbs was the kind of boy you would be proud to have as your own," San Bernardino County supervisor Paul Young said. "The kind you'd like your own to grow up to be."

The Hubbs family never quite recovered from the shock of their loss. "Every time the front door opens, I expect to see Ken walking through," Eulis Hubbs said. "Part of me just doesn't believe it. For a long time, I'm going to be looking for his name in the Cubs' box scores."

———

On June 14, 1964, Lou Brock hit a two-run home run as the Cubs beat the Pirates, 5–2, at Wrigley Field. On June 15, he was traded.

"There go the majors," thought Brock, who had been worrying he would be sent to the minors, when John Holland called to tell him his contract was being transferred. "Here I go: Tacoma."

But the Cubs weren't demoting Brock. They were sending him to the Cardinals in exchange for the left-handed starting pitcher they had needed for so long—Ernie Broglio, who had won eighteen games in 1963 and sixty in the past four seasons.

The reaction to the trade was unanimous. The Cubs had picked the Cardinals' pocket. "Thank you, thank you, oh you lovely St. Louis

Cardinals," Bob Smith wrote in the *Daily News*. "Nice doing business with you. Please call again any time."

"This gives us as good a pitching staff as there is in the league," said Kennedy, who, noting that the Cubs were only five and a half games out of first place, was almost giddy as he contemplated the remainder of the season. "We're taking more than a shot at the flag," Holland said. "We're blasting it open with both barrels."

Some of Brock's teammates professed to feel sorry for him. When he arrived at Wrigley Field to pack his bags for a hurried trip to Houston where he would join the Cardinals, he found a note pinned to his locker that read "See you at the World Series."

In St. Louis, fans showed up at Sportsman's Park carrying a banner that read, "Broglio for Brock. Who could make such a deal?" and a number of the Cardinals' players agreed they had been robbed. "A proven eighteen-game winner, who once won twenty-one games for a .251 hitter who can't field," one said. "Bing Devine! You have reached the living end!" one sportswriter wrote of the Cardinals' general manager. "This is your ex–Executive of the Year," Devine joked when a reporter called him. And, in fact, he was fired in August.

The Cardinals, who had lost sixteen of their previous twenty-three games at the time of the trade, were in danger of falling into ninth place when Brock joined them. Their greatest problem was replacing the bat of Stan Musial, who had retired after the 1963 season. And then, in the blink of an eye, their problems were solved.

Brock pinch-hit in his first game with the Cardinals and struck out. In his first start the following day, he had a single and a triple and walked twice. The next day, he drove in the winning run with a single. After two weeks, he was hitting .390 and had six stolen bases in seven attempts. He would finish the season hitting .348 for the Cardinals—he was batting .251 when he left the Cubs—with twelve home runs, eighty-one runs scored, and thirty-three stolen bases.

On the final day of the season, after the Cardinals had won one of the most thrilling of all National League pennant races—the Phillies blew a six-and-a-half-game lead with a dozen games left to play—Brock had two hits, scored two runs, made a shoestring catch against the New York Mets, and was carried off the field by delirious Cardinals fans. In the World Series that followed, Brock hit .300, and in the Game 7 victory that made the Cardinals world champions he hit a home run almost as hard as he had in the Polo Grounds three years earlier. The Cardinals, their manager Johnny Keane said, couldn't have won without him. To which Musial added, "We never would have won if I hadn't retired."

Brock said there was one major reason for his astonishing debut with the Cardinals: getting away from the Cubs. Under Kennedy, the players would be called "to heel" after a loss and told to sit and contemplate their sins. "It was like police court," Brock told Schulze. Keane's attitude in St. Louis, on the other hand, was, "Let's get 'em tomorrow." And, whereas in Chicago Brock was only allowed to steal a base on command, Keane told him to use his own judgment. After rubbing his eyes in disbelief, Brock never looked back.

In his nineteen years with the Cardinals, Brock won three National League pennants and two World Series, and broke Ty Cobb's career stolen-base record, which had stood for forty-nine years. He was elected to the Hall of Fame in his first year of eligibility.

———

As the Cardinals were celebrating their 1964 World Series championship in Musial's restaurant in St. Louis, one of the players called a former teammate who was feeling a little blue. "They passed the phone around and I really appreciated it," Ernie Broglio said. "I popped open my own bottle of champagne and drank along with them. I looked at it like they won the pennant by one game and I won three games before I was traded, so I thought I helped them win it."

Broglio's introduction to his new team was as disastrous as Brock's was electrifying. Unknown to the Cubs, he had hurt his elbow a month before the trade, and while at first Broglio didn't consider the injury to be serious, it kept getting worse. After losing his first four starts, he woke up in a New York hotel room in August to discover his elbow had swollen to the size of a grapefruit. He was sent back Chicago for treatment and then returned to the starting rotation.

After the season ended, Broglio underwent surgery to remove bone chips and repair a damaged ulnar nerve, and he was back in spring training three months later. He would always believe that not being given more time to recover destroyed his career. Broglio spent four more years with the Cubs, winning ten games and losing twenty-four. At the age of twenty-four, Broglio had led the National League in victories. At thirty, he was out of baseball.

———

Just as Bobby Thomson and Ralph Branca were joined at the hip for the rest of their lives after the former's home run off the latter in the historic 1951 National League playoff game, so were the two men involved in the historic trade between the Cubs and the Cardinals. Brock-for-Broglio became not just a reminder of what some regard as the worst trade in baseball history, but also a kind of shorthand for judgment so bad it could never be expunged. "The Broglio deal? What Broglio deal?" Banks once said. "I don't want to talk about that. Nobody on the Cubs wants to talk about that. That deal never occurred, you understand? What is there to say about something that never happened?"

Over the years, Brock and Broglio occasionally made appearances together during which Broglio would play his role with good humor. Before an old-timers' game at Wrigley Field in the 1990s, Broglio bowed to the crowd amid a chorus of boos, then stepped aside as Brock was introduced to cheers that rattled the old ballpark to its foundation. And, at his home in California, Broglio displayed an autographed picture of Brock and said he hoped his friend would not die before him.

"As long as people remember him," he said, "I know they are also going to remember me."

Chapter 23

The Most Unpopular Man in Chicago

The first thing Leo Durocher did when the Cubs began spring training in Long Beach, California, in 1966 was ban Charlie Grimm from the clubhouse. The players were stunned.

"I was humiliated for him," Randy Hundley says of Grimm, who at the age of sixty-seven no longer had any official position with the team other than to spread good cheer and serve as a reminder of days gone by. "It was astonishing to us. Why would he do that?"

The second thing Durocher did was bawl out Yosh Kawano. The players could scarcely believe their ears.

"Yosh, I don't give a damn what the players want, you get it for them," Durocher told the Cubs' beloved clubhouse man, whose white T-shirt and floppy white hat made him an incongruous presence in the dugout for many years, and whose work ethic bordered on the heroic.

"Yosh came to me crying," says Joe Amalfitano, who played sparingly for the Cubs in 1966 and would become a coach for Durocher the following season. "He said, 'I'm getting out of here. He can't talk to me that way.' I told him Leo was just trying to get everyone's attention, to tell them that he was going to be the boss."

The third thing Durocher did was to challenge Ernie Banks. The players were dumbstruck.

"I was astounded," Hundley says. "I'm a rookie on the team and I was just sitting there thinking 'Holy Cow!'"

Durocher's demands of Banks seemed pointless and silly. "When the pitcher throws over to first base, you don't ever tag the runner," the manager told him. "From now on, I want you to tag the runner."

Tag the runner? While he was standing on the base? Why? Was he testing Banks? Was he testing all of them? But for the rest of his career, Banks tagged the runner every time he received the ball. "He could be standing on the base for two minutes and Ernie had to tag him," Hundley says.

"For five years when I was there," says Phil Regan, a veteran relief pitcher who joined the Cubs in 1968, "I never saw a ball thrown to first base when he didn't put the tag on him."

But Durocher wasn't through. "When you get on first base, you never take a lead," he told Banks. "You're so close, fucking Houdini couldn't pick you off. I want you to take a lead. Got it?" That gave the players a laugh, but it too seemed ridiculous. Banks was thirty-five years old now and his knees were a constant problem. Did Durocher *want* him to get picked off first base? Was his goal simply to embarrass him?

"You didn't have to be Einstein to know he wasn't going to steal any bases," says Ferguson Jenkins. "So Ernie took tiny leads off first base, like three inches." For much of his first season, Durocher would yell across the diamond to first-base coach Rube Walker, demanding that Banks take a longer lead. "The rest of us sitting on the bench listening just wanted to tell Leo, 'Give it a rest!'" Jenkins says. "But nobody did."

Durocher's campaign against some of the Cubs' most venerable and admired figures included Jack Brickhouse, who during his long career in Chicago called the games of the Cubs, White Sox, and Bears, and it could be comically cruel. "Visualize Mr. Wrigley sitting there and on one knee is Charlie Grimm and Ernie is on the other knee," Durocher told his first clubhouse meeting. "Now Yosh is trying to find a place to sit and so is Jack Brickhouse."

"Jack is an institution in Chicago," Amalfitano says of Brickhouse, who would come to detest Durocher. "So tell me, why did he do that? Those are four pillars there. He's telling them that from now on they were all going to be in second place." The fact that Durocher's Friars

Club roast was aimed so specifically at Banks was not lost on the rest of the team. "I think he did it because Ernie was the big star," Billy Williams says. "He's thinking, 'If I get on the big guy, the younger guys are going to fall in line.' I told that to Leo once and he just smiled."

And indeed Durocher's plan was to knock down the Cubs' sturdiest pillar once and for all. "He would nitpick him," says Byron Browne. "He'd say, 'You're not fast enough. Your focus is not like it used to be. We're going to find somebody else.' He was trying to retire him."

"I found it a little disturbing," says Hundley of Durocher's treatment of Banks. "But I'm just a player."

Which was Durocher's point. He wanted Banks to be seen as just a player, too, a player no different from any of the others. And in Banks's case, a player he didn't want on his team, stealing his thunder. How could he be number one if one of the most admired players in all of baseball was standing in his way?

"Mr. Cub, my ass," Durocher would sometimes say to any reporter within earshot. "I'll give Banks a hundred dollars any time he even attempts to steal second." "Why don't you knock off that Mr. Cub stuff?" he would also say. "The guy's wearing out. He can't go on forever."

Durocher came up with pejorative nicknames for Banks—Gramps or Grandpa. He was getting old, the manager was saying. It was time for the Cubs, and for Banks, to move on. And no sooner had he instructed Banks how to play first base than it became clear that his real goal was to remove him from it entirely.

"Leo tried to give Ernie's job away five times," says Jenkins. "I'll name the players for you. John Boccabella, Dick Nen, Lee Thomas, Willie Smith, Jim Hickman. Ernie was always going to spring training and someone had his job. But he always won it back." Jenkins missed a few of Durocher's attempts to replace Banks—George Altman, Clarence Jones, and Norm Gigon also took their turn at first base—and it is possible that, given time, one of them might have succeeded. But Durocher was so impatient that at the first sign of failure he would go on to the next man, or admit defeat and return to Banks—for the moment.

Thomas and Boccabella, who got their chance in 1966, were cases in point. A left-handed hitter who had twenty-two home runs with the Boston Red Sox in 1965, Thomas was traded to the Cubs late in May, and Durocher said, "I'm going to give Lee every chance to play regularly at first base." Six weeks later, he gave the job to Boccabella, who had been unable to stick with the Cubs the previous three seasons.

He failed, too, and Banks, who had had fluid drained from his knee during spring training and gotten off to one of the worst starts of his career, reclaimed the position. Banks's hitting rebounded nicely as the season wore on, and his batting average rose from .167 near the end of May to .272 at the end of the season. He tied a modern major league record with three triples, even on his bad knee, in a single game in Houston in June and drove in fifty runs after the All-Star break. And, despite his manager's machinations, Banks played in 141 games in 1966, and early-season speculation that his career might be over faded away. Durocher, one Chicago writer noted about his search for a new first baseman, changes his mind more often than his ball club wins.

Banks credited his resurgence at the plate to a conversation in St. Louis with Stan Musial, who said he should start hitting to right field more often. But regaining his batting stroke did nothing to deter Durocher's determination to embarrass him. In the first game of a doubleheader against the New York Mets on June 26, Ron Santo was hit by a pitch thrown by Jack Fisher that fractured a cheekbone. Santo was taken to the hospital for surgery, and Banks was sent to third base for the second game, a position he had played only a few times in recent years. He committed three errors, two on the same play.

Durocher responded by benching Banks for a week, leading one Chicago columnist to say the manager was vying for the title of most unpopular man in Chicago. Durocher was so determined to denigrate Banks that in a series in Atlanta he used reserves Jimmy Stewart and Marty Keough, who were hitting .153 and .069 respectively, as pinch hitters while Banks, who had a nine-game hitting streak, sat on the bench.

There were times when Durocher's complaints defied belief. In May

1968, reporters were stunned when Durocher pinned a 9–2 loss to the Cardinals at Wrigley Field on the fact that Banks hadn't scored from third base on a ball hit to the infield. "Banks should have walked home," Durocher said of a run that would have reduced the margin of defeat from seven runs to six. "He's been in the league sixteen years, but he just won't get off the bag." But once again, Banks turned the other cheek. "Leo's right," he said. "Taking the extra lead or the extra base helps the club."

If Durocher's strategy was to make Banks begin to doubt himself, it was working. "I won't say it doesn't hurt, because it definitely does," Banks said. "As we get older, we have to make way for younger players. I simply have to adjust to it."

Durocher's animus was a constant subject of speculation among Banks's teammates. Did the fact that Banks always seemed so relaxed while he was playing upset the manager? they wondered. "You got the sense he didn't like Ernie because he wasn't one of those guys who was going to spit tobacco juice and then go out and play," says Rich Nye. "He wasn't someone who would strike out with the bases loaded and say, 'Goddamit!' and break the bat over his knee. Leo liked guys like Santo, who would smack his bat to the ground and kick the dirt to show his disappointment. I think Leo wanted to light a fire under his ass because he never threw his bat or flipped his helmet down on the ground."

In the end, though, everyone saw the most obvious reason for Durocher's animus. "Leo wanted to be number one in Chicago," Blake Cullen says. "That's all there was to it. As much as I admire Leo, I have to say Ernie did nothing to cause him not to like him, except jealousy."

There was another problem casting a cloud over Banks's relationship with Durocher—he was not Willie Mays.

"Leo managed Willie when he was real young," says Amalfitano, who had a ringside seat for Durocher's interactions with both Mays and Banks. This allowed Durocher to take credit for Mays's rise to stardom with the New York Giants, Amalfitano says, whereas Banks was already a star when he came to the Cubs. And while Mays was painfully shy in his early days, staying in the background and letting Durocher speak for

Ernie Banks was one of twelve children. Here they all are at home in Dallas, along with his mother, father, and assorted nephews and nieces, in 1955. *Courtesy of Edna Warren*

Football was Banks's main sport at Booker T. Washington High School, which didn't have a baseball team. He drew a line to number 30 and scribbled the word "Me" above it. *Courtesy of Jerry Banks*

Banks played for the Kansas City Monarchs in 1950 and 1953. He is standing fifth from the right in this photo, taken not long before he was signed by the Cubs. Monarchs manager Buck O'Neil is at the far right. *Courtesy of Larry Lester*

Banks's determination is written all over his face in this rare solo portrait of him in a Monarchs uniform. *Courtesy of Jerry Banks*

Banks, far right in the front row, was lucky the army sent him to Germany instead of Korea when he was drafted after his first season with the Monarchs. His duty consisted mainly of playing for the 242nd AAA Group Barons. *Courtesy of Jerry Banks*

Cubs manager Phil Cavarretta with his new double-play combination, Banks and Gene Baker, in 1954. Baker, who was six years older than Banks, joined the Cubs at the same time and helped him adjust to the big leagues. *Bettmann/ Getty Images*

Banks and Hank Aaron, shown here at Wrigley Field in 1957, led a revolution in batting when they began using lighter bats than most sluggers did—and hitting home runs with them. *Bettmann/Getty Images*

Banks was a superb—and underrated—shortstop before a knee injury robbed him of his speed and forced him to play first base. Here he is leaping over Gino Cimoli of the St. Louis Cardinals to complete a double play in 1959. *Associated Press*

Banks and his wife Eloyce were running out of display space after he won his second consecutive Most Valuable Player award in 1959. Banks lost the trophies in a divorce settlement, and though he later got them back, they went missing again and have not been recovered. *Associated Press*

Cubs owner Philip K. Wrigley had a paternal attitude toward Banks, often helping him with financial advice. Here, they chat at a team lunch in 1962. *Chicago Sun-Times*

Buck O'Neil's only season wearing a major league uniform came in 1963 when the Cubs made him the first black coach in big-league history. His main job was to help Banks adjust to playing first base. *Courtesy of Don Sparks*

Banks with his wife Eloyce, twin sons Joey and Jerry, and daughter Jan, in 1963. *Sporting News via Getty Images*

Leo Durocher became manager of the Cubs in 1966. His body language in this photo, and that of Banks, says all we need to know about their relationship. *Focus on Sport/Getty Images*

Ron Grousl was the undisputed leader of the Bleacher Bums, a group of Cubs fans who rose to fame with their over-the-top antics during the 1967 season. *Courtesy of Jack Herbon*

Cubs outfielder Willie Smith became a fan favorite after helping a not-entirely-sober Ron Grousl back into the stands after he fell during a game in 1969. *Chicago Tribune*

Banks often teased Willie Mays from his position at first base when the Giants star took a day off at Wrigley Field. Mays would hide in the dugout to escape Banks's taunts. *Bettmann/Getty Images*

Banks was sobered by his trip to Vietnam in 1968. Assisted by *Chicago Daily News* foreign correspondent Georgie Anne Geyer, he wrote reflective stories home. *Courtesy of Jerry Banks*

The 1969 Chicago Cubs. For all sad words of tongue and pen... *Courtesy of the National Baseball Hall of Fame*

Banks with Billy Williams and Ron Santo, one of the great power-hitting triumvirates in baseball history. *Chicago Tribune*

In 1962, still in the midst of his career, Banks surprised everyone when he announced he was running for alderman—as a Republican. He was routed in the election and went back to baseball. *Chicago Sun-Times*

Banks was named to the Chicago Transit Authority board in 1969. He said his main job was making sure the "L" stopped at Wrigley Field. *Courtesy of Chicago Transit Authority*

Banks was inducted into the Baseball Hall of Fame in 1977, his first year of eligibility. "There's sunshine, fresh air, and the team is behind us," he told the crowd, pointing to the Hall of Famers in attendance. "Let's play two." *Chicago Tribune*

Banks enjoyed the company of Chicago celebrities. Here, with his wife Liz (center) in a photo taken in 2007, he is at the top of his game. *Courtesy of Jerry Banks*

It took a while—and a previously erected statue of announcer Harry Caray—before the Cubs got around to putting up a statue of Banks outside Wrigley Field. "Even when I'm not here, I'll be here," he said when the statue was dedicated in 2008. *Associated Press*

Banks first met Barack Obama when the future president was an aspiring politician in Chicago. Obama presented him with the Presidential Medal of Freedom in 2013. *Win McNamee/Getty Images*

In his later years, Banks was a constant presence at Wrigley Field. *Timothy Hiatt/Getty Images for BMW*

Banks's celebration of his 500th home run in 1971 showed how he felt about playing baseball—if not always about life. *Chicago Sun-Times*

him, Banks could speak for himself. Durocher took justifiable pride in the way he had boosted Mays's confidence by praising him to the skies when, as a nervous rookie in 1951, he got off to a slow start. "I think it does something for Mays if I keep telling him, 'You're the greatest, no one can carry your glove, nobody can put your shoes on,'" Durocher had told Mays's teammates about why he was babying him along. "I think it makes him a better player and as long as it does he puts money in your pocket and mine."

But it was not in Durocher's nature to see that Banks would also have responded positively to this type of sweet talk. Though Banks and Mays were at different points in their careers when Durocher was their boss, some wondered why the aging manager and the aging player couldn't have joined forces. Amalfitano thought he knew. "Nobody in Leo's mind or eyes or heart was better than Mays," he says. "Until his dying breath he always loved him and believed he was the best player ever. Was he using him to try to fire up Ernie, to get him pissed off? I don't know what his philosophy was. I just don't know."

Amalfitano, who had half a century to ponder the destructive relationship between the manager who gave him his career and the player that manager couldn't abide, thinks something else may have been eating at Durocher. "Remember the scene in *Patton* where he says, 'War, God help me, I do love it so'? That was Ernie. He loved coming to the park, loved talking to people, loved playing the game. Maybe Leo was envious of that."

Durocher grudgingly acknowledged that Banks's positive outlook was the real thing. "He did love to play the game," the manager wrote in his autobiography, *Nice Guys Finish Last*, a book in which he said Banks's skills were gone by the time he became the Cubs manager and that Banks manipulated the press against him. "That part of the Ernie Banks legend was true." Durocher also admitted that Banks never confronted him. "He knew I wanted to get rid of him and it didn't affect our personal relationship a bit," wrote Durocher, who couldn't help adding, "But then, why should it?"

The Cubs were unanimous in their agreement that Banks never responded to Durocher. They were also amazed. "He never argued with him, never said anything back to him," Hundley says. "I think Leo was trying to keep him on edge and see how much he could stir Ernie up, but Ernie never gave him anything to go on. He didn't allow himself to show any disrespect to Leo. I admired the daylights out of him because I couldn't have done it myself."

"He just went about his business," says Bill Hands. "Whatever Leo tried to do didn't seem to affect him one way or the other."

"It was never made public," Williams says of Banks's chilly relationship with Durocher. "Nobody talked about it, but everybody knew it. The only time you noticed it was in the clubhouse. You'd look around and see that Ernie didn't have anything to do with Leo and Leo didn't have anything to do with Ernie."

There were times, in fact, when Banks's teammates seemed more upset than Banks himself, and occasionally they found themselves unwittingly caught up in Durocher's vendetta. "I don't know why the hell Ernie's not playing. He can still help us win games," Williams told Jim Enright one day. Enright repeated the comments to Durocher, who, rather than confront Williams directly, complained to John Holland, who reprimanded Williams, angering the usually even-tempered Cubs outfielder. "I told Leo he was trying to start some shit with me," says Williams, who didn't appreciate being caught up in clubhouse politics. "It didn't go any further."

George Altman was also offended by Durocher's treatment of Banks. After working through a number of injuries and having a fine season for the Cubs' Tacoma farm team in 1967, Altman was invited by Holland to spring training the following season. He asked if Durocher would be returning, and when Holland said yes he declined the offer. "The way I looked at it," Altman says, "was that if Leo would treat Ernie like that I had to get away from him because I know he'd treat me even worse." Altman went to Japan, where he had seven fine seasons and retired at the age of forty-one.

Throughout his life, Banks never publicly acknowledged being upset by Durocher's treatment of him. Leo was simply trying to motivate him, he said. He was the best manager he'd ever had. He only wished he could have played for him earlier in his career. "Leo wasn't jealous of me," he said in 1985. "I think he was just trying to push me. When you're in the latter stages of a career like I was, sometimes you get lackadaisical. I understood what he was trying to do. He wasn't trying to embarrass me."

Time after time, Banks would praise Durocher, sometimes with his trademark over-the-top enthusiasm. "I like his positive approach to base-ball," he said without any apparent irony. "He makes everybody think he's the greatest." Banks even made jokes about his relationship with Durocher. "I learned from my mother that if somebody comes after you, just kill them with kindness," he said. "So I would sit by Leo on the plane, sit by him on the bench, sit by him occasionally in the locker room. I'd just sit right beside him and never say a word."

But those close to Banks knew he was hiding the truth, which was that he was deeply wounded by Durocher's insults and his campaign to get rid of him. "I think it hurt Ernie really badly, his feeling that Leo would rather he wasn't the big hero that he was," says Don Kessinger. "I felt bad that Leo did things that put Ernie down and made him look bad."

The first evidence of Banks's unhappiness appeared in quiet mut-terings to Jenkins, his roommate on the road, who Banks knew would keep his confidence. "That damn Leo, he doesn't think I can still play," Banks would say when Durocher benched him. "I should be in the lineup today."

"He'd say it to me in the room," Jenkins says. "He wouldn't say it in front of the ball club or in front of the press. Not ever."

After he retired, Banks's wounds began to emerge when he was with friends, who were startled when he steered the conversation to Durocher. Banks could seem almost analytical as he tried to piece it all together. In one of the first intrasquad games in Long Beach, the manager asked him and Santo to manage the teams, and though Santo was given most of the Cubs' regulars, Banks's team won. "I think that was the beginning of the jealousy," Banks said. "I think Leo thought I was a threat. Sometimes, a veteran player can have more influence on the team than the manager. I think he thought that I had more control over the players than he did."

Durocher's refusal to tell him whether or not he was in the lineup also rankled, as did the manager's comments to reporters. "He's too old, he can't run" was what Banks would remember about Durocher's comments, and the hurt in his voice would be obvious to his listeners.

Banks recalled one incident in great detail, and there was no doubt about how hurtful the memory was. Though he said the game was in St. Louis in 1970, he appears to have been referring to one in Wrigley Field on June 25 of that year when the Cubs ended a home stand with their fifth straight loss to the Mets and fell out of first place. The Mets scored six runs in the third inning as the Cubs made three errors, the last of them on a pop-up that fell between Banks and Glenn Beckert at second base. The error was charged to Beckert, but after the game Durocher went after Banks.

"You're the veteran player!" he shouted. "You've got to make that play! My mother could have caught that ball!" Durocher's tirade went on and on, and as Banks looked around the locker room he saw his teammates sitting in silence, eyeing him with pity. "We got dressed, got on the bus, and didn't say a word," Banks said. "Every one of those players felt so bad for me."

Banks knew what this was all about, of course. He was close to the end of his career, and once again Durocher was using him to send a message to his teammates that said, "If he can get on Ernie Banks, he can get on anybody. Me, too." This is what it had come to, Banks realized. He had become a bad example Durocher was using to motivate younger players.

In Banks's telling, he redeemed himself by hitting two home runs off Steve Carlton of the Cardinals the following day, although records show the game took place in St. Louis four days later. Whatever the case, he had for the moment redeemed himself in his own eyes and those of his teammates, if not his manager's.

Over the years, a story was passed down among Cubs players about the one time Banks was said to have abandoned his policy of suffering in silence and confronted Durocher.

"The way I hear it," says Browne, "is that Ernie said, 'Leo, if this keeps up, one of us is going to go, and it's not going to be me.'"

"I heard that," Randy Hundley says. "I don't know if it's true, but I hope that it is. Nobody should disrespect Ernie the way Leo did."

In all probability, though, the story is only wishful thinking on the part of the Cubs who heard and repeated it.

Banks was, after all, the boy who never complained about the poverty and segregation in which he was raised.

He was the dutiful son who, rather than argue with his mother, gave up playing football.

He was the teenager whose friends called him Casper the Ghost because of his ability to melt away at the first sign of trouble.

He was the batter who never questioned, or even looked back at, an umpire after a questionable call.

He was the father who said, "I'm gone," got in his car, and drove away at the first sign of family discord.

He was the black man who refused to engage in the great public struggle over race during the time of his greatest celebrity.

He was the player who never once complained about wasting his finest seasons with a team that had no hope of winning a pennant.

So it seems highly unlikely that Banks would change the habits of a lifetime, the very essence of who he was, at this stage of his life.

And besides, he had a perfect understanding of all that transpired between Durocher and himself.

"It was him," he said, "not me."

Chapter 24

"This Is Not an Eighth-Place Team"

The 1966 season began with Leo Durocher comparing the Cubs' roster favorably to those of the New York Giants of 1951 and 1954, which he managed to National League pennants. It ended with the Cubs winning fifty-nine games and losing 103, which tied the record set in 1962 as the worst performance in the team's history, and finishing tenth and last in the National League standings.

"That was my fault," Blake Cullen says of Durocher's preseason quote, "This is not an eighth-place team," which was roundly mocked when the Cubs lost eight of their first nine games and sank into last place. "Rip Collins told me to write the press guide, and I was trying to think what Leo would say and how he would say it. When the press guide came out, Leo said, 'Where did you get this quote?' I said, 'I don't know, Skip. I'll find out who did it.' Of course, the writers had a field day with it, saying Leo was right, it was *not* an eighth-place team, it was a tenth-place team. I've always been sort of proud that I came up with Leo's second most famous line."

All season long, the Cubs were laughingstocks as they traveled around the league, and Durocher's detractors wallowed in their enjoyment of his misery. "Welcome back, Leo. How is it down there?" a headline in the *Los Angeles Herald-Examiner* asked when the Cubs arrived for a series against the Dodgers. Later in the season, the paper ran "Leo's timetable," comparing the Cubs' record to that of the New York Mets the year before when they won just fifty-one games.

Some Chicago baseball enthusiasts have playfully called the 1966 Cubs the best tenth-place team ever assembled, as Ron Santo and Billy Williams each drove in more than ninety runs, Don Kessinger and Glenn Beckert hit .274 and .287 respectively, Randy Hundley caught 149 games, the most ever by a rookie catcher, and Banks came on strong in the second half. And, in fact, the Cubs did finish somewhere in the middle of most of the National League's batting statistics.

But their pitching was another story, as none of their starters or top relief pitchers won more games than they lost. Dick Ellsworth, who had won fifty games the previous three seasons, led the league in defeats with a record of 8–22 while Ken Holtzman, who was in his rookie year, led the team in victories with a modest mark of 11–16. The Cubs' pitching staff finished last in earned run average and gave up more hits, runs, and home runs than any other team in the league. During one six-game stretch in June, the team used a total of twenty-four pitchers and gave up forty-nine runs. To add to the humiliation, the Cubs finished last in the league in attendance at 635,891, and on a wet and chilly afternoon near the end of September they drew only 961 fans to Wrigley Field, the smallest crowd of the season in baseball.

As might have been expected, Durocher did not respond well to his team's performance. "Leo was tougher than a night in jail," says Ferguson Jenkins, who was traded to the Cubs early in the season. "We'd have a meeting every day and it got to the point where we'd take batting practice after games on the road. We'd get shut out and he'd say, 'Go get dressed, boys. We're taking BP.' He'd make the other team leave the lights on and the pitchers would be out there shagging fly balls or running the bases." By the time the team got back to its hotel, the restaurant would often be closed, room service would have shut down, and the players would go to bed hungry. "We were all pissed off," Jenkins says. "But we did it and nobody argued about it, either."

Durocher was unorthodox in other ways, too, warning Chicago sportswriters before the season, "Don't be surprised at some of the moves I make, because I'll try anything." "Anything" included benching

Kessinger, moving Santo to shortstop and Banks to third—an experiment that ended quickly—and trying to make a catcher out of John Boccabella. Durocher also made public the fines he assessed players for dropping fly balls or not running the bases aggressively. When Joe Amalfitano failed to score from third on a ball that bounced over the pitcher's head in a game in Philadelphia, Durocher asked him what he thought his fine should be. "Joe said two hundred dollars," Durocher said. "I told him it would be one hundred dollars because I appreciated his frankness."

Durocher's efforts to control the Cubs, to insist that things be done his way, often materialized inning-by-inning and even pitch-by-pitch. And if it meant embarrassing a player in front of his teammates, so much the better.

"How in the hell could you take that pitch?!" he would roar at Santo from the dugout. "It was right down the middle!"

"Why did you throw that guy a high fastball?!" he'd yell at Holtzman, who shouted back, "Because I threw him a high fastball last time and struck him out."

"Why did you call for a curveball?!" he would shout at Hundley in the dugout after an opposing batter hit a home run. "I want an answer!"

"In his first year, Leo would tell Hundley to argue with the umpires," says Williams. He'd say, "Go get on them so you can make them mad enough so I can come out and protect you." This was, Williams says, Durocher's way of trying to make Hundley the Cubs' field leader.

"My first year, he absolutely drove me nuts," Hundley says. "I can't begin to tell you the times he would holler at me on the field. He'd want to call a pitch—up and in on one guy, low and away on another—and he would throw towels out on the field to get my attention. I thought, if this is major league baseball, you can take it and shove it."

One night in Philadelphia, Durocher became so angry at Hundley that he jumped up and hit his head on the low dugout ceiling. "We were all laughing about it after the game," Hundley says. "He's upstairs in the training room dealing with the cut on his bald head after the game."

Durocher's impulsiveness did occasionally work to the team's benefit, though. When Kessinger got off to a slow start at the plate, he reminded the manager of his switch-hitting experiment and suggested he try it full-time the following season. But Durocher told him to start batting from both sides of the plate immediately, and his hitting quickly improved. "I think the second half of the year I hit a little over .300," says Kessinger, whose .274 average for the season was a personal best. "It took a lot of courage for him to do that and it enhanced my career."

But even when he was helping a player, Durocher only went so far. Kessinger was an All-Star shortstop and a more than adequate hitter, but his impassive demeanor on the field and in the locker room were at odds with the way Durocher liked his players to carry themselves, and he made it clear over the years that Kessinger was never one of his favorite players. "He wanted guys with fire in their belly," says Chuck Shriver. "So he didn't like Kessinger particularly, the same way he didn't like Ernie."

Nor did Durocher attempt to control himself off the field. "We were having a drink in the Netherland Hotel in Cincinnati and some lady gets up and starts singing," says Cullen, who, as the team's traveling secretary, had been told by John Holland to keep an eye on Durocher. "She wasn't a paid singer, just someone from the audience, and she wasn't very good." Annoyed at having his own conversation interrupted, Durocher stopped the music, and every other sound in the bar, by shouting, "Throw her a fish!"

"Oh, Lord, here we go," Cullen thought as the woman and her angry-looking escort came over to their table. But before the man could confront Durocher, the woman said, "You're Leo Durocher. When I was a little girl, I used to stand outside the Polo Grounds, and I used to see you. Do you remember me?"

"I don't remember you, dear," Durocher replied, "but the dress is familiar." The couple laughed and walked away.

As the 1966 season drew to a merciful end, the Cubs realized something drastic had to be done. So John Holland announced they were prepared to do something drastic indeed: trade Billy Williams.

"I had my bags packed and was ready to go," Williams said. "If they want to trade you, there is nothing you can do to stop it."

Though his batting average fell from over .300 the previous two years to .276 in 1966, Williams hit twenty-nine home runs and drove in ninety-one runs. It was his sixth excellent season in a row, he hadn't missed a game in three years, and he continued to play well in left field. But with the Cubs unwilling to break up their infield—and with Banks, at the age of thirty-five, not a factor in the trade market—Williams, who was twenty-eight, was their most marketable commodity.

Holland's public announcement brought other teams running, but the only serious contender was the Baltimore Orioles. They offered several players, but not the one the Cubs wanted most—a promising young slugger in their minor league system named Mike Epstein—and the deal foundered. Just a few months later, the Orioles could have kicked themselves when Epstein left the team early in the 1967 season rather than be sent down to the minors, and they were forced to trade him to the Washington Senators for Pete Richert, a pitcher who remained with them for seven years but was hardly the player Williams was. Epstein went on to have a decent career, hitting 130 home runs in nine years, but Williams hit many more than that in the remaining ten years of his career, and the Cubs could only shudder at the idea of how close they came to losing him. "It turned out to be the best deal I never made," Durocher said.

The Cubs did add a few players as the season ended: Al Spangler, a thirty-three-year-old outfielder who came in a trade with the California Angels, and pitchers Joe Niekro and Ray Culp and outfielder Ted Savage. But as they entered the 1967 season, they couldn't point to many changes in their lineup from their historically bad season the year before— certainly none that would indicate how quickly things were about to change.

V

THE BEST OF TIMES, THE WORST OF TIMES

Chapter 25

"Change the Flag!"

The ball had barely settled into Al Spangler's glove in right field for the final out when the fans made their charge. They leaped over barriers separating them from the field, dodged ushers and security guards, and ran out onto the grass in celebration. The Cubs players escaped the onslaught by racing to their locker room under the left-field stands. The fans who remained in their seats, and in the standing-room areas behind them, clogged the aisles and the ramps between the two levels of the old ballpark and shouted with delight as a few police officers and ushers tried to tackle the interlopers on the field.

One young man who remained apart from the general mayhem stripped to the waist and began running around imaginary bases in an outfield covered from foul line to foul line with newspapers, game programs, and paper cups. He slid into each base, jumped up, and then raced toward the next one. "He did his own umpiring," said Leo Durocher, who was watching from inside the locker room door that opened out onto the outfield. "Every time, he was safe. I'll never forget it."

"Look at them, forty thousand people and they won't leave," said Randy Hundley as he peeked out the door. "Hey, don't you guys know we're only playing one game today?" he shouted. "The game's over."

"Don't go out there," said Ron Santo, who, accompanied by several policemen and ushers, had had to fight his way through the crowd after a post-game interview in the broadcast booth upstairs. "I'm lucky to get back here alive."

"Did you see them?" Billy Williams said as he held a cup of beer. "Hanging on the television stand, sitting on top of the roofs across the street. I wish this was champagne in here."

"I think they want a sacrifice," said Glenn Beckert. "We're going to have to sacrifice one center fielder," and he pointed to Adolfo Phillips, the Cubs regular at the position. Phillips declined but Dick Radatz, the Cubs' hulking relief pitcher, charged back out onto the field wearing an army helmet with his arms raised above his head in a V for victory signal.

Rookie pitcher Rich Nye went to the clubhouse door to take a look and returned shaking his head. "If we never win another game..." he said, and left his words hanging in the air.

Another Cubs pitcher, who had recently been recalled from the Texas League for his fourteenth and last major league season, might have had the best frame of reference for the noise that continued to rain down from the stands above. It reminded him, Don Larsen said, of the day at Yankee Stadium eleven years earlier when he had thrown the only perfect game in the history of the World Series.

In the upper-deck stands behind home plate came another cry from spectators who had earlier spotted Ernie Banks wearing a headset in the broadcast booth, where he had spent the game offering commentary after being spiked in the heel in a play at first base a day earlier by Cincinnati Reds outfielder Pete Rose. The injury had been Banks's fault— he had left his foot hanging too far over the base and Rose had almost twisted his ankle trying to avoid him—and Rose's apology was sincere. But the fans in Wrigley Field would make his life miserable whenever he appeared there for the rest of his career.

And then there was another cheer, which started in the left-field bleachers and quickly spread to every corner of the ballpark. "Change the flag! Change the flag!" came the shout. It continued for many minutes until the Cubs' grounds crew, which usually waited until some hours after the game before changing the position of the flags that flew above the center-field scoreboard to signify the current National League standings, set things right. Down the flags came and, moments later, up they went again, the one carrying the word CHICAGO above all the others. "Once in our lifetime, we wanted to see the Cubs' flag on top," says Mike Murphy, a member of a group of fans who gathered daily in the left-field bleachers and called themselves the Bleacher Bums.

Listening to the cheers in the locker room, many of the Cubs, led by Ferguson Jenkins, who had allowed just three hits and also hit a double and a triple in a 4–1 victory over the Reds, went back out onto the field and watched the flag go up. It was July 2, 1967, and the Cubs were tied for first place in the National League.

There was a different feeling when the Cubs began spring training in Scottsdale, Arizona, in 1967, and it began with the pitching. Jenkins, who had been converted to a starter during the previous season with indifferent results, suddenly showed signs of adapting to his new role. In his first exhibition game, he struck out five San Francisco Giants, including Willie Mays and Willie McCovey. "The ball's just jumping out of my hand," he said. "He's learned how to pitch," said Durocher. Ken Holtzman, who had pitched his near no-hitter against Sandy Koufax and the Dodgers at the end of the previous season, was just twenty-one years old, and though he had a National Guard commitment that would force him to miss more than half the season, the Cubs had every reason to believe he would continue to improve. Rich Nye, who had pitched well after moving from the University of California baseball team to the minors the previous summer, was also put into the starting rotation, as were new arrivals Joe Niekro and Ray Culp.

Perhaps reacting to the anticipated improvement of his pitching staff, or perhaps because his young catcher had passed his test, Durocher eased off Hundley. "You're my general on the field," the manager told him. "If you need anything, you come to me. I will back you up." Durocher was as good as his word as his hollering from the dugout and throwing towels to get Hundley's attention ceased. "Holy cow, this is certainly different from last year," Hundley thought. "I certainly welcomed it because he just drove me nuts." Hundley responded with a superb season, hitting .300 in the first half, handling the Cubs pitchers with confidence and playing in all but ten of the team's games.

One thing that did not change during this promising spring was Durocher's campaign to get rid of Banks. The manager simply ignored him, refusing to let him play in any early exhibition games and saying John Boccabella would get a "good shot" at the position. That plan lasted six days as Boccabella hit only singles, and Durocher, forever impatient, moved on, sending Lee Thomas, Clarence Jones, and Norm Gigon out to play first base one after the other. One Chicago writer called this parade "further evidence that Ernie Banks is likely to be in the background this year."

But Durocher had another scheme to force him into retirement. Banks, he said, was now a coach. He "would still play a lot of baseball for us," Durocher said, but few were fooled. Banks, who wasn't consulted about his new position and didn't even learn about it until shortly before it was made public, was given no particular assignments, nor did he ever perform any duties as a coach. It was clear that this was just one more gambit to push him aside. Once again, Banks held his tongue. "I'm very happy about it," he said. "I'm looking forward to working with the younger players. It's all very gratifying."

Banks was more forthcoming about a trip to Europe he and Eloyce had taken during the off-season. "Florence," he said. "What a city! It's paradise for women but purgatory for men. All those shops. And just imagine, fifteen years ago I'm a kid in Dallas and there I was in Vienna—eating goose liver with violin and gypsy music in the background." The highlight of the trip was an audience with Pope Paul VI at the Vatican, which was arranged by the pope's translator, Paul Marcinkus, a Chicago priest and lifelong Cubs fan who years later would become president of the Vatican Bank and be implicated in financial scandals that created headlines around the world. "He asked about Kessinger, Beckert, and Santo, all the guys," Banks said. "He said he listened to the Holtzman-Koufax game on shortwave radio and was hoping Holtzman would get the no-hitter." Marcinkus explained Banks's occupation to the pope, who replied, "You are very famous."

———

As his search for a first baseman floundered, Durocher finally returned to Banks, who ended all discussion. With seven exhibition games left to play, he was hitting .419, and reporters wondered if he would be in the opening day lineup after all. "It all depends on my grandfather over there," Durocher said, but when Banks had eight hits, including six in a row, in three exhibition games late in the spring, he had no choice. A week before the season opened, Durocher announced Banks would be at first base on opening day. "Old Grandpa blasting away," one reporter wrote when Banks hit two home runs in the first three games of the season. "Leo Durocher leads the league in ill-advised remarks," another writer noted. But Durocher hadn't given up. Despite Banks's good start, he found himself being platooned with Clarence Jones until the end of April, at which point Jones had only two hits in thirteen at-bats. Banks played the rest of the season at first base while Jones finished the season in the minors. After two at-bats with the Cubs the following year, his major league career was over.

By the end of June, Banks was hitting .310 and had fifteen home runs and forty-four runs batted in. It was his fastest start since his Most Valuable Player years almost a decade earlier, and some observers thought he was playing first base as well as he was hitting. "Banks at his advanced age is incredible," one wrote. Banks was exultant, too. "I can't remember when I hit like I'm hitting now," he said. "It's a lot of fun to be young again."

Banks credited his resurgence to losing a few pounds and to abandoning the light bat that had served him so well for so long. "It forces me to take a more rhythmic swing," he said of his new thirty-six-ounce bat. "I don't swing so hard now." The bigger bat helped Banks concentrate on just meeting the ball rather than trying to pull it, counting on pitches that strayed into the inner part of the strike zone to provide him with home runs. Banks finished the season with a .276 batting average, twenty-three home runs, and ninety-five runs batted in. Once again, he had followed a mediocre season that encouraged speculation his career was coming to an end with one that defied actuarial charts and his manager's wish to get rid of him.

A few opposing managers also needed convincing, and Banks counted a game against the New York Mets at Wrigley Field on June 9 as one of his most satisfying of the season. With the scored tied, 5–5, in the ninth and Williams and Beckert on base, the Mets' manager Wes Westrum ordered Lee Thomas walked to bring up Banks with the bases loaded. Banks responded to this effrontery by singling in the winning run. Other managers had no doubts, however. "The one reason why the Cubs are in the first division," said Walt Alston of the Los Angeles Dodgers, "is Ernie Banks."

Just as Banks sneaked up on the National League in 1967, so did the Cubs. As May gave way to June, they were winning about as many games as they were losing and were firmly embedded in fifth place. Five victories in seven games on the road in the middle of June raised their record to 34–28 and lifted them to third place, five and a half games behind the league-leading St. Louis Cardinals. They then returned to Wrigley Field for twelve games none of them would ever forget.

On June 23, the Cubs beat the Houston Astros, 9–8, on a pinch-hit single by Thomas in the ninth inning. Banks hit his twelfth home run of the season.

On June 24, they beat the Astros 3–2, after a two-hour rain delay. Santo hit a two-run home run and Jenkins struck out ten batters. Banks doubled and scored a run.

On June 25, they won a doubleheader, 4–1 and 8–0, as Hands and Niekro allowed a total of eight hits. Banks finished the day with five hits, two home runs, and two standing ovations. "It makes you feel like a kid again," he said.

On June 26, they beat the Philadelphia Phillies 4–2, on home runs by Williams and Santo. Banks doubled and scored a run. It was the Cubs' seventh win in a row, their longest winning streak since 1954, Banks's first full season with the Cubs.

On June 27, the streak ended with a 4–2 loss to the Phillies, but the Cubs immediately started another one with their third sweep of a double-header at Wrigley Field on June 28 as Jenkins pitched his ninth complete game against Pittsburgh and Culp pitched a three-hitter.

On June 29, Banks hit a two-run home run in a 4–3 win over the Pirates. On June 30, Santo and Williams hit home runs in a 7–5 win over the Reds.

On July 1, the largest crowd of the season to date, 31,833, showed up to see the Cubs beat the Reds, but that figure was topped the following day when 40,644 showed up to see the Cubs close out a home stand in which they won eleven of twelve games and moved into a tie for first place.

Chicago's reaction to the Cubs' resurrection was a mixture of hysteria and wonder. After Banks's home run beat the Pirates on June 29, he was told that several hundred fans outside the ballpark were yelling, "We want Ernie!" With a grin, Banks pretended to brush his hair with his hands and straightened his sweater, then walked outside to find police holding back a crowd composed largely of screaming youngsters. He escaped ten minutes later when his car was brought to a side entrance. Other players were warned to wait inside until the mob dispersed, and those who made a run for it were besieged by autograph seekers.

"Home of the National League champions," trainmen on the L told joyous fans arriving at Wrigley Field, while the Chicago Police Department sent detectives wearing Bermuda shorts to the right-field bleachers at the base of the scoreboard near seats occupied by members of a suspected gambling ring. "They were old guys in strap undershirts with cigars in the corner of their mouths," says John Schulian, who was in the army at Fort Sheridan, north of Chicago. "Right out of Central Casting." Their bets sometimes exceeded one hundred dollars, Sergeant Joseph Shaughnessy reported, and the gamblers bet on everything imaginable: innings when runs would score, balls and strikes, curveballs or fastballs, and the performance of individual players, as well as the outcome of the games. Seven men were arrested, including the alleged ringleader, an investigator for the Illinois Department of Revenue.

Cubs mania even reached City Hall, where the installation of a large, odd-looking statue by Pablo Picasso on the plaza outside the Civic Center was provoking a puzzled response. Was it a bird? A woman? A dog? Alderman John Hoellen called it an ugly hunk of iron and introduced a resolution demanding that it be shipped back to France and replaced by one of a true Chicago hero, Ernie Banks. The *Chicago American* responded with a cartoon of a huge statue of Banks looming over tiny citizens walking through the Civic Center.

Perhaps not surprisingly, the Cubs' front office was unprepared for this excitement. Even as the games were selling out, the team persisted in its tradition of Ladies' Day and, on the final game of the triumphant home stand, it promoted a Family Day on which fathers paid $1.50, mothers a dollar, and children fifty cents if they arrived as a family. The result was 10,000 people without children crowding the streets around the ballpark unable to buy tickets.

Two weeks later, the Cubs returned home from a road trip that had ended with three consecutive victories in San Francisco and were startled to discover hundreds of fans waiting to greet them at O'Hare Airport. Some carried signs reading, "Yea, Cubs, World Champions" and "Pennant Fever." As the crowd surged in for autographs, Durocher took a stray elbow to the stomach, while Lou Boudreau, who had been a part of a World Series celebration in Cleveland, called it the most hysterical crowd he'd ever seen. "I've never seen anything like it," said Eloyce Banks, who had come to the airport to pick up her husband.

Banks responded to being in first place midway through the season for the first time in his career with delight. On July 5, when he was named to his tenth National League All-Star team, he said he planned to enjoy it more than any of the others. "The general topic of conversation at All-Star Games among the players is the pennant race, and before I never had much to say," he said. "But this time I'm going to have a chance to talk."

The dream unraveled slowly. The Cubs won the first game after their glorious home stand, beating the Braves, 12–6, in Atlanta, which gave them their second seven-game win streak and fourteen victories in their last fifteen games. They then lost seven in a row to the Braves and Houston Astros, more consecutive defeats than they had suffered even in the disastrous 1966 season. A drop in the fan-fueled adrenaline they felt in Wrigley Field might have been partly responsible for this decline, but some suspected that Durocher, with his insistence on playing for the moment and dismissing all consideration of the long road ahead, was pushing his players too hard. Hundley, for instance, caught every inning of seventy-three consecutive games. Not until the Cubs lost their seventh in a row in Houston did Durocher finally give him a day off.

Beginning with the three victories in San Francisco at the end of the road trip, the Cubs rebounded with seven wins in eight games, and as late as the first of August they were only three and a half games behind the first-place Cardinals. They then lost nine of their next ten games and were done. They finished in third place, fourteen games behind the Cardinals, who won the World Series as Lou Brock hit .414, with two home runs, five runs batted in, and seven stolen bases.

Still, the Cubs finished in the first division for the first time since 1946, which gave them World Series shares of their own, $1,080.88 per player, and instilled in them the belief that better days were ahead. Banks, Williams, Hundley, Santo, Beckert, and Phillips all had fine years at the plate, and the young pitching staff had shown great promise. Jenkins had the first of what would be six straight seasons with twenty or more victories; Holtzman, who was limited to twelve starts because of his military commitment, won nine of them without a loss; and Nye and Niekro won thirteen and ten games respectively.

The Cubs' fan base reacted in kind as attendance climbed to 977,226, a gain of more than 50 percent over the year before. Mere numbers, however, don't begin to tell the story.

Chapter 26

Bleacher Bums

Howard Herbon was sitting in his usual spot in the left-field bleachers when he decided the time was right. The Cubs were in the middle of their magical 1967 home stand, Wrigley Field was filled with delirious fans, and those near Herbon were happy to help unroll his sign. "MEL ROACH FAN CLUB," it said, in large blue letters spray painted onto a bedsheet, and while only the savviest Cubs fans understood the reference, Ron Santo, who was standing at third base, doubled over in laughter.

"Not only was Roach one of the worst players the Cubs ever had," Mike Murphy says of the utility man who had five hits in forty-two at-bats in twenty-three games for the Cubs in 1961, "the name itself was funny back then, when marijuana was starting to get out to the bleachers and everybody knew what a roach was."

Delighted with Santo's response, Herbon returned to the garage in his suburban Morton Grove home and made another sign. "HIT THE BLEACHER BUM," it said. Herbon's wife, Doris, cut a hole in the middle and sewed a fringe around it to keep it from ripping. The Herbons were part of a group of fans who had been gathering in the left-field bleachers for several seasons, and Howard knew just the man to wear his new sign. "Here, Ronnie, put this on," Herbon told Ron Grousl the following day. Grousl put his head through the hole and, while the Cubs were at bat, stood up in the crowded bleachers for everyone to see.

"Billy Williams or Ernie Banks would come to bat and Ronnie would stand and the fans next to him would pull the sign out so you could read it," says Jack Herbon, Howard's son. "What greater love can a fan have than to sacrifice his face for a Cubs' home run?" Murphy says. The Cubs' winning streak had brought a large number of photographers to Wrigley Field, and one of them zoomed in on Grousl standing bare-chested in the middle of the sign and holding a bat in each hand. The picture ran in newspapers throughout the country the following day, and the Bleacher Bums were born.

Though Grousl was the Bleacher Bums' leader, nobody knew much about him. One story was that he was on unemployment. Another was that he didn't even have a Social Security card. Yet a third was that he'd once had a job riding bikes off the assembly line at the original Schwinn bicycle factory on Chicago's West Side, where to avoid monotony he rode clockwise in the morning and counterclockwise in the afternoon. One day, it was said, he went to lunch and never returned.

Grousl's dubious finances didn't prevent him from being generous, though. Sometimes, he would buy out the entire inventory of a vendor selling Wrigley Field's signature Frosty Malts and give one to everyone around him. "Back then, they cost twenty-five cents," says Jack Herbon. "He just started tossing them to the crowd." Grousl also enjoyed his celebrity in other ways. Occasionally during the seventh-inning stretch, he would put on a turban and, as fans chanted "Swami! Swami!," make predictions through a battery-powered megaphone. One constant prediction was that the Cubs would win the World Series.

Grousl controlled the membership of the Bleacher Bums, handing out gold metal cards he'd had made to about fifty people. Some of them acquired nicknames, such as Foghorn Ralph, whose voice could be heard all over the ballpark, Cheap Earl, Spider Man, Larry the Rebel, Race Track Stanley, Wild Bill Duncan, and Captain Hook. In deference to the

Herbons' advanced age—they were in their forties—Howard was called Big Daddy and Doris was Ma Barker.

———

Mike Murphy was intimidated by Grousl and his friends, who always sat in the same spot in the bleachers, behind the "368" sign painted on the brick wall in left field. They were older than he was and tough city kids who hung together, whereas he was a shy youngster from the suburbs who came to Wrigley Field alone. But in late September 1966, as Murphy sat off to the side away from the group, he screwed up his courage and pulled out the bugle he had bought years ago for two dollars at a junk shop. There was hardly anyone in the ballpark to see the Cubs finish their disastrous first season under Leo Durocher, so Murphy was fairly conspicuous when he stood up and began to play notes he had first heard on a late-night broadcast from Dodger Stadium on a transistor radio he kept under his pillow.

Da-da-DA-da-da/DA-da-da/da-da-da-DAAA, Murphy played, and the sound ricocheted through the all but empty ballpark. "It was echoing back from the grandstands and the box seats, off all that concrete," says Murphy, who was startled at what he had done. Grousl was tickled at the absurdity of it—the "Charge!" theme being played before the mopiest of Cubs teams with so few fans to respond to it. "Hey, come over here," Grousl told Murphy, and suddenly he was officially a Bum and with a nickname to prove it: Bugles Murphy.

———

The Bleacher Bums came of age in 1967 and, as Wrigley Field began filling up when the Cubs began winning, the Bums were a major attraction as well. They sang songs, such as "Give Me That Old-Time Durocher" ("If he's good enough for Santo, he's good enough for me"). And "Mine eyes have seen the glory of the coming of the Cubs" ("They are trampling down the Cardinals with their balls and bats and gloves"). And, later on, "We've Got the World Series in Our Hands."

They also borrowed the civil rights anthem "We Shall Overcome" on occasion and, as the black power movement gained prominence, they even adapted a chant from the Black Panthers for their own use.

Abeebee!

Ungowa!

Cub Powuh!

They had other moments of inspiration, such as the day Hank Aaron hit a home run into the bleachers and Grousl picked up the ball, looked at it for a second, then threw it as hard as he could, all the way back to the infield. "I don't want no fucking enemy home run ball," he said. "The crowd went nuts," Murphy says. "They couldn't believe what they had just seen. This was when getting a baseball was a big deal. What Ronnie did was crazy, but of course it's global now." Soon, the Bums were chanting "Throw it back!" to anyone who caught an opposing player's home run hit, and the entire ballpark was joining in. Even opponents' batting practice home runs were being thrown back onto the field.

The Bums conducted precarious parades along the top of the outfield wall, which was no more than eighteen inches wide, as Murphy played "Reveille," "The Call to the Post," "You're in the Army Now," and, inevitably, "Charge!" "There would be ten of us and we'd have ten beers under our belts," Murphy says. "At first, we'd get up on the wall and dance and I'd play music. But we got tired of just standing there so we started marching. We'd go from left center to the 400-foot sign in center to the '368' sign in right center and we'd turn around and come back again. We're walking and singing right when the ball game is going on. Can you imagine that today?"

Mercifully, few Bums fell from the wall, one exception coming when Grousl slipped as the Cubs were winning a doubleheader from the Phillies in July 1969. "He didn't get hurt," Don Alger, one of the original Bums, said. "He more or less floated to the ground." Cubs left fielder Willie Smith forever endeared himself to the Bums by boosting Grousl back up into the stands before security guards could apprehend him.

After games, the fans began hanging onto the wall with their hands and dropping the few remaining feet to the ground. "They were flooding the field and intercepting the players on their way to the clubhouse," says Phil Regan. "Some of them started grabbing everybody's stuff. Hundley came in one day minus his shin guards."

Despite the danger, the Cubs waited until 1970 before stretching a wire basket out from the top of the wall to keep the fans off the field. Not every Cub was happy about the change. "I gave up nine or ten home runs to that stupid net," Ferguson Jenkins says. The Cubs also built a concrete pyramid on top of the wall to foil the marchers. "We contemplated making a wooden box with a triangle cut in it so we could at least sit on the wall," Murphy says, "but nobody was that industrious."

The Bums rented buses and took road trips to Cincinnati, Pittsburgh, and St. Louis, where they would stay in the team hotel, sometimes as many as ten in a single room. "The safest place to sleep was in the bathtub," Murphy says. "You didn't want to be sleeping on the floor and get stepped on by the drunks coming in. The only downside was some joker would get up at six in the morning and turn on the hot water in the shower."

Looking back, they marvel at how they were allowed to sit in the bars of the most elegant hotels, looking like ragamuffins in their T-shirts and cutoff jeans and nursing their twenty-five-cent beers. But they were accepted by the players as well as the Cubs manager. "Hey, Bleacher Bums," Durocher said one evening in the Tack Room, the bar at the Chase Park Plaza Hotel in St. Louis as he pulled out a twenty-dollar bill and threw it on the table. "Tonight, you drink on Leo."

"All us combined probably didn't have that much money," Murphy says. "We drank all night on that twenty dollars."

A few of the most intrepid Bums accompanied the Cubs to spring training in Arizona, where the setting was more relaxed. They used their gold cards on unsuspecting ushers to get into exhibition games and even took part in the Cubs' morning practice sessions.

"Hey, Bleacher Bum, how come you're not out there shagging fly balls?" Ernie Banks asked Don Flynn one morning as he saw him standing near the left-field foul line at Scottsdale Stadium while other Bums were chasing balls hit to the outfield.

"I didn't bring a glove, Ernie," Flynn said.

"Hold on a minute," said Banks, who went to the locker room and returned with an old beat-up glove and tossed it to Flynn.

"It had probably been retired years ago," Flynn recalls, "but I got to go out and catch fly balls with Ernie Banks's glove."

Perhaps nobody took greater advantage of the Cubs' hospitality during the spring than Flynn's friend Tommy Foley, who, lacking the funds for even a shared hotel room, pitched a pup tent in left field. "When the grounds crew got there in the morning, they'd get on the loudspeaker and say, 'Okay, roll up the tent. Let's go,'" Flynn says.

But not every road trip was so innocuous. The Bums still tell the story of a trip to Cincinnati where Foghorn Ralph went to ground. "He didn't come home for two or three weeks," Murphy said, "and when he finally resurfaced he lost his job. After that, his wife wouldn't let him have anything to do with the Bleacher Bums. We held a reunion in 1989, and she wouldn't even let him come to that."

The Bums' raucous cheers for the Cubs made them conspicuous in other National League cities, particularly when Murphy played his bugle, and hometown fans were seldom amused. On one trip to St. Louis, they were pelted with paper cups, fruit, and other objects. "Luckily, they weren't selling beer in bottles," Murphy says, but the barrage gave Grousl an idea. He acquired a number of yellow hard hats, and when the Bums returned to St. Louis on a hot and humid Sunday afternoon in August 1968 and discovered a large crowd gathered outside Busch Stadium for the dedication of a statue of Stan Musial, he was ready.

"Cover me, boys," Grousl said as the ceremonies were ending. He worked his way through the crowd to the base of the statue and shimmied up to the top, where he took off his yellow hard hat and placed it on Musial's head. It was a perfect fit. "He was waving a Cubs flag," says Jack Herbon. "It was like the photo of Iwo Jima." Pandemonium ensued as Cardinals fans, outraged that a monument to their beloved hero should be so rudely defaced, sought out anyone in a yellow helmet, and fists began to fly. Fortunately, enough police were on hand to prevent serious injuries, and the Bums sneaked away, their helmets hidden in their shirts, where they remained during that afternoon's game.

In the end, the yellow helmets served less as protection than as identification, particularly when the wife of one of the Bums, a graphic artist, created a stencil for them using the psychedelic lettering made popular on the television show *Laugh-In*. "They were like our flags," Murphy says. "It said, 'I've got my helmet. I'm a Bleacher Bum and you're not.'"

The Bums had their own gathering place, Ray's Bleachers, a bar across the street from the right-field stands. It was owned by Ray Meyer, whose son, Little Ray, ran hot dogs to the ballpark before he became old enough to serve drinks. Inspired by Grousl's helmets, Meyer installed fifty pegs on a wall so the Bums wouldn't have to carry them home. "It was like a coffee shop where you have your own mug," Murphy says.

Meyer was a charter Bum himself, and he mixed business with pleasure when he made his Ballpark Special for friends in the bleachers. "He'd take a twelve-ounce Styrofoam cup, put in a shot of vodka, and top it off with lemonade and ice," Flynn says. "We'd be rolling back and forth to Ray's for refills. You could leave the ballpark during the game and come back in and nobody said a word. It was all so loosey-goosey then."

Buying beer in the ballpark was equally stress-free. "There was a sweetheart of a lady by the name of Clara who ran the beer concession under the center-field scoreboard," Flynn says. "Their inventory was based on the number of cups they used, but she'd give us refills. Of course, we tipped her well."

When the games were over, fans jammed Ray's Bleachers, which accommodated no more than fifty people at best. An hour or so later, the bar would be left mostly to the Bums and their friends, and before long Cubs players began dropping by. Santo, Jenkins, Glenn Beckert, Dick Selma, and others all became close to Meyer and enjoyed winding down over a beer and chatting with the Bums. Not surprisingly, the one player who did not frequent Ray's Bleachers was Banks. "He never came in,"

Murphy says. "It was the same thing on the road. We took a couple of dozen road trips in four years, and we never saw Ernie in the lobby of the hotel unless he was getting on the team bus or he was going to his room after a game. Sometimes I wondered if he had any friends."

As the Bleacher Bums continued to attract attention, they found themselves becoming celebrities. Chicago sportswriters mingled with them during games, and soon reporters from around the country began appearing in the bleachers. The Bums were featured in articles in the *New York Times, Wall Street Journal,* and other newspapers and became such a phenomenon that the press began looking for new ways to pursue the story. Food editors came to sample the cuisine in the bleachers. Theater writers showed up to compare the Bums' antics to the offerings in the city's playhouses. "One paper sent its architecture writer, who asked me how I liked the way the bleachers were conformed," Murphy says. "I said, 'What?' Pretty soon, we were turning down interviews so we could watch the game."

But despite this adulation, or perhaps because of it, the Bums created hard feelings and drew angry protests from opposing players who thought they sometimes crossed all barriers of good fun, and even decency. Cardinals outfielder Curt Flood said the Bums threw batteries, ball bearings, marbles, chicken bones, and even bras from a few women in the stands. "They were *mean*," says Dodgers pitcher Mudcat Grant, pointing to a missing upper molar. "Here's the tooth they knocked out when they threw a hard rubber handball at me. Fortunately, one of my teammates saw who it was, and I fired it back at him and hit him right in the sternum. He went down."

One of the Bums' missiles, a baseball, hit Reds pitcher José Peña in the face while he was climbing the stairs to the visitors' locker room after a game in 1969. Pena suffered a broken nose and was badly shaken, which caused Banks, who was writing an occasional column for the *Chicago Tribune,* to chastise the Bums and ask for "a little kindness for the players on the other teams. After all, some of them may become Cubs some day!"

Sitting in Ray's Bleachers after a game against the Braves one afternoon in June 1969, Grousl hatched a plan to attack Hank Aaron, who he thought had slid too hard into Beckert at second base. Leading the Bums outside and finding the Braves boarding their bus, Grousl yelled, "Hey, Aaron, this is from Glenn Beckert!" and threw his gin and tonic in his face. With drops of moisture dripping from his face onto his elegant suit, Aaron angrily took two steps toward Grousl, and the Bums scattered. "I never ran so fast in my life," says Jack Herbon. "We were all wearing our Bleacher Bums helmets and yelling, 'Hank Aaron's after us.' Grousl was running like an Olympic sprinter."

The Bums were also fixated on Pete Rose, whom they had never forgiven for spiking Banks in 1967. "Rosie! Rosie!" and "Rose is a fairy!" they chanted, and they hung a mannequin of the Reds outfielder from the left-field wall. Rose responded to these insults by pretending to make an easy catch in left field look difficult, then turning around, holding up his glove, and grinning at the Bums. During warm-ups in the outfield the next day, Rose was showered with hot dogs provided by Meyer. "I guess we threw about a dozen," Flynn says. "Pete laughed and picked a few up and threw them back at us." Hot dogs weren't the only objects thrown in Rose's direction. Rick Monday, who played for the Cubs in the early 1970s, said he once saw someone throw a crutch at Rose in left field. "You have to be a little off-center if you need a crutch to get around and you throw it at Pete Rose," Monday said.

The Bums also harassed the players about their off-the-field activities, purporting to know which of them had been out drinking the night before or had been seen in the company of a woman whose name they would shout. "Those fans in left field are crazy," Dodgers outfielder Willie Davis said after a game in May 1969. "They've been yelling at me for three years about a girl named Ruthie, and I don't know any girl by that name. They made me mad. I wanted to hit one right in the middle of them so bad." Davis accomplished his mission by hitting a game-tying home run off Jenkins in the sixth inning into the first row of the left-field bleachers and another in the twelfth to give the Dodgers the victory. After the second home run, Davis raised a middle finger to the Bums while rounding second base. "Willie Davis is telling the fans that he's number one," Jack Brickhouse told the Cubs' television audience.

Remarkably, none of the Bums can recall being ejected from a game or even receiving a warning. "There were only two security guards in the entire bleachers," Murphy says. "They had name tags—Officer Woods and Officer Scalaraga—and we became their best friends. Any time they walked into Ray's, the drinks were on us, and if they did occasionally chase us, they would always be one step behind and couldn't quite catch us." And in fact, Cubs management was so delighted by the publicity the Bums generated, and so tolerant of their excesses, that on one fateful weekend when the Cubs were riding high in 1969 it took them on the road trip of their lives, all expenses paid.

Chapter 27

In the World

Two things occurred in 1968 that set the stage for the great morality play Ernie Banks and the Cubs would become involved in the following year.

The first was the Cubs winning more games than they lost for the second straight season, the first time that had happened since 1946. The season bore none of the excitement of the one that preceded it, however, as the Cubs lost seven of their first ten games, had two five-game losing streaks and another of seven games in June alone, and one stretch when they were shut out for forty-eight consecutive innings, a National League record. Even when they went 21–11 in July and moved into second place, the Cubs remained a dozen or more games behind the St. Louis Cardinals, who breezed to their second straight National League pennant as Lou Brock led the league in doubles, triples, and stolen bases.

Still, there was reason for hope. Billy Williams and Ron Santo each drove in ninety-eight runs, Randy Hundley caught 160 games, and the pitching continued to improve as Ferguson Jenkins won twenty games, Bill Hands sixteen, Joe Niekro fourteen, and Ken Holtzman (whose season was interrupted ten times by his National Guard commitment) eleven. The Cubs won their last five games of the season to sneak into third place ahead of the Cincinnati Reds with a record of 84–78.

Also promising was the fact they beat the Cardinals seven times in a row in the last half of the season. "We began to believe we could beat them out for the pennant in '69," says Phil Regan, who won ten games out of the bullpen for the Cubs in 1968 and saved twenty-five.

The Cubs fans were believers, too. Despite the disappointing season, the team's attendance surpassed a million for the first time since 1952, the high point coming on July 28 when a crowd of 42,261, the Cubs' largest in twenty years, arrived at Wrigley Field for a doubleheader against the Dodgers. "There was no promotion, no gimmick, and not much of an opponent in the ninth-place, weak-hitting Dodgers," noted George Langford of the *Chicago Tribune*, and when the Cubs won both games in less than two and a half hours each, Banks couldn't help saying, "Let's play three."

Banks's batting average sank to .246 in 1968, his lowest mark since 1963, but a home run binge in the second half of the season gave him thirty-two for the season, his highest total since 1962, and third in the league behind Willie McCovey and Richie Allen. "It looks like Ernie is going to go on forever," Billy Williams said, and even Leo Durocher professed to being impressed. "Whatever he's taking," the manager said, "I want some myself."

The season had begun with Durocher calling something of a truce. "I've tried to retire him several times," he told reporters, "but Ernie just won't hold still for it. He's amazing. I wish I knew the secret of his youth." But when Durocher blamed the 9–2 loss to the Cardinals in May on Banks's inability to score from third on an infield grounder, it was an indication that he would never truly give up the fight.

On May 26, Banks hit two home runs against the Giants at Wrigley Field in a game that Willie Mays, claiming exhaustion, sat out. Asked about Mays's absence after the game, Banks drew a curious, almost wistful, comparison between the great Giants star's career and his own. "Don't forget that Willie has been playing under the pressure of pennant winners almost since the day he came to the majors," Banks said. "That takes a lot out of a guy. You sweat and grow tired, and you age. Until last year—and it didn't last too long, really—I have never known what that kind of pressure and tension can do to a guy."

He would soon find out.

The second transformative event Banks experienced in 1968 was a trip to Vietnam. The visit, which was arranged by the baseball commissioner's office, was not a series of quick-hit appearances at large, well-fortified bases. For sixteen days in November, Banks and Baltimore Orioles pitcher Pete Richert, New York Mets outfielder Ron Swoboda, and retired pitcher Larry Jackson rode in armed helicopters to as many as six or seven base camps a day, where they chatted with troops, who were amazed to see them.

"Why are you here?" one soldier asked Banks.

"Because you're here," he replied.

The players realized the danger they faced when they landed at a forward base north of Da Nang, which had been hit by rockets the night before. At another base they were told, "We haven't been attacked recently, but if mortars come in, roll over and pull the mattress over you."

As the best-known player on the tour, Banks was the center of attention wherever he went, and he responded enthusiastically. "If anybody batted a thousand on the trip it was Banks," said Al Fleishman, a St. Louis Cardinals' executive who made the trip. "When we walked into a hospital or a mess hall, Ernie simply took the place by storm." Wearing military fatigues and combat boots, Banks, Richert, and Fleishman split from the others, who went off on their own tour, and flew to the deck of a battleship, where, surrounded by soldiers, Banks stripped to the waist in order, he said, "to soak up a little sun."

The war was at its height then—the enemy's Tet Offensive had occurred earlier in the year—and Banks was surprised that men in such fraught circumstances wanted to talk about baseball. "Can you imagine?" he said. "They'd been on top of a hill where they'd been in battle and they ask you, 'Who's the toughest pitcher you ever faced?'" Banks was particularly moved when a sergeant who had lost his right leg during a battle just two weeks before he was to go home asked for his autograph. He asked for the soldier's autograph in return.

Banks returned home full of upbeat stories about the fine young soldiers he had seen. Many young people at home were shiftless by comparison, he told reporters. "He spent an entire day telling me about it," Eloyce said. "Ernie talked more that day than all he has said since we've been married."

But Banks had a deeper, darker response to his trip to Vietnam, which might have gone unrecorded but for an editor at the *Chicago Daily News*, who told the paper's correspondent in the country to travel with him and write some dispatches in Banks's name. "I thought, 'How stupid,'" Georgie Anne Geyer says of her reaction to the assignment. "'Be a ghost writer for a *baseball* player?' I was very young."

Whatever feeling Geyer had that accompanying Banks was beneath her—she was there to cover a war, after all—disappeared when she and Banks met. She quickly saw that watching soldiers respond to his visit was an excellent way to get a different look at the war and to elicit reactions that might otherwise remain hidden. What she did not understand was that Banks would tell her things to write in his name that he would not have said for himself.

Banks and Geyer quickly fell into a routine. At the end of each day, they would sit together and he would tell her what he had seen and what he thought about it. Geyer never suggested any topics—"I'm very serious about journalism, and when they told me to write through his eyes, I wrote through his eyes," she says—but Banks soon began addressing topics that could only have made the army brass wince.

Marijuana was everywhere, he said. "It's a way of life and everybody's got it. It's because you don't live the kind of life here which, when you finish cleaning your weapon, you just go to bed. You need something to assist you."

Black soldiers felt they weren't treated fairly, he said. Many of them had never received rest-and-recreation leaves. One had been busted in rank for something he hadn't done. Their officers sent them into danger zones unnecessarily. And they wouldn't mind having some black "donut dollies" to talk to among the young Red Cross volunteers who traveled around the country cheering up the troops.

Banks also expressed his concerns about being the only black player on the trip. "I went to the commissioner's office and told them, 'You people have built up this integration business,'" he said. "'I don't care who you send, just so you don't send Ho Chi Minh.'"

Banks also came to understand how the soldiers coped with the existential threat they lived under by developing their own language. "In the world," he said. "I picked up that phrase in Phu Bai up north where I first heard a couple of guys using it. To them, 'the world' means anyplace but here because this is the end of the world."

Banks saw how the danger of the soldiers' lives could elicit a kind of eloquence. "One kid said to me, 'Courage and fear are a little the same,'" he said in one dispatch. "Life has a flavor the protected will never know," he said in another. "The whole rhythm of life changes," he said in a third. "Each man's going through his own countdown until the day he gets on that freedom bird. It's different at home—there you don't want the days to pass."

Banks concluded Geyer's final story by saying, "I'm not disappointed in everything I saw in Vietnam. I'm not like a politician who's going to try to give any solution, when there is none. And I'm not going to go home and prop up my feet and talk about Vietnam, because everybody knows that it is a terrible war, that it is a slaughter. I know I'm not going to influence people one way or another. I just wanted to tell what I saw."

In later years, Geyer would occasionally visit Banks in Chicago, where they would tell war stories, including one he favored about how she had saved his life in Vietnam. "He had a cold," she says. "I think I gave him an aspirin."

Geyer's own career as a foreign correspondent took her around the world—to Eastern Europe, the Middle East, Africa, and the mountains in Guatemala, where she hid with guerilla fighters. And over the years, she interviewed Fidel Castro, Saddam Hussein, Yasser Arafat, Anwar Sadat, King Hussein of Jordan, Muammar Gaddafi, and the Ayatollah Khomeini. But nothing, she says, quite compared with the time she spent with Ernie Banks.

Back "in the world," Banks celebrated his thirty-eighth birthday in January, and shortly thereafter he reported to his sixteenth Cubs spring training camp, where he seemed sobered by the tenuous existence of the
young men he had seen in combat. "The end's coming," he told an interviewer. "I feel it. It scares me. It saddens me."

Chapter 28

"Break Out the Champagne"

Ernie Banks received four standing ovations on the first day of the 1969 season—one during pregame introductions, one when he took the field, and one after each of his two home runs.

It was the wildest opening day anyone could remember. The fans began lining up at eight a.m. for the 27,000 bleacher and grandstand seats that had been held back for game-day sale, and the 40,796 people who pushed their way into Wrigley Field—4,000 of whom had to stand—comprised the largest opening-day crowd in forty years. The sun broke through the clouds as the game began, and a chilly Chicago morning turned into a bright, sunny day. The spectators took off their coats and settled in to watch the Cubs play the Philadelphia Phillies.

Banks's three-run home run in the first inning put the Cubs ahead, 3–1, and his second, with a runner on base in the third inning, raised the lead to 5–1. It was the 476th of his career, sending him past Stan Musial into tenth place on the all-time home run list. Ferguson Jenkins protected the lead into the seventh inning when Don Money, the Phillies' rookie second baseman, hit a ball that just cleared the railing at the left-field foul pole. There was no doubt about Money's second home run, though, a three-run shot in the ninth that sailed over the left-field wall, bounced onto Waveland Avenue, and sent the game into extra innings. And when Money had yet another run-scoring hit, a double off Phil Regan in the eleventh inning, the Phillies led for the first time. Barry Lersch, another Phillies' rookie, had retired ten straight Cubs batters when Randy Hundley singled with one out in the eleventh and forced Leo Durocher to make a decision—let Jim Hickman bat or send up a left-handed pinch hitter.

———

Willie Smith's teammates adored him. A thirty-year-old outfielder and pinch hitter, Smith had joined the Cubs during the 1968 season, and his constant chatter and upbeat personality made him the life of the party. Smith was also an accomplished singer, who would burst into blues melodies at any given moment. "He'd start singing, laughing and kidding everybody," Banks said. "He'd get our minds off what we were thinking about and make us relax."

Smith was anything but relaxed when Durocher told him to pinch-hit, however. One of his practice swings was so energetic he got a cramp in his side and limped to the plate at a painful angle.

"Just hit a dying quail over third," Durocher said as Smith took Lersch's first pitch.

"Hell, Skip," said Bill Hands, who was sitting next to him, "he'll hit it out."

Which Smith did, hitting a hard line drive into the right-field bleachers to win the game, 7–6.

Pandemonium!

Cubs fans screamed with joy, jumped over the infield walls, and joined the players who had rushed from the dugout to greet Smith at home plate. Smith muscled his way through this reception committee to step on the plate and was spiked in his right big toe by one of his teammates. "He threw one I kind of liked," Smith said of Lersch's pitch once he made it to the safety of the clubhouse.

Sitting at his locker after the game, listening to the muffled noise of the fans who refused to leave the ballpark, Banks watched his teammates' joyful celebration and turned to the man next to him, who had made a rare trip from Dallas to be a part of it.

"This is a great life, ain't it, Daddy?" he said. "Thanks for making me a ballplayer."

"You're welcome, Ernie," Eddie Banks said. "Just keep it up."

"Those were the days, my friend..." Banks sang softly.

After getting dressed, Banks returned to the dugout, where ushers handed him slips of paper to sign for fans in the stands above who didn't want to leave the scene of so much excitement, so much promise for the season ahead.

"I'm happy," Banks said. "Is everybody happy?"

———

And so it began, a season that would forever define two iconic baseball franchises—one that had been a part of the game since the major leagues were formed nearly a century earlier, and another that was entering its eighth year of existence.

———

Despite his trepidation about the approaching end of his career, Banks was heartened by the spirit of the Cubs' 1969 training camp. He was famous for his optimism at the beginning of each season, of course— "The Cubs will shine in '69" was this year's slogan—but now he saw something different. "Spring training was very well managed," he said. "There was a real focus on what we were doing. Everybody was working on improving their weaknesses and getting in shape. It seemed like there was a different atmosphere. We were more settled, more centered on playing each game." The fact that the core of the team had been together for some years was another positive factor, Banks thought. "We knew each other—we knew each other's kids—and we were more at ease with each other," he said.

But Banks had another, more tangible, reason for feeling hopeful. The Cubs were loaded. Along with Jenkins and Ken Holtzman, their pitching had been bolstered by the emergence of Hands as a front-line starter and the reacquisition of reliever Ted Abernathy, who had led the league in games pitched the past two seasons, and Hank Aguirre to join Regan, who had pitched in sixty-eight games in 1968, in the bullpen.

No team in baseball had a better infield than Banks at first, Glenn Beckert at second, Don Kessinger at shortstop, and Ron Santo at third base, and Randy Hundley was unsurpassed as a defensive catcher and at calling a game. Billy Williams remained the very essence of a power-hitting left fielder, while two savvy veterans, Hickman and Al Spangler, would take turns in right field. The Cubs were particularly intrigued by Hickman, who had been a powerful but streaky hitter during his five seasons with the original New York Mets, and who was a dependable outfielder with a powerful arm. Hickman's quiet demeanor and Tennessee drawl made him a clubhouse favorite.

The only question mark was center field. After Adolfo Phillips, who had played the position the last three seasons, broke a bone in his hand early in the spring, the Cubs tried a number of players, and the situation remained unresolved as Durocher left camp at the command of Richard J. Daley, who summoned him back to Chicago to be grand marshal of the city's St. Patrick's Day parade.

"What the hell is that?!" Durocher asked Pete Reiser, his second in command, when he returned during an exhibition game a few days later. The Cubs were playing their regulars now in preparation for the upcoming season and, as Durocher looked out to center field, he saw Reiser had put Don Young in the starting lineup.

Young had been scuffling since his brief tenure on the Cubs' roster in 1965, during which he made his major league debut by striking out three times in Sandy Koufax's perfect game. He spent the next three seasons in the minors, and by 1968 had sunk as low as Class A ball in Lodi, California. Had it not been for a brief players' strike over pensions during the pre-season, he would not even have been invited to spring training. But with Phillips wearing a cast, Oscar Gamble considered too young, and no other candidates emerging, Durocher's hands were tied. Young would open the season in center field. He was under no illusions about his role or what was expected of him, though. "Why do they call me a glove man? Maybe it's because for four years in a row I hit .170 or less?" Young told Robert Markus of the *Chicago Tribune*, exaggerating slightly.

Banks's hopes for the coming season grew stronger, and soon he was playfully fantasizing about filling in the gap in his baseball resume.

"World Series! Sixty-nine! The Chicago Cubs versus the Detroit Tigers," he told reporters, and he began conducting his own mock post-Series press conference.

"What kind of ball did you hit for your home run, Mr. Banks?"

"Oh, a mediocre fastball, Mr. Newspaperman."

The Tigers were on his mind, he said, because after fifteen years of frustration their great star, Al Kaline, had finally played in his first World Series in 1968 and performed brilliantly as the Tigers beat the St. Louis Cardinals. "I lived through the World Series with Al Kaline," Banks said. "Every time he came up, I was helping him out. That's why he had such a great Series. There were two of us getting the job done."

"No kidding, the Cubs are going to win the pennant," he told Willie Mays during the spring.

"What league?" Mays replied with a grin.

But Banks ignored him. It was his turn now. He could feel it in his bones. "This is my biggest chance to be on a pennant winner," he said. "This year we really have a chance to do it and I want to do everything I can to make it happen."

In the second game of the season, Williams tied a major league record with four doubles as the Cubs beat the Phillies, 11–3.

In the third game, Santo hit two home runs and the Cubs won, 6–2.

In the fourth game, Joe Niekro and Abernathy combined for a twelve-inning shutout as the Cubs beat Montreal, 1–0, on Williams's run-scoring single.

The Expos handed the Cubs their first loss the following day, but when a lazy fly ball by Banks eluded three Montreal outfielders, the Cubs prevailed, 7–6, in the final game of the series, and fans stormed the field once again.

The home stand ended with two victories over the Pittsburgh Pirates, one of them saved by a fine running over-the-shoulder catch in deep center field by Young. "That catch could have been the turning point for us," Williams said. "Don has really done a job for us. You can see him gaining confidence every day." The Cubs left for their first road trip leading the National League's East Division by two games.

After winning eleven of their first twelve games, the Cubs were off to their best start in thirty-five years, but it was not just that they were winning, it was *how* they were winning. Close games, blowouts, it didn't seem to matter. They would find a way.

On April 28, Ted Abernathy survived a bases-loaded, no-out dilemma in the tenth inning in Philadelphia when Banks threw a runner out at the plate and the Cubs won, 2–1.

"I can't ever remember getting out of a spot like that before," Abernathy said.

"Had 'em all the way, Skip," a player told Durocher after the game.

"I wish you had told *me*," the manager replied.

The following day the Cubs beat the Phillies, 10–0, as Jenkins pitched a four-hitter and Kessinger scored four runs. On their way out of town they left behind a sign in the visitors' locker room for the Tigers, who were coming in to play an exhibition game. "See you at the World Series if you can make it," it read.

The fact that John Holland remained active in the early-season trade market offered even more encouragement. The Cubs picked up Dick Selma, a starting pitcher, from the San Diego Padres, and Nate Oliver, a shortstop the Los Angeles Dodgers had once compared to Pee Wee Reese. Oliver quickly stepped in to replace Beckert, who had taken a fastball to the chin that required fifteen stitches in a game against San Diego. Oliver drove in four runs in a 19–0 win over the Padres during which Banks drove in seven runs with two three-run home runs and a double, Young also hit a three-run homer, Williams had two triples, and Selma allowed only three infield singles. The game tied the record for most lopsided shutout in National League history. Two days later, Oliver scored the winning run in the ninth inning of a 3–2 win over the Padres, and when the Cubs beat the Astros 11–0 two days later, they had scored forty-three runs in their last five games and given up only two.

On June 11, Durocher ceded center field to Young by trading away Phillips to Montreal for Paul Popovich, who had been the Dodgers' regular second baseman in 1968. Durocher had feuded with Phillips, whom he had raved about for his occasionally spectacular play but who was moody and inconsistent. Popovich immediately entered the Cubs' lineup replacing the luckless Beckert, who had broken his thumb in a play at second base a few days earlier, and performed well both in the field and at the plate.

Cub veterans seemed to take turns rising to the occasion. By the middle of May, Kessinger was hitting well over .300 and had more doubles than during the entire 1968 season, which allowed Santo, who hit behind him, to have more runs batted in than hits. "Every time I look up, Kessinger is on second or third," he said. It continued on through the lineup as Williams, Hundley, and Beckert were all hitting close to .300; Jenkins, Holtzman, and Hands were winning their starts; and Regan and Abernathy were pitching well in relief.

But nobody responded to the challenge early in the season more than Banks. On May 24 in San Diego, he hit the twelfth grand-slam home run of his career in a 7–5 win over the Padres. "Those grand slams really do something special to you because they usually put your team ahead or tie the game," he said. "Is there anything better than playing baseball in the major leagues?" In the Cubs' first fifty-three games, Banks had fifty runs batted in and moved past Mickey Mantle on the all-time RBI list.

Banks was in his glory now, reveling in the spotlight and, as reporters from national publications began covering him and the Cubs on a regular basis for the first time in his career, he made the most of it.

"One minute he is crawling around the clubhouse floor in a hilarious demonstration of what it feels like to play on a second-division team for so many years," a story in *Time* said at the end of May. "The next, to show the comeback powers of the Cubs, he leaps up and sings out in his quavery baritone, 'Chicago, Chicago, that toddlin' town...'"

"Banks is particularly animated during batting practice," wrote Mark Kram in *Sports Illustrated*. "The area around the cage is Banks's stage, where he performs like some aging vaudevillian. If he is in St. Louis he will say: 'St. Louis! Home of the mighty Cardinals and the great Stan. Meet me in St. Looie, Looie...' If he is in New York he will say: 'New York, the Big Apple, the Melting Pot of the World. Home of *Oh! Calcutta!* and those pesky Mets! East Side, West Side, all around the town.'" And asked if travel had become a grind after all these years, he said, "My goodness, no. Nothing could be fin-ah than baseball by air-linah."

He was having a ball on the field, too. "If I'm on second and he's on first," Santo said, "he'll yell over to me, saying I better put on some steam. 'Now, Ronnie, don't let me pass you.'"

"He'd be at first base and he'd yell over to me, 'Joe, you like it here, don't you?' Joe Amalfitano says. "'You like it here. You *like* it here. Don't you, Joe?'"

Banks also made calls to players on other teams, always within earshot of his teammates or reporters. He told Lou Brock the Cardinals' two-year World Series run was over. He told Frank Robinson he would see him and the Baltimore Orioles in the Series. He told Willie Mays to give his best against the Cardinals and Bob Gibson. "You always hit him," Banks said. "When you come up to the plate against Gibson, it's murder. I feel sorry for him tonight."

Banks especially enjoyed teasing Mays when the Giants came to Wrigley Field. "First base was right next to the visiting dugout, and every once in a while Willie would take a day off," says Jack Hiatt, who was then the Giants' backup catcher. "Ernie would stand at first and say, 'Hey, Willie, what's wrong with you? You can't play? You're tired? We're out here in God's light. Come out and play.' Willie would be down near the end of the tunnel, hiding almost, putting his finger up to his mouth, going, 'Shhh, keep it down.' It was priceless."

Banks also paid a visit to the Royal London Wax Museum in Chicago's Old Town to view a wax statue of himself that had been sent over from London. "The thing stares back," he said.

But Banks didn't need a crowd or a spotlight to vent his excitement. There were times, in fact, when it seemed he could hardly contain himself. "We landed in Pittsburgh at two in the morning and were walking through an empty airline terminal," says Blake Cullen. "A guy is cleaning up with a vacuum cleaner and Ernie walks up to him and says, 'We're going to beat them Bucs tomorrow. Come out and see us beat the Bucs.' Leo was just shaking his head as if he was saying, 'I don't believe this.'"

Wasn't there *someone* he disliked? a reporter asked him. Banks thought a moment and said, "Oh, maybe Mao Tse-Tung."

———

Throughout June and into July, the Cubs remained the class of the league. There was no way they could lose the pennant, Astros manager Harry Walker said, to which Dodgers manager Walt Alston added it would save time if the entire Cubs infield, including Hundley, were named to the National League All-Star team. Hundley and Kessinger were voted starters for the game, which was played in Washington, D.C., in July, and a few innings later Banks, Beckert, and Santo joined them on the field. It was, Kessinger said, one of his biggest thrills in baseball.

The Cubs' celebration continued with the cutting of a record with some of the Bleacher Bums that included narration by Jack Brickhouse, Banks, and Santo, and such songs as the National Anthem, "Take Me Out to the Ball Game," their "Hey, Hey, Holy Mackerel" theme song, and two original blues tunes by their most adept singers, Willie Smith and Nate and Gene Oliver, a backup catcher. As demands on their time grew, the players enlisted Chicago businessman Jack Childers to help them devise an all-for-one system of dividing the spoils. Reserves would be paid as well as the stars from the proceeds of Cubs T-shirts, mugs, pictures, posters, autographed baseballs, and other items. The deal netted $150,000, which amounted to just a few thousand dollars each when divided up. But for players who were earning $12,000 to $15,000 a season, it was a welcome dividend as well as an expression of the camaraderie only a team that is marching to a championship can know.

Soon, Cubs games became as much performance art as baseball. Returning from the clubhouse bathroom down the left-field line during a game late in May, Selma noted an unaccustomed silence in the stands. "Start yelling!" he shouted, and he waved his arms. Just then Banks hit a home run, and the following day Durocher, superstitious to the last, told Selma to leave the dugout where starting pitchers typically sit and go to the bullpen.

"Get those Bums going!" Durocher ordered.

"So I go down and start waving a towel around. From then on when I wasn't pitching, that was my job," said Selma, who would theatrically whirl the towel, leap into the air, and point his finger at the ground as the Bleacher Bums sang, "Every day I go to town, the boys all kick my dog around. Makes no difference if he's a hound, you'd better stop kicking my dog around."

Santo made his contribution to the theatrics on June 22 after Hickman hit a home run to cap a four-run ninth-inning explosion against the Expos. Santo ran out onto the field and, without really knowing whether he could do it, jumped up and clicked his heels. Then he pounded Hickman on the head so hard he later complained of a headache.

"I'm watching TV that night and the first thing they show is me clicking my heels," Santo told *Sport* magazine's Bill Furlong. "I couldn't believe it. And then I started to get phone calls and stacks of letters: 'Don't forget to click your heels.' I'd be going along in my car and kids would be running alongside me, clicking their heels. One couple wrote—they must have been in their fifties—and said the man had jumped up and clicked his heels after we won a ball game and he fell down and broke both his ankles."

Four days later, after Hickman hit yet another game-winning home run, in the tenth inning against the Pirates, Banks joined in the fun by singing, to the tune of "The Tennessee Waltz," "I introduced Jim to the Pirates, and while they were pitching..."

As for Hickman's counterpart in right field, the Bleachers Bums sang, "Oh, say does that *Al Spangler* banner yet wave" during the National Anthem.

On July 20, during the second inning of a doubleheader in Philadelphia, another sort of patriotism was exhibited when the news came over the public address system that the crew of *Apollo 11* had landed on the moon. The teams were called off the field, lined up on the foul line, and, after a moment of silence for the safe return of the astronauts was observed, a record of Kate Smith singing "God Bless America" was played. The Cubs then swept the doubleheader as reporters in the press box exchanged jokes about a man landing on the moon before the Cubs won the pennant.

———

Half a century later, eyes of Cubs fans no longer young grow misty and their mouths turn up in smiles as they recall the sweet lost Chicago summer of 1969. They remember the routes they took to Wrigley Field, the sandwiches their mothers packed for them, the reaction of the fans that took on a new urgency, the excitement of, at long last, cheering for a winning team. They remember it all.

Ned Colletti, who was in his early teens and lived in Franklin Park near O'Hare International Airport, remembers the train and two buses he took to the ballpark, arriving early, lying down outside the bleacher wall, waiting for the gates to open. The field would be empty when he went in, and then the players would emerge from the clubhouse in left field in small groups, some of them occasionally coming over and chatting with the early-arriving fans. "But not Ernie," Colletti says. "He would wave, tip his cap, walk down the third-base line, get in the batting cage, and hit balls at us in the bleachers."

John Schulian remembers Regan and Aguirre running in the outfield before games and Aguirre reaching in his pocket, pulling out a bottle of Vitalis, holding it up, and pointing at Regan, who had been accused of doctoring his pitches. "There was such a level of intimacy," Schulian says. "If it was a doubleheader, you'd be there at ten-thirty in the morning and you'd leave at six or seven at night, sunburned and full of hot dogs. It felt like the greatest afternoon you'd ever had in your life."

There are other, more complicated, memories as well. "I was a college kid, an antiwar hippie with long hair, and my dad and I didn't agree
on a lot of things," says Dennis Paoli. "One of the few things we could
agree on was the Cubs. He was a screamer of a fan and we could still go
to games and root for the Cubs."

Cubs fever became inescapable as attendance jumped by more than
600,000 over 1968 to 1,674,993, a Wrigley Field record that would not
be broken for fifteen years. Longtime fans used to a nearly empty ballpark were joined by newcomers who wanted a seat on the bandwagon.
A bus carrying fifty blind children came to a game in July, and they were
guided to seats behind home plate. Nobody seemed to mind that they
were all wearing Oakland A's caps.

"One fellow came in pretty upset because he couldn't cart his own
beer into the park," said Chicago police lieutenant Ed Mowen, who commanded a force of more than thirty officers on the busiest game days. "I
asked him if he didn't know ballpark regulations, and he said this was the
first time he had been to Wrigley Field in twenty-five years."

Parking in the neighborhood was extremely tight, and the nuns at
the nearby House of the Good Shepherd, which had been established in
1859 to minister to former slaves and now took in the victims of domestic violence, reaped some of the benefit as they stood in their parking
lot wearing Cubs hats atop their habits and accepting donations. "You'd
give them a dollar and they were happy," says Jack Herbon. In 2013, the
lot was sold to the Cubs for the use of season ticket holders, who paid as
much as sixty dollars per game for parking.

The players reacted to Cubs mania with astonishment. "You'd get
there at ten in the morning and people would be lined up around the ballpark," says Rich Nye. "There was always this positive energy when you
walked into Wrigley Field. The other teams would be booed and they
could feel the energy coming to their opponent. I think it had an effect."

"It's something to be in a crucial situation and hear twenty-five thousand people behind you," said Selma, who continued waving his towel in
the bullpen. "It gives you a strength you never knew you had."

———

Could there possibly be anything better in life than being a Cubs fan at Wrigley Field in 1969? Actually, there could.

"We had free rein," says Jerry Banks. "We knew all the crevices under the stands and ran around in them before the park opened. There was nobody watching us, nobody stopping us, nobody saying, 'Get out of there.'"

"Wrigley Field was like a playground," says Ron Santo, Jr. "We'd get there early and play catch and run around the field and go out to left field during batting practice. Trying to catch major league pop-ups was a lot of fun if you were eight or nine years old. The Bleacher Bums knew who we were and they'd always ask, 'How's your dad doing?'"

Though the boys had assigned seats, they found it hard to sit still and ran from place to place, often entering the Cubs' locker room through a door on the concourse and, when they were feeling particularly brave, wandering into Durocher's office. "Sometimes we'd watch the game from the clubhouse door in the left-field corner," Santo says. "We'd stick our heads out and watch the last inning from there. It was incredible. Everything that went on, just incredible."

As the summer wore on, the fans' lionization of the Cubs players began to border on something close to madness. "We could hardly leave the ballpark," says Kessinger. "We'd park across the street and there would be thousands of fans outside. They knew which way we went home and literally at every corner there would be people waiting and you had to sign autographs before you could move on."

"It was almost impossible to get across the street to our cars," says Regan. "The fans would line up and make an aisle so we could get to the parking lot, and because people knew our cars they would stop us and it took two or three hours to get to the expressway."

Some of the Cubs' less recognizable players developed a getaway strategy. "We'd come out of the locker room and point and holler, 'Here comes Ernie!' or 'There goes Santo!'" says Spangler. "Then we'd run the other way to get to our cars."

For Banks, there was no escape. "They'd pull the car up to the wall of the door at Wrigley Field and we would literally have to jump in," says Jerry Banks. "They'd be mobbing the car and I'd be thinking, 'Oh my God, these people are crazy.' It was pretty scary. I was wondering, 'Do you really have this much influence on people?'"

Once they got away from Wrigley Field, a few of the Cubs discovered there were certain perks that helped ease the strain. "There was a little side street one block north of Irving Park Road and there was a package store that we stopped at and got a six-pack," says Hands, who carpooled with Hickman. "We'd share a couple of beers on the way home. We never had a problem with cops."

One day while the Pirates were in town, Banks stood near first base talking to Roberto Clemente, who had just singled.

"We've got a chance to win," Banks told the great Pirates outfielder.

"Just wait until you get to September," Clemente said. "It's going to be tough for you then. You're going to have guys shaking."

"What?" Banks said. "We ain't going to shake. Look at how we're playing." Clemente just smiled.

Hank Aaron had a similar warning. "When you get to September, they're going to be hitting ground balls and you aren't going to be able to catch them," he told Banks. "Just wait until you get there. It's different."

Why is it different? Banks wondered. Baseball is baseball, and the Cubs were playing the best baseball of their lives.

The peak moment arrived on August 19 when Holtzman, whose fastball deserted him and didn't record a single strikeout, pitched the second no-hitter of his career, against the Braves at Wrigley Field. The milestone almost came undone in the seventh inning when Aaron hit a ball so hard that Williams, standing in left field, was certain it would land deep in the bleachers. But a ferocious wind blew the ball back, and Williams caught it at the wall. "It was like it went into the hand of God and fell into Billy Williams's glove," says Paoli, who had driven down with friends from the University of Wisconsin, where he was in summer school. "You should have seen the look on Aaron's face when that ball was caught," Banks said. "He couldn't believe it."

Two innings later, Aaron grounded sharply to Beckert for the final out, and Santo leaped into Holtzman's arms just ahead of a group of fans who had raced onto the field. "We were in the right-field bleachers and we jumped over the wall and ran out onto the field," says Paoli. "I found myself between second and third, cutting one way and then back, dodging the cops and the ushers and thinking, 'I'm on the field!' I found myself next to Leo Durocher, who up close looked really old, and I whacked him on the ass and said, 'Great game, Mr. Durocher!' He looked at me like I was this terrible threat. I felt really bad about it and I ran off the field."

A cordon of ushers finally helped Holtzman make his way to the locker room, where, after his teammates mobbed him, he was handed a telephone to receive congratulations from Sandy Koufax. "Break out the champagne!" Willie Smith shouted.

The Cubs' lead was now up to eight games, and there were just six weeks left in the season.

———

One summer day, Blake Cullen made his way into the left-field bleachers and found Ron Grousl.

"John Holland wants to talk to you," he said.

"Oh, shit," Grousl said, wondering what he had done now.

Three innings later, he returned with a large smile on his face.

"Mr. Wrigley is going to take us on a road trip, all expenses paid, to thank us for everything we've done for the Cubs," Grousl said. "He said to pick fifty of your most loyal Bleacher Bums. We're going to Atlanta."

"Not since the arrival of General Sherman had Atlanta seen anything like it," said the *Chicago Tribune,* which assigned a society writer, Stephanie Fuller, to cover the Bums' journey to the three-game series. Fuller posed for a picture that ran next to her first dispatch holding a Bleacher Bums membership card and wearing a yellow hard hat.

The trip began on August 29 with a send-off breakfast of grilled cheese sandwiches and champagne at Ray's Bleachers, and that afternoon the Bums announced their arrival in Atlanta by marching six abreast through the airport, singing, "Give me that old-time Durocher." They sneaked down to the hotel lobby in the middle of the night to fill up the elevators with large flower arrangements that had been set up for a florists' convention.

The series was as important to the Braves as it was to the Cubs. After three desultory seasons following their move to Atlanta from Milwaukee, they were now just a half game out of first place in the National League West—which they would eventually go on to win—and their fans were excited, too. More than 96,000 of them showed up for the series. None of that mattered to the Bums, though, who swung into action during the first game of the series when one of their members who was proficient in throwing a lasso flung a rope from the left-field stands. It snagged a tentpole of the teepee belonging to the Braves' mascot, Chief Noc-A-Homa, who did a war dance at the pitcher's mound before each game and rushed out of his teepee to celebrate after each Atlanta home run. A few tugs of the rope and the teepee toppled over, revealing the chief wearing a T-shirt, drinking beer, and monitoring the game on television. It took him half an inning to restore the structure.

Shortly thereafter, one of the Bums, Norm Bartczak, tried to descend the twenty-foot wall to the teepee, only to fall onto the field when his rope broke. "Oh, Lord, how many mothers are watching television in Chicago and wondering if it was their son?" Grousl said. Bartczak was taken to the hospital but was not seriously hurt.

The Bums' final stunt, which Grousl had previously worked out with Jenkins over beers at Ray's Bleachers, came on the last day of the trip. They cleared the plan with Durocher, who saw no harm in Grousl planting himself in the bullpen before the game, watching Chief Noc-A-Homa do his pregame dance, and then, costumed from head to toe as a bear, running out onto the field.

"The chief is running back to his teepee and Ronnie jumps out of the bullpen and runs over and tackles him near third base like he was Dick Butkus," Murphy says.

"They were really whacking each other," says Herbon. "The chief was trying to get Ronnie off him and they're rolling around in the grass and the ushers and the cops just let them go at it. It was like a barroom fight and everybody was just watching and wondering, 'Is this the pre-game show?' "

The battle ended when an usher picked up Grousl's Cubs hat and ran across the field as the fans howled at the sight of a bear chasing the usher and tripping over second base. Shortly thereafter, the bear and the chief stood at home plate during the playing of the National Anthem, after which Morganna Roberts, a busty young woman who was gaining noto-riety throughout baseball as "The Kissing Bandit," rushed onto the field and planted a smooch on Braves' third baseman Clete Boyer.

"Let the Bums top that," the Braves' public address announcer said.

"Enough is enough," Grousl said. "I don't want to kiss Clete Boyer anyway."

As the Bums returned home from what Grousl pronounced "the best road trip we'd ever taken," they could take satisfaction in knowing they had cheered the Cubs to victories in all three games. And when the team won the first game of a series in Cincinnati on September 2, their lead in the division was five games. This was a bit of a comedown from their nine-game margin in mid-August, but twice during the season, once early in June and then again at the end of the month, they'd had a lead of eight and a half or nine games, seen it dip to five games or less, and built it right back up again.

At about this time, the Chicago papers began running the Cubs' "magic number," the combination of victories coupled with their closest pursuer's defeats needed to win the pennant, and the National League office told the team to print tickets for the postseason. Cullen designed a World Series program with a picture of Beckert completing a double play on the cover. "All we were wondering about was who we were going to play in the playoffs," Cullen says. "The way Leo Durocher was going in

Chicago, he was one up on God and only a step and a half behind Mayor Daley," Bill Furlong wrote in *Look*.

They were on their way now, on their way to the pennant and the World Series. On their way to what Cubs fans had been waiting for all their lives—and to fulfilling Ernie Banks's destiny at last.

What could possibly go wrong?

Chapter 29

A Bunch of Old Men

In May 1969, the New York Mets played their first series in Chicago, and it was old home week for Billy Williams. Three of the Mets' outfielders—Cleon Jones, Tommie Agee, and Amos Otis—were from Mobile, Alabama, Williams's hometown, and he invited them over for dinner. "Shirley cooked for them and we talked about baseball, about home, about old times," Williams says.

He had every reason to be magnanimous. The Mets were born as baseball's laughingstocks in 1962 when they lost 120 games, a modern record, and remained so as the 1969 season began. They had never finished higher than ninth place—they would avoid that ignominy this year because the league had been split into two six-team divisions—and never come close to winning even half their games. Their 73–89 record in 1968 was a high-water mark, but only their most devoted fans could take any hope from it.

The Mets had long capitalized on their mediocrity, which was captured by their first manager, Casey Stengel, who called them "The Amazin' Mets" and "The Youth of America." Bumblers in the field, hapless at the plate, devoid of pitching, they had nevertheless developed a devoted following that packed Shea Stadium. The Mets drew more than 1,750,000 fans in four of their first seven seasons, fans who made them baseball's most lovable losers, a sort of latter-day, East Coast Cubs.

The Mets' 1969 roster didn't foster any great hopes for a change in fortune, as it was virtually the same as the year before and contained only one truly excellent player, the twenty-four-year-old pitcher Tom Seaver, and two others, Jones and Agee, who had performed well at times but were inconsistent. Their infielders were young and inexperienced and their pitching appeared particularly vulnerable, as only Seaver, who had won sixteen games in each of his first two seasons; Jerry Koosman, who had won nineteen games in 1968, his second year in the majors; and Ron Taylor, an experienced reliever, were proven major leaguers.

Nor had the Cubs' first series against the Mets been any problem when they met in New York at the end of April. Ferguson Jenkins beat Seaver, 3–1, in the first of four games, Bill Hands went the distance in a 9–3 victory the next day, and when the Cubs scored four runs in the ninth inning on two Mets errors to win the first game of a Sunday doubleheader 8–6, they were on the verge of sweeping the series. Only when Rich Nye, who had pitched eight scoreless innings, gave up a three-run home run to Jones in the ninth inning of the second game did the Mets salvage a 3–0 victory.

The first two games in Chicago a week later were more of the same as Ken Holtzman won the first game 6–4, and the Cubs scored two runs off their former teammate Cal Koonce in the eighth inning the next day to win, 3–2. The Cubs had now won five of the six games they had played against the Mets, and eighteen of their first twenty-five overall. Their sixteen victories in April were the most in team history and gave them a two-and-a-half-game lead in the National League East and produced the first fan stampede of the season.

An estimated 60,000 people made their way to Wrigley Field on May 4 for a Sunday doubleheader, and 20,000 of them were disappointed. Of the 40,484 who did gain admission, a few brave souls stood precariously on the railings behind the last row of seats in the lower deck to get a glimpse of the action. What they saw was Seaver taking matters into his own right hand.

"I brushed him back on purpose," Seaver said of the 0–2 pitch in the second inning of the first game that sent Ron Santo, who had driven in ten runs in six previous games against the Mets, sprawling into the dirt.

"The man hits me hard. I wanted him to know I was protecting myself."
Seaver became the target the following inning when Bill Hands hit him
on the left arm. Seaver responded by hitting Hands in the left leg in
the bottom of the third, which brought umpire Frank Secory out from
behind home plate pointing at Seaver.

Was Secory going to throw Seaver out of the game? Was he indicating a fifty-dollar fine that was supposed to be automatic in retaliatory
situations? The Mets' manager, Gil Hodges, left the dugout to defend his
pitcher and, wonder of wonders, won the argument. He was issuing an
"unofficial" warning, Secory said. Seaver would not be punished. The
beanball war ceased, but the Mets' momentum did not. "I think when
Hands hit me, it helped the whole ball club," Seaver said after the Mets
won both games by identical 3–2 scores. "The whole dugout came alive."

But the Mets had done more than win a doubleheader on the road
against a team that had beaten them repeatedly early in the season.
Though they were fourth place in the National League East with an
11–14 record, they had shown they were not to be trifled with and that
the Cubs were not the only team dreaming of better days.

The Cubs and the Mets didn't play again until July, and while the Cubs
continued to post victory after victory, the Mets began to make some
modest noise of their own. The first sound was heard on May 21 when
Seaver shut out the Braves in Atlanta on three hits, 5–0, to raise the Mets'
record to 18–18. Never before had they been at .500 this far into the season. The Mets lost their next five games, but then they went on a tear,
winning seven straight at home from the Padres, Giants, and Dodgers,
three more at San Diego, and the first game of a series in San Francisco
for eleven consecutive victories. Though their 29–23 record was far
behind the Cubs' mark of 37–17, the Mets had slipped into second place
in the division. More important, however, was a change in their attitude.

"We had always had trouble with the West Coast teams, but we beat
all three of them at Shea and then went out to the Coast and beat them all

again," Mets relief pitcher Tug McGraw told Stanley Cohen in his book *A Magic Summer: The Amazin' Story of the 1969 New York Mets*. "At that point, I think we began saying, 'Hey, we're not doing this with mirrors, we're not doing this with miracles. We're playing good baseball. We can beat anybody if we play our game.'"

The Mets completed their road trip with eight victories in twelve games and then returned home to some even happier news: a trade with Montreal for Donn Clendenon. A thirty-three-year-old first baseman in his ninth year in the majors, Clendenon brought the Mets the right-handed power hitter they craved and something more—the cool head of a veteran player who could communicate a calm wisdom to his younger teammates. "Clendenon was probably the key to our whole season because when he came over we really came alive," Mets third baseman Wayne Garrett said. "He gave us the potential to score four, five, six runs a game. He kept us going when we were down on ourselves. He was just the ingredient we needed, the last piece of the puzzle."

"He was our exorcist," said McGraw. "He scared the demons right out of the clubhouse." Clendenon went right to work, driving in nine runs in five consecutive Mets victories over the Cardinals and Pirates between July 2 and July 6. And when the Cubs lost three games during a misbegotten weekend in St. Louis, their lead was down to five and a half games as they made their way to New York for a series that would reverberate through the remainder of the season.

The Cubs were stunned when they arrived at Shea Stadium on July 8. What was this? they wondered when they saw the horde of writers, television cameras, and interlopers crowding the field and locker rooms. National magazines based in New York were out in force, and some sportswriters had come in from out of town to chronicle the series between two bedraggled franchises that had been doormats for so many years and were now occupying the top two spots in the National League East. The Mets had estimated that 110,000 fans would attend the three-game series; the final count was more than 140,000.

The Cubs were also startled by how much attention was focused on the Mets. They were the second-place team, after all, and only lately had they shown any signs of life. The frenzy seemed so premature. "We'd pick up a paper and all they talked about were how good they were," Santo told *Sport*. "They made your Al Weises, your Harrelsons, your Garretts all look like they were Babe Ruth. I'm sure any one of those ballplayers picked up a paper and they *felt* like Babe Ruth. And they were five and a half games behind *us*."

Jenkins had won eleven games when he took the mound in Shea Stadium the afternoon of July 8, and he proceeded to pitch his best game of the season. He retired the Mets' first eleven batters, and as the ninth inning began he had given up just one hit, a home run by Ed Kranepool, in the fifth. Home runs by Ernie Banks and Jim Hickman off Koosman had given the Cubs a 3–1 lead, and the 55,096 fans who had jammed Shea Stadium had little to cheer about as the Mets came up in the bottom of the ninth.

Ken Boswell, pinch-hitting, opened the inning with a fly ball to short center field, where Don Young took two steps back before realizing his mistake and racing in to try to correct it. The ball fell in front of him as Boswell alertly ran to second base. "The ball was in the sun and he didn't have his glasses on," said Williams, who had the best view of the play from left field.

Jenkins retired Agee on a foul pop-up, but Clendenon, the Mets' second pinch hitter of the inning, brought the fans to their feet with a long drive to left center that appeared likely to be an extra-base hit until they saw Young running back and heading straight for the ball. "My heart went up in my throat when I saw it looked like Young was going to make the catch," Koosman said. "Then I saw the ball fall out of his glove when he hit the fence. It was a beautiful sight." Young had gotten a quick start this time, but as he made a backhanded catch his right shoulder hit the fence, and the impact jarred the ball loose. "I thought he was going to run through the fence," Williams said. "So I run over and say, 'Hey, you gotta take it easy, man. Relax a little out here.'"

Boswell, holding up on the play, stopped at third base and, with two men out, Durocher had a decision to make: pitch to Cleon Jones, who had been burning up the league with a .354 batting average, or walk him and force Hodges to go to his bench. "Battle him," Durocher told Jenkins. Jones hit a hanging slider to left field that drove in both runners and tied the score. Durocher then ordered that Art Shamsky be walked, and when Garrett grounded to second, the runners moved to second and third. Jenkins got two quick strikes on Kranepool, but when his next pitch came in low and away, Kranepool punched it into short left field. "I just threw my bat at it," Kranepool said. Jones scored the winning run and was mobbed at the plate by his teammates as Shea Stadium erupted over the improbable 4–3 victory. "Somebody said the Cubs weren't taking us seriously," Jones said in the jubilant Mets' locker room. "Maybe they'll take us seriously now."

For fifteen minutes after the game, the Cubs' locker room was silent until Phil Regan stood up and yelled the only thing worth yelling after such a dispiriting defeat: "We'll get 'em tomorrow." In the manager's office, Durocher fumed at Young. "My three-year-old could have caught those balls," he said.

And that might have been the end of it if Santo hadn't poured gasoline onto the embers. "He was just thinking of himself," Santo told reporters. "He had a bad day at the plate, so he had his head down. He is worrying about his batting average, not the team. He's out there thinking about how he didn't hit anything out of the infield and forgot that we had a 3–1 lead and were going to win the game."

Hearing his teammate's rant as he emerged from the shower, Young, already disconsolate, was in disbelief. *Santo* was ranting at him? *Santo*, who had been so friendly in spring training, who had spoken up for him when center field was up for grabs, who had always encouraged him? And it wasn't true that he'd been preoccupied after going 0-for-4 and striking out twice. He'd run out to the outfield in the bottom of the ninth, clapping his hands, and shouting, "Let's go!" Unable to face his teammates, Young dressed quickly, left the ballpark, walked for a bit, and suddenly realized he was lost. Finally, he found a drugstore, where he called a cab that took him back to the team hotel, the Waldorf Astoria. "He can keep on going out of sight for all I care," Santo said when he learned of Young's departure.

"When I got back to the hotel, Don already had his bags packed," Rich Nye told Rick Talley for his book *The Cubs of '69: Recollections of the Team That Should Have Been.* "He was going home. After a couple of drinks, I talked him out of it."

It was all so unfair, Nye thought. Yes, Young had failed to make the two catches, but neither of them had been ruled an error and no runs had scored on them. The Cubs were still leading by two runs. "It wasn't Don Young who threw the hanging slider to Cleon Jones," Nye said. "It was Fergie Jenkins."

But perhaps the most discerning defense of Young came from Agee, the Mets' center fielder, who said, "It got awfully hard to see out there the last two innings. A ball could easily have been lost in the sun and in the white shirt background."

The repercussions of the defeat spread. In tears, Jenkins called Williams and begged his friend to come to his room. Williams complied, and they talked of the game into the night.

What the Cubs needed now was someone who could take control, rally the team, make it realize it was just one loss, no matter how difficult, and there was still more than half the season to play. But there seemed to be no one willing or able to assume the task—not the manager and not the team's biggest star, who sat next to Santo as he delivered his rant, remaining silent and making no attempt to intervene, to try to calm the waters. "Of all the years I've been with the Cubs, this was the toughest defeat I've ever seen this club take," Banks said later.

After a sleepless night, Santo called the four writers traveling with the team to his hotel room. He had apologized to Young personally, he said, and would do so in front of the team before that evening's game. "What I said about Donnie, I didn't mean," Santo said. "I said it because I was upset." His accusation that Young had let his bad day at the plate affect

him in the field was unfair, Santo said. It was his *own* failings he was
thinking about, the times *he* had lost control after making an out and
neglected to bear down in the field. He had transferred his own problems
to Young. He was sorry, he said, so sorry.

The game was a tonic to the Mets. "That might have been the turning point of the season," Kranepool told Cohen. "From then on, we kept
applying the pressure and the Cubs knew they were in a pennant race."

"You could see the difference in the Cubs after that, the way they
reacted, like, 'Oh, my God, we're choking,'" said Duffy Dyer, the Mets'
third-string catcher. "I don't think they were the same after that series."

Young all but vanished from the Cubs' lineup the rest of the season,
and the Cubs would go on to employ a total of eight players in center
field. But Young's disappearance came one day too soon for Tom Seaver.

Seaver would always maintain he never pitched a better game than he
did on July 9, 1969, and the Cubs could hardly disagree. With more than
50,000 people roaring on every pitch, the Mets took a 4–0 lead into the
ninth inning and Seaver, who had retired twenty-five Cubs in a row and
had not had a three-ball count on a single batter, faced a player none of
them had ever heard of.

Jim Qualls, who was batting eighth and playing center field in just his
eighteenth major league game, had spent part of the season in Tacoma,
and part of it in the army, before joining the Cubs a week earlier in Montreal. But despite his lack of experience, Seaver was wary because Qualls
had hit the ball hard his first two times up. "So I pitched him outside," he
said. Outside the pitch may have been, but it was also a little higher than
Seaver wanted, at Qualls's waist, and he was ready. "I hit a fastball and I
hit it good," he said. The result was a single to left center that landed in
almost the same spot as Kranepool's game winner the day before. Standing at first base, Qualls could see tears in the eyes of Seaver's wife as she
sat in her box seat. "You little shit," Seaver told him while running in the

outfield before a game the following week in Wrigley Field. "You cost me a million dollars." Seaver would have four more one-hitters before finally pitching his sole no-hitter in 1978. He never pitched a perfect game.

Qualls was front and center the following day, too, as the Cubs finally beat the Mets and broke a five-game losing streak. He stretched a single to a double, kicked a ball out of Mets shortstop Al Weis's glove at second base, and scored on a single by Kessinger in a five-run inning that featured a home run by the penitent Santo. The resulting 6–2 victory featured two Mets errors and several other bobbles in the field. For the moment, the Cubs' confidence was restored, and as they left New York four and a half games ahead of the Mets, they were full of bravado.

"Were those the real Cubs we saw out there today?" a writer asked Durocher.

"No, but those were the real Mets," he said.

"I wouldn't put the Mets' infield in Tacoma," said Santo. "Wait until we get them back home before the Bleacher Bums."

The Mets read these words and seethed. "He really pissed us off," said pitcher Jim McAndrew. "No one liked Santo. During the course of a season, it's hard to get up for every game, but when it came to playing the Cubs it was easy because of just one man. He was a great competitor but if I was his teammate, I would have been taping his mouth shut."

Young, who had the lowest moment of his career in the series, and Qualls, who had the highest, were both gone from the major leagues the following year. It wasn't the two dropped balls that ended his career, or Santo's outburst, said Young, who would enter Cubs lore as one more symbol of their futility. "I just wasn't good enough."

More than 37,000 fans, a huge number for a Monday afternoon, came to Wrigley Field July 14, when the Cubs and the Mets met again, and they were rewarded with a superb performance by Hands. A bunt by Kessinger, a hit-and-run grounder by Beckert, and an RBI single by Williams gave the Cubs their first run off Seaver in twenty-one innings, and the 1–0 victory increased the Cubs' lead in the National League East to six games. "I'm kicking the habit," Santo said as he jumped up and clicked his heels after the game. "The losing habit. I'm working on a double click for the World Series."

But the series turned sour the following day when Weis hit a pitch from Selma over the left-field fence that bounced on Waveland Avenue and came to rest on a porch across the street. It was his first home run of the season, and only his fifth in seven years in the majors, and it drove in three runs in a 5–4 Mets victory. Asked what he was thinking as he saw the ball leave the park, Weis replied, "To touch every base." On July 16, the Mets drove Jenkins from the mound after he faced just one batter in the second inning, and Weis hit another home run, his second and last of the season, as the Mets won the final game of the series, 9–5. Asked after the game what kind of stuff he had, Jenkins said, "I wasn't around long enough to find out."

The victory was the Mets' eleventh in their last fourteen games, a two-week span during which they had cut the Cubs' lead from eight games to four. Perhaps more important was the fact they had won four of their last five games at Wrigley Field. In the locker room, they giddily burlesqued Santo clicking his heels and Selma's towel-waving leadership of the Bleacher Bums' cheers.

"Let's hear it for Leo."

"Fuck Leo."

"Let's hear it for Santo."

"Fuck Santo."

"Let's hear it for Ernie."

"Fuck Ernie."

"Let's hear it for the Bleacher Bums."

"Fuck the Bleacher Bums."

Cleon Jones summed up the mood of the club when he said, "When we left Chicago, our feeling was, 'We're going to beat you guys. You're just a bunch of old men.'"

Banks's extraordinary production continued for the first four months of the season. He had twenty-four RBI in May, twenty-six in June, and by the first of August his total was eighty-four, a remarkable number for a thirty-eight-year-old man. But the excitement he felt over finally being in the thick of a pennant race was accompanied by another emotion, one that shocked the few people he shared it with. It was an unease, a discomfort that might even be described as bitterness.

Several times during the summer, Banks would approach a sportswriter he trusted—George Langford of the *Tribune* or Jerome Holtzman of the *Sun-Times*—during pregame workouts, and they would walk across the field to a spot near the visitors' dugout, away from the Chicago side where they might be overheard. His remarks were elliptical, never fully spelled out, but his meaning was plain. At what should have been the greatest moment of his baseball career, he was not a happy man.

"He'd say things like, 'They spend a lot,' and I'd wonder if he was talking about his family or his wife," Langford says. "Or he'd talk about Durocher. He'd say, 'I can deal with it. I know I need pushing but it hurts.' These were short insights, something to escape the happy talk, but I think they reflected an inner turmoil that was very real. I got the feeling he wasn't spending much time at home and with his manager being such a bastard that his only joy was playing the game."

What was behind this? his listeners wondered. Was finally being on a winning team making him wonder about all the wasted years, all the bad moves the Cubs had made? Was finally seeing the good side of baseball reminding him how awful the bad side had been back when he was in his prime? But just as they were coming to terms with a side of Banks they had never seen before, he would revert to form. "Hey, the sun is shining and I'm getting paid to play a game. Do you believe it?" he would say. Or he would chirp, "The sun will shine in '69" at a fan in the stands, then wander away. The reporters understood that Banks's musings were not to be repeated, but it was clear that he was reaching out, that he wanted someone, anyone, to realize the toll the years and the stress were taking on him.

———

The Mets struggled after leaving Wrigley Field, winning only eleven of their next twenty-five games and even falling into third place for a day. By August 13, they trailed the Cubs by ten games, and Mets catcher J. C. Martin asked his teammate and fellow Chicago resident Al Weis if he wanted to go to the World Series. "Al said, 'Sure, let's go,'" Martin said. "So we made arrangements with some of the Cubs players to get tickets for the Series."

And then the Mets got hot. Returning home after three consecutive defeats in Houston, they won four in a row from the Padres by scores of 2–0, 2–0, 3–2, and 3–2. Then they beat the Giants twice and the Dodgers three times for a 9–1 home stand, which was followed by a 6–4 West Coast swing, and three victories out of four at home against the Phillies for a record of 18–6 since their low-water mark in the middle of August. And, just as the Cubs had done early in the season, the Mets were winning all kinds of games in all kinds of ways. McAndrew, who had won three games all season, won two more in one week. Koonce had five consecutive victories out of the bullpen. Ron Swoboda, platooned all season for his inconsistency at the plate, was hitting everything thrown his way and now playing every day. And on and on through the lineup.

The Cubs in the meantime stopped hitting, stopped pitching, and stopped winning. In the twenty-one games they played after taking a nine-game lead over the Mets on August 16, Williams drove in twelve runs, Santo nine, Banks eight, and Randy Hundley just one as all of their batting averages fell, along with those of Beckert and Kessinger. Only Hickman, who was on one of his hot streaks, was hitting. Hands lost four of five starts while Jenkins and Holtzman lost about as often as they won, and Selma, after winning a game on August 17, lost six straight through the end of the season. By the time the Cubs played the Mets again in September, their nine-game lead had shrunk to two and a half.

The Cubs were in a foul mood when they arrived in New York for games on September 7 and 8. They had just lost three games at home to the Pirates and were still replaying the last one in their minds. They had been one strike away from victory after a two-run homer by Hickman in the eighth inning when Willie Stargell hit a home run off Regan that tied the score. And when Kessinger, who earlier in the season had set a record for shortstops with fifty-four errorless games, booted a ball in the eleventh, the Pirates were on their way to a 7–5 victory. "To me," Santo said, "that was the turning point."

More than 50,000 people and reporters from twenty-seven newspapers crowded into Shea Stadium on a wet September evening and, after a fifteen-minute rain delay, the game began and the animosity between the two teams spilled over. A pitch from Hands sent Agee, the Mets' first batter, down into the dirt, and Koosman retaliated in the second inning by hitting Santo just below his right elbow. "That's when we should have gotten into a fight," Hank Aguirre, who was in the Cubs' bullpen, told Rick Talley. "It hurt me deeply that Santo just walked to first base and nobody did anything. That's when I knew we were in trouble." But neither team seemed interested in engaging in battle after the two purpose pitches, nor did home plate umpire Satch Davidson issue a warning. The teams settled down to business.

The Mets struck first when Agee hit a two-run home run in the third inning, but the Cubs tied the score with two runs in the sixth on an RBI single by Williams and a sacrifice fly by Santo, who'd had a painkiller sprayed on his arm after being hit by Koosman's pitch. In the bottom of the inning, Agee sent a ground ball through the soggy grass in left field and raced to second base, barely beating Williams's throw. Garrett followed with a single to right field that bounced twice in front of Hickman, who grabbed it and threw a strike to the plate as Agee rounded third and headed for home.

"It's in the middle of my mitt and I slap the tag on Agee and I could feel it all the way up his blooming body from his leg to his armpit," Hundley says. "I checked Garrett at first and he's disgusted because he sees the tag and then I turn to give the ball to Bill Hands and all of a sudden I heard this roar go up and I said, 'Oh, crap.' I turned around and Satch Davidson had the safe sign and I went ballistic."

"When he heard the umpire call Agee safe, he jumped about a mile in the air," Williams says.

"I had to maintain myself and not touch him in any way so jumping straight up and down was the only thing I could do," Hundley says.

"How in the world could you miss that call?" Santo shouted at Davidson.

"If you think that's a bad call, you take that ball and cram it in your stomach," the umpire said. "Then you'll have more brains in your stomach than you do in your head."

"That aggravated me, to say the least," Hundley says.

In the years to come, Agee would tell Hundley and several other Cubs that he'd been tagged out, but that meant nothing now. Koosman struck out six batters in the last three innings and the Mets won, 3–2. They were now within one and a half games of the division lead.

Except for Banks, the Cubs had little to say to reporters who jammed their locker room after the game, and even he didn't say much. "We're still in front," Banks said, and then he said it again. His lack of enthusiasm might have had something to do with the fact the Cubs would face Seaver in the final game of the series the following night.

With Holtzman missing his regular turn because of the Rosh Hashanah holiday, Jenkins pitched on two days' rest and gave up two quick runs in the first inning. Then, as Santo stood in the on-deck circle with his bat on his shoulder before the top of the second, he was startled to see something moving on the ground in front of him. It was a black cat that had emerged from the stands and was playing its role to perfection. The cat ran directly in front of Santo, then turned and walked within a foot of the Cubs' dugout, where it stopped and stared before reversing field and running off to safety under the stands near the Mets' dugout.

"I saw the cat come out of the stands and I knew right away we were in trouble," Santo said later. "I just wanted to run and hide."

The game was a 7–1 rout as Seaver set the Cubs down on five hits for his twenty-first victory of the season, and as the Mets piled up run after run their fans rose to the joyous occasion. Inning after inning, they sang, "Goodbye, Leo, goodbye, Leo, goodbye, Leo, we hate to see you go," a clever reference to the taunts New York Giants fans had been singing for years to Allie Sherman, the football team's coach who had recently been fired.

"The chorus swelled by tens of thousands of voices," Red Smith wrote. "On all four levels, the park blossomed with handkerchiefs fluttering in derision. Whistles and hoots arose. The voices were strident, unfriendly. It was extraordinary."

In the jubilant Mets' locker room, a cry went up for the players to get out of the shower and put their clothes on. A distinguished visitor had just arrived.

"Mrs. Payson!" said a started Gil Hodges as the dowager owner of the Mets entered his office.

"That's me," Joan Payson said. "I'm so happy, so thrilled, that I can hardly stand it. Can I kiss you?"

The Cubs' locker room by contrast was sullen. "It just makes me want to play harder," Williams said, "and we've got the Bleacher Bums for them when they come to Wrigley Field."

"They're going to regret this," said Kessinger. "They're going to eat their words."

Durocher had the last word when, asked about the chorus of taunts directed at him, he said, "Who gives a shit? When those fans go after me, they're not going after any maiden."

As the Cubs' bus left the parking lot, some fans raised their fists and threw objects, and a few of them even sat down in its path. The driver gunned the engine, the fans scattered, and the Cubs made their escape from New York.

The end came with the swiftness of an executioner's sword. The Mets won a doubleheader from Montreal the day after the Cubs left town and moved into first place for the first time in their eight-year history. The Cubs' 155-day hold on the position that had begun on opening day was over. "What am I doing with this?" Mets second baseman Ken Boswell said as he drank from a bottle of champagne. "My father drives a beer truck."

The Mets' winning streak reached ten games, and they won three more in a row after it was broken, while the Cubs lost ten of eleven games. Within ten days, they had gone from leading the Mets by one and a half games to trailing them by five.

Succumbing to the pressure of the chase, the Cubs simply came unglued. Their hitters couldn't get on base, their pitchers couldn't get anyone out, and their fielders made disastrous errors. Beckert's inability to catch a routine grounder led to a loss in St. Louis. Williams's failure to hit the cutoff man led to another the following day. Banks's inability to catch a pop foul was one of four errors in an 8–2 defeat in Montreal. But perhaps the greatest symbol of their futility came on September 11 in Philadelphia when Selma threw a ball to third base, when there was neither a runner nor a fielder in sight. He thought the Phillies' runner at second might be off with the pitch, he explained, and called out a signal to Santo to cover third. But Santo didn't hear Selma, and the ball sailed down the left-field line. The umpires held a long conference about whether Selma had balked—which would have allowed the runner to advance to third, but no farther—before deciding he hadn't, and the runner on second was allowed to score. "For much of that season, we knew we couldn't lose," Santo said. "Then things started to happen and there came a time that we were *waiting* for something to happen."

The Mets, in the meantime, were playing with great precision and even better luck. They won a doubleheader against Pittsburgh on

September 12, 1–0 and 1–0, as their pitchers drove in the only run in both games. "I've never seen such a performance, in the majors or anywhere else," Hodges said.

"You begin to say, 'What's going on here?'" said Regan, when word of the sweep reached the Cubs in St. Louis.

The Mets beat the Pirates the following day when, after Clendenon was intentionally walked in the eighth inning to load the bases, Swoboda, who'd had just six home runs all season, hit his seventh, a grand slam. In St. Louis, where the Cubs lost the first of three consecutive games to the Cardinals, a recording played at full volume in the home team's locker room. "That's life," Frank Sinatra sang. "If there's nothing shakin' come here this July, I'm going to roll myself up in a big ball and die."

Two days later, Beckert picked up a newspaper in Montreal and read that Steve Carlton had struck out nineteen Mets in St. Louis, a major league record for a nine-inning game.

"You're kidding," Santo said when his roommate read the news out loud.

Beckert took the paper into the bathroom and moments later shouted, "Oh, no!"

"What?!" Santo yelled back.

"The Mets *beat* him."

Swoboda had homered twice, once in the eighth inning, and the Mets had won, 4–3. "The game against Carlton was the high point," Swoboda told Stanley Cohen. "It always will be. He was having the best day of his life. I came to bat four times and he had two strikes on me all four times. He got me twice and I got him twice. Each home run put us ahead when we were behind a run."

"Swoboda is what happens when a team wins a pennant," said Detroit Tigers manager Mayo Smith.

On September 18, Seaver won his twenty-third game of the season, 2–0 over the Expos. It was the fifth shutout for the Mets' pitching staff in their last eight games, and Seaver would go on to win six games in September, two of them shutouts, while giving up just five runs. He would finish the season with a record of 25–7, and in all the Mets would have ten shutouts among their last twenty-five victories. "You can't be lucky every day," Casey Stengel said, "but you can if you get good pitching."

The Mets lost a doubleheader to Pittsburgh the following day, and Bob Moose of the Pirates pitched a no-hitter against them on September 20, but it hardly mattered, as the Cardinals scored four runs in the eighth inning when Santo fumbled a double-play grounder and the Cardinals beat the Cubs 4–1 at Wrigley Field. The Mets' lead in the division remained at four games.

———

As the Mets became America's darlings, the little team that could, the symbol of triumph to underdogs everywhere, the Cubs became the objects of derision throughout the league. "The Expos were laughing at us," Nye said after a game in Montreal. "It really made me mad. I wanted to do something about it." But he couldn't.

Perhaps no team enjoyed the Cubs' decline more than the Cardinals, who had won the last two National League pennants and viewed the Cubs' celebrations earlier in the season with disdain. They were scornful of Santo's heel clicking and the antics of the Bleacher Bums, whom they accused of throwing objects at them from the stands. "We didn't act that way when we were running away with the pennant," one Cardinal said. "If we can't win, I hope the Mets do," said Bob Gibson. "The Cubs ran off at the mouth."

The Cardinals took special pleasure in adding to the Cubs' woes late in September by winning two games in Wrigley Field. "Not on our watch," said Lou Brock, who had once sat in the home-team dugout.

Through it all, Banks put up a brave front, even boarding the Cardinals' bus before it left for the airport to shake hands with a few players and say, "We're still going to win this thing. We're going to win it right here, when the Mets come in to finish the season." The Cardinals booed him.

One St. Louis player in particular had a personal stake in the Cubs' plight, especially after Young's misadventures against the Mets. "I would have caught those balls," Byron Browne says, and when he saw Jenkins over the years he would say, "Remember that black cat that jumped up in front of Santo and snarled at him? That was me, saying, 'You've got the wrong guy out there.'"

Many of the Cubs fans were booing by then, too, and hurling abuse from the box seats at Santo, Beckert, Kessinger, and others by name, while elsewhere fights broke out in the stands. "It was brutal," one Cub said, "the most brutal I've ever seen." "You guys blew it!" a fan yelled at several Cubs players at one of the pregame autograph sessions that had once been so popular, and Holtzman opened a letter in the locker room to find his autograph had been returned. "It's too bad you and Holtzman didn't die in the plane crash in Indiana," read one letter to Santo, referring to a current headline. Years later, Santo said he had received death threats, including one that said he would be shot during a game in New York. Asked if he wanted extra security, Santo said, "No, it just sounds like somebody who wants me out of the lineup."

The Cubs' wives, who had been making plans for the World Series, were miserable, too. "My wife was expecting our second child shortly after the season, and when I got home she'd be crying because we were blowing the pennant," Kessinger says. "So I'd come home heartbroken and have to make *her* feel better."

The Cubs players surrendered to their fate with grace. They sat quietly at their lockers after each defeat, patiently answering questions and explaining their actions on the field. Even Durocher's customary fire was dampened. Whereas earlier in the season he would rant and rave and rip his uniform shirt off, sending buttons flying, now he was almost mute. "He wouldn't say a thing when we were losing," Regan said. "The more we lost, the quieter he became," says Blake Cullen, who had always admired Durocher's ability to turn the page once he had vented his anger after a loss. But now, Cullen wondered where the anger had gone. "He just let everything go," Cullen says.

The Mets clinched the pennant on September 24 with a 6–0 victory over Carlton before more than 54,000 fans in New York. "This stuff burns," Koonce said as champagne got into his eyes during the locker-room celebration. "I don't drink this stuff," said Weis. "I just pour it." "Here's to you, Leo," said Mets pitcher Don Cardwell, the former Cub who won eight games during the season.

Earlier in the day, the Cubs won a meaningless game against the Expos, 6–3, before 2,217 listless fans at Wrigley Field. "We shall overcome," Beckert sang softly as he leaned back in his chair in the Cubs' locker room. "We shall overcome some day-ay-ay."

"Next year, I'm going to keep my mouth shut," Santo said. "Somewhere the Sun Is Shining," read the headline in the *Tribune* the following day. Driving home after the game, Banks stopped his car along Lake Michigan and wept. "I thought it was in the bag," he said later. "But the bag broke."

The Cubs' final two games of the season against the Mets in Wrigley Field, which had once seemed so important, degenerated into an angry, riot-filled anticlimax. "It's hard to admit you weren't good enough, isn't it?" Swoboda yelled at Cubs fans who climbed on top of the Mets' dugout before the game to taunt the visiting players. Turning to a reporter, he said, "Frustration and envy manifest themselves in strange ways."

As the game progressed, many in the Ladies' Day crowd of more than 12,000 brushed past outnumbered ushers, crowded into the lower stands, and climbed on top of both dugouts, shouting and chanting angrily. The end of the game was their signal to rush out onto the field, where they slid around the bases, waved phantom runners home, and remained for the better part of an hour. "Happy Days Are Here Again," the Wrigley Field organ sounded during the chaos, which some sportswriters blamed on the Bleacher Bums, saying it was a fine way to thank a team that had treated them so well. The Bums said it was a bad rap. "That wasn't us," says Mike Murphy. "We were back in school. You want to know why? So we wouldn't go to Vietnam. We had to keep that deferment. And besides, what was I going to do? Blow a bugle?"

––––––––

The Cubs beat the Mets, 5–3, in the final game of the season as Banks hit a triple in the second inning and a three-run home run in the sixth. The runs batted in gave him a total of 106 for the season, which was third in the National League and more than he had driven in since he was in his twenties. It was also the most in baseball history by a thirty-eight-year-old man. Babe Ruth and Ty Cobb, by comparison, drove in 103 and 102 runs respectively at that age. Willie Mays drove in fifty-eight. And though Banks's range in the field had diminished considerably, he led all National League first basemen with a .996 fielding percentage

When the Mets played the Orioles in the World Series, the Cubs invited Banks to join their front-office personnel at the games, and though it was unusual for players to be a part of this contingent, Banks decided to go. "It was my last chance," he said many years later, "and I thought I might as well go see it."

He enjoyed watching the Mets win four straight games after losing the Series opener, he said, as well as the enthusiasm of the fans and the players and their families. But he was discomfited by some of the people sitting around him, who occasionally glanced his way to see how he was reacting. What were they thinking? he wondered. Were they feeling sorry for him?

You never thought, "That should have been us"? he was asked many years later.

"What I saw was that to win everybody's got to like each other, just one time," he replied. "The owner, the general manager, the coaches, the players, the fans, the writers, everybody. Just one time."

Chapter 30

Questions and Answers

How could it have happened?

How could a team of All-Stars, a team with four future members of the Hall of Fame, have lost to this ragtag bunch of journeymen plus Tom Seaver?

The question would haunt the Cubs down through the years, as would the search for answers.

Their hats were off to the Mets, no argument there. They had seized every opportunity and squeezed every ounce of talent out of their players, stars and scrubs alike. From August 13, when they trailed the Cubs by ten games, to September 24, when they clinched the pennant, they had won thirty-four games and lost just ten. And their pitching, particularly late in the season, had been sublime.

Seaver, with twenty-five victories, Jerry Koosman, with seventeen, and Ron Taylor, with nine wins and thirteen saves, had performed as advertised. But Gary Gentry, a twenty-two-year-old rookie, also won thirteen games. Jim McAndrew won important games down the stretch. Tug McGraw, who hadn't distinguished himself in his three previous major league seasons, won nine games and saved twelve more. Former Cubs Don Cardwell and Cal Koonce also stepped up, and so did a twenty-two-year-old pitcher with an astonishing fastball but serious control problems whom the Mets didn't seem to know what to do with.

Nolan Ryan started ten games in 1969 and relieved in fifteen others, winning six while losing three. It was the only one of his four seasons with the Mets in which he won more games than he lost, and two years later they would trade him in frustration to the California Angels for Jim Fregosi, who had once been an All-Star infielder but whose best days were behind him. Ryan would pitch for twenty-seven seasons, win 324 games, and pitch seven no-hitters. Any team, it seemed, was capable of making a Brock-for-Broglio trade.

But was the brilliance of the Mets the only answer? Was it the only thing that accounted for what amounted to the greatest fall from grace in baseball history? The 1951 New York Giants were celebrated for having made up a thirteen-and-a-half-game deficit over the Brooklyn Dodgers, but it took them six weeks to do it. The 1969 Mets went from ten games off the lead to three and a half in front in just a month. Leo Durocher, it was noted, had now managed one of the worst performances in a stretch drive as well as the best.

The search for answers continued.

Was it all those day games at Wrigley Field? Joe Amalfitano, who was a Cubs coach in 1969, thought playing in the heat of the summer may have hurt, but Ernie Banks pointed out that the afternoon games gave the players regular hours and, since most of them were married, let them spend their evenings at home and get the rest they needed.

Did the fifteen doubleheaders they played, several of them within one week, sap their strength? But the Mets had played twenty-two double-headers, many of them to make up for rainouts, and two of them on successive days.

Was it all the outside activities the Cubs participated in, the money-making gigs Jack Childers had arranged for them? Did they tire them out and affect their concentration? Philip K. Wrigley subscribed to this theory. "I think it's all the TV appearances, the speaking engagements, the recording sessions, the autograph parties, and other activities that took the players' minds off the game," the Cubs owner said. "They're all young and aren't used to being celebrities. They don't know how to handle it."

Was overconfidence the key to what went wrong? "I think some of the players took something for granted in August and instead of playing out the year we just worried too much about going to the World Series," Al Spangler says. "Some of the players had tentative gigs out in Las Vegas for the winter and some of the wives were buying World Series clothes."

"The Cubs' wives had already spent their World Series checks," Koonce told Stanley Cohen. "They thought they had it in the bag. I kept reading in the papers that Mrs. So-and-so was going to buy this and Mrs. So-and-so was going to do that. I said, 'I think these guys might just be jumping the gun a little.'"

"The truth is we ran the flag up the pole too soon," Gene Oliver told Rick Talley. "No doubt about it. We celebrated too soon."

Did the Cubs' antics when they were winning—Ron Santo's heel clicking, Dick Selma's towel waving—and the over-the-top enthusiasm of the Bleacher Bums infuriate other teams and make them more determined to beat the Cubs? And had Santo's tirade against Don Young shown a fundamental inability to come together for a common purpose?

Did the fact that the Mets were not expected to win, did not expect it themselves, while the Cubs, by running up an early lead in the standings, put themselves in the ironic position considering their decades of failure of being the team to beat? "We had the innocence of someone who had never been there before. What did we have to lose?" Ron Swoboda said. "We were ingenues. We had that wonderful, clear-minded innocence of not having the responsibility of winning it, of not having to doubt ourselves if we stumbled."

"Maybe we're too inexperienced at winning to know what pressure is," Seaver said. "Maybe we're mistaking it for excitement."

The Cubs' feeling was different. "None of us had been there," said Billy Williams. "Most of the time there is somebody on a club who can tell you how to feel. We had nobody. Just a bunch of guys who made it so far and couldn't get over the hurdle."

But the more the players and fans peeled back the onion of despair surrounding the disaster, the more it became clear that the Cubs' biggest problem was one from which there was no escape: their manager.

Almost from the start of the 1969 season, Leo Durocher had seemed curiously indifferent to his responsibilities. For some years, it had been noticed that he was seldom on the field for pregame warmups, preferring to stay in the locker room until the game began while his coaches oversaw drills. And while he had occasionally missed games in past years claiming illness, and sometimes left the dugout early, one reporter counted six times during the season he failed to show.

One came when he left Pittsburgh in June to attend a bachelor party in Chicago the night before his wedding to Lynne Goldblatt, leaving Pete Reiser to manage a 3–2, ten-inning defeat to the Pirates. More than 200 guests and a number of reporters and photographers attended the ceremony the following day, including Banks, who sang "Get Me to the Church on Time." Among the gifts was a silver ensemble from the players with the bride's name spelled incorrectly, ten dollars in nickels and dimes from the Bleacher Bums, and, as a gag, a bullet for Durocher to use on himself if the Cubs lost the pennant.

Durocher's commitment to Goldblatt was such that before a game in Montreal less than two weeks after the wedding, he saw Ken Holtzman chatting up one of the young French-Canadian usherettes who worked for the Expos and asked the pitcher to see if she had a friend. After the game, they went on a double date that ended up with Durocher entertaining his usherette by throwing up the following morning and then again in the afternoon. "I think he missed the last two games of the series, holed up in his hotel room," Holtzman told Talley. "Everyone thought he had the flu. The French flu maybe."

But while most of the games Durocher missed were ignored or unremarked upon, there was one in July that almost got him fired. In the third inning of a game at Wrigley Field against the Dodgers, he told Reiser to take over the team and to tell anyone who asked that he was ill. He then took a private plane 330 miles to Eagle River, Wisconsin, for Parents' Weekend at Camp Ojibwa, where Goldblatt was visiting her ten-year-old son. One parent in attendance called Jim Enright of the *Chicago American* with the news, and it soon became the biggest story in town.

Wrigley was furious and, according to Jack Brickhouse, was prepared to fire Durocher, but calmed down when the manager apologized. "I agree that Leo could feel just as lousy up in Wisconsin as in his apartment," Wrigley said. "My concern is that some of the players who have been hustling their boilers to win the pennant might wonder if the manager is equally dedicated." Durocher blamed the uproar on Enright and feuded with a number of the reporters covering the Cubs, sometimes lying to them about who would be playing the next day, which led to angry confrontations and hard feelings that never healed.

Nor were the Cubs players spared Durocher's wrath. At one point late in the season, he called Ferguson Jenkins, who started forty-two games in 1969, the most since Joe "Iron Man" McGinnity of the 1903 New York Giants, a quitter. "I nearly fell over," Holtzman says. "That's when I thought Leo had lost it." Holtzman also confirms a story told by a few of his astonished teammates that Durocher once called him a "gutless Jew" in front of the team. "It was hard to tell sometimes when he was kidding and when he was serious," says Holtzman, who didn't respond to his manager's slurs. "He did the same with Santo and Banks."

Durocher also engaged in bizarre behavior that baffled his players. At one point late in the season, he banned card games in the clubhouse. At another, he told the players he was lifting curfew and would fine anyone he found *in* his room. Randy Hundley, who was not a drinker, dutifully complied, but after trying to match his teammates as they barhopped by drinking Cokes, he was up all night with a caffeine headache and was worn out when he got to the ballpark.

"It was crazy," says Williams, who recalls one moment when Durocher almost went berserk. "We'd lost five or six ball games and Leo said, 'Sit by your locker and put your head between your legs and think about what you're doing,'" Williams says. As they sat in silence, a doctor who had been called to check on some of the players entered the room. "About a minute later, Leo had the guy by the neck and the belt and shoved him out of the clubhouse, shouting at Yosh Kawano, 'Don't let anyone in this damn clubhouse!' There was just a lot of tension."

But if Durocher's impulsive behavior worried his players, the way he ran the team into the ground left them positively bewildered. Game after game, week after week, the same lineup took the field with never a day off. If a hitter was doing well, he continued to play. If he fell into a slump, he played on. Every position player on the team suffered from this overwork, but none more than Hundley, who hit .276 with fourteen home runs and forty-four runs batted in during the first half of the season and paid the price as the summer, and the schedule, heated up.

"I'd lose ten pounds a day and drink water to get back five pounds of it," says Hundley, who played in 151 games and in both games of nine doubleheaders. "I finally had to go to a department store and ask for suspenders. I didn't even know what they were until then."

"He would wear red suspenders one day, then yellow, then blue," says Jenkins. "He was proud of that. You played until you dropped."

There was no question of a player suggesting to Durocher that he might benefit from some occasional rest. Baseball's macho code—best expressed by Reiser, who liked to say, "Rub some dirt on it"—forbade it. So did the manager.

"We were playing in St. Louis one day and it's unbelievably hot and I'm sitting at my locker flat worn out," Hundley says. "They take me down the runway of the dugout and ice me down and Leo pops his head around the corner and says, 'How do you feel?' I said, 'Skip, I want you to look at me and you tell me how I feel.' He said, 'You're all right. Get out there.' And that's the way it went. I'm not going to tell the manager I can't play. I just couldn't do that."

Holtzman was another Cub who learned not to admit he was tiring. "He accused me of being lackadaisical and not being enough of a competitor," he said at the start of the season. "Well, from now on it'll be different. If he comes out to talk to me in the seventh or eighth inning, I just won't tell him I'm tired. No pitcher is as strong in the late innings as he is at the start. Not if he's really pitching. But I'll never admit I'm tired again."

Kessinger also lost an alarming amount of weight during the season as he joined Banks, Hundley, Santo, and Williams in playing more than 150 games while players who might have spelled them from time to time languished on the bench. The only Cubs reserves who played in more than half the games were Willie Smith, who appeared in 103, and Al Spangler, who played in eighty-two. "Leo was just not bringing everybody into the fold," says Rich Nye. "We're playing .500 ball, the Mets are playing .800 ball, and you've got to make a change, give everybody a rest. It got to where the reserve players weren't thinking about how they could contribute, thinking about the game. It was so frustrating."

Particularly galling to some players was the way Durocher ignored Paul Popovich, who hit .337 and played brilliantly at second base while Glenn Beckert was on the disabled list. But when Beckert came back, Popovich all but disappeared from the lineup. Other reserves hardly played at all, such as backup catchers Bill Heath and Ken Rudolph, who might have spelled Hundley, but had only forty-five and forty plate appearances respectively. "I watched the whole gory thing," Heath told Talley. "It wasn't sad, it was stupid. You could see what was happening, everybody getting tighter and tighter and nobody doing anything about it. Leo went into a trance. It was really sad to see Kessinger missing those ground balls. Beckert, too. Sometimes I think it was tougher on those of us on the bench who had to watch."

Durocher's insistence on staying with his lineup boiled over in August when *Chicago Tribune* writer Richard Dozer approached the manager while he was shaving in front of his office mirror after a loss to the Astros and asked whether the Cubs starters might benefit from some rest. "Don't ask me that fucking question," Durocher said. "If you've got a silly fucking question, go ask the players." His face still lathered, the manager went into the locker room and shouted, "I want all my players out here!" A few Cubs emerged from the shower to see what was going on.

In his autobiography, Williams describes the scene: "'Does anyone want to come out of the lineup because you are tired?' Durocher yelled. 'Beckert! Are you tired?' 'Nope,' Beckert said. 'How about you,

Kessinger? Is the heat getting to you? Are you tired?' Kessinger shrugged his shoulders and answered, 'No, I'm not tired.' One by one, each of our starters told Durocher exactly what he wanted to hear as he turned and sneered at Dozer for daring to challenge his strategy."

Durocher's handling of the Cubs pitchers was just as inflexible. Along with Jenkins's forty-two starts, Bill Hands had forty-one, Holtzman thirty-nine, and Dick Selma thirty-six, pitching for the most part on three days' rest. Phil Regan pitched seventy-one times out of the bullpen while, particularly toward the end of the season, Ted Abernathy, Hank Aguirre, Nye, and others were forgotten. At one point after the All-Star break, Regan pitched in seven consecutive games and was within two games of the record for pitchers when Jenkins pitched a complete-game victory. "I shook his hand twice when he came off the mound," Regan says. "That's one record I didn't want."

"It got to be a joke the way Leo would telephone the bullpen and say, 'Get Regan up.'" Nye says. "Sometimes Don Nottebart and I would start warming up on our own, just to get mentioned in the press box."

"He plum forgot Aguirre and me the second half of the season," Abernathy said. "I pitched my best when my arm was real tired—that's when the submarine sinker worked best—but my arm sure didn't get very tired that year."

"I won a game in relief on May fourteenth in San Diego and lost one on May seventeenth in Houston and that's all I pitched, baby," said Nottebart, who was coming to the end of a ten-year major league career. "Leo forgot about me. I just sat there and watched it all go down the tubes. I wasted my entire last year of baseball on the Cubs' bench."

"Leo tried to bury me," said Jim Colborn, a Cubs rookie in 1969, who would win twenty games for the Milwaukee Brewers four years later. "I can remember after the trade saying to myself, 'What a load off my mind.'"

Nye, who had won thirteen games and pitched 200 innings in 1967 and 132 in 1968, was held to just sixty-eight innings in 1969, which frustrated him as it did other members of the bullpen, who found it hard to pitch effectively when they were called on after long layoffs. But once again the idea of taking the matter up with Durocher was out of the question.

"Why didn't I go to Leo and tell him my arm was healthy and I could give him two hundred innings?" Nye says. "The answer is Leo himself. He was unapproachable. He had this tough-guy image to maintain and you just didn't question him."

Certainly the team's biggest star didn't. Banks's hot start at the plate eased Durocher's negative attitude toward him and ended any doubt about his place in the lineup. Banks played in 155 games, came to the plate 629 times, and never once told Durocher that he, or anyone else, might benefit from a day off. Banks's teammates were amazed at his consistent run production—"I wouldn't be surprised if he's hitting home runs when he's eighty," Kessinger said—but none of them dared to suggest that he approach the manager on their behalf. It was simply not in his nature, they knew, and so they played on.

———

Gil Hodges was everything Durocher was not. He was a certifiably great baseball player who hit 370 home runs during his eighteen-year career and was considered the best first baseman of his era, while Babe Ruth himself had called Durocher "the All-American out." Hodges was tall and ruggedly handsome while Durocher, for all his charm, was hardly a matinee idol. He was quiet and soft-spoken in contrast to Durocher's ceaseless bombast. There was one other contrast between the two managers. Hodges's players loved him.

"He was a pillar of strength," Tom Seaver told Stanley Cohen. "He never rattled. He was always in complete control. Every player felt he had his complete support. He didn't show his emotions. He was a father image, someone the players could always count on."

Hodges's command of the Mets was absolute. After Cleon Jones failed to hustle after a ball hit to left field and then made a weak throw in a game the Mets were losing to the Astros late in July, Hodges left the dugout as if he was going to the pitcher's mound. But instead, as everyone in the ballpark watched in amazement, he continued walking into the outfield until he reached Jones. After a short conversation, Hodges left the field with Jones trailing behind him. "It might have looked like he was trying to embarrass me, but he wasn't," Jones said. "We were getting our ass kicked and something had to be done." Jones hit .340 for the Mets in 1969 and finished third in the National League batting race.

In a sense, Hodges was lucky the Mets had so few established, reliable players. Their unimposing roster left him free to improvise and innovate, to make sure everyone played, and everyone rested. Jones and Tommie Agee were the only Mets to come to bat more than 400 times in 1969 while fifteen other players batted more than 160 times. Ron Swoboda, who performed so well late in the season, played in just 109 games and batted only .235. And so it went through the lineup, as statistics meant nothing and opportunity everything.

Ed Kranepool and Donn Clendenon shared first base, Ken Boswell, Bud Harrelson, Wayne Garrett, Al Weis, Ed Charles, and Bobby Pfeil took turns in the infield. And, in contrast to the daily punishment Hundley took, Jerry Grote, the Mets' first-string catcher, played in just 109 games as J. C. Martin and Duffy Dyer spelled him regularly.

At times, Hodges seemed almost uncanny in his ability to identify players who could help. Rod Gaspar, a rookie outfielder who wasn't considered likely to make the team in the spring, played in 118 games, had ten assists, and led the league with six double plays started by an outfielder. Gaspar also made several brilliant plays when Jones left the lineup with an injured hand during the Mets' key winning stretch in August.

Hodges was equally deft at handling his pitching staff. Using a five-man rotation at a time when the practice was not widespread, he held Seaver to thirty-six starts, a contrast to Jenkins's forty-two that would make a big difference during the final months of the season. Koosman, with thirty-two starts, Gentry, with thirty-five, and Don Cardwell, with twenty-one, were similarly kept fresh with good results. Cardwell, for instance, was ineffective early in the season but came on strong in the second half, and the Mets won eleven of his last fourteen starts.

The same was true in the bullpen. In contrast to Regan's seventy-two appearances, Ron Taylor pitched fifty-nine times while Tug McGraw was used in relief forty-two times and Cal Koonce forty. Koonce lost three games early in the season, but later won six games and saved seven. It was, he said, a big difference from the six seasons he spent with the Cubs. "During one period, I warmed up in the bullpen fourteen days in a row," Koonce said. "With the Mets it was different. We took turns. If you were brought in one day, you knew you would have a day or two to get ready before you were called on again. That's why we were fresh at the end of the season."

But it wasn't only the Mets who revered their manager. Hodges's reputation for fairness, honesty, and humility had spread throughout baseball during his playing career, and the Cubs thought it might even have spread to the umpires. "You had the feeling they wanted to see Gil Hodges and the Mets beat out Durocher and the Cubs," Al Spangler says. "I can't prove anything. It's just a feeling. Leo was not well liked among the umpires and Hodges was."

Though Hodges seldom showed emotion, it was clear to his players how much the season meant to him. He had suffered a heart attack the previous fall, and while he had given up smoking and began taking long walks, he now had a sense of his own mortality that led to a great compassion for his players. When McAndrew injured his shoulder, Hodges told him, "If you have a physical problem, I want to know about it. There's no pennant that's worth your career. It's *you* that I'm responsible for and *you* that I care about." The contrast with Durocher's attitude toward injuries was stark.

Other Mets noted how Hodges never humiliated a player for a mistake, but took him aside afterward to conduct an almost Socratic dialogue, or none at all. "He would make you tell yourself what was wrong," Garrett said. "He could just look at you and you knew something was wrong," said Gentry. "He never had to tell you."

J. C. Martin got a close-up view of the difference between Hodges and Durocher when he was traded to the Cubs in 1970. Martin was happy to be going home and excited about being on a team with so much talent, but he was quickly disappointed. Whereas Hodges would never react to a bad play, Durocher would throw towels and berate the miscreant who had betrayed him, continually creating the kind of pressure no team could overcome. "They were so tight and wound up they could not perform in the late innings," Martin said. "It was different with the Mets in '69. Hodges kept us believing that we were never out of a game."

In the years to come, there would be many summations of the Cubs' storied defeat by the Mets in 1969—Enright suggested their epitaph should be "Died from a lack of leadership"—but perhaps the most cruel, and the most accurate, came from Martin. "I think Gil would have won with the Cubs," he said. "I think it was the manager that made the difference."

———

The 1969 season resonated with the Cubs and Mets players for the rest or their lives. Wherever they went, they encountered reminders.

More than forty years later, Phil Regan became a minor league pitching coach for the Mets, and when he walked into the clubhouse in Port St. Lucie, Florida, he saw a small plaque dedicated to the 1969 World Series champions. "I turned and went the other way," he said. Regan had a different emotion when he read a letter from a woman in Chicago. She was born in the summer of 1969, she said, and her mother had wanted to name her Holly or Kathleen. But her father was a rabid Cubs fan who insisted that she be named after his favorite player. It was an honor to be named Regan, she wrote, and she would be a Cubs fan forever. Later, she and her father visited Regan in the Mets' spring training headquarters. They have stayed in touch ever since.

———

In the 1980s, Hundley got in on the ground floor of baseball's newest growth industry—adult fantasy camps for which grown men pay large sums to go to Arizona or Florida, wear uniforms, and receive instruction from, and play alongside, the players they cheered for when they were young. In 1986, Hundley added a special wrinkle to his camp—a charity game in Phoenix between members of the 1969 Cubs and Mets.

"I can hit! I can hit! I still got it!" said a fifty-five-year-old Banks after hitting a two-run double off Koosman in the first inning. Hundley followed with a run-scoring double, but the Mets scored seven runs off Holtzman in the second and went on to win, 11–3. "Now you can see why we won and they lost," Kranepool said.

Though many members of the 1969 Mets and Cubs attended the game, there were two notable exceptions. One was Hodges, whose death of a heart attack in 1972 two days short of his forty-eighth birthday had rocked baseball. Ten thousand mourners attended his funeral, and Jackie Robinson, who had long been in ill health himself, said he had thought he would be the first of the Dodgers' fabled Boys of Summer to die and that he was "absolutely shattered." Robinson died six months later at the age of fifty-three.

The other missing link in Phoenix was Ron Santo. "I wouldn't go to *anything* that had to do with the Mets," he said. Nor would he watch the telecast back in Chicago. "The game would have brought back bad memories for me."

As the years went by, Holtzman began to notice a curious phenomenon. The great fun Cubs fans had enjoyed during the first five months of the 1969 season, which had been lost during the team's collapse, seemed to be returning in their memories. "Now, as parents and grandparents," he says, "that team remains a link to their youth."

"We'll never get away from 1969," Kessinger says. "It was the best of times for us, and the worst of times. I've never had a summer I enjoyed more, even though it ended not so good."

"People say, 'I was there in 1969,'" says Jenkins of his encounters with Cubs fans over the years. "I tell them, 'So was I.'"

Chapter 31

Riding the Pines

Not long after Jack Hiatt reported to Montreal after the San Francisco Giants traded him to the expansion franchise before the 1970 season, Expos manager Gene Mauch called him in his New York hotel room before a game against the Mets.

"I've got some good news for you, Jack," said Mauch, whose team had gotten off to a dismal start and was en route to its second consecutive last-place finish in the National League East. "Randy Hundley has been hurt, and you've been traded to the Cubs. Better get there right now." Hiatt packed quickly, hurried to the airport, caught a plane to Chicago, and arrived at Wrigley Field shortly after the Cubs' game against the Atlanta Braves had begun. He hastily put on a uniform and ran out to the bullpen.

Moments later, a huge roar went up from the stands as Ernie Banks hit a home run off Braves pitcher Pat Jarvis that barely cleared the left-field wall, struck the concrete floor below the second row of seats, and bounced back onto the field. The cheering continued as the game was stopped and Braves left fielder Rico Carty picked up the ball and tossed it into the Cubs bullpen. It was retrieved by Willie Smith, who ran to the dugout and presented it to Banks, who accepted it with a shy grin, looking, one observer thought, like the little boy he no longer was.

"What's going on, Rube?" Hiatt asked Cubs bullpen coach Rube Walker. "Ernie's hit a million home runs."

"Jack, that's his five hundredth," Walker said as the celebration continued.

"Congratulations," Hank Aaron, who had hit his 500th home run two years earlier, told Banks at first base when he was walked later in the game.

"Thanks, Hank," Banks replied. "I'm just happy to be in the same category as you."

Banks's teammates were thrilled for him—"Too bad we didn't have some champagne to pour over his head," Ron Santo said—and even Leo Durocher got into the spirit of the occasion. "How many times did I try to retire him?" he said. "How many first basemen did I try? He'd sit there on the bench and I'd look at him and he'd look at me and I'd look at him again and finally I'd say, 'Okay, go out there and play first base.' What a man." But Durocher couldn't help adding that he was glad the ball had been well hit, rather than being aided by the wind. It was a subtle suggestion, some thought, that many of Banks's home runs at Wrigley Field through the years had been cheap.

After spending almost an hour doing postgame radio and television interviews, Banks came back out onto the field, took a groundskeeper's hose, sprinkled the infield, and said there was time for another game. Then he jumped up and clicked his heels and said, "I'm twelve years old again." Banks remained in the Cubs' locker room answering questions for so long that when a reporter returned the following day and found him in the same spot he wondered if Banks had ever left. "I was going to pitch a tent and spend the night," he said. "But my wife called and said I had to come home."

A 500th home run was a game-stopping event in 1970. Only eight players in baseball history, Hall of Famers every one, had hit that many prior to Banks in the era before performance-enhancing drugs twisted the record book out of shape. The replay of the event, along with Jack Brickhouse's call, would become the signature moment of Banks's career, replayed on what seemed to be an endless televised loop in Chicago for the rest of his life and beyond.

In truth, Banks's 500th home run should have come three days earlier, because one had been stolen from him the year before on a murky evening in Montreal. Banks hit a low line drive that cleared the fence and rattled in the right-field seats but went unseen by second-base umpire Tony Venzon, who ran into the outfield to get a closer look. Seeing Venzon's confusion, Expos' right fielder Rusty Staub stuck his foot into a small hole at the bottom of the fence and enlarged it.

"Maybe it went through here," Staub said as Durocher raced to the scene of the crime. Venzon was fooled and told Durocher, "Look. It went under the fence through the hole."

"I had to turn away to keep from laughing out loud," Staub told Rick Talley. "I mean, it's not like I misled the umpire. I didn't actually *say* the ball went through the hole." Durocher's protest was ignored, and Banks would enter baseball's record books with 512 home runs, tying him with Eddie Mathews, instead of one ahead.

Ten days after the milestone, Banks pulled a muscle in his left leg during a game in New York and left the Cubs' starting lineup for eight days. He returned on May 30 and hit another home run while playing in both games of a doubleheader, but then went back to the bench for two more weeks. His knees were betraying him on every front now—painful bone chips, pulled muscles, strained tendons, the formation of fluid that required repeated draining. Doctors told him he had the legs of a sixty-year-old man.

Banks was also still jittery from death threats that had been called into the Cubs' Arizona spring training headquarters. The perpetrator was quickly arrested—hardly a criminal mastermind, he had called from a Chicago YMCA where FBI agents had no trouble finding him—but Banks was confined to his hotel room, which he said was like being in jail. "It's great to be alive," he said when he was set free. "Let's play two."

Banks was back in the lineup on June 13 in Los Angeles, and in his first at-bat he hit his 502nd run off Dodgers' pitcher Claude Osteen, a twenty-game winner the year before. "Jesus, he hadn't played all this time and look at him," Hiatt thought. "It's not that easy." And though his batting average remained below .250, Banks hit six home runs and drove in sixteen runs in fifteen games through the end of June. Two of the homers were off Steve Carlton in St. Louis, but neither Banks nor the Cubs could celebrate as the Cubs lost their eleventh straight game, 8–6.

Any hope that Banks's legs might stop troubling him ended quickly when, after playing in both games of a Fourth of July doubleheader at Wrigley Field, his left knee began to swell. "It's painful, like a toothache, especially when I turn on it," he said. The only prescription the Cubs' doctors could offer was cortisone shots and rest. He played in only two more games in July, the last one in Atlanta on July 20 when, after a nine-day layoff, Durocher let his anger at the writers covering the team, whom he believed Banks manipulated against him, get the best of him.

He was putting Banks in the lineup "against my better judgment," Durocher said, because a Chicago sportswriter had told him Banks was ready to play. He was tired of "taking this kind of criticism," the manager said. "If Banks should get hurt out there tonight, the sportswriter will have to take the blame for ruining his career." Banks took two pain pills during the game and went hitless in three at-bats.

Two days later, Banks and the Cubs surrendered to the inevitable, and for the first time in his career he was placed on the disabled list. He needed "complete rest and physiotherapy," team physician Jacob Suker said, adding that surgery "would not enhance the chances of furthering his playing career."

Banks took the news hard. He didn't want to be a hindrance, he said, or embarrass himself or the Cubs. Perhaps he should retire. The Cubs reacted to the suggestion with horror. He should not even think about it, John Holland said, certainly not while his knees were hurting. All he needed was some rest. And besides, the Cubs were going to need him in August and September for the pennant race.

―――

It was hard to know what to make of the 1970 Cubs. After losing three of their first four games, they won eleven in a row, the team's longest win streak since 1945, and moved into first place. Late in June, they lost twelve straight, one short of the club record, and fell into fourth.

Billy Williams had his finest season, hitting .322 with forty-two home runs and 129 runs batted in. His 137 runs scored were the most in the major leagues in twenty-three years, and he finished second in the Most Valuable Player balloting. Ron Santo, Glenn Beckert, and Don Kessinger all had fine years at the plate, and Ferguson Jenkins, Bill Hands, and Ken Holtzman won twenty-two, eighteen, and seventeen games respectively. The Cubs also made two midseason acquisitions who helped immediately: Milt Pappas, who won four of his first five starts, and Joe Pepitone, who drove in thirty-one runs in his first thirty-one games. Another newcomer, J. C. Martin, was advised to dispose of his New York Mets bag and, when he showed his 1969 World Series ring to some of his new teammates, they muttered, "That's nice." Besides Banks, only Hundley, who had played in 612 games in the previous four years, missed a large portion of the season. He suffered a fractured thumb and torn knee cartilage that required surgery in the first month of the season and played in just seventy-three games.

The Cubs veterans declared a new sense of purpose after the 1969 debacle. "We're more mature now," Santo said. "We're taking things more calmly and not going on any emotional binges."

"Last year, we *thought* we could win it," said Kessinger. "This year we *know* we can."

During the heady early days of the season, the fans did their best to recapture the magic of the previous summer, and for a time they succeeded. Dick Selma had been traded away, but Pepitone was there to pick up the slack. A hugely free-spirited soul—he owned hair salons and was famous for wearing one of his two toupees under his baseball cap—Pepitone had played for the New York Yankees for eight tempestuous years before being traded to the Astros after the 1969 season. But late in July, the Astros committed the unpardonable sin of assigning him a roommate on the road, and he demanded to be put on the voluntary retired list. The Astros traded him to the Cubs instead. Arriving in

Cincinnati, where the Cubs were playing a doubleheader, Pepitone was immediately put in center field and had two hits in five at-bats. He lit up a cigarette in the locker room between games and said, "Man, I'm tired. I think what I need is a week off."

With his bell-bottom pants, man purse, and hair dryer (a *hair dryer?* In the *locker room?*) Pepitone quickly became a favorite among his teammates. "He keeps us laughing so hard we don't have time to think of our troubles," Santo said.

Soon, Pepitone was a Chicago celebrity and man about town, which he occasionally toured on his motorcycle. "I like making people like me," he said. "Going out and having a good time—it's my thing."

Cubs fans were happy to oblige him, and one admirer even hired a chauffeur-driven limousine to take him to the ballpark. "The limousine had a horn that played 'Take Me Out to the Ball Game,'" Hiatt says. "The kids would come flying after Joey."

Some older fans also found Pepitone irresistible. "He had a bevy of beauties waiting for him all the time," says Greg Carlton, a Cubs batboy.

The one member of the organization who didn't care for Pepitone's antics was Durocher. The clothes, the women, the constant need for attention, the trouble that followed wherever he went, they all hit perhaps just a little too close to home. The manager may not have known that Pepitone had ridden the team bus in St. Louis wearing a button that said "Fire Durocher," but it was clear they were never going to get along for the simple reason that they were too much alike.

Durocher couldn't argue with Pepitone's production, though. He drove in forty-four runs in fifty-six games and gave them a significant upgrade on defense. "He did a hell of a job in center field," Hiatt says. "The fans who remembered Don Young knew we were going to be in business when we got Joe."

As far as personality went, Jim Hickman was Pepitone's polar opposite—quiet, unemotional, a player who went about his business without drawing attention to himself. He was also the Cubs' top offensive threat in 1970, when he had the season of his life—a .315 batting average with thirty-two home runs, 115 runs batted in, and 102 runs scored. This was an inexplicable outlier from Hickman's other twelve years in the majors, during which he never batted higher than .272, hit more than nineteen home runs, drove in more than sixty-four runs, or scored more than sixty. No one could explain it, least of all Hickman. "It happens every once in a while that I get into one of these hot streaks for two or three weeks and then, just as fast as it comes, it goes away," he told Robert Markus of the *Tribune*. "I guess that's the difference between the good ballplayer and the average player. When the good player loses it, he always manages to find it again. I've never been able to." But now he had found it for an entire season, during which he drove in the winning run in the All-Star Game in Cincinnati with the single that sent Pete Rose barreling into Ray Fosse, severely injuring the catcher's shoulder. It is considered one of the most memorable moments in the history of the All-Star Game, and when Hickman died in 2016 his obituaries called him a footnote to baseball history.

Hickman split his time between first base and the outfield early in the season, but when Banks left the lineup he became a regular at first, which made him uncomfortable because he hadn't played the position much during his career, and never for the Cubs. After having problems catching two balls thrown straight at him during a game, he said, "I know that Ernie would have been able to handle those throws, but I just don't have enough experience."

Another player who knew something about the trials of age and injury was also pained at Banks's absence. He hoped his friend wouldn't prolong his career to the point where he began to hear boos, Willie Mays said when the Giants came to Wrigley Field in August. "The people in Chicago love him. I hope they always love him."

Banks's twenty-one days on the disabled list came and went, and he remained on the bench. "This is a great disappointment to me," said Holland. "The doctors said he was coming along real well, but that he needed two more weeks and probably three before his knee could take the twisting, turning, and punishment of a game." Perhaps, but some of the Cubs suspected that Durocher had made the decision to keep Banks out of action for so long, and they could hardly blame him. The team was better off with Hickman at first base.

On August 22, more than a month after he left the lineup, Banks replaced Hickman at first base in the fifth inning of a game in San Francisco. Two innings later, he hit a sacrifice fly to center field, and in the ninth he singled to left. He appeared in the starting lineup for the first time on September 2 and played in eighteen of his team's remaining thirty-two games, often as a pinch hitter, but also at first base as Hickman returned to the outfield. An eight-game hitting streak in September raised his batting average twenty points, but he finished the season with by far the worst production of his career: a .252 batting average, twelve home runs, and forty-four runs batted in. The most glaring number, however, was seventy-two. Banks had played in fewer than half the Cubs' games, and his knees had never stopped hurting.

The Cubs were cruelly mocked by two vagaries of the 1970 National League schedule. The first was that they would play their final fourteen games on the road, a brutal trip that started in Montreal and moved on to St. Louis and Philadelphia. The second was that they would finish the season playing the Mets in New York.

The trip got off to a promising start when they won three closely fought games from the Expos and crept within one and a half games of the first-place Pittsburgh Pirates. And when they took a 4–2 lead into the eighth inning of the final game of the series, their hopes continued to rise. But with one out, the Expos hit three consecutive singles off Phil Regan, cutting the margin to one run. Ron Fairly followed with a sharp ground ball near Hickman at first that might have been turned into an inning-ending double play. But the ball shot by him, rolled into foul territory down the right-field line, and drove in the runs that put the Expos ahead. "All a man can do is try his best," said Hickman, who had performed so brilliantly all season but had come up short at a key moment.

The defeat seemed to take the heart out of the Cubs. They lost two games in St. Louis, two more in Philadelphia, and were eliminated on September 27 as they sloshed through a muddy field in Philadelphia for a victory that had no greater reward than Jenkins's twenty-first win. Unhappily, they trudged to New York, where all that remained of the season was the battle for second place.

"Fergie, do me a favor. Let's win this one," Hiatt told Jenkins before the final game of the season. "I need the money." Jenkins laughed at the idea that the rivalry that had inflamed the nation a year earlier had come to this—tied in the standings on the final day of the season and little more to play for than pride and the extra $500 the winners would receive as the second-place share of World Series receipts.

The Cubs were no longer startled that a crowd of 48,314 Mets fans showed up for the game, but they couldn't get over the reception the fans gave Pepitone. "I have never seen a ballpark that booed like that," Hiatt says of the screams that arose every time Pepitone came to bat. "I don't know what he ever did to New York. I have no idea why they disliked Joe Pepitone."

Pepitone did. "Those are affectionate boos," he said, recalling the home runs he had hit in the Yankees' annual exhibition games against the Mets. "Every time, I'd jump on home plate with both feet and give the fans the peace sign," he said.

The Cubs led the Mets 2–1 in the seventh inning when Williams singled and Pepitone followed with his twenty-sixth home run of the season. As the boos rained down, he ran slowly around the bases, jumped on the plate, turned to the crowd, and flashed one last peace sign from the Cubs to the Mets for old times' sake.

Chapter 32

Sunday in America

Early on a March morning in 1971 at the Cubs' spring training camp in Scottsdale, Ernie Banks was finishing his drills at first base and trotting across the field to the dugout when he heard his manager calling to him.

"Hey!" Leo Durocher shouted. "Didn't you use to play shortstop?"

Banks replied that he had.

"Well, go to short and take ten balls," Durocher said. "I'll bet you a Coke I can get a few past you."

Banks traded his first baseman's glove for an infielder's and trotted out to left side of the diamond, where he had not played for a decade, as Durocher walked to home plate with a bat in his hand.

Blake Cullen describes the scene:

"Leo smashes a couple right at him and Ernie handles them cleanly. Then he starts hitting them near second base, near third base, and Ernie handles them all, ten in a row. He even backhands a few. Everybody in the ballpark—there weren't any fans there yet, but there might have been a few stragglers—has stopped what they're doing to watch. Finally, Leo smashes a one-hopper right at him and Ernie fields it. Leo throws his hat down and he says, 'Damn! I take my hat off to you, old man.'"

Banks went into the clubhouse and collapsed.

———

Banks was almost defiant when spring training began. "I'm going to surprise some people," he said in a tone reporters had never heard from him before. "He was biting off the words," Jerome Holtzman wrote in *The Sporting News*, "almost spitting them out, as if defying anyone to tell him he had reached the end of the baseball road."

He was undergoing extensive treatments to improve his legs, Banks said. He was using special exercises to build up the muscles in the upper part of his legs to lessen the formation of fluid in his knees and ten-pound weights on his feet to strengthen his thigh muscles. He was getting regular heat treatments and exerting himself in practice day after day. "It's going to be the hardest program I've ever had to follow, but I've got to do it," he said. A few days later, he was struck in the face with a batted ball, which required seven stitches and left him with a black eye to go with his aching legs for the remainder of the spring.

Banks was forty years old now and knew he could only be a part-time player. He would pinch-hit and play first base occasionally. And when he had five singles in twelve at-bats in the few exhibition games he played, he dared to hope. But then his knees gave out again, and it was announced he would start the season on the disabled list. Durocher had to make a point of saying that, yes, Ernie Banks was still a member of the Chicago Cubs. "He can play as long as he wants to," the manager said. "I'm not going to decide for him."

Banks didn't appear in his first game until April 23, when he was used as a pinch hitter against the Mets and struck out. Another week went by before he pinch-hit again, but then he was feeling well enough to play four games in a row at first base. The last one was on May 4 at Shea Stadium, where Nolan Ryan was the Mets' starting pitcher.

Banks might well have been given the day off, as no aging hitter could hope to keep up with Ryan's remarkable fastball. The San Francisco Giants, for instance, allowed Willie Mays to face him only three times during the three years they crossed paths in the National League. But Banks had had two hits in five previous at-bats against Ryan, including a home run in 1968, so perhaps Durocher was playing a hunch. Or perhaps he was playing a perverse joke.

If Banks hadn't already had a stomachache, Ryan's fastball would have given it to him, and he struck out on three pitches in the second inning. But Ryan's chronic problems finding the strike zone had not abated, and Banks walked in the fourth. Trailing 1–0 in the fifth, the Cubs tied the score on a pair of two-out doubles, and Joe Pepitone was walked intentionally to bring up Banks. Once, such a move would have been an insult; now, it was the obvious strategy, and Ryan struck him out again. The Mets regained the lead in the bottom of the seventh and Ryan, who had seven strikeouts and allowed only three hits, was taken out of the game. The seven walks he allowed in an otherwise fine performance seemed to sum up the frustration that would lead the Mets to trade him when the season ended.

Ryan was followed to the mound by Ray Sadecki, a twelve-year veteran who had once won twenty games but who was now a spot starter and reliever. Cubs right fielder Johnny Callison walked to open the top of the eighth, and Pepitone singled him to third. It was the chance Banks had been waiting for, a chance to face a left-hander who didn't have much of a fastball and to get his first runs batted in of the season in an important situation. And then a shadow fell across him as he stood in the on-deck circle.

"I'm sorry," Jim Hickman said as he approached home plate. "I've got to hit for you." Banks walked back to the dugout, put his bat in the bat rack, and, without a word, sat down next to Durocher.

Years later, Hickman would sigh as he recalled the moment when Durocher called his name. "I didn't enjoy that too much," he said. "You kind of feel funny playing in place of somebody that was the kind of player he was." Pinch-hitting for Banks, Hickman hit a weak grounder back to Sadecki, who threw Callison out at the plate, and the Mets went on to win, 2–1.

Reporters scrambled to recall if Banks had ever been removed for a pinch hitter before—the answer was twice, in 1954, the time Warren Spahn struck him out two times, and in 1963 when, in the midst of a slump, he had given way to Merritt Ranew—and a few wondered if Durocher would have made such a move before the fans in Wrigley Field. At first, the manager seemed somewhat penitent. "I did it for two reasons," he said. "Number one, he had an upset stomach, and number two, to keep out of the double play." But then, unable to help himself, Durocher took it back. Even if Banks's stomach hadn't been bothering him, he said, "I would have hit for him anyway."

Banks was of two minds about the indignity, too. "I'm not discouraged," he said. "Baseball is still fun to me and I'll keep playing as long as I'm wanted." But then, he added, "If I'm not wanted anymore, well then, in that case I'll have to move on."

The season was a disaster for Banks—thirty-nine games played, a .196 batting average, three home runs, six runs batted in—and for the Cubs. Injuries to Randy Hundley and Joe Pepitone offset excellent seasons by Billy Williams, Glenn Beckert, and the starting pitching rotation, and the team did well to finish third, fourteen games behind the division-winning Pirates, with a record of 83–79. But along the way, they engaged in a shocking rebellion that showed all the world they were a franchise spinning out of control.

It began with Pepitone's motorcycle.

"Come here, let me show you something," Durocher told Hundley after calling him into his office at Wrigley Field before a game against the Cincinnati Reds on August 23. The manager opened the door, pointed outside, and said, "See this? This is why Pepitone is not hitting. He's wearing himself out riding this motorcycle. I'm calling a meeting after batting practice and I'm going to get on him a little bit. I want you to tell him to just sit there and not say a word."

Hundley sat at his locker as the meeting began, hoping Pepitone would follow Durocher's instructions and suspecting he would not. Pepitone listened to Durocher berate him for several minutes until he finally stood up and said, "Leo, Ralph Houk would never get on his players the way you get on us," and began a diatribe of his own.

Infuriated that Pepitone would invoke the name of the New York

Yankees manager who had considered him a troublemaker and gotten rid of him, Durocher shouted back, and soon the argument spread to other players. Durocher chastised Milt Pappas for a pitch he'd made during a loss to Houston the day before. Pappas answered back and Pepitone yelled, "Why pick on *him?*" and profanely challenged Durocher's ability as a manager.

"I took you off the streets of New York and brought you here, Joe!" Durocher shouted, referring to Pepitone's short exile after leaving the Astros two years earlier. And to Pappas he yelled, "I took you from Atlanta when nobody wanted you!"

The shouting continued until Durocher's attention turned to another target, the worst possible one he could have chosen had he wanted to deflate the tension in the room. "You're not there for batting practice," he told Ron Santo. "Maybe if you came out there and practiced, you wouldn't get into those slumps. Look at Beckert. He just goes out there and works his ass off!"

"I'm working, Leo!" shouted Santo, who had begun hearing boos from the stands during his occasional struggles at the plate and in the field. "And I've got this day coming up and I've got that on my mind."

"Well, Ronnie, when you negotiated your contract, didn't you *ask* to have a day?" Durocher said. "Aren't you the one who *wanted* to have it?"

The news stunned Santo's teammates. After much soul-searching, he had only recently disclosed that he had been diagnosed with diabetes as a teenager, and a day in his honor had been arranged as a benefit for the Diabetes Association of Chicago. A fine gesture, to be sure, but he'd had Ron Santo Day put into his *contract?* Durocher was calling him out as vain and distracted while his teammates were fighting for a pennant. Santo stood up and loudly denied he had negotiated for the ceremony. Durocher shouted back, and for a few moments it appeared that the Cubs' two most volatile personalities might come to blows. Then Durocher demanded that John Holland be summoned from the front office to settle the matter.

"John!" Durocher demanded when Holland appeared. "Did Santo want to have this day when he was negotiating his contract?!"

Holland tried to evade the question and calm things down—"Leo is your manager," he told the players—but Durocher wouldn't have it.

"John, *did* he?"

"Yes, I do think I remember that entering the conversation," Holland admitted.

"That's it!" Durocher shouted. "I resign! You don't need me!" and he stormed out of the room.

The Cubs sat in stunned silence. The clubhouse was filled with veteran players—Banks, Williams, Hundley, Kessinger, Beckert, Jenkins, and more—but none of them seemed to know what to do. As Jenkins surveyed the room, all he could think was, "Wow!"

And then came a voice from a most unlikely corner. "Boys, we can't let this happen," Hickman said. "If we do, the fans, the newspapers, everything will destroy us. This is not what we want."

It was precisely because Hickman was usually so quiet, Phil Regan thinks, that the players saw the wisdom in his words. "He told the players what they had to do and they listened to him," Regan says.

Joe Amalfitano seconded Hickman's motion. "Ronnie, we have to get him back," the Cubs coach told Santo, and the two men went to Durocher's office, where he had changed out of his uniform and was preparing to leave. "He felt he had lost the club," Amalfitano says. "Leo was tough as a roofing nail, but we are all sensitive at times."

"You can't do this, Leo," Amalfitano told Durocher. "We need you here." He then encouraged the two men, their tempers spent, to shake hands. Durocher put his uniform back on, returned to the locker room, and, as if nothing had happened, shouted, "Let's go out and kick somebody's ass!" The Cubs proceeded to beat the Reds, 6–3, as Santo had two doubles, a single, and three runs batted in. Ron Santo Day was held six days later and was a huge success, as Santo was praised by civic officials, cheered by the fans, applauded by his teammates, and showered with gifts. The Diabetes Association of Chicago received one check for $25,000 and many other smaller contributions.

A few days after the locker room battle, the Great Cubs Mutiny of

1971 descended into farce when Philip K. Wrigley took out a large ad in all four Chicago newspapers, saying the "Dump Durocher Clique would not succeed" and "if some of the players do not like it here and lie down on the job, during the offseason we will see what we can do to find them happier homes." The message ended, "P.S. If we could only find more team players like Ernie Banks."

Once again, the players were in disbelief. The storm had passed. Why stir things up? Sportswriters spent the next few days dissecting Wrigley's remarks, and so did the players. Pappas said he wished the subject had been dropped. Jenkins called the ad "a bunch of junk." Others were furious at having been called loafers. But Banks held his tongue. He would defend his owner unconditionally, and if that meant defending Durocher as well, so be it. "Leo put us in contention and we owe him something for that," he said.

As the Cubs' 1971 season wound down to a merciful end, Banks sat on the bench. He played in just three games in the first ten days of September, pinch-hitting in two of them, and came out of the lineup for two weeks. But it was announced he would start at first base in the last three home games of the season against the Philadelphia Phillies. He was hitless in the first one, but when he had a single and a double and made several good fielding plays in a 4–2 victory the following day, he was in a chipper mood as the final game approached.

It had already been announced that Banks would miss the last three games of the season in Montreal to remain with Eloyce, who was undergoing foot surgery, so a question loomed over the game. "Banks Swan Song?" a headline in *Chicago Today* asked. "Has Ernie's Sun Set at Last?" the *Sun-Times* wondered. Banks said no. "I'm ready to play next season. Of course, I haven't done much this season, but Mr. Holland told me he'd like to see me play twenty years. That's my objective, too."

The speculation over Banks's retirement had actually begun the year before when, as the Cubs were losing to the Cardinals in the final home game of the season, Banks came to the plate in the ninth inning. A huge ovation greeted him, and it rose to the skies when Banks singled to center and grew even louder as he left the field for a pinch runner. "It was obvious that many in the crowd felt they were seeing their long-time hero in action for the last time," Robert Markus wrote in the *Tribune*.

But now it was a year later, and even while Banks's body and his performance were telling him it was time to go, he and his employers seemed trapped in a bubble of delusion, hoping that past glories might somehow be rekindled. Outside the bubble, however, reality was taking hold.

"Maybe you remember a little about 1953," Rick Talley wrote in *Chicago Today* on September 26. "The year you were married? Graduated? Maybe the year you were born." The benediction continued as he ran through the batting order of Banks's first major league game eighteen Septembers earlier. And Banks, for all his bravado the previous day, sensed the truth, too.

"There'll be no nostalgia," he said as he sat in the dugout before the game. "Let's just play this one to win. Let's have everyone go home happy, except the Phillies." He was joined by Paul Pryor, who would be the game's first base umpire, and two children for whom he signed autographs while he and Pryor chatted. Later at the batting cage, Banks shouted, "Isn't it a beautiful day?" and began to sing, "On a clear day, you can see forever." Then he jumped into the batting cage and said, "Let's go, let's go. Sunday in America."

The game was about to begin when the voice of Pat Pieper came over the public address system. "Your attention, ladies and gentlemen. Your attention, please," he said. A modest but lively Wrigley Field crowd of 18,505 quieted down. "Today marks the end of a distinguished baseball career..." Pieper said. Then he paused as the crowd grew deathly still. (*"He wouldn't?! Not today?! Not like this?!"*) "...for umpire Al Barlick, who spent thirty-one years in the..." Pieper continued as deafening cheers of relief spread throughout the ballpark, drowning out the rest of the tribute.

Banks received a standing ovation when he came to the plate in the first inning and responded with a weak grounder to third base that Deron Johnson of the Phillies fumbled, recovered, and threw wildly to first. "Only a nostalgic official scorer could rule that Ernie deserved a base hit on that play," wrote Tom Fitzpatrick in the *Sun-Times*. "It turned out the official scorer was nostalgic."

The crowd stood and shouted again as Banks walked in the third inning and once more when he hit a ground ball to shortstop in the sixth. By now, the Wrigley Field organist was playing a different song each time he returned to the field—the theme from *Midnight Cowboy* in the sixth inning, *Love Story* in the seventh, "Sunrise, Sunset" in the eighth.

The Cubs were losing 5–1 when Banks came to bat in the bottom of the eighth as the organist played "Hold That Tiger" and the crowd stood. It remained on its feet as he took a called strike from Phillies pitcher Ken Reynolds and cheered hopefully when he connected on the second pitch. The ball flew high in the air into foul territory behind third base, where it was caught by John Vukovich, who had replaced Johnson as a pinch runner an inning earlier, no more than ninety feet from the plate.

The cheers continued as Banks returned to the dugout, and when the Cubs finished batting he picked up his glove and trotted out onto the field one last time. Only the most observant fans saw Pryor greet him at first base by removing his umpire's hat and holding it over his chest in salute.

Chapter 33

Coda

At first, neither Ernie Banks nor the Cubs could accept the fact that his career was over. He would be there next season, Banks said in November, and Leo Durocher said he would not hesitate to use him as a pinch hitter. Even when the Cubs made Banks their first-base coach for the 1972 season, it was a ruse. "If we get into the World Series," John Holland explained, "the only way Ernie can get in is to start on the coaching staff and then be activated. Mr. Wrigley wants him to be a part of it." A note was added to Banks's contract indicating he would be paid an extra $20,000 if he played again.

But the Cubs' hopes died early when they lost nine of their first eleven games, and they finished eleven games behind the Pittsburgh Pirates in the National League East. Banks's only at-bat of the season came on August 14, when he entered a charity game between the Cubs and White Sox at Comiskey Park in the bottom of the seventh inning. He was given a standing ovation and struck out.

Over the next few years, his teammates left, too, one by one. Billy Williams and Ken Holtzman went to Oakland, Ferguson Jenkins to Texas, Glenn Beckert to San Diego, Don Kessinger to St. Louis, Randy Hundley and Bill Hands to Minnesota, Ron Santo a few miles south to the White Sox. At times, it seemed as if they took the heart of the team with them.

The Cubs fell to fifth place in 1973 and didn't post another winning record for more than a decade.

———

Before the 1972 All-Star Game, Leo Durocher and Philip K. Wrigley decided it was time to part. "If I had said I wanted to finish the season Mr. Wrigley would have backed me," Durocher said. "But I told him that maybe for all concerned it would be better if I stepped aside."

Showing some grace, Durocher appeared at a press conference because "I want to give the boys one more shot at me." He praised Wrigley as a good man and said he regretted he had been unable to bring a pennant to Chicago. When he resurfaced a month later as the manager of the Houston Astros, a Cubs fan sent the team's general manager, Spec Richardson, a button that said "Leo must go." "She told me the button had served its purpose in Chicago and we'd be needing it in a couple of years," Richardson said. After one desultory season in Houston, Durocher's career in baseball, which had lasted for nearly half a century, was over.

———

The Bleacher Bums and other hardcore fans also melted away. They had families now, jobs, responsibilities. "Nothing lasts forever," Mike Murphy says.

Murphy went on to become one of Chicago's first radio sports talk show hosts. Jack Herbon drove a forklift for a company that made medical supplies. Don Flynn bought a restaurant. John Schulian became a sportswriter in Chicago and later a television writer in Los Angeles. Ned Colletti talked his way into a job in the Cubs' public relations department and rose through baseball's ranks to become general manager of the Los Angeles Dodgers.

Dennis Paoli became a college professor in New York and wrote for the movies and television. One day, he received a call from Stuart Gordon, a friend from high school who had founded the Organic Theater Company in Chicago. Gordon said he was intrigued by an idea from Joe Mantegna, an actor in the group, for a play based on life in the Wrigley Field bleachers. Paoli summoned up his memories and received a credit for supplying additional dialogue to *The Bleacher Bums*, which opened in Chicago in 1977. The play toured the country for years and was made into a movie.

Ron Grousl disappeared. "He completely fell off the map," Herbon says. "Last I heard, he was living in California somewhere. I googled his name and used all the people searches, but no luck. He could be dead for all I know."

———

Philip K. Wrigley, whose father's will had ordered him not to sell the team, did not impose the same condition on his son. At nine a.m. on June 16, 1981, William Wrigley III, who had taken over the team upon his father's death four years earlier, called Joe Amalfitano in the manager's office at Wrigley Field. He was leaving his office in the Wrigley Building and walking across Michigan Avenue to the Tribune Tower, Wrigley said. He was going to sell the Cubs to the company that owned the *Chicago Tribune*.

Amalfitano wondered whether it was his fault that Wrigley was selling the team that had been in his family for sixty years. He was in his first full season as manager, and when Wrigley had asked him in the spring how long it would take the Cubs to win again he had said four years. Wrigley assured him that was not the reason. The Cubs were losing too much money, he said, and estate taxes following the death of his parents were a serious problem for the family.

The idea of a newspaper owning a baseball team was greeted with mirth—would the *Tribune* print the standings upside down?—and trepidation. Was the era of individually owned teams coming to an end? Had baseball become a permanent part of the corporate world? William J. Hagenah, Jr., Philip K. Wrigley's son-in-law and president of the Cubs, indicated that it had. "You've got to just have an awful lot of money to play ball these days," he said.

The *Tribune* paid $20.5 million for the Cubs, second only to the $21.1

million the New York Mets had sold for in 1979. A generation later, when William Wrigley IV, known to his friends as Beau and the last member of his family to run the gum company that had made his great-grandfather one of America's richest men, sold the jewel in the family's crown, there were no concerns about cash flow or estate taxes. The Mars food and candy conglomerate, along with Warren Buffett's investment firm, Berkshire Hathaway, paid $22 billion for the William Wrigley Jr. Company, and Beau Wrigley became a billionaire twice over.

Tom Ricketts, whose family bought the Cubs in 2009, was chatting with Beau Wrigley once, and they began to reminisce. Everything had changed in and around Wrigley Field by then. The ballpark had lights, tickets were expensive and often hard to come by, the neighborhood had become a food-and-fun mecca, and the Cubs had built a solid foundation of players and front-office personnel that offered hope for the future.

Did he ever wish his family still owned the team? Ricketts asked. No, Wrigley said. He wouldn't want to endure the torment his grandfather had when the Cubs lost.

Leo Durocher's friends were surprised at how frail he became as he aged, and how mellow. He had begun to think about God, he said, and about all the curses he had uttered in his life. It was clear he was facing his mortality. He was still capable of bringing a room to its feet, though, as he did at one last baseball writers' Diamond Dinner in 1983. He spoke lovingly about the Cubs who had played for him in those glory days gone by and received by far the loudest ovation of the evening.

A year later, Durocher made another, more private, goodbye at Randy Hundley's fantasy baseball camp in Arizona, where he joined many of the 1969 Cubs. He spoke with great emotion and brought tears to many eyes as he finished. He was sorry he had given Ron Santo such a hard time that day in the locker room, Durocher said. And he regretted the way he had treated Ernie Banks.

VI

BEING ERNIE BANKS

Chapter 34

Man at Work

In the summer of 2012, a young baseball player named Yasiel Puig walked into a Mercedes-Benz dealership in Glendale, Arizona, where he was about to join the Los Angeles Dodgers' Rookie League team, the lowest rung on their organizational ladder. Puig, who had survived a harrowing journey to the United States from Cuba via Mexico earlier in the year, was carrying a magazine ad that pictured a particular Mercedes model. Puig showed the ad to a salesman and, through an interpreter, asked if it was available in red.

"No," the salesman said. "We don't make that car in red."

"Do you have any other cars on the lot in that color?" Puig asked.

"Yes, but they're more expensive."

"That's okay. I'll take it."

Puig, who had just signed a contract for $42 million, had yet to play in a game in the United States. He was twenty-one years old.

The most money Ernie Banks made during a single season was $85,000—Billy Williams became the Cubs' first $100,000 player in 1971— and Banks's total career earnings were about $800,000. Adjusted for inflation, Banks made a little more than $400,000 per season during his nineteen-year career, or about one-tenth of the average major league salary in 2017, which was $4 million. Banks's inflation-adjusted career earnings are about $3 million less than Anthony Rizzo, the Cubs' star first baseman, had coming to him in 2019 as part of a seven-year, $41 million contract. Rizzo, who signed a long-term contract early in his career, was considered vastly underpaid.

Like virtually every other player of his era, great stars and journeymen alike, Banks's contracts were for one year, which gave ownership the upper hand if a player was injured or his production fell off. After Mickey Mantle hit .304 and led the American League with forty-two home runs in 1958, for instance, he was forced to take a pay cut because he hadn't matched his .365 batting average of the year before. And Hank Aaron was given his first two-year contract only as a reward for breaking Babe Ruth's career home run record in 1974. "That's the way baseball was played back then," Aaron says. "There just wasn't any money. At least there wasn't any money for the players."

Since few players could survive on their salaries alone, most of them held jobs during the off-season and continued working when they retired. "In 1957, after we won the championship, I had two jobs," Aaron says, "selling beer and selling insurance. Many times, I borrowed money from the team to pay my light bill. They had you on a string. That's just the way life was."

The Cubs of Banks's era were an industrious bunch. Ron Santo opened a pizza parlor, owned gas stations and Kentucky Fried Chicken franchises, and had other investments. Glenn Beckert sold life insurance. George Altman sold used cars and new homes and was a substitute teacher in the Chicago school system. In 1968, Ferguson Jenkins celebrated his second consecutive twenty-victory season by touring with the Harlem Globetrotters. Lou Brock's off-season job with an oil company after the 1962 season required him to go down into basements and bang on furnaces. "Based on how it sounded, it either needed a filter or a part needed to be replaced," Brock said. "I got to be that good."

Banks came up with a clever moneymaking idea following his breakthrough season in 1955 by putting an ad in the *Chicago American* stating, "Mr. Grand Slam Himself, Ernie Banks, is available for a limited number of select talks and appearances at luncheons, dinners and Christmas parties during December and January." There is no record of how successful this endeavor was.

It came as no surprise to the people who knew Banks best that he held scores of jobs during and after his baseball career. "Ernie never stayed with anything," Williams says. "He kept moving on from one business to the next. He did the same with his wives."

"He would always talk about business," says William Marovitz. "I can't tell you how many times he said, 'What can we do together?' He figured the more business ventures he got into, the more he'd have coming in from different directions. But he had trouble focusing. Today, we'd say he had attention deficit disorder."

Aaron ran into this problem when he tried to introduce Banks to a wealthy man in Atlanta who had helped him in several business ventures, including the ownership of several restaurants, that had given him a degree of financial independence. "He wanted to meet Ernie, and I said I'd arrange it," Aaron says. Banks eagerly agreed, but he didn't show up for the meeting. "I thought, 'Boy, you just don't do that,'" Aaron says. "The guy felt betrayed. But that was a typical Ernie Banks thing. He would say one thing and do something else."

Banks admitted his inability to concentrate on his business affairs many years later when he said, "When I got out of baseball, I was brain dead. I said, 'Gosh, I don't know anybody outside of baseball and I don't have any skills.'" It was different, he said, with the younger generation of players who were entering the game as he was leaving it.

Once, when he was working as a minor league hitting instructor for the Cubs, he was giving tips to an infielder named Dave Hill, who had graduated from Amherst with a degree in criminal justice. "Ernie, you've got to prepare yourself," Hill said, as the pupil became the teacher. "I was shocked," Banks told the *Dallas Morning News*. "The kids in the minor leagues had degrees in engineering and mathematics and prelaw. Here I was with a high school education. They had more to offer than I did. Who wants a forty-year-old ex-shortstop? It was frightening."

So Banks moved from one job to the next, beginning each one with a fanfare of publicity and quietly moving on some time later. Over the years, he worked for banks, insurance companies, moving companies, film-promotion companies, a firm that developed executive benefits packages for corporations, and more. He ran a gas station and, along with Chicago businessman Bob Nelson, opened the first minority-owned Ford dealership in the United States in 1966. After three years of selling cars largely to his teammates and other major leaguers, the partnership was dissolved. "My own attorneys got Ernie Banks straightened out on his automobile agency," Philip K. Wrigley later said.

In nearly all of these jobs, and in his position on the board of the Chicago Transit Authority from 1969 to 1981, Banks felt lost and insecure. "Most people felt that I was going to fall in the gutter or live under viaducts," he told the History Makers, a Chicago-based African-American oral history project. "It seemed like they were hoping that." Banks said he tried to cope by seeing a psychologist at one of his banking jobs, but all she could tell him was to enjoy his celebrity status.

One problem was that while he would join a new firm hoping to learn the ropes and become a useful employee, he was trapped in his public identity. "They always thought of me as Ernie Banks, the ballplayer," Banks told Ira Berkow of the New York Times. "There was always the company softball team, and racquetball with the bank president, and functions to attend. It was hard to make a new identity and people don't help when they keep talking to you about your past."

Banks was also frustrated that he didn't have the national profile that led to well-paying television commercials. "Can't we do things like Willie Mays is doing or Hank Aaron?" he once asked Yale Gordon, a Chicago advertising man who became his business advisor. Gordon had to explain that because of their World Series championships and their signature moments—Mays's iconic catch in the 1954 World Series, Aaron's breaking of Babe Ruth's home run record—they were larger national figures than he was.

Banks also had a profound misunderstanding of how his celebrity carried with it responsibilities that could not be monetized.

"George W. Bush just called me," he told Gordon one day in 2007. "He wants me to be an ambassador. How much should I charge him?"

"Ernie, he's the president of the United States," Gordon said. "He's asking you to represent your country. He's not going to pay you." Banks dutifully went off to Shanghai as part of a U.S. delegation to the Special Olympics.

———

There was one job Banks had often been mentioned for, which, given his long service to the Cubs and Philip K. Wrigley's love of experimenting, seemed like a natural.

As early as 1960, Bill Veeck had predicted that Banks would become baseball's first black manager. "Ernie has both the ability and the talent to be the first member of his race to manage in the majors—and he'd make a good one," Veeck said.

Many Cubs fans felt the same way. "During his last year, people were yelling from right over the dugout, 'Ernie, are you going to be the manager?!'" says Cubs' batboy Greg Carlton. "He wouldn't say anything because Durocher was still the manager, but they kept yelling."

Banks loved to tell the story about the day he did become baseball's first black manager, if only briefly. It happened on May 8, 1973, when he was serving as a Cubs coach, and manager Whitey Lockman was ejected from a tie game in San Diego in the eleventh inning. Neither of the Cubs' senior coaches, Pete Reiser and Larry Jansen, was with the team, so Banks took over. He took the job seriously, calling for a bunt that sent Don Kessinger to third in the twelfth inning, bringing in Joe Pepitone, who drove in the winning run with a pinch-hit double, and sending relief pitcher Bill Bonham out to earn the save. Banks celebrated the win by notifying the front desk at the Cubs' hotel that he was not to be disturbed.

But Banks's claim to being the managerial Jackie Robinson was incorrect. This time, Gene Baker had beaten him to it.

Baker's playing career all but ended in 1958, the year after the Cubs traded him to the Pirates, when he slipped while charging a ground ball hit by Curt Flood in St. Louis. "There was a crack that sounded like a thirty-thirty rifle," Baker said. He underwent surgery for a torn ligament, and though he managed a comeback he was never the same. He pinch-hit three times in the 1960 World Series, which the Pirates won, without reaching base. The Pirates kept him around, however. "He knows more about baseball than fellows twice his age," manager Danny Murtaugh said, and Baker became an instructor and scout, then moved on to manage in Pittsburgh's minor league system. Two years later, he joined the Pirates as a coach.

On September 21, 1963, both Murtaugh and coach Frank Oceak were thrown out of a game in Los Angeles after protesting an umpire's call, and Baker took over. The Dodgers scored three runs in the ninth to win the game, 5–3. The milestone escaped the attention of almost everyone in baseball at the time, including Banks, who wouldn't take his turn as manager for a day until ten years later.

But whenever the idea of managing for real was mentioned, Banks couldn't seem to make up his mind.

"I definitely believe there will be a Negro manager in the major leagues eventually," he said in 1966. But he wasn't interested. "I'd rather be a coach because I would be closer to the players," he said. "If you manage, you have to be aloof. You can no longer be one of the boys."

But Banks only coached the Cubs for one year and then moved on to other roles with the team—minor league hitting instructor, scout, fixture at spring training—without any indication of higher aspirations.

Later, though, he seemed to be changing his mind. "I can't live the rest of my life in a cocoon, being coddled," he told New York sportswriter Dick Young in 1972, when he was coaching first base for the Cubs. "I think I'd like to step up and meet the challenge of managing. I'll just risk being booed. I want to reach out for the next thing in life. That's what living is all about." A year later, Banks told Hank Hollingsworth of the *Long Beach Press-Telegram* much the same thing. Whether he was the first black manager didn't matter, he said, but he could do the job if it was given to him. And in 1976, when he was serving as a minor league instructor for the Cubs, he told *Jet* magazine, "I like working with young players and seeing them develop," and then he added, "I sure would love to manage the Cubs."

But Banks didn't pursue becoming a manager with any more sense of purpose than he did his other jobs. In 1969, he turned down an offer to manage in the Puerto Rican winter league, saying he needed to spend more time with his family and to look after his business interests in Chicago. Another of baseball's great stars, Frank Robinson, showed no such reluctance and spent seven full winter league seasons managing in Puerto Rico before finally becoming the first black manager in the major leagues in 1975.

But if Banks's ambivalence played a role in his failure to become the Cubs manager, it was matched by Wrigley's. "If that's what he wants, then we'll start him off in the minor leagues and see how he does," Wrigley said in 1974, "but to be perfectly frank, I think he's too nice a guy to manage. Ernie has such a beautiful reputation, it would be a shame to ruin it by making him a manager. It's the next thing to becoming a kamikaze pilot."

On the face of it, Wrigley's reluctance seems suspect. During his long ownership of the Cubs, the surest way to become manager was to be a long-tenured star. Not only did Wrigley keep bringing Charlie Grimm back to the dugout, but Gabby Hartnett, Phil Cavarretta, and Stan Hack, all Wrigley Field favorites in their day, also took their turn at managing. For all the innovations Wrigley had come up with over the years, was he drawing the line at hiring baseball's first black manager? Jesse Jackson charged as much when the Cubs replaced Lockman with Jim Marshall during the 1974 season. Their failure to give the job to Banks, Jackson said to the team, was "racism at its height."

But perhaps it is best to take Wrigley at his word. He had always acted paternally toward Banks, promoting and protecting him, giving him financial advice and helping him with his business dealings. But in assessing his capabilities as a manager, Wrigley was probably right. Banks's aversion to confrontation would not have served him well in the role of manager, who must challenge some players, build up the confidence of others, bench or demote still others, and deal with difficult personalities and situations on a daily basis. It was one job where he couldn't simply disappear. And while Banks was an exemplary leader as a player, he was never a strong presence in the locker room, one known for speaking up and motivating his teammates.

Nor was Banks a gifted instructor, someone who could watch a hitter's swing, for instance, and suggest improvements. From the day he told a young Lou Brock that all he needed to do was relax, to conversations he had in the last years of his life with Tom Bongiorno, who lived next door to him in Chicago's Trump Tower, Banks's approach to hitting was never analytical. A former minor leaguer himself, Bongiorno was fascinated by the use of complex computer-generated statistics that had revolutionized baseball and wondered if it had any relationship to players of Banks's era.

"When you faced pitchers like Don Drysdale, how did you prepare?" Bongiorno once asked Banks.

"Tom, it's hitting a little white ball," Banks replied. "You go up there and you see that little white ball and you hit that little white ball. What preparing are you talking about?"

There was another factor that might have prevented Banks from succeeding as a manager. "He was coaching first base in St. Louis once and Leo Durocher and Joe Amalfitano were yelling at him, 'No, Ernie, no! That's not right!' " says Carlton, the batboy who adored Banks because, unlike some others in the clubhouse, he could make even a minor contributor to the club like him feel special. "He was giving the wrong signals and they were both yelling at him. He just wasn't into that part of the game. He was into being Ernie Banks, home run hitter, all-around nice guy. Ernie was never meant to be a manager."

In the end, Banks was probably fortunate he never managed the Cubs. He would not have been able to stem the mediocrity they descended into during the decade following his retirement, and the fans who had loved him as a player despite the team's failures might not have been so forgiving had he been responsible for them managerially.

Still, it might have been interesting to see him try, if only because he could hardly have done any worse than the other seven men who took the job during that period and failed at it.

———

There was, of course, one job Banks was supremely fit for, and he performed it with gusto: being Ernie Banks.

It is hard to overstate the effect Banks had on many of the people who had grown up watching him play. Though they were adults now and had moved on with their lives, Banks was a reminder of more innocent, idealized days. Marcel Proust ate a cookie to remind himself of his childhood. Chicagoans remembered Ernie Banks.

Bradley Borowiec, the general manager of the Wrigley Building, where Banks had an office late in his life, invited his father, a lifelong Cubs fan, to lunch with Banks and, as the two men spoke of the games he had attended and the players he had admired, Borowiec realized he was seeing his father in a way he never had before. "He was seventy-five, and it was the first time I'd seen him as a young boy," Borowiec says. "He just had this glow and excitement and energy. It seemed like they talked forever. I just sat and listened."

Other more exalted Chicagoans had the same reaction. "A CEO of a Fortune 500 company would walk into the restaurant and see Ernie and start shaking uncontrollably, quivering and saying, 'Oh my God, oh my God,'" says Grant DePorter, who runs Chicago's Harry Caray's restaurant chain. "Ernie would flag him over and have him sit down and talk to him and I would hear him say when he was leaving, 'I can't believe I was just with Ernie Banks.' He had that effect on a lot of people."

One of them was John Canning, the cofounder of Madison Dearborn Partners, a multi-billion-dollar private equity fund in Chicago, who was the leading candidate to buy the Cubs when the Tribune Company sold them in 2009 before he lost out to the Ricketts family. A self-confessed baseball groupie, Canning had a tryout with the Milwaukee Braves in his youth—"I batted about .195," he says—and went on to add six minor league teams and a portion of the Milwaukee Brewers to his investment portfolio.

As the bidding for the Cubs began, Banks called Canning to ask if he could be a part of his ownership group. He had no interest in how the team was run, he said, but wanted to be an ambassador, spokesman, organizer of baseball clinics for children, and the like. Canning readily agreed, and as he listened to Banks make his pitch, he saw an urgency behind it. "Desperate isn't the right word, but he was very intent on selling himself as an asset that would be good for our group," Canning says. "I could see that it was revisiting the glory days, of being recognized again as Mr. Cub. He seemed to me to be kind of lost."

Still, Canning was delighted to meet Banks, and in one of their conversations Banks stopped him cold when he asked if Canning would be his mentor. "Can you imagine that?" Canning says. "Ernie Banks is sitting in my office asking me to be his mentor. It was like God asking you if you'd like to go to church with him."

Banks had a similar effect on John Rogers, who founded Ariel Investments, the largest minority-owned mutual fund in the United States, and met Banks through Rogers's mother, who was active in Republican politics. "I joked that they were both black Republicans, so that's how it got started," Rogers says. His own politics differed from his mother's, dating back to his days playing basketball at Princeton with Craig Robinson, whose sister, Michelle, would later marry a young aspiring Chicago politician named Barack Obama. Later, Rogers was drawn further into Obama's orbit through his then wife, Desirée Rogers, who would become White House social secretary when Obama became president.

Banks and Rogers quickly developed a rapport, and Rogers was delighted when Banks showed up unannounced at a dinner where he was being honored, and later at his wedding. "I was in heaven," Rogers says. "Mr. Cub was interested in me? He would call me sometimes and we had long conversations. It's funny, but I'll try to remember things

Barack and I did twenty years ago and I have ten times more memories over that period of Ernie."

And so with one job title or another, and under one financial arrangement or another, Banks represented and became the symbol of the Chicago Cubs for the rest of his life.

It was a job he was born to do. His instant rapport with people, his genuine interest in them, his patience, his constant smile, his optimistic attitude and pleasant chatter made him a crowd favorite wherever he went. And he had one other attribute that put his job performance over the top: a photographic memory.

"He remembered names as good as anybody you ever saw," says Jack Hiatt. "The man could walk through an airport and say, 'Hey, Mr. Jones, how are you? Good to see you.' I don't know how many times I saw that."

"He would remember the most obscure details about people," says Borowiec. "He would know that someone's wife had a baby, or their daughter had graduated from college. If one of the executives in the building said, 'Ernie, we met on a golf course,' he'd say, 'Oh, sure, that was at Shady Oaks.' I saw this time after time."

"I wrote a speech for him once to deliver before a game from the pitcher's mound at Wrigley Field," says Yale Gordon. "He's standing there with Jack Brickhouse and the governor and other dignitaries, and he picks up the mic and I'm pointing to my hand as if to say, 'Where's the speech?' He points to his head, meaning 'It's in here,' and he proceeds to state it verbatim. I stood there with my mouth open, thinking, 'I don't believe this.'"

"A customer walked into the restaurant and started talking to Ernie and told him his wife wasn't doing well," DePorter says. "They only met that once. A year later, the customer is here, Ernie walks in and goes right over to him and says, 'How's your wife? Is she doing better?' The guy couldn't believe it."

"Once he asked me, 'How's your mom? Is she still working at the hospital?'" says Rebecca Polihronis, who booked some of his public appearances. "I had told him she worked there five years earlier. How would he remember something like that, something we just talked about in passing?"

"I don't know how he did it," says Regina Rice, Banks's friend who became his caretaker during his final years. "He didn't do speed dial, none of that. He would just look at the phone and call whoever he wanted to talk to. I would go, 'What's so-and-so's number?' and he'd say, 'You *would* ask me that,' and I would think maybe he didn't know. And then he would rattle it right off."

But Banks's ability to represent his team and himself was undermined by one maddening flaw—his irresponsibility. It began near the end of his playing career, when he would agree to make public appearances and then not show up. "Some little kid or father would come down to the wall at batting practice, and they were having a banquet in November," says Chuck Shriver. "He'd always say yes, and I'd find out later he said yes to two different events on the same night."

"People would say, 'Ernie, will you speak to my high school?' and he'd say yes and not have any intention of doing it," says Blake Cullen. "It was not out of meanness, he just couldn't say no."

The Cubs would apologize and arrange for a substitute if possible, but now that his entire job revolved around public appearances, the situation became untenable. "Last year was constant apologies—from Ernie to us and from us to the people who expected him," a team spokesman said at one point. "You should see the letters that came in."

In 1983, Dallas Green, the team's executive vice president and general manager, decided to take a stand. The Cubs would continue to pay Banks his six-figure salary, but on a per-appearance basis. For every event he missed, his pay would be docked. Banks refused, the story became public, and Green soon found himself dealing with a public relations nightmare that made him seem callous toward the Cubs' greatest star. "Cubs Fire Ernie Banks," one headline read. "Cubs Snub Mr. Cub" said another.

True to his nature, Banks took the high road. The split was amicable, he said. The Cubs "said they had to make some budget cuts." Green, stung by the public reaction, was less magnanimous. " 'There are always two sides to every story," he said. "The Ernie Banks story also has two sides, and he apparently has chosen to let the newspapers do his talking for him."

Banks's friends could also be disappointed at his failure to follow through on commitments. Charley Pride recalls attending a ceremony honoring Banks in Dallas and making frantic phone calls when he didn't appear. "I tried to reach him in Chicago and California," Pride says. "None of the numbers worked."

And Bill Blair became angry when the man whose career he had set in motion agreed to be grand marshal of the large Martin Luther King Day parade in Dallas, which Blair had initiated some years before, but reneged. "We had announced it, it had been printed up, it had been given to all the media and he stood us up," says Blair's son, Darryl.

But the Cubs could no more turn their backs on Banks than he could sacrifice his public identity, and before long he was back with the team. In the years ahead, the front office would exercise tighter control of his schedule, often working with his third and fourth wives, Marjorie Lott and Liz Ellzey, to make sure he was where he was supposed to be. "I trained my interns that the players should never say no, you say no for them," says Polihronis. "If somebody asks, you say, 'I'm sorry, we can't commit right now. Please send a letter to the office.' So we got that straightened out, and Ernie had very strong wives who kept him on schedule."

Banks had another maddening habit that sometimes complicated his public appearances—taking things that didn't belong to him.

"Where did you get this picture?" he asked a friend of Sander Esserman, Banks's lawyer in Dallas, who had a treasured photo of Banks he wanted him to sign. "I'm going to keep it."

"Wait a minute, it's my picture," the fan protested. "I've had it for years."

But Banks kept the photo, and when the fan complained to Cubs employees overseeing the appearance, he was told, "It's Ernie Banks. What do you want us to do?"

Another fan, Mark Long, tells of the time he wanted Banks to sign a portrait his son had given him as a Father's Day gift several years earlier. "My thought was to 're-gift' it back to my son as a Christmas present signed by Ernie Banks," Long said in a Facebook post. But Banks folded the portrait and put it in his pocket. "I certainly was not going to inform Mr. Cub that he had misconstrued our conversation and ask him to return the drawing," Long said. "I only hope it brought him a smile or two over his final few years."

Sue Schwerin, a rabid Cubs fan who had met Banks on a team-sponsored trip to Disney World, was sitting with friends at a table at a winter Cubs convention when Banks approached, charmed her by saying, "You haven't aged at all," sat down, and, as fans swarmed around, began signing autographs. One of Schwerin's friends produced a bottle of Ernie Banks 512 wine, which was being sold for $75 a bottle, for him to sign. Banks took the bottle and put it under his coat. "We sat there thinking he'd sign it and give it back," Schwerin says. But when Banks left, he took the wine with him. "We laughed and wondered if we were going to read in the paper the next day that Ernie Banks was found passed out in a stairway with an empty bottle of wine," Schwerin says. "I hope he drank it at least."

Chicago Fire Department lieutenant John Sampson, who has worked in Engine Company 78, which is located just beyond Wrigley Field's left-field wall, for nearly four decades, was surprised when Yosh Kawano showed up one afternoon a decade after Banks retired and even more surprised by the Cubs' equipment manager's request. Banks had shown up for an old-timers' game without a black belt for his uniform, Kawano said. Could he borrow Sampson's black fireman's belt? "I'm not giving anybody my belt unless Ernie Banks comes over here," Sampson says. "So they brought Ernie over, I took my belt off, gave it to him and that's the last I saw of it."

Eventually, Banks's kleptomania was brought under some measure of control through the intervention of Rice, who would tell unsuspecting fans who wanted Banks to sign something he coveted to put it in the mail. "Then I'd wink so they understood they could take it back home," Rice says.

But for all his idiosyncrasies, Banks was capable of remarkable acts of kindness that those on the receiving end would never forget. Hearing that Bret Laczynski, a nineteen-year-old Cubs fan in Chesterton, Indiana, had an inoperable brain tumor, Banks arrived with a personalized Cubs jersey, signed bat and ball, and photos. "He spent three and a half hours at the house," says Todd Laczynski, Bret's father. "Bret wasn't really coherent, and his eyesight was starting to go, so I don't know if he even saw Ernie. But Ernie was very loving and caring. He kept saying, 'How are you doing? You're going to do well,' even though we knew he only had a month to live."

Yale Gordon tells of the time Banks came to a Little League game in which his son was playing. Perhaps to impress his distinguished visitor, Brad Gordon, who was small for a ten-year-old, insisted on pitching, and when he couldn't throw the ball to home plate, the other players laughed at him and he ran off the field in tears. An hour later, Banks called Gordon and asked to speak with Brad. He told him of the disappointment of 1969, of how he had cried when he realized he was not going to the World Series. "You have your whole future ahead of you," Banks said. "Just because you had one crummy game doesn't mean that it's going to be a future of games like that."

"It was such a kind thing for him to do," Gordon says. "He gave us so many memories like that."

———

The first call Banks made when he was elected to the Hall of Fame in January 1977 was to Gene Baker. The second was to Buck O'Neil, the third to Philip K. Wrigley, the fourth to Billy Williams, and the fifth to Eddie Mathews, who had finished second to Banks in the voting and would have to wait another year before gaining admission to the Hall. He then called American Airlines and said he needed to fly to New York for the official announcement. "They told me they'd hold the plane for me," he said.

Only a dozen players had been elected to the Hall of Fame in their first year of eligibility prior to Banks—the number is up to more than fifty now—and they are among the greatest baseball has ever known: Babe Ruth, Ted Williams, Walter Johnson, Bob Feller, Jackie Robinson, Mickey Mantle, Ty Cobb, Christy Mathewson, Honus Wagner, Sandy Koufax, Stan Musial, Warren Spahn. Among those who were not selected in their first year on the ballot are Joe DiMaggio, Yogi Berra, Jimmie Foxx, Mel Ott, and Roy Campanella.

So Banks was sobered and more than a little nostalgic as the day of his induction approached. He spoke of the ballparks he had played in around the league—Crosley Field in Cincinnati, Forbes Field in Pittsburgh, Seals Stadium in San Francisco, the Polo Grounds in New York. He spoke of the encouragement his mother had given him and of his father working from dawn to dusk. He spoke of being hit in the back by Jack Sanford and of the thrill of watching the Cubs move into first place for the first time in twenty years in 1967 from the press box where he was nursing a spike wound. He said how glad he was to be inducted as a fairly young man. "Most people have to wait until late in life to get this honor," he said. "Many times they are in poor health. I'm lucky. I feel good."

"This means you're a legend, Ernie," a reporter told him.

"My life is a legend to me," he said.

The sun peeked through rain clouds in Cooperstown, New York, as Banks stepped to the microphone on August 8, 1977. A sign reading "America Loves Ernie Banks" rose from the crowd, which gave him a loud ovation. He drew a laugh when he thanked the "thousands of Cub fans" and, pointing to the Hall of Famers in the nearby grandstand, said, "There's sunshine, fresh air, and the team is behind us. Let's play two."

Banks then gave a short speech thanking his family, the players and coaches who had taught and encouraged him, the fans, and "one of the finest gentlemen I ever met," Philip K. Wrigley, who had died four months earlier at the age of eighty-two. "A person's success is dependent not only on the talent God gave him," he said, "but also upon the people who believe in him."

But not even receiving the greatest accolade a baseball player can aspire to was enough to overwhelm Banks's basic character and instincts. Peter Clark, the Hall's registrar for more than forty years, was one of the few non-players invited to a dinner for Hall of Famers in Cooperstown for the weekend, and he was startled when he found himself having a lengthy conversation with Banks. "He was asking personal questions about where I lived, if I was married, if I had children, and how I came to Cooperstown," Clark says. "How many players would be that friendly and go out of their way to talk to just a common person, particularly on Hall of Fame weekend when they are kind of into themselves? He just seemed so human and modest. Ever since then, he's been my favorite Hall of Famer."

Banks would return to Cooperstown many times over the years and would enjoy the company of his fellow Hall of Famers, who traded war stories and joshed each other about days gone by. After a time, though, he began to feel out of place as he took part in these exchanges. He was, he realized, the only one in the room who had never played in the World Series.

"I think it bothered him," says Jeff Idelson, the president of the Hall of Fame since 2008. "He was so proud to be a part of the Hall and the players he played against. I think he felt a little left out in the conversations about not being able to speak about World Series moments."

And in truth, Banks was never able to escape the one great failure of his career. It was a hole in his life, he said, and whether in Cooperstown or at old-timers' games, he would ask Mickey Mantle or Lou Brock or Reggie Jackson or Warren Spahn or Harmon Killebrew or Gene Baker what it had been like to play in the World Series. Their answers never satisfied him. "They'd just laugh," Banks said. "It was almost like it was funny to them that I played for the Cubs, and you'll never get in the World Series if you play for the Cubs."

Sometimes, Banks would dream of being in the World Series. "It was always the seventh game and we were playing the Giants and I hit three homers and Willie Mays said, 'Man, how'd you get those kind of pitches to hit?'" And when, at a banquet or golf tournament, he ran into Jackson, who *had* hit three home runs in one World Series game, he would say, "Reggie, that was me." Jackson, like the other Hall of Famers, just laughed.

Banks's anguish over not playing in the World Series once weighed on him so much that he saw a psychiatrist. "There wasn't much he could say," Banks said. "Just that I'd done the best I could and it wasn't meant to be."

Chapter 35

Family Ties

Ernie, come get your shit!" Eloyce Banks shouted at her ex-husband over the phone. "We're cleaning out the garage and it's going to be thrown away if you don't come get it."

True to what she had told her children several years earlier, Eloyce held off before filing for divorce in 1981. "She waited until we got out of high school," Jerry Banks says. "She said, 'When you go to college, that's when I'm going to file.'"

The fact that Eloyce and the children lived in Arizona while Banks was spending much of the year in Chicago contributed to the separation, but Jerry and Joey had seen enough of a baseball player's life during the summers they worked in the visitors' locker room at Wrigley Field not to be surprised. "Ballplayers get divorced more than any other profession except for maybe a firefighter or somebody in the service," Jerry says. "You're committed to your job. There are a lot of external pressures that weigh on a family."

Though press accounts said Eloyce was awarded $500,000 in the settlement, it seems unlikely that she ever received that much. Court records are sealed, but documents from Banks's divorce from his third wife, Marjorie Lott, indicate Eloyce received $950 of Banks's $2,085 monthly baseball pension and $1,150 a month in alimony. But even that money didn't arrive regularly, and in 1994 Eloyce claimed he was constantly falling behind.

Banks didn't heed Eloyce's call to collect his trophies and other memorabilia, and she sold what she had to an auction company, which began a merry-go-round of sales and resales. In 1993, all eighty-five items in her collection, which ranged from Banks's 500th home run ball to his wooden shower clogs, were sold for $82,000. In later years, this would prove to be a bargain-basement price.

If Banks's divorce from Eloyce maintained at least some measure of outward decorum, the same cannot be said for the dissolution of his two subsequent marriages. Not only were bitter charges hurled back and forth, but the proceedings seemed endless and Banks's legal expenses were considerable, though court documents indicate he was often slow to pay his lawyers. Lott, whom Banks married in 1984, filed for divorce in 1993, but the marriage wasn't dissolved until 1997. Banks left Liz Ellzey, whom he married in 1997, in 2007, but the divorce wasn't finalized at the time of his death eight years later.

The divorce from Lott was particularly ugly. It was set in motion when she showed up a day early at the Cubs' spring training hotel in 1993, went to Banks's room, and, as she delicately puts it—and as Banks acknowledged in court documents—"found out all I needed to know." In testimony that followed, Banks accused her of threatening to write a tell-all book that would ruin his reputation, of saying she would charge him with infidelity and child molestation, and of threatening to kill him. Lott said these allegations were "absolutely untrue." In return for her silence, and for agreeing to keep the record of the proceedings secret, Banks agreed to give her his two Most Valuable Player trophies, which had not been included in the memorabilia Eloyce had sold. It was a decision that would come back to haunt him.

Despite all the angry words hurled back and forth, Lott looks back on her life with Banks with a mixture of fondness and regret. "I thought we had a happy marriage and a happy life," she says. "I'm grateful to Ernie for the opportunity he gave me to go to all the wonderful places we went and for all the wonderful people I was allowed to meet because of him." Among the highlights was a banquet in Chicago for Princess Diana, for which Lott took lessons on how to curtsy.

On the other hand, Lott says, "I probably should have been more sensitive to his need to have a closer companionship. He needed to have things to do and I didn't realize that until after the fact. I take responsibility for that and I think others should, too. A lot of us failed to connect with him. It was always, 'What can I get from him?' 'What can he do for me?' 'Can I just be with him so people will think highly of me?'"

Banks's separation from Ellzey was also contentious. She had "committed extreme and repeated acts of mental cruelty . . . which occurred without provocation," he charged, and he demanded that she "cease and desist exploiting his name and likeness for her benefit."

Banks's divorce from Eloyce took a heavy toll on his relationship with his sons. They were devoted to their mother and didn't much care for the women who entered Banks's life afterward. "They weren't our mom, we didn't know them and I didn't want to know them," Joey Banks says. "We didn't come over for Thanksgiving, there were no presents at Christmas, there wasn't any of that. It wasn't anything to do with me and him. It was his relationship with other women."

"Once the divorce was completed, there were about five years we didn't have much contact," says Jerry, who, like his brother, lives in Los Angeles. "He was in Chicago and I was here." So in the years following the divorce, Banks's relationship with his sons was an estrangement based on distance. They had their own jobs, their own families, their own lives. Even during the years when Banks lived in Los Angeles, there was none of the warmth they all may have craved.

In time, though, attitudes began to soften. There were more phone calls, more golf dates, more evenings together. "Over the years, we became closer," Joey says. "I was kind of his psychiatrist on the golf course. I knew when he was feeling good or not feeling good when we talked about what club he should hit." And when on other occasions Banks invited them to dinner, "Boom, we were there," Joey says. Occasionally, Marjorie, Liz, or Regina Rice would arrange family evenings, and everyone would be polite to each other and get along.

Some of those who knew Banks well regretted he did not have a closer relationship with his children. "There couldn't be a greater contrast than the one between Billy Williams—a fifty-year marriage and so many grandchildren he loves—and Ernie," Tom Ricketts says.

Williams too wished that Banks had developed the kind of bond he had with his own children. He had often brought his wife, Shirley, and daughters to the Banks home at 8159 South Rhodes when the children were young so both families could enjoy an afternoon together. Later, he took Banks's sons fishing and took pride in the warm feelings they had for each other. "Right now, if I see them, they run up to me and hug me," Williams says.

Years later, after two of Williams's four daughters, Valarie and Nina, graduated from high school, he packed them off to Clark University, a historically black college in Atlanta, and told them to stay there. "It was a growing city, on the move," he says. The girls took jobs in Atlanta after college and seemed to be settling in, but when they returned to Chicago to celebrate Williams's fiftieth birthday in 1988, they had a surprise for him. They were moving home, for no better reason than they wanted to be with their mother and father. "I guess it tells you that there's something that you did right because they all wanted to be around us," Williams says with a smile. Now his daughters and grandchildren all live nearby, a blessing he was particularly grateful for when Shirley began slipping into the fog of illness.

―――――

Back in Chicago after leaving Liz and their home in Marina del Rey, California, Banks spent the remaining eight years of his life amid the company of old friends and some new younger ones, such as Rebecca Polihronis of the Cubs; Sylvia Menias, who coordinated flights for United Airlines and booked the Cubs' charters; and his next-door neighbor, Tom Bongiorno, who owned a restaurant bearing his name near Trump Tower on North Wabash Avenue.

Banks's financial situation stabilized somewhat during this period thanks to two outside forces. One was a relationship of mutual respect with Ricketts, who signed him to a six-figure contract that the new Cubs owner felt was well worth the money. "He always wanted to do more," Ricketts says. "We would have lunches where he would say, 'What else do you guys need? I can show up for more games.' A lot of people sign personal service contracts, then we don't see them much. Ernie was just the opposite." Banks's deal with the Cubs later included his lodgings in Trump Tower. "He needed a place to live so we got him the apartment," Ricketts says. "You should take care of your Hall of Famers."

Banks also received help in navigating the one steady source of income available to famous athletes—appearing at card shows and other events where fans paid to meet and obtain their favorite players' autographs.

Banks had not always profited from these shows. A deposition in his divorce from Lott lists four occasions in 1993 alone when he was cheated by promoters who were in over their heads. "He's a friend and former athlete," Banks said of one man who owed him $25,000. "I said, 'First time you've done it? Fine.'" Another novice was a Los Angeles County deputy sheriff who owed him $15,000, but paid Banks much less. "I was more or less protecting him from losing his job," Banks testified. "I had a lot of empathy. He was one of the few black promoters in the business."

Another problem was that much of what Banks did earn was paid in cash. "I saw him walk out of card shows with handfuls of cash or envelopes full of bills," says Jerry Banks. "A lot of players got in deep shit with the IRS over unreported income." And in fact, when the promoters of a New York card show pleaded guilty to tax fraud in 1989, Banks was named along with several other former players—Joe DiMaggio, Ted Williams, and Willie Mays among them. "Sources say there is an ongoing dispute in the U.S. attorney's office over whether to indict Banks on allegations he failed to report $10,000 in cash," Newsday reported in 1994. "The dispute is over whether $10,000 is a large enough sum to indict a person of the Hall of Famer's stature." There is no record of Banks facing any charges related to the IRS.

By the time Banks returned to Chicago for good, the business of card shows and other personal appearances had become professionally run and quite lucrative, once he began working with people who knew the ropes. "Some of them were basically trade shows," says Yale Gordon, who arranged many of Banks's appearances in Chicago. "Companies would come in and exhibit their products and they needed somebody to draw a crowd." Willie Mays and Hank Aaron could make $15,000 to $20,000 for appearances at these events, Gordon says, while Banks earned $7,500.

In 2011, Banks began working with Mollie Bracigliano, the owner of MAB Celebrity Services, a sports marketing firm in Fairfield, New Jersey, who set up appearances outside of Chicago for which she was able to negotiate larger amounts. "He was a thirty-thousand-dollar commitment if you wanted him to show up for two hours," Bracigliano says. "And he attended the annual event at Cooperstown I do every year. I'm pretty sure the last thing he did for me there—it was the July before he died—his check was for over fifty thousand dollars."

Bracigliano says Rice was instrumental in making sure Banks appeared at these events on time, but even as he finally overcame his earlier habit of not honoring his commitments there was another problem: his inability to adhere to the card shows' business model of signing the most autographs in the shortest amount of time.

"The promoters would say, 'Just sign the autograph and move on,'" Gordon says. "But Ernie wanted to talk to each person, learn about their life, were they married, did they have girlfriends. He just wanted to know about people."

"He would go to the other athletes and just talk," says Bracigliano. "And if Willie Mays was in the room, forget it. Ernie just couldn't focus. He had ADD in the worst way. How he ever played baseball on a daily basis is beyond me."

"Ernie was frustrating because he insisted on talking to people instead of keeping the line moving," says Ricketts of Banks's appearances at events sponsored by the Cubs. "I'm sure he was one of the least effective autograph signers in history."

For the most part, Banks missed out on another potential source of income—the sale of his trophies and other memorabilia. In part, this was due to Eloyce's dispersal of so much of it after they divorced, but it was also a matter of timing. Baseball collectibles didn't become a big business until the mid-1980s, and like many other players of his era—and like the boys whose mothers threw out their baseball card collections—Banks would come to rue the fact he hadn't taken better care of his awards and other items, which were now worth a small fortune. In 2014, for instance, an autographed uniform jersey from 1969 signed by Banks was sold for $150,000 in an online auction. And in 2018, a mint edition of his 1954 Topps bubble gum rookie card sold for $74,400.

"These things had no intrinsic value until about thirty years ago," says Chris Ivy, the director of sports collectibles at Heritage Auctions, a large auction firm in Dallas that has sold some of Banks's memorabilia. "So trophies were often tossed in the trash or lost somewhere in time."

The one great mystery surrounding Banks's baseball memorabilia concerns his most precious items, his two Most Valuable Player trophies. Lott had won custody of them during their divorce, but later that part of the agreement was set aside when a Los Angeles Superior Court judge ruled she had obtained them under duress. After the hearing, Banks dismayed his attorney, Sam Perlmutter, by going into one of his impromptu filibusters.

"I had walking pneumonia and my head was throbbing," Perlmutter says. "I said, 'Ernie, we've won the case so let's get in and get out.' But the judge was a big baseball fan and he said, 'Why is this trophy so valuable to you?' and Ernie started talking about how he won the trophy, who he beat out, and it went on for half an hour. Finally, he was done and I took him by the arm and said, 'Let's go, Ernie,' but then the judge said, 'Wait a second. What about the second trophy?' Well, the second one was probably more important to him than the first one and that discussion took even longer. I was afraid I was going to go out of there on a stretcher. Finally, Ernie finishes, winks at me, and says, 'I did a good job, didn't I?' I was so sick I made him drive me home."

But soon the trophies disappeared again.

Banks's sons suspect they ended up with Marjean Tanaka, who

worked for Banks as a bookkeeper. The twins hunted for them, and Jerry even drove to where he thought Tanaka lived but found only an empty house. On the open market, the trophies would be worth a great deal of money—Andre Dawson's Most Valuable Player trophy was sold for $117,000 in 2015—but whoever has them might have a hard time profiting from them.

"I've never seen a case when an MVP award went missing," says one investigator who searches for valuable lost and stolen items. "Selling them in public would maximize the price, but there would be high exposure. I'm sure my phone would ring." There is, of course, the possibility that the trophies are simply lost. "To older players, the awards weren't what they are today," he says. "They were viewed more as trinkets. They could just be sitting in a storage unit. A player falls on hard times, doesn't pay the storage fee, and somebody buys it. It happens all the time."

Regina Rice received a call from an old boyfriend one day asking her to dinner. "I think he only called because he liked to hear me say no," says Rice, who had refused his requests several times.

"Well, would you have dinner with me and my friend Ernie Banks?" he persisted.

"Who the hell is Ernie Banks?" she said.

But Rice agreed to the date and, though she was amused by Banks's conversation, she found herself more drawn to his demeanor. "Ernie reminded me of my grandmother, even though he was a man," she says. "My grandmother had a certain way of communicating and gesturing, and he reminded me of her. He would even say my name the way my grandmother said it."

Banks was in his early seventies when he and Rice met, and though she was several decades younger they developed an easy rapport. Rice occasionally sings in Chicago clubs—her Facebook handle is Vocalist Regina—and she is an accomplished seamstress, but she also worked for many years as a manager in Chicago law offices. This led to Banks asking her to look over some contracts and to make some calls for him, and before long she was helping arrange his schedule.

Banks was alone and somewhat despondent when he separated from Liz and moved back to Chicago, and he shared some of what was troubling him with Rice. "I went into my rescue mode, encouraging and pushing him," she says. "I could see that he wanted to be in charge, so I found every way possible to make him feel like he was still in charge."

Banks was having trouble getting around during this period, and though he had long considered having his arthritic knees replaced, he was fearful of an operation. But Rice encouraged him. "You're still a young guy," she said. "You don't want to walk like that." Finally, he agreed, and in 2004 he was fitted with the latest in rotating platform knees. He was back on the golf course not long afterward.

In the years ahead, as Banks grew older and his health declined, Rice's role in his life changed in ways, and with results, she could not have anticipated.

Chapter 36

"How's Your Wife?"

Living alone in Chicago, separated from his family, with few close friends and no daily responsibilities, Ernie Banks retreated into a caricature of the identity he had created for himself. His need to hide his loneliness by being part of a crowd resulted in behavior that sometimes bordered on manic. Wherever he was and whomever he met, Banks was always "on," always seizing the opportunity to be Ernie Banks.

His signature phrase during the last decade of his life was no longer "Let's play two." Instead, it was "How's your wife?" Or sometimes, "How's your mother?" or "How's your family?"

Banks's friends laughed it off, understanding it was his way of initiating conversation, but those who didn't know him were perplexed. Patrick Kane, the young star of the Chicago Blackhawks who lived in Trump Tower, once asked John McDonough about the old man who was always asking him "How's your wife?" McDonough, who had left the Cubs to become president of the Blackhawks, told him it was just Banks's way of saying hello.

"If he got you in an elevator, you were done," says Jerry Banks of his father's fondness for talking to strangers. The two men were walking through the Trump Tower lobby one day when Jerry saw a huge man rolling a suitcase whom he recognized as Martellus Bennett, the Chicago Bears' newly acquired tight end. "We all get on the elevator—there were nine or ten of us—and we start going up forty floors, the guy's minding his own business, and I know what's coming," Jerry says. "I've seen it a hundred times."

"How's your wife?" Banks asked Bennett.

"She's fine," he answered.

"Where are you from?" Banks asked.

"Houston," Bennett replied.

"I'm from Dallas," Banks replied, and soon the two men were having a lively conversation.

"He doesn't know who this old man is, even if he is wearing a hat that says 'Ernie Banks,'" Jerry says. "We got out of the elevator and I said, 'You just had to do that, huh? You had to say something.'"

The corollary of "How's your wife?" was "Are you married?" and Banks attacked it with a vengeance. Every unmarried young woman he knew was fair game.

"He was always trying to marry me off to Mark Grace," says Sharon Pannozzo, who worked for the Cubs when Grace was one of the team's biggest stars. "Now, Mark is dating model types—at one point he was dating Janine Turner, the TV star—but he'd call me Mrs. Mark Grace. I'd say, 'Ernie!' but he'd just say, 'Yeah, yeah, but you'd be perfect for him.'"

"He'd say, 'What about Rick Wilkins?' 'What about Jim Bullinger?'" says Rebecca Polihronis. "He'd run through the whole lineup. I'd say, 'Ernie, why do you want to marry everybody off?' and he'd say, 'Love is good, love is in the air,' and then he'd starting singing to you."

"There was a pitcher for the White Sox and he would say, 'You should marry him, he makes good money,'" says Martha Black, the childhood friend of Banks's daughter who was now working in the White Sox front office. "I said, 'Uncle Ernie, that's not what it's all about,' and he said, 'Yes it is,' and I said, 'Oh, good grief, you sound just like my mother—and your ex-wife.'"

Banks's greatest flight of matrimonial fancy came when he offered to set up Sylvia Menias with Dennis Rodman, the professionally outrageous player for the Chicago Bulls. "I said, 'Dude, what are you thinking?

He's crazy,'" Menias says. "He said, 'I think you'd do great with him. You have a lot in common.' I wasn't embarrassed by it. It was just comical."

Occasionally, Banks would be called on this foolishness. "I used to break his chops," says Tom Bongiorno. "He'd tell everybody, 'Get married, get married,' and I'd say, 'Ernie, you're the guy to talk. You've been married four times. Leave these people alone.'"

But for all of Banks's garrulous chatter, those paying close attention could see the method behind it. From his earliest days as a player, Banks had learned how to deflect conversation away from himself, as Jerome Holtzman described in *The Sporting News* in 1958: "There is probably no other major league star who minimizes and soft-pedals his achievements the way Banks does. He almost never speaks about himself, especially when in a group. Ask him about hitting and he'll talk in surprisingly vivid detail of Stan Musial or Willie Mays. He almost never mentions Ernie Banks."

Banks maintained this distance throughout his career, as Paul Hemphill noted when he wrote about Banks's final game at Wrigley Field in *Sport*: "I tried to remember some of the things he had said the day before, well before the game, under the grandstand in a dank private corridor near the umpires' dressing room, tried to piece them together and make some sense of this man who had managed to show not a sliver of his inner self in nearly two decades of being in the spotlight."

Off the field, it was the same. "Ernie was the most selfless superstar I've ever met," McDonough says. "He was not comfortable talking about himself. I tried. I would ask him questions about growing up in Dallas, about the Negro Leagues, Buck O'Neil, his early years with the Cubs, the back-to-back MVPs, the Hall of Fame, being Mr. Cub. But the next thing you knew, you were talking about you and not him. There was never a time where he expounded on his brilliant career or being Mr. Cub. I've met accomplished, decorated people who are like that, but I've never met anyone who did it as well as Ernie."

"You would bring Ernie to meet somebody and they'd come back an hour later and say, 'I had a great conversation but I talked all about myself,'" says Tom Ricketts. "I think the reason Ernie was so well loved, the reason that he was Mr. Cub, was people loved him and he loved them back."

But there were those who wondered if Banks's unwillingness to talk about himself was healthy. Marjorie Lott thinks it was one more illustration of the unhappiness he kept hidden and, again, wondered if a therapist might have helped. "He needed someone who could make him look at himself, put everything on the table and deal with it so the real him could come out," she says, "so he could get to the point where he *could* talk about himself."

———

At leisure now, Banks became a master of the art of hanging out. He would spend hours in a barbershop on East Walton Place run by Peter Vodovoz, where they discussed any subject under the sun, but never himself. He also became friendly with Peter's brother, Greg, a tailor who would occasionally come to Banks's apartment with fabric samples so he could choose a new suit. Later, as Banks began losing weight, Greg would alter the suits to make them smaller.

Banks would also spend afternoons at a table at Harry Caray's restaurant on West Kinzie Street and hold court or, when there was no one around, simply sit alone. Occasionally, someone who knew him would stop to chat, or sit down and spend some time with him. "Thank you for taking care of Ernie," the hostess would say as the person left him sitting by himself in the restaurant.

Banks would spend afternoons in his office at the Wrigley Building or sitting in its outdoor plaza, where people would either come over to talk to him, or, daunted at the thought of disturbing the great Ernie Banks, would walk past him, then later regret they had missed their chance to speak to him. "He would sit in my office and we would talk," says Bradley Borowiec. "I recognized it as a gift, an opportunity that not many people had. He talked about overcoming obstacles in life, about not losing your focus, and most of all to always be kind. They were very *Chicken*

Soup for the Soul conversations. I was young when my grandfather died and I began to think of Ernie as my grandfather."

He was also a regular presence at Wrigley Field. "He basically had carte blanche there," says Pannozzo. "He'd be everywhere—down on the field, up in the offices. He was part of the fabric of the place."

Banks spent many afternoons with Bongiorno at his restaurant, where the two men would talk and later adjourn to Bongiorno's apartment on the forty-ninth floor to watch television. One night, they found themselves watching an old black-and-white telecast of *Home Run Derby* from many years earlier in which Banks had competed against Mickey Mantle.

"What are you doing?" Bongiorno asked Banks. "It's a home run contest and you're hitting line drives off the wall. Mickey's killing you."

"Ah, in those days you had to let the New York guys win," Banks said with a smile.

Sylvia Menias sat with him in Bongiorno's, too, and he talked about his days with the Cubs and how they were finally going to win this year. He spoke about his father and mother, too, and about the difficult life they had all had many years ago in Dallas. "Do you realize how blessed you are?" she told him one day. Banks smiled and said he was going to find someone for her to marry.

The golf course was another place where Banks liked to spend time. Most often, he played at Cog Hill, thirty miles southwest of Chicago, where the owner, Joe Jemsek, had welcomed black athletes in the 1950s when it was difficult for them to find a place to play. "My grandfather never discriminated against anybody," says Joe T. Jemsek, who runs Cog Hill today. "If you had a dollar or a dollar and a half to play golf, you were welcome."

Banks had long been an avid golfer, and not a bad one, capable of impressive, if not always accurate, distance off the tee. True to form, his passion for the game did not permit displays of anger. He left the curses and club throwing to others. "A lot of golfers are frustrated when they hit a bad shot," says Darryl Blair, who played with Banks in tournaments in

Dallas. "But if he hit a bad shot or missed a putt, he would just make fun of it."

"He never got mad or upset," Jemsek says. "Whatever the game gave him is what he got out of it."

As a teenager, Jemsek had caddied for Banks in celebrity charity tournaments, and he noted that even though first-place prize money could be as much as $10,000, Banks was indifferent to the outcome. "If he hit the ball down the middle, he'd walk down the side of the course instead of the middle of the fairway and say hello to people," Jemsek says. "He was less interested in talking to his celebrity partners than the general public. He was too busy talking to people and signing autographs to focus on trying to make a score."

When Tiger Woods began dominating professional golf in the late 1990s, Banks became obsessed with the new young star. He was part of Woods's gallery at the Western Open in Chicago and later at Augusta National in 1997, when Woods became the first black player to win the Masters. "I just had to be here to see this," Banks said, and, recalling the other fine black pro golfers he had played with over the years, he said it was a Jackie Robinson moment. When the 1999 PGA Championship came to Medinah Country Club west of Chicago, Banks said, "I'll be stalking him. Wherever you see Tiger, you'll see me."

Banks saw something of himself in Woods and recalled the days when he felt as if he were alone at Wrigley Field, standing at the plate, waiting for the pitch. "He plays as if nobody is out there but him and the ball," Banks told Ed Sherman of the *Chicago Tribune*. "I began to see he was a little bit like me."

———

Later in life, Banks began making ambush phone calls. None of his friends were safe from an early-morning call that began with him loudly proclaiming his victim's name, following with his own, and proceeding with some over-the-top flattery. After several minutes, he would lower his voice and finally say what was on his mind.

"You always knew the conversation was going to be entertaining but you never knew where it was going," says Jeff Idelson, the president of the Hall of Fame. "He called me once and said, 'How you doing?' 'How's Cooperstown?' 'How's your wife?' 'How's your mother?' The usual. Then he asked, 'Who's in charge of the Seven Wonders of the World?' I tried to look it up online while we were talking to see if it was determined by a government agency or was just mythical and I said, 'I don't know, Ernie. Why do you want to know?'

"Because I understand they're going to rerank them. I don't know if that's true or not."

"But why do you want to know?"

"Because Wrigley Field belongs on that list. It's truly one of the Seven Wonders of the World."

——

In 1998, the Cubs unveiled a statue of Harry Caray, their voluble play-by-play man whose off-the-cuff remarks and mispronunciations of players' names made him a cult figure in Chicago, on a sidewalk outside Wrigley Field. To some observers, this seemed odd. An *announcer* was the subject of the first statue ever erected at Wrigley Field? But the idea of a statue of the greatest Cub who had ever played in the ballpark was almost casual in getting started.

"Why doesn't Ernie Banks have a statue at Wrigley Field?" Mike North, a popular sports radio talk show host, said one day, and the comment was replayed for a week. Later, North invited Jesse Jackson on his show to discuss the matter, and things began to move.

"I went to a shareholders meeting and put it on the table," says Jackson, who thought the Cubs treated Banks shabbily in the latter years of the Tribune Company's ownership. "We threatened to picket on opening day. But I've got to give John McDonough credit because he did not procrastinate."

"When we put up the statue of Harry Caray, we knew we had to honor Ernie and we had to do it soon," says McDonough, who was then the president of the team. "The clock was ticking on us. We knew it was important to our franchise."

"I just wish this had been done fifteen years ago," said Hank Aaron, whose own statue outside the Atlanta Braves' stadium was erected in 1982, when the monument to Banks was finally dedicated on March 31, 2008.

"Maybe he felt like it was a little late in coming," says John Rogers, "but he was thrilled. His positiveness, his joy, overtook whatever disgruntlement might have been in his mind. He just put it behind him and looked forward with optimism, which so many people can't do."

And indeed Banks was forgiving and delighted as his former teammates, civic dignitaries, and fans gathered in the rain. "Is that me?" he said when the statue was uncovered, showing him standing with his bat cocked and a grin on his face. "It's the best. Even when I'm not here, I'll be here."

Banks liked to tell friends and reporters that his ultimate goal in life was to win the Nobel Peace Prize. In 2013, he settled for the Presidential Medal of Freedom instead. Banks was particularly pleased that the award would be presented by Barack Obama, whom he had come to know in Chicago and whom he greatly admired for having broken America's ultimate racial barrier. Banks wondered if he would have to make a speech at the White House ceremony—he did not—and when he expressed his concern to Grant DePorter at Harry Caray's, he was surprised to find himself leafing through a huge stack of clippings that DePorter, an inveterate collector, had been saving for him.

"When he was traveling with the team, he didn't see what the Chicago papers were writing about him and he was reading them for the first time," DePorter says. "Every single story was so complimentary and his eyes started watering. You could see how touched he was. The final one was by Bill Gleason of the *Sun-Times* and the headline was 'Ernie Banks, the Apostle of Love.' That meant a lot to him."

The day of the ceremony got off to a rocky start when, after Banks and his party arrived at the White House, Secret Service agents discovered that the birth dates of Billy Williams and his wife were transposed on a form, and it took forty-five minutes to straighten things out. "Really?" Tom Ricketts thought. "He's a Hall of Famer and we're waiting for *this*?"

Once inside, Banks, wearing a navy blue suit specially made for the occasion by Greg Vodovoz, took his seat alongside Bill Clinton, Oprah Winfrey, Gloria Steinem, and the other recipients of the award that year. He listened as Obama teased him about "his cheer and his optimism and his eternal faith that someday the Cubs would go all the way" and as the president repeated one of the imaginary stories Banks had invented about the origin of "Let's play two." A proclamation was read saying Banks had "slugged, sprinted, and smiled his way into the record books." He smiled as Obama draped a ribbon holding the award around his neck, then shook the president's hand, appearing genuinely touched.

The guest list Banks had chosen to attend the ceremony with him included a number of friends—Billy Williams and Ferguson Jenkins and their wives, Tom Ricketts, Regina Rice, John Rogers, and a few others—but no members of his family. No wife, no children, no brothers or sisters, no cousins, no nieces or nephews. It was as if he was proclaiming on a national stage that he was alone in the world.

"Absolutely, we were hurt," Jerry Banks says of his and his brother's response to not being invited to the ceremony. It would not be the last time his father would disappoint them.

Chapter 37

Rounding Third

The first sign that Ernie Banks's health was beginning to trouble him appeared when he was in his sixties and was diagnosed with hypertension. He should lose weight, doctors told him, change his diet, exercise regularly, remember to take his medication. Soon, Banks was traveling the country as part of a blood-pressure awareness campaign, issuing warnings that hypertension is a leading cause of heart attacks and strokes. He blamed his own elevated blood pressure on his retirement from baseball so many years earlier. "I wasn't used to change, so when I had to deal with change it affected my whole immune system," he said.

A dozen years later, Banks received a more sobering diagnosis. He had myelodysplastic syndrome, a cancer of the bone marrow that can lead to leukemia. Edward-Elmhurst Health in the west Chicago suburb of Naperville, where Banks was treated, denied several requests, including one from his son Joey, to examine Banks's medical records and speak with his doctors, but his condition seems clear enough.

"It's a type of cancer that has a variable prognosis," says Yogesh Jethava, a hematologist at the University of Iowa who specializes in bone marrow transplants. "Some patients can progress very fast to leukemia and some can remain with myelodysplasia for five, seven, even ten years. So the fact that he lived for seven years means he didn't have acute leukemia, but he definitely had myelodysplasia." Accompanied by Regina Rice, Banks made regular visits to Edward Cancer Center in Plainfield, where Jethava says doctors would have checked his blood levels and, if necessary, given him blood transfusions.

Joey Banks confirms that his father's cancer was not life-threatening, and there were no outward manifestations. "It didn't seem to affect his energy level or where he was going or what he was doing," he says.

But Joey and Jerry both thought that if their father had cancer he should be cared for by his family. "We got into a heated argument," Jerry says. "I said he couldn't stay in Chicago by himself, he needed to come to California. We were going to put him up in a spare room in my house."

But Banks refused. "I haven't made any money in California in fifty years," he said, and that was the end of the discussion.

In hindsight, Jerry believes his father's decision to remain in Chicago was probably for the best. "His whole life was being surrounded by the public everywhere he goes. If he comes here, he's just another guy on the streets. Nobody would come up to him and say, 'Hey, Ernie!'"

As Rice began accompanying Banks to his doctors' appointments, her role evolved from friend and part-time employee to caretaker. She visited him regularly and often went to dinner with him, though it could be painful to watch him eat. "He was always a finicky eater, but now he just lost his appetite," she says. "He'd say, 'I don't eat that stuff,' and I'd say to myself, 'Yes, you do.'" The result was that Banks, who had become heavy, was now painfully thin. "My doctor wanted me to lose some weight," he told a concerned Grant DePorter. "Don't worry about it."

Rice also helped arrange Banks's daily schedule and public appearances. Many of his friends, believing he would have been lost if he had to fend for himself, thought he was lucky to have her.

"She just seemed so good with Ernie," John Rogers says. "There just seemed to be genuine love and respect there."

"She's a caring person and she put in a lot of time and effort," says Yale Gordon. "She made sure that everything was on the up-and-up, that the events he participated in were above board and he got paid. She policed it."

"She was extremely protective," says Mollie Bracigliano, who become close to Rice as they coordinated many of Banks's public appearances. "They talked three or four times a day and she made him eat good healthy snacks and carried his bag. She was the only one who went the extra mile."

As for those who noted Banks's relationship with Rice with raised eyebrows, Bracigliano says they were off base. "She wasn't his girlfriend," she says. "She was like a daughter to him. She had a significant other the whole time she was with him. She took care of him and didn't want anything from him. She told him that."

Banks's sons were not so sure. What was her role? they wondered. How was it defined? "We appreciated everything she was doing for him because she was definitely doing a lot," Jerry Banks says, "but my brother had skepticism of her motives as he did with all women other than my mother."

―――

He was slowing down now, and his friends could see it. Not all the time—there were still flashes of the convivial, outgoing Ernie Banks they all loved—but more and more there were signs that he was succumbing to old age.

"Every time I saw him, he was getting around a little slower," William Marovitz says. "His weight, his color, and his vibrancy were consistent, but he was moving a little slower."

"He would get confused," says Sharon Pannozzo. "You would have the same conversations with him over and over again. I felt bad for him because I felt like a daughter to him. He was very sweet to me."

"He was starting to get a little forgetful," says Ron Santo, Jr., who arranged private autograph signings for Banks with collectors who preferred them to large, crowded card shows. "But it was still amazing he got around and did so much."

"I ran into him walking between the Wrigley Building and Trump Tower," Rogers says. "We stopped and talked, and I could tell he had slowed down. He just wasn't as sharp. It was the first time I felt like he was struggling."

Randy Hundley grew concerned when he met Banks backstage in the summer of 2013 at a concert at Wrigley Field by Pearl Jam, whose lead singer, Eddie Vedder, is a rabid Cubs fan. "He seemed to be a little bit distant," Hundley says. "He'd go off on these tangents of silly stuff that didn't mean anything—why don't I get married again, things like that. You couldn't tell him, 'Hey, Ernie, let's talk about you and how you're doing. Let's talk about baseball.' It was a different Ernie Banks from the one I knew. I wanted him to be the old Ernie and he wasn't."

Later in the evening, Vedder introduced Banks as a surprise guest, and as he stood on the stage wearing his uniform jersey, the crowd, which filled the field as well as the stands, began shouting, "Ernie! Ernie! Ernie!" They were the last cheers Banks would ever receive at Wrigley Field.

As Banks's condition got worse, Rice convinced him to stop driving and, though he put up a fuss at first, he soon decided he liked being a sightseer while others drove. By now, a touch of self-pity was beginning to show in conversations with some of his closest friends.

"Do you love me?" he asked Georgie Anne Geyer during a long lunch at the Drake Hotel in the spring of 2014.

"Yes, Ernie," Geyer answered. "I do love you."

"Well, why didn't my four wives love me?"

Geyer changed the subject.

One of those wives, Marjorie Lott, who had not spoken with Banks in twenty years, was initially reluctant to break the silence when one of Banks's attorneys called to say he would like to hear from her. "He used a word that made me think differently," Lott says. "He said Ernie was suicidal. I called him a few times and finally gave him my number. The last time he called me was Christmas Day. I still have the message on my phone."

In the summer of 2014, Banks began showing signs of dementia.

Among the first indications was something no one had ever seen from him before: a public display of temper. "We were in Cooperstown and he got real cranky," says Bracigliano. "He shouted, 'I don't want to do it!' at Regina—he just yelled at her—and she handled it with the utmost respect. She said, 'You will not speak to me like that. I don't deserve it and you have to stop.'"

Banks began calling Rice several times a day, asking such questions as how to warm up the coffee she had left for him and laboriously following her directions of how to use his microwave oven. "He'd ask, 'How do I warm up this food?'" she says. "I could hear him pushing the buttons."

"Ernie's lonely," Rice would tell Ferguson Jenkins, who would call him and arrange to have lunch or just sit in the Trump Tower courtyard.

Jenkins observed the change in his friend with sadness. "He was always on top of the world, always joyful," Jenkins says. And now he wasn't.

Banks's sons could also sense the change from long distance. "He would call and ask me things he should know," says Jerry Banks. "One time, he called and said, 'What's your number?' I said, 'You just called me at my number.'"

Soon, some of Banks's friends were having encounters with him that were simply heartbreaking.

"The last time we were together was when President Obama invited all of us who had received the Medal of Freedom from him back to Washington," Hank Aaron says. "I was sitting across the aisle from him and I shouted, 'Hey, Ernie!' He looked at me and then put his head down and completely ignored me. My wife said I should go over and talk to him, but I said no. I didn't think he knew what he was doing."

Sylvia Menias saw it, too. "We were sitting in Bongiorno's one day and he said he wanted me to arrange a trip to Greece," she says. "He was going to gather up Oprah and Warren Buffett and we were all going to Greece. In the end, I think he just wanted attention."

As they sat in the restaurant on another occasion, a fan approached to take a picture. Angrily, Banks put his hand in front of the camera to block the shot. Menias couldn't have been more surprised if he had slapped her.

Once during the summer, Rice and Yale Gordon arranged a barbe-cue at Gordon's home, but as the date grew near Banks began to balk. "Regina told me that he was declining very quickly and that he did not want to be around people and he was very depressed," Gordon says. "He didn't want people to see him that way."

At home, Banks would grow silent, and Rice would try to cajole him into conversation.

"You don't talk anymore," she told him.

"There's nothing to talk about," he replied.

"You don't laugh anymore."

"Nothing's funny."

———

The one place where Banks always felt alive and at peace during this period was Wrigley Field. His job was to enter a suite on the mezzanine, chat with fans for a few minutes, and then move on to another suite. But once he began talking, he didn't want to leave.

"He came in about the seventh inning and stayed the rest of the game," says Donna Wakefield, a Cubs fan who was in a suite that sum-mer. "They kept giving him mai tais and he was having a good time, chatting and goofing around, but he kept turning around to watch the game. I'm a speech pathologist and I know a lot about dementia and I didn't see it. He was bright-eyed and bushy-tailed. He was totally there."

On September 24, 2014, Banks ran into his old friend Sue Schwerin in one of the suites during the Cubs' final home game of the season. They chatted and drank mai tais awhile and then Schwerin took out her cell phone and called Shelly Ladd, a friend who at that moment was sitting in the bleachers at Yankee Stadium watching one of Derek Jeter's final games.

"Shelly and I have a friendly competition about who can outdo each other in terms of great experiences," Schwerin says. "So if she was watch-ing Derek Jeter, I had to call and tell her I was sitting with Ernie Banks. I got hold of her—I didn't know if she'd be able to hear me, but she did—and we chatted for a minute and then I gave the phone to Ernie and said, 'Say hi to Shelly. She's watching Derek Jeter.' "

Unlike the end of Banks's playing career, which had passed with so little notice, the great Yankee shortstop's retirement had been meticulously choreographed and monetized the entire season. During the countdown, Gatorade created an affecting commercial in which Jeter walks the streets of New York as Frank Sinatra sings "My Way" in the background. Banks, who had surely seen the commercial, proceeded to sing the song in its entirety ("Regrets, I've had a few, but then again, too few to mention") to a woman he didn't know in the bleachers at Yankee Stadium. Later, Schwerin realized it was the last time Banks was ever at Wrigley Field and wondered if he was singing "My Way" for Jeter or for himself.

Banks and Tom Bongiorno were walking through the lobby of Trump Tower one fall day when Banks lost his footing. "He grabbed my arm like it was a freaking vise," Bongiorno said. "He nearly broke my hand. That's how strong he was—an eighty-three-year-old man."

"Do not call an ambulance," Banks said.

"All right, now let go of my freaking arm," Bongiorno said, and he called paramedics to Banks's apartment to check him out.

Soon, Banks began falling more often. In October, he hit his head, drawing blood and requiring a trip to the hospital. In November, he fell out of bed, and his mattress was moved so he could sleep on the floor. His sons were concerned and so were some of his friends, who thought he should be in a nursing home or other facility where he could receive full-time care and have ready access to doctors. But he was becoming increasingly cantankerous and probably wouldn't have gone.

"He kept walking and acting like he was in charge," says Rice, whose son, Tony, sometimes helped her care for Banks. "We were watching every move he made to make sure he didn't fall, but he would push us away and say, 'I can walk, just get away.' " Simple things like getting him in a shower were an ordeal, though once he submitted he perked up and enjoyed watching television, particularly if a golf tournament was being shown.

Looking on from the apartment next door, Bongiorno despaired as he watched Banks's decline. "He couldn't go out anymore, although he wanted to badly. When a guy lives to speak with people, to deal with people, and can't do it anymore . . ." Bongiorno says, his voice trailing off.

Occasionally, Rice would ask friends to visit—Jenkins or Billy Williams, or John Rogers, who was pleased to be invited.

"I brought him some cupcakes and a book on Wrigley Field," Rogers says. "He was more vulnerable than I had ever seen him." Improbably, the two men began talking about their respective divorces and why they were taking so long and costing so much. Banks's divorce proceedings from Liz had been dragging on for years while Rogers's divorce from his second wife also seemed to be taking forever. "We were going through similar frustrations," Rogers says. "We were both wondering why it should be so hard."

While some of Banks's friends visited during this period, others felt they were being kept away. "Regina isolated him," says William Marovitz. "She cut him off from a lot of his friends, and who knows what that did to his mental state. If you don't see familiar faces, it can certainly hasten dementia."

Another of Banks's friends put it more bluntly: "She separated him from everybody he loved."

The Cubs' first indication of how much Banks's condition had deteriorated came late in the year when they were told he could not attend their annual winter convention.

"Ernie loved the Cubs Convention," Tom Ricketts says. "It was his element, he was the king of the convention. We asked if we could film him just saying hello to everybody, but they said he couldn't do that either. That's when we knew it was pretty serious."

One day in January, Bongiorno visited Banks in his apartment, where he was sitting in his underwear, wearing a fedora, and complaining that he wanted to go outside. "They won't let me get out of here," Banks said. "Come on. Let's go."

To divert him, Bongiorno, who had listened to so many of Banks's stories, mentioned something he had been thinking about.

"You should write a book," he said. "The Ernie we don't know. Forget about this 'Let's play two' bullshit and get to the real guy."

"Yeah, yeah, that's a good idea," Banks said.

"You've got to open up, though. You've got to let people know everything."

"Yeah, yeah, yeah, let's get some people and do that."

But it was too late—just as it was for the documentary film Banks had often spoken of—and Bongiorno later thought it might have been for the best. "I'm not sure people want to hear the other part of it," he says. Perhaps it was better, he thought, if Banks's life remained unexamined, if his "Let's play two" image remained intact.

Banks needed a walker to get around his apartment now, and during a particularly arduous trip to a doctor's office in January Rice bought a wheelchair. With Tony's assistance, she eased him into it.

"We get him in the wheelchair, we get him home, and he's so weak he can only lay down," she says. "But he's in no discomfort. That was Monday. Tuesday, he can sit up. Wednesday, he can't feed himself or hold a cup. I told my son to get him a sippy cup and we put liquids in it and I said, 'Can you hold this, Ernie?' He's not talking now, but he understands. Now it's Thursday and I'm feeding him. He's still able to eat, but he can't put his hand up to do it himself. He just declined so fast."

On Friday, January 23, 2015, Rice was at an aunt's funeral when she had a premonition. "Something said, 'Go now,'" she says.

As she drove to Trump Tower, a trip she had made many times, she missed her expressway exit and found herself going the wrong way in bumper-to-bumper traffic. "I came to a calm right then," she says. "I thought this was by design. Just be patient."

When she finally arrived, she found Banks in bed, barely breathing, his eyes closed. She called a security guard in the lobby and told him to call 911. She propped open a door to Banks's apartment so the paramedics and guards could enter, went into the bedroom, turned Banks on his side, and checked to see if there were any obstructions in his mouth. The security guards arrived just then and, to prevent them from hearing, she whispered in his ear, "Ernie, it's me. I'm here. It's okay. You can go. It's okay to go."

"I looked at his face and I saw a little tear coming out of one eye, so I know he heard me," Rice says. She made sure he was warm and wearing a hat, and the paramedics took him downstairs. She expected to ride to the hospital in the back of the ambulance, but the chief of the operation told her to wait in the lobby for a moment.

"What's going on?" she asked, reading the urgency of his body language.

"We'll let you know in a few minutes," he said.

Moments later, the ambulance driver took her by the arm and guided her to the ambulance. "I want you to sit in the front, but I need you to be calm," he said, and he shut the door. She cried uncontrollably for a moment, then quickly fixed her face so the driver wouldn't notice during their ride of half a mile to Northwestern Memorial Hospital.

As she waited in the emergency room, Rice was approached by two volunteer church women stationed at the hospital. "We just want to be here with you while you go through this," one of them said. She wasn't sure how she felt about that but said nothing. A doctor emerged from Banks's room to say they had found a pulse but it was weak and they would continue working on him. Not long afterward, the doctor returned to say they had lost Banks's pulse but would keep trying. "He was calm, so I was calm, too," Rice says.

Finally, the doctor came out and said, "I'm going to have to pronounce him."

"I just sat there," Rice says. "I thanked the two ladies and I sat there. My mind was saying, 'What do I do now?' "

———

Banks's death certificate listed myocardial infarction—a heart attack—myelodysplastic syndrome, and hypertension as the causes of death. Dementia was noted as a significant contributing factor. He died eight days before his eighty-fourth birthday.

Graceland

In October 2016, as the Cubs were en route to their first World Series championship since 1908, reporters from around the country visited Ernie Banks's grave in Graceland Cemetery, half a mile north of Wrigley Field. The fact the Cubs were ending a century's worth of curses less than two years after Banks died was a bittersweet irony that made for a number of touching stories and columns. Cubs fans visited the grave, too, often leaving flowers behind or white flags with "W" printed in blue, which the team flew above Wrigley Field whenever it won a game. When the Cubs won the World Series, the crowds at Graceland were so large that the police controlling traffic had to spend the night.

"I sure hate that Ernest is not here to see this," Edna Warren thought as she watched the excitement from a nursing home in Lancaster, Texas, just south of Dallas. "This is what he always dreamed of. It took my brother's death for it to happen."

———

For a time after he died, Banks's grave went unmarked, with only fresh grass and a faint coffin-shaped outline giving away its presence. By the time the reporters arrived, a small black marble headstone in the shape of a baseball diamond with the dates of his birth and death and his uniform number on the top had been erected. A year later, a more elaborate memorial was dedicated, a four-foot-tall solid rose marble structure with

a cast of Banks's glove on top. His statistics, his Hall of Fame membership, Presidential Medal of Freedom, and "It's a beautiful day for a ball-
game. Let's play two" were noted on three of the monument's sides. On
the fourth side, an inscription read, "Loving Husband, Father and Friend
to All." With some coaxing from her mother, young Alyna, whom Liz
and Banks had adopted as an infant shortly before he left California for
good, read from her composition "Memories of My Father."

Graceland's 120 acres are a popular Chicago tourist attraction, and
a number of the many people buried there were famous in their time.
Among them are such sports figures as the boxing champions Jack
Johnson and Bob Fitzsimmons, and William Hulbert, one of the found-
ers of the National League. Tucked away in a back portion of the cemetery, away from the entrance, is an area reserved for some of the people
who built Chicago and shaped its destiny. Titans of business—Cyrus
McCormick, George Pullman, Phillip Armour, Marshall Field, Charles
Wacker—are here along with giants of architecture—Louis Sullivan,
Ludwig Mies van der Rohe, Daniel Burnham—and former *Chicago Tribune* owner Joseph Medill and legendary Illinois governor John Altgeld.
Banks's grave is on the shore of Lake Willowmere and across the lake
from the sixteen-column mausoleum that contains the remains of Ber-
tha and Potter Palmer. He is the only athlete buried in this prime real
estate, and no one was heard to say he didn't belong there.

———

The period between Banks's death and the Cubs' World Series victory
had not treated his memory kindly. Though his memorial service a week
after his death was the closest thing to a state funeral Chicago had at
its command, a dynamic was playing out underneath that foretold the
battle that lay ahead.

The service was held in the Fourth Presbyterian Church, a large 104-
year-old gothic building on North Michigan Avenue, and was aired in
its entirety on local television. His coffin sat in front of the pews, draped
with a large replica of his uniform—"Banks, 14"—while a picture of an

impossibly young Ernie Banks smiled shyly behind it. Hank Aaron was a pallbearer, as were Randy Hundley and Glenn Beckert.

Chicago mayor Rahm Emanuel and Illinois governor Bruce Rauner spoke. Tom Ricketts spoke, as did Billy Williams and Ferguson Jenkins. Jesse Jackson spoke, and John Rogers and Joe Torre, who was representing Major League Baseball. Jerry and Joey Banks were particularly eloquent and funny in their remarks. "Thank you, Dad, for letting Mom do the spanking," Joey said, "because with those big hands that would not be a good thing." Joey thanked a number of people, including Buck O'Neil, Ricketts, and Regina Rice and Tony, "who took care of him until the bitter end." After the service, Banks's coffin was driven south to Daley Plaza, where his statue, which had been in storage during construction at Wrigley Field, was on display. The televised procession then moved north to the ballpark and finally to Graceland. "You've never seen more grown men cry than the ones standing in line to say goodbye to Ernie Banks," Ricketts said of a visitation the day before.

But as moving as Banks's memorial service was, it was also a private battleground between two determined women. From California, Liz Banks made several decisions. One was that Banks's ashes would not be scattered over Wrigley Field as he had requested; he would be buried at Graceland instead. Another was that his coffin would be closed during the ceremony. In Chicago, Rice could not counter the first command, but she bitterly fought the second one.

"Ernie's got friends that need closure," she told the Cubs. "She doesn't even want his *kids* to see him? If I get in that church and I can't see his face, it ain't going to be pretty." Liz was just as adamant, and the stalemate continued until the Cubs, caught in the middle, came up with an ingenious solution. In the hours before the funeral, Banks's coffin would be open and placed in a small communion room near the back of the church where Rice could invite anyone she liked. "I beat the heck out of whoever I was communicating with," she says, "but, baby, those Cubs stepped up to the plate." (They did so in other ways as well, paying for

Banks's burial, the memorial service, and the travel expenses of his family. "He's Mr. Cub and he deserves it," Ricketts says. "We did Ron Santo's funeral a couple of years ago. We have a subspecialty in state funerals.")

Rice called some of Banks's relatives, who had arrived from around the country, and told them to come to the church early if they wanted to see him and say goodbye. "They were really appreciative because he looked so good," says Rice, who had asked Greg Vodovoz to make one last suit for Banks, a gray number that was set off by a tie in blue and red—Cubs colors. And when Banks's closest friends arrived at the funeral, she brought them in, too.

"Come back here," Rice told Yale Gordon when he arrived at the church. "Bring your kids with you."

"What's this about?" Gordon said as he entered the room. Then his elbow bumped into the open coffin.

"I thought you might want to see him one last time," she said.

All Gordon could think as he looked at Banks was how frail he had become since the last time they had been together.

Rice remained in the back of the room during the service while Liz and the people with her were seated prominently up front. Almost unrecognized, Marjorie Lott slipped into a seat in the row behind her. As the ceremony began, no one in the church was prepared for the greater drama that would soon unfold.

———

Joey and Jerry were angry when they learned they had been cut out of their father's will and that he had left everything to Rice. And they were cut to the quick by the language he used to explain his decision: "not for a lack of love and affection for them and for reasons best known by them."

"Those aren't his words," Joey says. "Just listen to the cadence. It's some lawyer's voice. He would never say that. I want to know the date he was diagnosed and I want to know what the diagnosis was. How many thousands of senior citizens have been taken advantage of?"

Rice, for her part, was wounded when she was portrayed by Banks's family and on social media as a designing woman who had taken advantage of an old man suffering from dementia. "It was very challenging to live through that," she says, "but all it did was give me a thick skin. I never thought I would be portrayed that way because that's not how it was."

Rice says she hadn't known Banks was going to change his will when they saw a lawyer three months before he died. "I had no clue what he was going to do," she says. "I was shocked. I said, 'What about Jan and Joey and Jerry?' He said, 'I don't want them to have anything. They've never done anything for me.' A week later, we went back, he sat down and reviewed everything, and the lawyer said, 'Now here's the part nobody likes. Are you of sound mind? Are you making these decisions on your own?' There were two witnesses there. I never opened my mouth, never said a word."

Liz filed suit, but the will was declared valid. The legal battle continued, even after a settlement was believed to have been reached. In September 2016, Liz's lawyers withdrew from the case, but she pressed on. By then, however, the fight was essentially over, as Rice was given the rights to the only items Banks had left of any real value: his memorabilia. She consigned twelve items to Heritage Auctions, including two "Mr. Cub" license plates, a signed photo of Banks with Barack and Michelle Obama at the Medal of Freedom ceremony, and the tie he wore at that event. Ten of them sold for a total of $47,897, while the other two were retained in anticipation of a higher price at a later date.

Banks's friends were appalled at the public spectacle of the dispute and considered it a blot on his memory.

"I was not a happy camper," says Jesse White, who as a minor leaguer had sat at Banks's feet and now, so many years later, was Illinois's secretary of state.

"The man can't die in peace," says Billy Williams.

The arguments after Banks's death were the only personal unpleasantness associated with him to be played out in real time before a large audience. But just as Banks was able to deflect all public discussion of the problems, mistakes, and disappointments that beset him during his life, so are these posthumous complications sure to be overlooked whenever his memory is invoked in his adopted city.

"He had a persona in this town like nobody else," says William Marovitz. "There was Mayor Daley, maybe, but some people didn't like his politics. But it was impossible not to like Ernie. He always had a smile on his face. He never said anything negative about anybody. He made us feel good about the Cubs and Chicago and ourselves. How could you not love a guy like that?"

Acknowledgments

This project began as a "with" or an "as told to" book. Ernie's name was to appear prominently on the cover and title page while mine would trail inconspicuously behind. That it did not work out that way is a subject I explored at length in an article in the October 2015 edition of *Chicago* magazine. For now, let it simply be said that an autobiography was one more project Ernie began and then abandoned.

After Ernie died, I saw that what I learned during the time I spent with him might be expanded into the biography he deserves, and I returned to our interviews with a mixture of elation and sadness. Elation because as we began work on his autobiography he had dug so deep. Memories from every period of his life came spilling out, story after story he had never told before, many of them remarkable in their detail and introspection. Sadness because we'd had so little time—only a few weeks, as I remember it—with a tape recorder sitting between us on his dining room table. If only we'd had more time, I thought.

But as I began calling around to some of the people who knew Ernie from his earliest days in Dallas to his final years in Chicago, I made a fascinating discovery. Nearly everyone I spoke with was not only willing to tell me about their experiences with Ernie but eager to do so. And many of them gave me the names of other people they insisted I must talk to. Those people in turn put me on the trail of still others, and so on down the line.

I wondered about the urgency of these recommendations until I realized that the closer people were to Ernie, the more they shared my frustration that the joyful, melancholy, humble, complicated, companionable, lonely man they knew remained imprisoned in an image of one simplistic dimension. In the end, I spoke with more than one hundred people who knew Ernie well, and I saw that their perceptions were leading me to a more complete portrait than he and I could have achieved on our own. Though Ernie remembered and explained a great deal—and our conversations permeate every section of this book—those who knew him best remembered and explained even more.

I am particularly grateful to Edna Warren, Walter Banks, Jerry and Joey Banks, the other members of Ernie's family, and his friends from Booker T. Washington High School who spoke with me so frankly. And I appreciate the forthright discussions I had with Marjorie Lott, Ernie's third wife, and Regina Rice, his friend and caretaker in his final years. I regret that Liz Banks, Ernie's fourth wife, declined to speak with me. She is, she said in a brief conversation, working on her own book about her life with Ernie.

During my travels, I learned a great deal about Texas hospitality in Dallas, where I was warmly received not only by Ernie's family and high school classmates, but also by Darwin Payne, a historian, author, and retired journalism professor at Southern Methodist University. He graciously drove me to a number of places where Ernie spent time as a boy and young man and directed me to other people he thought I should speak with and to some useful historical records.

One of the joys of working on this book was being able to speak with many of Ernie's Chicago Cubs teammates. I am indebted to Billy Williams for putting me in touch with many of them and for giving me so much of his time. And it was a great pleasure to meet with my favorite Cubs manager during my sportswriting days in Chicago, Joe Amalfitano. I am also honored that Hank Aaron, Charley Pride, Jesse Jackson, and Timuel Black spoke with me about their memories of Ernie, and I appreciate Keith Hubbs's willingness to share his memories of his brother's tragic death. Thanks also to Tom Ricketts, William Marovitz, John Canning, Jesse White, John Rogers, John McDonough, Georgie Anne Geyer, Grant DePorter, Tom Bongiorno, Bradley Borowiec, and the other prominent Chicagoans who made time for me.

I am grateful to a number of people who went out of their way to facilitate interviews that were helpful in re-creating Ernie's life. These include Grant DePorter, Tom Ricketts, Bill Caplan, Arlene Gill, Sharon Pannozzo, Ned Colletti, Gromer Jeffers of the *Dallas Morning News*, and Glenn Pait, the director of the T. Glenn Pait Spine Clinic at the University of Arkansas for Medical Sciences, who referred me to his colleagues, C. Lowry Barnes and Yogesh Jethava, who were so helpful in explaining Ernie's medical condition.

Ernie gave four long interviews to oral historians after he retired. These were conducted by Renee Poussaint at the National Visionary Leadership Project, Raymond Dodson at the Negro Leagues Baseball Museum, Timothy J. Gilfoyle at the Chicago Historical Society, and an unnamed interviewer at the History Makers in Chicago. Ernie was far more forthcoming in these conversations than he was in his own autobiography, *Mr. Cub,* which he wrote with Jim Enright in 1971 and must be approached cautiously. Though the book is entertaining, it is also, as I note in the text, marred by several notable omissions and errors. More reliable is *Ernie Banks: Mr. Cub and the Summer of '69* by Phil Rogers, which frames Ernie's story in the context of the 1969 season.

———

Anyone seeking to write about a Major League Baseball player before the digital revolution changed newspaper and magazine sports pages forever must begin with *The Sporting News.* From its first brief mention of Ernie when he was playing for the Kansas City Monarchs, the paper followed his career week by week in illuminating detail, and I spent many profitable hours searching its archives. Chicago's newspapers—the *Tribune, Sun-Times, Daily News,* and *American* (reborn in 1969 as *Chicago Today*)—were all helpful sources as were *Sport, Sports Illustrated,* and *Look.* The

Baseball Biography Project of the Society for American Baseball Research is a fine reservoir of detailed information about hundreds of baseball figures that I found useful. And the papers of Kansas City Monarchs owner T. Y. Baird, which are at the Kenneth Spencer Research Library at the University of Kansas, helped unravel the story of the Cubs' pursuit of Ernie while he was playing in the Negro Leagues.

A number of books were helpful in describing the various eras of Ernie's life. Darwin Payne's book *Quest for Justice: Louis A. Bedford Jr. and the Struggle for Equal Rights in Texas* describes North Dallas during the time Ernie lived there, and *Dallas from a Different Perspective* by Ernie's friend Dr. Robert Prince gives a personal view of that time and place.

The Negro Leagues have received the attention of historians they deserve in recent years as exemplified by such books as *Negro League Baseball: The Rise and Ruin of a Black Institution* by Neil Lanctot, and *Shades of Glory: The Negro Leagues and the Story of African-American Baseball* by Lawrence D. Hogan. I was particularly drawn to *The Negro Leagues Revisited: Conversations with 66 More Baseball Heroes* by Brent Kelley, a fascinating collection of oral histories of the leagues' stars and journeymen alike.

American Pharaoh: Mayor Richard J Daley: His Battle for Chicago and the Nation by Adam Cohen and Elizabeth Taylor provides a comprehensive history of Chicago during the Daley years, while on a smaller scale *Philip K. Wrigley: A Memoir of a Modest Man* by his friend Paul M. Angle is an excellent source of information about the Cubs' owner. While amusing, Leo Durocher's autobiography, inevitably titled *Nice Guys Finish Last*, must rank among the most self-absorbed and self-absolving books ever written. *Leo Durocher: Baseball's Prodigal Son* by Paul Dickson weighs the evidence and helps to set the record straight.

Bookshelves fairly groan under the weight of books about, and memoirs by, the 1969 Chicago Cubs and New York Mets. Two of the best are *The Cubs of '69: Recollections of the Team That Should Have Been* by Rick Talley and *A Magic Summer: The Amazin' Story of the 1969 New York Mets* by Stanley Cohen. Talley and Cohen both had the happy idea of reaching out to the 1969 Cubs and Mets two decades later, and they found many of them in reflective moods and full of memories. As I note in the text, I found these books helpful in re-creating that historic season, and I have listed the other publications I consulted along with the interviews I conducted in the Sources section that follows. Because I mention so many sources in the text, it did not seem to me to be necessary to footnote every quotation in the book.

It is customary in acknowledgments such as these for writers to thank their agents, but in this case the recognition is more than perfunctory. Tim Hays sought me out after reading my previous writings about Ernie, insisted they contained the makings of a book, and proved it by quickly producing an offer I couldn't refuse. So very simply, the equation is: No Tim = no book. To which I can only say thanks. At Hachette Books, I am grateful to vice president and publisher Mauro DiPreta, who immediately saw the book's potential, to executive editor Brant Rumble for the careful attention he paid to the manuscript and his many extremely valuable editorial suggestions, and to copy editor (and Cubs fan) Becky Maines for her excellent work. Thanks also to associate publisher Michelle Aielli, director of marketing Michael Barrs, marketing associate Odette Fleming, art director Amanda Kain, and assistant editors Lauren Hummel and David Lamb for their assistance.

Others I would like to thank are, in Dallas, John H. Slate, the city archivist; Kerry Adams, collections and exhibits director at the Old Red Museum; Alan P. Olson, interim executive director of the Dallas Historical Society; and C. Paul Rogers III, professor of law and former dean at the Dedman School of Law, SMU.

In Chicago, thank you to Fred Mitchell, Jason Meisner, Rick Kogan, Paul Sullivan, and Anthony Dudek at the *Chicago Tribune*; Joe Goddard, Toni Ginnetti, Len Ziehm, and Lynn Sweet at the *Chicago Sun-Times*; Terrance Noland at *Chicago* magazine; Nick Shields of the Cook County Clerk's Office; Phil Costello, archivist at Cook County Clerk of the Circuit Court; Don Terry at Operation Rainbow/Push; Lorraine Swiatly at the Chicago Cubs; Bob Vorwald at WGN; Al Yellon at Bleed Cubbie Blue; Dave Druker at the Illinois Secretary of State's Office; Emily Ward at John Canning's office; Jillian Smith at the Chicago Blackhawks; Ellen Keith at the Chicago History Museum; Jared Wyllys at BP Wrigleyville; Cody Lowe at the Chicago Transit Authority; and Nancy Haff at the House of the Good Shepard. Thanks also to Ed Sherman, George Castle, Ellen Dease, Mary Craig, Andy Zavelson, Cathy Karp, Diane Simpson, Paul and Adrianne Johnson, Richard Cahan, Marielle Sainvilus, and Alan Cubbage.

In Los Angeles, thank you to my friends John Schulian, Mike Downey, Ned Colletti, and Charley Steiner for allowing so many of our regular lunch dates to become Ernie Banks seminars. And thanks to Ernie's lawyer, Sam Perlmutter, for showing me his files and explaining some of his client's legal problems. Thanks also to Byron Browne and his representative, Dani Green, for putting me in touch with Browne's father, who was Ernie's teammate, and to David Davis, Ina Jaffe, Mark Langill, Ruth Weisberg, Bob Lieber, Jon Leonoudakis, Diana Michael, Terry Cannon, Andy McCue, Steve Brenner, and Linda Gross.

Thanks to Bob Kendrick, Raymond Doswell, and N'Deda Mozee at the Negro Leagues Museum in Kansas City; Jeff Idelson, Matt Rothenberg, John Horne, Peter Clark, and Tom Heitz at the National Baseball Hall of Fame in Cooperstown, New York; Deborah Dandridge at the Spencer Library, University of Kansas; Jim Kevlin at Freeman's Journal; Jacob Pomrenke, director of editorial content at the Society for American Baseball Research; Ann Baker and Joyce Gettman at the University of Nebraska Press; Harry Minium at the *Virginian-Pilot*; Susan Bailey at the Atlanta Braves; Debbie Nacito at the Philadelphia Phillies; and Rich Rice at the Texas Rangers. And thank you to Bill Madden, Paul Dickson, Jane Leavy, Fred Claire, Mark Purdy, Leigh Ann Young, Ira Berkow, Lonnie Wheeler, Steve Bisheff, Claudia Keith, Wayne Terwilliger, Jessica Zamperini, Jeff Brown, Gary Gilbertson, and Robert J. Lieber.

Thank you to Julie Rapoport and Barbara Isenberg for their careful reading of the manuscript, and to Mary Dease, whose knowledge of all things Chicago and all things Cubs proved invaluable in putting this book together.

Ernie had a favorite joke, which he often told to unsuspecting listeners, sometimes in one of his ambush phone calls: A skeleton walks into a bar and tells the bartender, "Give me a beer and a mop."

My thanks to everyone in these pages for helping me to put some meat on Ernie's rhetorical bones.

Sources

EPIGRAPH
Publication: *Time Out Chicago,* Tim McCormick.

PROLOGUE: *Omaha*
Interviews: William Marovitz.
Publications: *Chicago American, Chicago Tribune.*

CHAPTER 1: *1717 Fairmount*
Interviews: Ernie Banks, Edna Warren, Walter Banks, Jack Price, Robert Prince, John Slate, Darwin Payne, Dolores Law.
Publications: Dallas Housing Authority, *General Survey of Housing Conditions,* August 1938.
Quest for Justice: Louis A. Bedford Jr. and the Struggle for Equal Rights in Texas by Darwin Payne, 2009.
Dallas from a Different Perspective by Dr. Robert Prince, 1993.
Mr. Cub by Ernie Banks and Jim Enright, 1971.
National Visionary Leadership Project, Ernie Banks, Interview by Renee Poussaint, 2004.
Chicago Historical Society, Ernie Banks, Oral History Interview, Timothy J. Gilfoyle, 1997.
Negro Leagues Baseball Museum Archives, Interview by Raymond Dodson, 2004.
The Sporting News.
Sport.

CHAPTER 2: *Booker T.*
Interviews: Scott Rudes, Sharon Cornell, Ernie Banks, Edna Warren, Jack Price, Joe Kirven, Gloria Foster, Robert Prince, Karen Ridge.

Publications: National Visionary Leadership Project, Ernie Banks, Interview by
    Renee Poussaint, 2004.
The History Makers, Digital Archive, 2000.
Mr. Cub by Ernie Banks and Jim Enright, 1971.
Dallas from a Different Perspective by Dr. Robert Prince, 1993.
Dallas magazine.
Dallas Times Herald.

CHAPTER 3: *On the Road*
Interviews: Ernie Banks, Darryl Blair, Jack Price.
Publications: *Mr. Cub* by Ernie Banks and Jim Enright, 1971.
Chicago Historical Society, Ernie Banks, Oral History Interview by Timothy J.
    Gilfoyle, 1997.
The History Makers, Digital Archive. 2000.
Negro Leagues Baseball Museum Archives, Interview by Raymond Dodson, 2004.
St. Louis Post-Dispatch.
Sportsday.dallasnews.com.

CHAPTER 4: *Leaving Home*
Interviews: Ernie Banks, Walter Banks, Sander Esserman, Marjorie Lott, Edna
    Warren, Karen Ridge, Jack Price, Robert Prince, Scott Rudes, Bobby Johnson,
    Jeremy Halbreich, Emmanuel Gillespie.
Publications: Associated Press.
Dallas Morning News.
National Visionary Leadership Project, Ernie Banks, Interview by Renee Pous-
    saint, 2004.
The History Makers, Digital Archive, 2000.
Texas State Historical Association.

CHAPTER 5: *Monarchs of All They Surveyed*
Interviews: Ernie Banks, Darryl Blair, Larry Lester, George Altman, Charley
    Pride, Robert Prince, Jack Hiatt.
Publications: *Chicago Tribune.*
Shades of Glory: The Negro Leagues and the Story of African-American Baseball by Law-
    rence D. Hogan, 2006.
The Negro Leagues Revisited, Conversations with 66 More Baseball Heroes by Brent
    Kelley, 2000.
Negro Leagues Baseball Museum.
Willie Mays: The Life, The Legend by James S. Hirsch, 2010.
Innings Ago: Recollections by Kansas City Ballplayers of Their Days in the Game by Jack
    Etkin, 1986.
I Was Right on Time by Buck O'Neil with Steve Wulf and David Conrads, 1996.

Elston and Me: The Story of the First Black Yankee by Arlene Howard with Ralph Wimbish, 2001.

National Visionary Leadership Project, Ernie Banks, Interview by Renee Poussaint, 2004.

The History Makers, Digital Archive, 2000.

Chicago Historical Society, Ernie Banks, Oral History Interview, Timothy J. Gilfoyle, 1997.

MLB.com.

Monarch Cheers, Integration Whimpers, and Loyalty Conflicts: Coverage of the Black Yankees in Black and White Kansas City, 1937–1955 by Eric M. Eames, Master's Thesis, Brigham Young University, 2008.

Ernie Banks: Mr. Cub and the Summer of '69 by Phil Rogers, 2011.

The Sporting News.

CHAPTER 6: *Army Life*

Interviews: Ernie Banks, Larry Lester, Edna Warren, Ted Knutson.

Publications: Howstuffworks,com, Paul Adomites and Saul Wisnia.

Satchel: The Life and Times of an American Legend by Larry Tye, 2009.

Jackie Robinson: A Biography by Arnold Rampersad, 1997.

Mr. Cub by Ernie Banks and Jim Enright, 1971.

I Was Right on Time by Buck O'Neil with Steve Wulf and David Conrads, 1996.

Voices from the Great Black Baseball Leagues by John Holway, 2010.

Curveball: The Remarkable Story of Toni Stone by Martha Ackmann, 2010.

National Visionary Leadership Project, Ernie Banks, Interview by Renee Poussaint, 2004.

The History Makers, Digital Archive, 2000.

The Sporting News.

Chicago Tribune.

Sport.

Dallas Morning News.

La Crosse Tribune.

Stars and Stripes.

CHAPTER 7: *"Going to Chicago, Sorry I Can't Take You"*

Interviews: Ernie Banks, Jack Price, Robert Prince, Phil Dixon, Hank Mason.

Publications: T. Y. Baird papers, 1913–1992, Kenneth Spencer Research Library, University of Kansas.

Society for American Baseball Research, Jeff Angus.

Society for American Baseball Research, Aaron Stilley.

Mr. Cub by Ernie Banks and Jim Enright, 1971.

I Had a Hammer by Henry Aaron and Lonnie Wheeler, 1991.

The Kansas City Monarchs: Champions of Baseball by Janet Bruce, 1986.

Saturday Evening Post.

Negro League Baseball: The Rise and Ruin of a Black Institution by Neil Lanctot, 2004.

Topeka Capital-Journal.

The History Makers, Digital Archive, 2000.

CHAPTER 8: *North Side, South Side*

Interviews: Ernie Banks, Timuel Black, Billy Williams.

Publications: *American Pharaoh: Mayor Richard J Daley: His Battle for Chicago and the Nation* by Adam Cohen and Elizabeth Taylor, 2000.

Get That Nigger Off the Field: An Oral History of Black Ballplayers from the Negro Leagues to the Present by Art Rust, 1992.

Mr. Cub by Ernie Banks and Jim Enright, 1971.

Chicago Historical Society, Ernie Banks, Oral History Interview, Timothy J. Gilfoyle, 1997.

Negro Leagues Baseball Museum Archives, Interview by Raymond Dodson, 2004.

The History Makers, Digital Archive, 2000.

Chicago Daily News.

The Sporting News.

Ernie Banks: Mr. Cub and the Summer of '69 by Phil Rogers, 2011.

CHAPTER 9: *The Master Builder*

Interviews: Ernie Banks, Billy Williams, Jesse White.

Publications: *Chicago Tribune* magazine, "P.K.: Philip Knight Wrigley Is More Than Just the Doublemint Magnate," by William Barry Furlong.

Philip K. Wrigley: A Memoir of a Modest Man by Paul M. Angle, 1975.

Chicago American.

Chicago Tribune.

Chicago Sun-Times.

The Sporting News.

Sports Illustrated.

Carrying Jackie's Torch: The Players Who Integrated Baseball—and America by Steve Jacobson, 2007.

Shades of Glory: The Negro Leagues and the Story of African-American Baseball by Lawrence D. Hogan, 2006.

Negro League Baseball: The Rise and Ruin of a Black Institution by Neil Lanctot, 2004.

Cruxresearch.com, "Don't Sequester Your Marketing Budget."

Winningerlawfirm.com, "Wrigley Field and an International Story of Litigation with William Wrigley III."

Arizona Republic.

CHAPTER 10: *Future Shock*
Publications: *The Sporting News.*
Chicago Sun-Times.
MLB.com.
Society for American Baseball Research, Lawrence Baldassaro.
The Sporting News.
Mr. Cub by Ernie Banks and Jim Enright, 1971.
The New York Times.

CHAPTER 11: *MVP! MVP!*
Interviews: George Altman, Dusty Baker, Wes Parker, Jeff Torborg, Joe Amalfitano, Doug Harvey.
Publications: *The Sporting News.*
The Saturday Evening Post.
Chicago Tribune.
Chicago Defender.
Austin America-Statesman.
Sports Illustrated.
Sport.
National Visionary Leadership Project, Ernie Banks, Interview by Renee Poussaint, 2004.
The History Makers, Digital Archive, 2000.
Ernie Banks: Mr. Cub and the Summer of '69 by Phil Rogers, 2011.
We Played the Game by Danny Peary, 2002.

CHAPTER 12: *The Slough of Despond*
Interviews: Arlene Gill, Mike Downey.
Prentice H. Marshall, letter to the author.
Publications: National Visionary Leadership Project, Ernie Banks, Interview by Renee Poussaint, 2004.
The Sporting News.
Chicago Tribune.
Baseball-Reference.com.

CHAPTER 13: *The Once and Future Cub*
Interviews: Hank Aaron.
Publications: *The Sporting News.*
Chicago Tribune.
The New York Times.

CHAPTER 14: *Let's Play Two*

Interviews: Billy Williams, Al Spangler, Don Kessinger, Bill Hands, Ferguson Jenkins, Rich Nye, Chuck Shriver, Ron Santo, Jr., Edna Warren, Ernie Banks, Marjorie Lott, Sharon Pannozzo, Wes Parker, John McDonough, Jerry Banks.

Publications: Joeposnanski.com.

Farmersalmanac.com.

Chicago Sun-Times.

Something to Write Home About by Seth Swirsky, 2003.

Once Upon a Game: Baseball's Greatest Memories by Alan Schwarz, 2007.

Ernie Banks: Mr. Cub and the Summer of '69, by Phil Rogers, 2011.

The Sporting News.

ESPN.com.

CHAPTER 15: *The Rock of the Family*

Interviews: Ernie Banks, Edna Warren, Hank Aaron, Karen Ridge, Billy Williams, Jerry Banks, Joey Banks, Chuck Shriver, Arlene Gill, Mary Dease.

Court Records: *Mollye Louise Banks v. Ernest Banks,* Case #59S-5954, Superior Court of Cook County, Archives of the Circuit Court Clerk of Cook County.

Publications: *Chicago Defender.*

National Visionary Leadership Project, Ernie Banks, Interview by Renee Poussaint, 2004.

Racine Journal Times.

Jet, Nov. 5, 1959.

Billy Williams: My Sweet-Swinging Lifetime with the Cubs by Billy Williams with Fred Mitchell, 2008.

Glory Days with the Dodgers by John Roseboro with Bill Libby, 1978

I Had a Hammer, by Henry Aaron and Lonnie Wheeler, 1991.

CHAPTER 16: *Bright College Days*

Interviews: Rich Nye, Mary Dease, Chuck Shriver, Blake Cullen, Ken Holtzman, Jeff Torborg.

Publications: *Chicago Tribune.*

The Sporting News.

Sport.

Society for American Baseball Research, Richard Puerzer.

The Hardball Times, "P. K. Wrigley and the College of Coaches" by Scott Ferkovich.

"Psychology Strikes Out: Coleman R. Griffith and the Chicago Cubs" by Christopher D. Green.

Veeck as in Wreck by Bill Veeck with Ed Linn, 2001.

CHAPTER 17: *"He Was Why We Fell in Love with the Game"*
Interviews: Joe Amalfitano, Bill Hands, Ken Holtzman, Dennis Paoli.
Publications: *Chicago Tribune.*
The Sporting News.
Sport.
Chicago Tribune.
The New York Times.
Gary Post-Tribune.
ESPN.com.
Society for American Baseball Research, Richard Puerzer.
The Hardball Times, "P. K. Wrigley and the College of Coaches" by Scott Ferkovich.
Stealing Is My Game by Lou Brock and Franz Schulze, 1976.
American Negro Press.

CHAPTER 18: *The Lull Before the Storm*
Interviews: Byron Browne, Jeff Torborg.
Publications: *The Sporting News.*
Chicago Daily News.
Sport.
The Last Innocents: The Collision of the Turbulent Sixties and the Los Angeles Dodgers by Michael Leahy, 2016.

CHAPTER 19: *Taking Over*
Interviews: Joe Amalfitano, Arlene Gill, Mary Dease, Wes Parker.
Publications: *Leo Durocher: Baseball's Prodigal Son* by Paul Dickson, 2017.
Day with the Giants by Laraine Day, 1952.
Nice Guys Finish Last by Leo Durocher with Ed Linn, 1974.
Philip K. Wrigley: A Memoir of a Modest Man by Paul M. Angle, 1975.
The Sporting News.
Time.
The Last Innocents: The Collision of the Turbulent Sixties and the Los Angeles Dodgers by Michael Leahy, 2016.
The Cubs of '69: Recollections of the Team That Should Have Been by Rick Talley, 1989.

CHAPTER 20: *"Daddy, Where Were You?"*
Interviews: Interviews: Ernie Banks, Jesse Jackson, Billy Williams, Hank Aaron, Chuck Shriver, Blake Cullen, Al Spangler, Ned Colletti, Oscar Gamble, Byron Browne, Rich Nye, Ken Holtzman, Marjorie Lott, Timuel Black.
Publications: The History Makers, Digital Archive, 2000.
Chicago Tribune.
Chicago Defender.

The Sporting News.

Sport.

Time.

Jet.

Dougwilsonbaseball.blogspot.com, "When Ernie Banks Ran for Alderman" by
    Doug Wilson.

Jackie Robinson: A Biography by Arnold Rampersad, 1997.

Up from the Ghetto by Phillip T. Drotning and Wesley W. South, 1970.

Newspaper Enterprise Association.

The Cubs of '69: Recollections of the Team That Should Have Been by Rick Talley, 1989.

The Last Innocents: The Collision of the Turbulent Sixties and the Los Angeles Dodgers
    by Michael Leahy, 2016.

Leo Durocher: Baseball's Prodigal Son by Paul Dickson, 2017.

Mr. Cub by Ernie Banks and Jim Enright, 1971.

Dallas Morning News.

Chicago Historical Society, Ernie Banks, Oral History Interview, Timothy J. Gil-
    foyle, 1997.

Carrying Jackie's Torch by Steve Jacobson, 2007.

CHAPTER 21: *Teammates*

Interviews: Ron Santo, Jr., Jesse White, Billy Williams, Ken Holtzman, Douglas
    Holtzman.

Publications: *Chicago Tribune.*

The Sporting News.

Los Angeles Times.

Chicago Reader.

Sports Illustrated.

Bleedcubbieblue.com.

The Cubs of '69: Recollections of the Team That Should Have Been by Rick Talley, 1989.

*1954: The Year Willie Mays and the First Generation of Black Superstars Changed Base-
    ball Forever* by Bill Madden, 2014.

CHAPTER 22: *And Yet So Far*

Interviews: Keith Hubbs.

Publications: *Stealing Is My Game* by Lou Brock and Franz Schulze, 1976.

Los Angeles Times.

Chicago Tribune.

Chicago Defender.

The Sporting News.

"Diamond Gems," George Castle, Chicago Baseball Museum.

Society for American Baseball Research, Russell Lake.

CHAPTER 23: *The Most Unpopular Man in Chicago*
Interviews: Randy Hundley, Billy Williams, Joe Amalfitano, Phil Regan, Blake Cullen, Rich Nye, Chuck Shriver, George Altman, Don Kessinger, Ernie Banks.
Publications: *Fergie: My Life from the Cubs to Cooperstown* by Ferguson Jenkins and Lew Freedman, 2009.
Chicago Sun-Times.
The Sporting News.
Willie Mays: The Life, The Legend by James S. Hirsch, 2010.
Banks to Sandberg to Grace: Five Decades of Love and Frustration with the Chicago Cubs by Carrie Muskat, 2001.
Nice Guys Finish Last by Leo Durocher with Ed Linn, 1974.

CHAPTER 24: *"This Is Not an Eighth-Place Team"*
Interviews: Blake Cullen, Ferguson Jenkins, Randy Hundley, Don Kessinger.
Publications: *The Cubs of '69: Reflections of the Team That Should Have Been* by Rick Talley, 1989.
The Sporting News.
Sport.
Billy Williams: My Sweet-Swinging Lifetime with the Cubs by Billy Williams with Fred Mitchell, 2008.
Society for American Baseball Research, Ted Leavengood.

CHAPTER 25: *"Change the Flag!"*
Interviews: Randy Hundley, Mike Murphy, John Schulian.
Publications: *Chicago Tribune.*
Ernie Banks: Mr. Cub and the Summer of '69 by Phil Rogers, 2011.
The Sporting News.
Milwaukee Journal.
Chicago American.

CHAPTER 26: *Bleacher Bums*
Interviews: Mike Murphy, Jack Herbon, Don Flynn, Phil Regan, Ferguson Jenkins, Mudcat Grant.
Publications: *The New York Times.*
Chicago Tribune.
Sports Illustrated.
Jet.
Chicago Daily News.

CHAPTER 27: *In the World*
Interviews: Phil Regan, Georgie Anne Geyer.
Publications: *Sports Illustrated.*

The Sporting News.
Chicago Tribune.
Sport.

CHAPTER 28: *"Break Out the Champagne"*
Interviews: Ernie Banks, Joe Amalfitano, Jack Hiatt, Blake Cullen, Rich Nye, Jack Herbon, Nancy Hawes, Don Kessinger, Phil Regan, Dennis Paoli, Jerry Banks, Ron Santo, Jr., Mike Murphy.
Publications: *Chicago Tribune.*
The Sporting News.
Sport.
Time.
Sports Illustrated.
The Cubs of '69: Recollections of the Team That Should Have Been by Rick Talley, 1989.
Look.

CHAPTER 29: *A Bunch of Old Men*
Interviews: Billy Williams, Rich Nye, George Langford, Randy Hundley, Bill Hands, Don Kessinger, Byron Browne, Mike Murphy.
Publications: *Sporting News.*
Chicago Tribune.
A Magic Summer: The Amazin' Story of the 1969 New York Mets by Stanley Cohen, 2009.
Sport.
The Cubs of '69: Recollections of the Team That Should Have Been by Rick Talley, 1989.
Sports Illustrated.
USA Today.

CHAPTER 30: *Questions and Answers*
Interviews: Joe Amalfitano, Ernie Banks, Al Spangler, Billy Williams, Ken Holtzman, Randy Hundley, Ferguson Jenkins, Rich Nye.
Publications: *Sport.*
A Magic Summer: The Amazin' Story of the 1969 New York Mets by Stanley Cohen, 2009.
The Cubs of '69: Recollections of the Team That Should Have Been by Rick Talley, 1989.
Chicago Tribune.
Look.
Billy Williams: My Sweet-Swinging Lifetime with the Cubs by Billy Williams with Fred Mitchell, 2008.
Jackie Robinson: A Biography by Arnold Rampersad, 1997.

CHAPTER 31: *Riding the Pines*
Interviews: Jack Hiatt, Jim Hickman, Greg Carlton.
Publications: *The Sporting News.*

Chicago Tribune.

Chicago Sun-Times.

The Cubs of '69: Recollections of the Team That Should Have Been by Rick Talley, 1989.

Sports Illustrated.

CHAPTER 32: *Sunday in America*

Interviews: Blake Cullen, Jim Hickman, Randy Hundley, Phil Regan, Joe Amalfitano.

Publications: *The Sporting News.*

Chicago Tribune.

Nice Guys Finish Last by Leo Durocher with Ed Linn, 1974.

Chicago Today.

Chicago Sun-Times.

St. Petersburg Times.

Sport.

CHAPTER 33: *Coda*

Interviews: Joe Amalfitano, Mike Murphy, Jack Herbon, Dennis Paoli, Tom Ricketts, Randy Hundley.

Publications: *Chicago Tribune.*

Sport.

New York Times.

Economist.com.

CHAPTER 34: *Man at Work*

Interviews: Ned Colletti, Hank Aaron, William Marovitz, Greg Carlton, Grant DePorter, John Canning, John Rogers, Tom Bongiorno, Jack Hiatt, Bradley Borowiec, Regina Rice, Blake Cullen, Chuck Shriver, Rebecca Polihronis, Charley Pride, Darryl Blair, Sander Esserman, Sue Schwerin, Todd Laczynski, Yale Gordon, Ernie Banks, Peter Clark, Jeff Idelson, Edna Warren.

Publications: "Diamond Gems," Chicago Baseball Museum, Lou Brock interview with George Castle.

Chicago Tribune.

The History Makers, Digital Archive, 2000.

The Sporting News.

Long Beach Press-Telegram.

Society for American Baseball Research, Gene Faber.

Dallas Morning News.

New York Times.

Chicago Sun-Times

ABC7Chicago.com.

CHAPTER 35: *Family Ties*

Interviews: Jerry Banks, Marjorie Lott, Tom Ricketts, Billy Williams, Yale Gordon, Mollie Bracigliano, Chris Ivy, Sam Perlmutter.

Court Records: Superior Court of Cook County, Case No. BD 113441, Circuit Court of Cook County, Illinois County Department, Probate Division, No. 2015 P 0594.

Publications: *Chicago Tribune.*

Newsday.

CHAPTER 36: *"How's Your Wife?"*

Interviews: John McDonough, Jerry Banks, Sharon Pannozzo, Rebecca Polihronis, Sylvia Menias, Tom Bongiorno, Bradly Borowiec, Todd Laczynski, Tom Ricketts, Marjorie Lott, Peter Vodovoz, Greg Vodovoz, Joe Jemsek, Darryl Blair, Jeff Idelson, Mike Murphy, Jesse Jackson, John Rogers, Grant DePorter, William Marovitz.

Publications: *The Sporting News.*

Sport.

Chicago Tribune.

ESPN.com.

CHAPTER 37: *Rounding Third*

Interviews: Yogesh Jethava, Jerry Banks, John Rogers, Yale Gordon, Mollie Bracigliano, Regina Rice, William Marovitz, Grant DePorter, Sharon Pannozzo, Ron Santo, Jr., John Rogers, Ferguson Jenkins, Hank Aaron, Randy Hundley, Georgie Anne Geyer, Marjorie Lott, Donna Wakefield, Sue Schwerin, Tom Bongiorno, Tom Ricketts.

Publications: *Orlando Sentinel.*

EPILOGUE: *Graceland*

Interviews: Edna Warren, Regina Rice, Yale Gordon, Joey Banks, Jerry Banks, Jesse White, Billy Williams, Chris Ivy, William Marovitz.

Publications: *Chicago Tribune.*

Dallas Morning News.

Index

436 · Index

Badu, Erykah, 23
Baird, T. Y., 53, 61, 71–75, 77–81
Baker, Dusty, 114
Baker, Gene, 74–75, 90–94, 97–98, 109–111, 133–134, 136, 215, 230, 365–366, 375, 377
Baltimore Elite Giants, 74
Baltimore Orioles, 96, 108, 203, 256, 280, 291, 322
Banks, Alyna (daughter), 409
Banks, Ben (brother), 12, 43
Banks, Donald (brother), 16
Banks, Eddie (father), 11–12, 14–20, 41–42, 60, 64, 82, 285–286, 376
Banks, Eddie, Jr. (brother), 43
Banks, Edna (sister). See Warren, Edna
Banks, Eloyce (second wife). See Johnson, Eloyce
Banks, Ernie
  army years, 64–67
  attending 1969 World Series, 322
  bullet fired through home window, 177
  business ventures and jobs
    after baseball, 362–365
    difficulties with, 27–28
    picking cotton, 5, 17–18
  Chicago Cubs
    1967 season, 263–266
    1969 season, 5, 284–294, 296–298, 301, 306, 313, 322, 329, 331
    1970 season, 336–340, 342–343
    1971 season, 351
    acclimating to Chicago, 88–91
    all-time RBIs, 290
    batting style, 113–115
    Bleacher Bums, 269, 272–275
    breakout year, 112
    broken window at public appearance, 177
    candidacy for Rookie of the Year, 110
    career earnings, 361–362
    Cavarretta's firing, 109
    as coach, 262
    College of Coaches, 180
    comeback after illness, 187–188
    consecutive game streak, 122–123, 139, 170
    Cubs' futility during Banks's stardom, 124–130, 178–179
    disabled list, 339–340, 342, 346
    double-play combination with Baker, 93–94, 110, 112
    Durocher's campaign against Banks, 242–251, 262–263, 279, 357
    Durocher's ten-ball bet, 345
    efforts to intimidate, 127
    Ernie Banks Day, 130, 188
    fastest start of career, 174
    first big-league home run, 92–93
    first spring training, 95–97
    five grand-slam home runs in a season, 124–127
    500th home run, 336–338
    Great Cubs Mutiny of 1971, 348–351
    hit by pitches, 127–128, 173–174
    Houston doubleheaders, 140
    Hubbs's funeral, 238
    importance of game, 130
    informal mentoring seminars, 98
    intentionally walked, 126–127
    last game, 352–353
    management role, 365–369
    meeting Wrigley, 98–99
    mentoring by Baker, 90–92, 133
    mentoring Taylor, 136
    as new arrival, 91–92
    permanent move to first base, 122, 174–175
    position changes due to knee problem, 170
    power hitting, 113–116
    prospect of being traded, 137–139
    removed for pinch hitter, 347–348
    representing after retirement, 369–373
    scouting and signing, 71, 77–79, 81–83
    set apart from other power hitters, 129
    six-season stats, 112
    speculation over retirement, 339, 351–352
    spiked by Rose, 260, 276
    stats for 1961 season, 172
    stats for 1965 season, 188
    stats for 1970 season, 343
    stats for 1971 season, 348